JOHN SLOAN

John Loughery

A JOHN MACRAE BOOK

Henry Holt and Company
New York

JOHN SLOAN

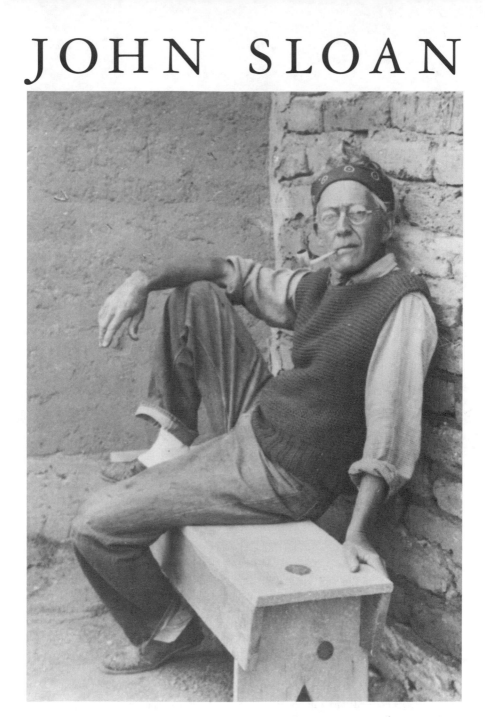

Painter and Rebel

Henry Holt and Company, Inc.
Publishers since 1866
115 West 18th Street
New York, New York 10011
Henry Holt® is a registered trademark of
Henry Holt and Company, Inc.

Published in Canada by Fitzhenry & Whiteside Ltd.,
195 Allstate Parkway, Markham, Ontario L3R 4T8.

Library of Congress Cataloging-in-Publication Data

Loughery, John.
John Sloan : painter and rebel / John Loughery. — 1st ed.
p.   cm.
"A John Macrae book."
Includes bibliographical references and index.
1. Sloan, John, 1871–1951. 2. Painters—United States—Biography.
3. Art and society—New York (N.Y.)—History—20th century. 4. New
York (N.Y.)—Intellectual life—20th century. I. Title.
ND237.S57L68   1995
759.13—dc20   94-39986
[B]   CIP

ISBN 0-8050-2878-1

Henry Holt books are available for special promotions and
premiums. For details contact: Director, Special Markets.

First Edition—May 1995

Designed by Kate Nichols

Printed in the United States of America
All first editions are printed on acid-free paper. ∞

1   3   5   7   9   10   8   6   4   2

For Thomas Orefice

Contents

"Though a living cannot be made at art,
art makes life worth living. It makes
living, living. It makes starving, living.
It makes worry, it makes trouble, it makes
a life that would be barren of everything—
living. It brings life to life."

—JOHN SLOAN

"Sloan called the other day. He is a new Sloan
every time I see him. He is a progressive man,
and therein the best kind of American, tho'
even here the progressive man is rare."

—JOHN BUTLER YEATS
to John Quinn
(1918)

Prologue:
To West Eighth Street

We are as distant from John Sloan's New York—from his America, in fact—as Sloan was from the New York of Whitman and Melville. Yet in a city that thrives on self-mythologizing and cultivates an indifference to the past in the hope of an ever busier, richer, *taller* future, the traces are still there, stark evidence of the time when the mythologizing began, when the patterns that would determine the future were just unfolding.

This is the world that John Sloan knew and chronicled and, in his way, helped to define before it vanished.

Begin at Andrew Carnegie's great gift to the metropolis. At the corner of Seventh Avenue and Fifty-seventh Street, Carnegie Hall is one of the few buildings in that part of the city left from the era of hansom cabs and the rumbling line of the "El." Dwarfed today by the black glass wedges and sandy brick of fifty-story apartment houses, it stood when Sloan arrived in New York as the preeminent structure of its neighborhood, two blocks south of Central Park. Indeed, Carnegie Hall was a kind of focal point for the men and women of Sloan's circle and generation. This building mattered then for the orchestras and conductors who performed there, but also for the drama of radical politics and passionate rhetoric it hosted in its early days and has since excluded: Emma Goldman and Margaret Sanger at the lecture podium, policemen in the aisles, a fashionable crowd downstairs, a balcony of Bolsheviks, Socialists, Anarchists, the young, the curious, the committed and indignant.

Here the Sloans regularly listened to speakers denounce a host of evils —the drift toward war in the Wilson years, the government's hostility to civil liberties and birth control, and the harassment of Sloan's old colleagues on *The Masses,* men such as Max Eastman, Floyd Dell, and Art Young. Here Dolly Sloan, the artist's wife, perennial fund-raiser for liberal and left-wing causes, took to the stage one night to help restore order to a gathering that threatened to get out of hand, mindful (like most of her colleagues in the movement) of the police commissioner's desire to curb the noisy "Reds." Here she and her husband celebrated with a thousand others the release of their friend Emma Goldman from prison in 1916. For the Sloans, life in the city before the sweeping changes of the 1920s and '30s meant guarded hope, useful conflict, and a willingness on the part of a clearly defined, genteelly impoverished group of intellectuals to work for the causes they believed in.

The Art Students League nearby is another incongruous survivor of urban progress. Only a half block to the west on Fifty-seventh Street, a few steps from Broadway, the League is a gray stone building just over a hundred years old, a four-story *hommage* to the French Renaissance. Its presence in an especially hectic stretch of Manhattan is even more unexpected than that of Carnegie Hall, but survive it has, almost in defiance of the real hub of the art world, three miles south.

The League versus SoHo, the traditional art school versus the politicized, postpainterly climate of the modern art world: this conflict of vision and values—realist nudes and carved sculpture in contrast to the more ambiguous, more lucrative products found in the land of Castelli and Sonnabend—is one that John Sloan, teacher at the League for more than twenty years, would have had cause to understand in a deeply personal way. An exhibitor in the legendary Armory Show, Sloan was keenly aware that he was living in a time of change and self-examination in the arts. The old tenets were under attack. New philosophies of art were evolving. His place in this new landscape, the ideas he wished to impart to his students as well as his own thoughts about Cézanne, Picasso, and the juggernaut of Modernism that was replacing the realism of his youth, was often more complicated than he was given credit for, and in the halls of the Art Students League for two decades—years that saw the disparate talents of Alexander Calder, John Graham, Adolph Gottlieb, and Jackson

Pollock pass through Sloan's classes—the debate was fierce. By the time of his angry resignation as president of the League, in 1932, Sloan had his doubts about the institution's commitment to a vital program. Yet the complex and important questions the new European artists had raised were not easily put to rest, nor was Sloan's role in the matter settled much before the advent of the New York School.

From the corner of Fifty-seventh Street down the corridor of Broadway through Midtown to Chelsea, New York City has always had less room for ghosts or landmarks. The staggering changes in this part of Manhattan would surprise the time traveler from 1950 and paralyze the visitor from 1930. The panorama Sloan painted in 1927 in *The White Way,* one of the last of his major city pictures, still allowed for sky, unthreatened pedestrians, the feel of the elements, a sense that the city (however aggressive its commercial interests were becoming) was not entirely indifferent to the pleasure and movement of its people. Sloan feared the passing of those qualities, with good reason. From the corporate towers of Sixth Avenue to the fortress-city of the Broadway Marriott, that sense of esprit, not to mention human scale, is harder to locate today. The energy of Midtown tends to be more daunting than invigorating. Yet, oddly, the angle of Broadway itself is the noteworthy vestige. A street that snakes its way diagonally through the island, breaking the grid and obscuring our view of the distance, suggests unexpected possibilities of experience and activity north and south of where we stand—and that promise is the real subject of *The White Way,* a force still felt in Manhattan, however diluted, at century's end.

To the south, office buildings and warehouses of the Garment District now occupy the streets that housed the seedy bars, the brothels, and the gambling dens of the area from Forty-second Street to Twenty-third—the "Tenderloin," as Sloan intimately knew it. One form of commerce takes the place of another. Bottlenecks of cars and trucks replace the heave and soot of the El. The old Penn Station, Stanford White's glory and a new addition to the skyline in the background of Sloan's *Pigeons* of 1910, has given way to a sixties skyscraper and a commuter's labyrinth. In Chelsea, though—the section from West Twenty-third Street to Greenwich Village with which Sloan's art is most identified—the fragments of the past come closest to forming a whole. The miraculous open space of Madison Square and the proud tower of the Flatiron Building have survived, and both Sloan's first and his last New York City residences—a battered brownstone on Twenty-third Street near Seventh Avenue and the redbrick Chelsea Hotel, a stately Gilded Age relic complete with iron balconies— stand today. These are the streets, no more genteel or less hectic in his own time, that Sloan walked to find the "bits of human drama" that he claimed as the theme of some of his most famous paintings and etchings. The richest "old money" families had left Chelsea by the time Sloan arrived in 1904, left it to just those mixes of people and shops, to the gentrifiers and the old-timers, that it is home to now.

Fourteenth Street, within sight of the spires of the Jefferson Market building, marks the northernmost point of Greenwich Village. The rakish Village that John and Dolly Sloan knew was still just that, a protected neighborhood, a sanctuary living on borrowed time. All direct north-south traffic on Sixth and Seventh Avenues ended at Greenwich Village before the First World War; the simple, inexpensive eateries, artists' studios, galleries, and bookstores were naively assumed to be a permanent characteristic of the territory. Within a short walk in Sloan's day were the offices of *The Masses* on Greenwich Avenue, the Provincetown Players, Mabel Dodge's salon, Romany Marie's and the Golden Swan, the Liberal Club and Webster Hall, and that percolating den of Socialism, the Rand School. The image of the Village as a center of art, intellect, and the bohemian good life, advertised by Sloan in some skillful etchings, lasted a bit longer than the equivalent images (whether suspect or real) of other areas of New York. No large modern city is willing to do without the illusion that it protects its special pockets, its countercultural glamour.

The Greenwich Village of the 1990s is a place that still represents relief from the conventions of Midtown, with its multicultural street life, its raucous energy—as well as the less fortunate attributes of drug dealing, gay bashing, noise, dense traffic, murderous rents, and omnipresent graffiti. In fact, to anyone walking the first block of Eighth Street east from Sixth Avenue, near the building where the Sloans lived from 1912 to 1927, the graffiti is often the most striking, most emblematic sight: it winds its way up the sides of the storefronts, along window frames, over awnings, climbing the fire escapes to heights and odd angles that surely require great agility and determination to reach.

Toward the end of this block (the main east-west artery of the Village), one building near Fifth Avenue stands out among the belt shops and shoe stores, the boarded-up movie house, the street vendors, the T-shirt displays. Number 8 West Eighth Street is a composite structure, a twentieth-century union of four nineteenth-century brownstones with a common front and four corresponding stables, later studios, attached to the back on Macdougal Alley. This building grew by degrees, as the occupant of a studio in the rear—the sculptor and heiress Gertrude Vanderbilt Whitney—acquired the properties and opened them in the present expansive configuration, in 1931, as the Whitney Museum of American Art.

Number 8 does not stand out because of any presumptuous stateliness in relation to its neighbors. The facade of the building is marred regularly by the graffiti that asserts itself everywhere else. The plaster shows its age. The once-uniform red of the four stories is more brownish at street level, where a severe, dark repainting tries to cope with recent vandalism. If anything, the building wears its decay more prominently than the less vivid architecture on the rest of Eighth Street. But even a casual pedestrian might intuit that this is a place with a distinctive history, a history that once mattered in New York. A look through the narrow glass doors, incongruously flanked by two white marble columns, shows a small entryway with a terrazzo floor, a double staircase with balusters in the shape of delicate tendrils, and niches in the wall for long-gone nymphs that formerly ushered visitors up and in.

This tight, eclectic lobby was a passage to rooms where almost every American artist of consequence in the 1930s was exhibited; where the *cause* of American art was most ardently advanced in a period when most Americans took for granted the inferiority of native talents to the European masters; where impoverished painters could turn for help and those working in isolation could find solidarity and support. Even before the building was expanded and opened as the museum proper, Mrs. Whitney exhibited painters and sculptors here as part of the adventurous program of her Whitney Studio Club. Many, like Sloan in 1916 at the time of his one-man show at the Club, enjoyed their first significant public exposure under this roof. An audience for American art was created and educated on Eighth Street between the wars; a framework for scholarship and professionalism that has transformed American culture took shape here. Controversies, ambitions, clashes of personality and ideology, the unique satisfaction of great paintings and sculptures—number 8 West Eighth Street was a forum, and at times an arena, for varying ends and diverse needs.

Gertrude Vanderbilt Whitney would be taken aback today by the state of her beautiful domain, whose decay was well under way by the 1960s, but she would be pleased—maybe compensatingly pleased—by one crucial fact. The old Whitney is not an abandoned site today, and it never gave up the ghost and saw the property relinquished for yet another co-op tower, another chain store, another video outlet. It lives on as the New York Studio School of Drawing, Painting, and Sculpture. The maze-like halls and ramshackle rooms have been home for the last twenty-odd years to just the kind of people the building was originally meant to guide and sustain. A heartening development was the announcement in 1992 that number 8 West Eighth Street had finally been granted landmark status by the city and that fund-raising for its renovation could begin—not, as one recent commentator aptly noted, with the intention of creating a spotless museumlike environment, but rather to preserve an art school "awash in dribbled paint and the baggage of artists who are living, not dead—very close to the spirit of the original institution." Surely this is a goal that everyone associated with the early life of the Whitney Museum of American Art would have appreciated, none more so than Sloan the artist and teacher, the eternal outsider.

In this same salmon-stucco building on West Eighth Street—minus the graffiti, minus the cracking plaster—the Whitney Museum's retrospective of John Sloan's career was held in January 1952, prior to its stop at the Corcoran Gallery of Art in Washington, D.C., and the Toledo Museum of Art in Ohio. Long announced but slow in coming to fruition, the exhibition was an event that Sloan himself had anticipated with decidedly mixed feelings.

After enjoying a critical success in his middle years followed by two decades of antagonism toward his later style of painting, Sloan felt that he had finally reached a point at which he could live and work in relative indifference to the judgments of his peers. "Official" praise for a man who had rarely had a kind word to say about American museums and curators —a man about to turn eighty, no less—seemed absurd. It was the kind of cultural embalming Sloan had always resisted. Yet throughout the spring of 1951 he helped the Whitney's associate director, Lloyd Goodrich, in the arduous business of rummaging through sixty years' worth of work to make his selections, submitting to the inevitable interviews and even, despite his curmudgeonly manner whenever the subject came up, allowing himself some pleasure in anticipating the honor. This exhibition was only the second one-man show the museum had devoted to a living American artist. Sloan's unexpected death in the autumn of 1951, however, made the celebration a posthumous one.

The crowds of guests who came to the museum late on the afternoon of January 9 for the opening, passing beneath Karl Free's white-metal eagle over the doorway, through the little foyer, and up the two weirdly Deco staircases, saw not only the great paintings of their own city that had made Sloan's reputation but the full, buoyant span of a career that encompassed an even larger number of paintings dealing with the coastline of New England, the arroyos and mesas of the Southwest, and the rituals of the Pueblo Indians. The ninety-eight paintings at the Whitney included classics like *The Haymarket, Three A.M., McSorley's Bar,* and *The White Way,* the later *Gloucester Harbor* and *Carnival, Santa Fe,* and a fair sampling of the controversial "cross-hatched" nudes and portraits of the 1930s and '40s. The etchings, an aspect of his work that Sloan had always approached with the same enthusiasm he felt toward oil-on-canvas, covered a forty-year span, from the first daring "City Life" prints through the renderings of Jazz Age speakeasies, from the majestic nudes of the early 1930s to the illustrations for a book-club edition of *Of Human Bondage,* which Somerset Maugham had praised for having "caught wonderfully" the spirit of his characters and the "tang of the period."

The surprise for almost all of those who had followed Sloan's work over the years lay in the cross-section of drawings Goodrich had chosen. The images of the Ludlow, Colorado, strike massacre or the pictures of the unemployed of 1913 that had appeared in the heady days of *The Masses* would not have been a revelation to anyone; though little had yet been written about it, the history of radical political journalism and political illustration in America had its pantheon already, and Sloan's was a name securely placed there. His graphic art had been as provocative as the best of Art Young's and Robert Minor's, as blistering as the prose of Jack Reed and Max Eastman that accompanied it. Rather, the pleasant shock came from the elegant, sinuous drawings Sloan had made in his twenties in Philadelphia for the daily papers he had worked for since 1892, in the heyday of newspaper illustration. That the man known as one of the founders of the school of "Ash Can realism" in American art (a term Sloan hated and a concept he thought ridiculous) had been, in his youth, a practitioner of Art Nouveau, a native version of an Aubrey

Beardsley or a Felix Vallotton, was news indeed to those who came to Greenwich Village that month for this exhibition, which *The New Yorker* called a "highly successful effort."

Not surprisingly, many of the notices of the show in the national press had a warmly respectful tone that would have set Sloan's teeth on edge. Billed by one magazine as the "painter laureate of Manhattan" and by another as an "important historian of the early years of the twentieth century," he was discussed in art-political as much as in aesthetic terms. The haunting light of *The "City" from Greenwich Village,* the able portraiture of *Yeats at Petipas,* the fluent brushstrokes in the best of the Gloucester and Santa Fe landscapes—none of these were pondered in much detail. "Sloan was one of the first American artists of the early twentieth century to force painting out of the salon and into the warm earthy life of the outdoors," the critic for the *Washington Post* wrote, before commenting on what seemed to him the dated qualities of the art itself. The *New York Times* reviewer wondered if "[Sloan's] influence may not outweigh his actual achievement as an artist." In the *New York Herald Tribune,* Emily Genauer was most direct about the climate of the moment and Sloan's place in the postwar scene: he was an eminently talented man and a "great and courageous personality," Genauer wrote, but she speculated about the timing of the retrospective. In a period that saw Abstract Expressionism transcendent over all other styles, how would Sloan's brand of realism fare among younger or more doctrinaire audiences? The implication—a perceptive one—was that Sloan might have to wait for another, later day for a more vigorous, appreciative response to his work. The advent of the New York School had meant the decline of any widespread interest for the moment in the circle of John Sloan, Robert Henri, Rockwell Kent, and Edward Hopper.

Still, the accolades at the time were considerable and meaningful in their own way. John Sloan was extolled on this occasion as a great painter who had helped the United States, just then emerging from the Gilded Age, to see itself in a new way, acknowledging the untidy reality of its urban social order while documenting a love affair with the American city when it was still something one could love. He was spoken of as a man who had inspired a generation of art students, fought the conservative museum establishment of his day, and tried to make a place for the experience of Native Americans in our cultural hierarchy. He was also remembered as an individual blessed in his friendships and vociferous, even belligerent, in his conception of what an artist should be: a man answerable only to his own interests and vision, unhindered by the demands of the marketplace. With American art entering a phase that involved high prices, well-oiled publicity machines, new fashion dictates, and limited tolerance for even the best figurative painting, Sloan began to look like the last of a line of truculent, independent, struggling painters raised on Whitman and Emerson, a nineteenth-century original who, like Alfred Stieglitz or Robert Frost, had somehow survived into the nuclear age.

What was barely mentioned, and not at all belabored, in the winter of 1952 was Sloan's earlier political affiliations with pacifist and radical Socialist groups. No one wanted to think about the file Mr. Hoover's agents had been amassing through the years. For even as Sloan was being honored in New York and Washington, he was about to be included in the next wave of attacks in Congress on "communistic" painters and the corruption of American life by wayward artists and "fellow travelers." Born in the era of Grant and Greeley, a spectator at Grover Cleveland's second inaugural and at the trials of Emma Goldman, he had lived to see the nightmare of Cold War rhetoric and the beginning of the McCarthy steamroller. Yet John Sloan, one of the most passionate chroniclers of American life, would have found in Congressman Dondero's infamous speeches about the evil influence of modern artists only confirmation of his belief (formulated in the days of McKinley and the first Roosevelt) that the leadership of the country had always been entrusted precisely to those who understood it least. To preserve what really mattered—art, personal and intellectual independence, civil liberties, the beauty of the city—was always a fight. But that, too, was an essential part of Sloan's America and Sloan's story.

JOHN SLOAN

Early Days

(1871–1891)

"We love the things we love for what they are."

—Robert Frost

In an interview late in his life, John Sloan remarked that he had been born "just about the time the French were shooting the Communists in Père Lachaise." The allusion was typical: vivid, offbeat, pointed, apt for a man with a sense of history (always rare among American artists), a boundless capacity for protest, and—in his seventies—a feeling of having narrowly been passed by, of having almost missed his place on the dynamic stage of his time. But to refer to the Paris Commune and to the brutality and bloodshed of 1871 was also, of course, a chance for John Sloan to take note of how far his *origins* were from that romantic arena. In Lock Haven, on the banks of the Susquehanna in central Pennsylvania, drama and challenge were in short supply, ambition had its limits, and the tensions were necessarily of a humbler sort.

Those tensions often had to do with money and social place, or the lack of them. When Henrietta Ireland, a schoolteacher who had lived in Lock Haven for two years, met, fell in love with, and married James Dixon Sloan in 1870, she was—by the standards of the Ireland family of Philadelphia—making a match that was by no means promising enough. The Sloan furniture and undertaking business (like most such establishments in nineteenth-century America, the local firm that provided desks and highboys was expected to deal in coffins as well) had experienced a slow decline since its peak in the 1850s. Competition from new factories, among them the Boyertown Casket Company, and two disastrous fires

1

had brought the concern to the brink of insolvency, and since his return from the Civil War and his recovery from typhoid fever, James Sloan had been doing his best to make a living as a photographer and bicycle repairman. The dignity of honest labor notwithstanding, the grand-daughter of Samuel Priestley, a well-to-do Pennsylvania paper merchant, was expected to aim higher. But with his warm smile, scraggly hair, and full, dark mustache (of a thickness that his son was never able to imitate), Sloan must have seemed a desirable partner for a woman of education, about to turn thirty: all accounts refer to a decent, caring, easygoing man, gentle, intelligent, and talented. No matter that Henrietta's sisters, purse-proud Episcopalians, had been sent to finishing school in Switzer-land. No matter that her younger sister Emma was soon to marry the wealthy William Hardcastle Ward, son of the founder of Marcus Ward & Co., a stationery and publishing business of greater renown than Priestley & Co. of Philadelphia. No matter that at thirty-five, James Sloan gave the impression of a man whose prime was quite possibly behind him and whose financial prospects were slim. Henrietta Ireland knew her own mind—she wouldn't have been on her own, teaching in a girls' academy in a lumber town two hundred miles from her parents' home, if she hadn't been an independent sort—and wed the man of her choice.

According to the conventional wisdom of the 1870s, a woman of thirty was assumed to have very little time to spare if she desired chil-dren, and Henrietta was pregnant soon after her wedding. A first child, a son, was born on August 2, 1871. That same month, James Sloan's father died, and the boy was named for his paternal grandfather: John French Sloan. Two years later, a girl—Elizabeth Priestley Sloan, called Bess—joined the family circle, and in 1875, Marianna, the last of Henrietta's babies to survive, was born. Four years later, a son christened Henry died in infancy.

John Sloan's recollections of his childhood, on those rare occasions when he discussed his early years, were almost uniformly benevolent. He would speak of a mother who never nagged and who loved a witty retort or a good joke, a religious woman but a much less severe figure than her sisters ("a born punster . . . a Dionysian at heart"). He would refer to his hapless father in terms that accorded the man the dignity he deserved but rarely enjoyed. And as a much-doted-on only son, so clearly his mother's favorite, John probably had less cause than his sisters to be critical or bitter. Yet the Sloans of Lock Haven were a markedly undemonstrative family, and not without their problems. Affection was never expressed in a physical way, not even to the extent of a simple kiss before bed for the children, and Marianna, the most high-strung of the three, was prone to fierce tantrums that led to unpleasant scenes and hours spent locked in her room or a closet. The pall of Ireland religiosity was to cast a wider shadow each year as well, dividing father and adolescent son from Henrietta's pious daughters, just as the uncertainty of James Sloan's income and ambition took its toll.

A common characteristic of the three siblings in their early years, though, was also a common source of joy in the narrow, almost yardless two-story brick house on North Grove Street and later, after they moved, in the bigger house on Camac Street in Philadelphia. To a remarkable extent, this was a family with a special feel for pencils, ink, and fine rag paper—commodities that the firm founded by Henrietta's grandfather and maintained for a while by her uncle could provide—and for well-made books of the sort that Marcus Ward & Co. produced. They all loved to read, to pore over the illustrations in their gift books (especially those containing the popular drawings of Walter Crane), and to sketch. A Sunday painter himself, their father was delighted with the interest John, Bess, and Marianna showed in art, and he encouraged them in the development of their imaginative and graphic skills. In this household, the practical had to make way on occasion for the aesthetic and the inventive side of life; allowing time for the young ones to play, to moon about, to putter with their father's tools, or to draw or paint with watercolor at the kitchen table was considered crucial. Whatever the other hesitations and misdirections of his life, of which there were many, James Dixon Sloan was in this regard decisively, purposefully, on the mark.

Although he lived for the first six years of his life in a small town, John Sloan was a creature of the city. Visiting Lock Haven in 1940, on his first trip back after the family's departure in 1877, he was surprised by how little he remembered and how little nostalgia his visit evoked. Not even the house seemed familiar. A much clearer and more exciting early memory was that of his first experience of Philadelphia in the year of the great Centennial celebration.

The excursion made by James and John Sloan in the summer of 1876 had a less than happy purpose for Sloan senior. For too long, at least since the catastrophic recession of 1873, it had been evident that there was not going to be a secure enough future for a growing family in tiny Lock

Haven. Indeed, James Sloan felt under a kind of cloud in his hometown. Part of that cloud was of his own making: he was a hopeless manager of money, and his decision to co-sign a promissory note for his brother—a note that John Nelson Sloan had been unable to repay—had irreparably set him back. Philadelphia meant a fresh start, and it was on this trip to look into job prospects in the eastern part of the state that his son had his first chance to see the world beyond the Susquehanna.

The Philadelphia Centennial Exposition, opened with much fanfare by President Grant and the Emperor of Brazil on the two hundred acres of Fairmont Park above the Schuykill, was the grandest spectacle the hundred-year-old republic had ever seen. Several million people attended the fair to bask in the artistic, scientific, and commercial glories of the age. A five-year-old was probably less interested in the paintings on view by John Singleton Copley, Gilbert Stuart, and Winslow Homer than in the pavilions devoted to more exotic and technological fare, but the Sloans certainly stopped by the prizewinning Marcus Ward & Co. display of stationery, calendars, posters, and greeting cards designed by European illustrators like Kate Greenaway and J. Moyr Smith. Now related by marriage, through Aunt Emma, to William Ward himself, the family had reason to be proud of and interested in this new and popular middle-class product. In an age that lacked the man-made visual stimulation, not to say the daily bombardment of images, that we live with in the twentieth century—no photographs in newspapers or magazines, no comic strips, no museum posters, no billboard drawings, no film or television—exhibitions of illustrated paper products at large fairs had an impact that is hard to assess and appreciate today. For a family with a flair for drawing, this was particularly true. Of course, what interested John Sloan most, he remembered, was the famous brass-and-steel Corliss Engine that set the walls quivering in Machinery Hall; like so many others in the crowd, he told of standing mesmerized before the power and heat of this duplex vertical engine with its fifty-six-ton flywheel, and of having to be forcibly led away by his father.

After such an introduction, when his parents announced the following spring that the family was moving to Philadelphia, John was just as likely to be excited by the prospect as not. The memories of the Exposition had cast their spell. Only when he was older did he learn there hadn't been much choice in the matter: the Sloans had lost their house in Lock Haven.

For several months John, Bess, Marianna, and their parents lived with Grandmother Ireland in Germantown, a comfortable suburb of Philadelphia, while James Dixon Sloan looked for work. This was a torturous period for the unemployed father of three; the Irelands, both collectively and in little ways, made their son- and brother-in-law feel the weight of their disappointment and disapproval. Economic realities should have called for some sympathy with the plight of this man who wasn't lazy and who was, after all, doing his best. A record nine thousand business failures were recorded in America the year the Sloans moved to Philadelphia —those dark months of a stolen presidential election and a violent nationwide railway strike—leading one journalist to describe the country as a "weary and aching mass of unemployed or half-employed capital, misdirected talent, and underpaid labor." The phrase *misdirected talent* fairly described James Dixon Sloan's predicament, and in any case it was not likely in such parlous times that he would find a position for himself on his own. Eventually, in a final indignity, his in-laws had to see that he was set up as a traveling salesman, a commission job for which he was woefully unsuited.

As John Sloan recalled with some terseness, "Mother's family got him a job as a traveling salesman for the Marcus Ward Company. My uncle Alfred Ireland [Henrietta's older brother] was the American representative for this firm [though he was still connected to Priestley & Co. for the moment]. . . . My father never made more than twenty five dollars a week, and I suspect that my uncle Alfred paid some of that salary out of his own pocket." But at least the family was able to move from Germantown into Philadelphia, to a rented house of their own at 1921 Camac Street, where John Sloan would live with his parents and sisters for the next fifteen years.

Life assumed a more outer-directed course for John Sloan once the family settled in on Camac Street. Taught to read by his mother and kept at home until he was eight, John went to a private school in the neighborhood that year and then to public school. Mrs. Sloan had a newborn son, Henry, to tend to in 1879—another reason to send her eldest out into the world—and the baby's health was, from the start, far from good. Indeed, Henry was dead by the end of his first year, an event that (along with James's poor return as a salesman) made for an initially somber and uneasy atmosphere in the Sloans' new home.

Henrietta, however, was not one to complain. If she lacked the power to make everything right, at least she showed more fortitude and humor than her own mother and sisters in the face of difficulty. As her son would later comment on several occasions, thanks to his mother, he hadn't known how financially pressed the family really was in their first years in Philadelphia. In front of the children, anyway, Henrietta made no complaints and never challenged her husband. It wasn't until he visited an adolescent friend whose parents invited him to stay for dinner that Sloan noticed how much food the friend's family had on the table for one meal, in contrast to the practice of his own house, where just enough for everyone was served. That a stigma might be attached to their family in the middle-class neighborhood where they lived, making do without hired help or any fineries, had never occurred to him. Mrs. Sloan would joke that she liked to have watermelon—because "it makes such rich looking garbage." Yet even the awareness that they were poor (a word Sloan himself much preferred to *underprivileged*) meant nothing to the Sloans in terms of the high expectations they had for their son. He might well be the doctor or lawyer of the family, his parents felt; he was certainly bright enough. His aunts thought they detected the makings of an Episcopal minister in their handsome, well-behaved nephew, and they made sure he took part in the boys' choir at the Church of the Annunciation.

Between the ages of nine and twelve, Sloan went on the first great reading binge of his life, devouring the works of Rider Haggard, James Fenimore Cooper, Robert Louis Stevenson, Dickens, and Shakespeare, a pleasure encouraged by everyone around him. Never an especially athletic or rowdy child, he had an affect—devoid of the tormenting instincts common in little boys, wistful, gentle, dutiful rather than rebellious— that encouraged the Ireland family's speculations that it had a budding High Church clergyman in its midst. His brushes with indignant authority, as on the occasion when he and another boy broke into an abandoned house down the block and were caught by a policeman, or the time an aunt reprimanded him for a prank in the choir loft, were few and far between. But an attentive observer among the Irelands would have noted that the drive toward the visual—toward a skilled use of the paper and pens to which the family fortunes were so bound—was a greater constant than religion in John Sloan's childhood. At twelve he was happily filling the blank sections of pages of his own edition of *Treasure Island* with fairly detailed, highly competent illustrations in watercolor.

John Sloan always maintained that his sister Marianna was the most

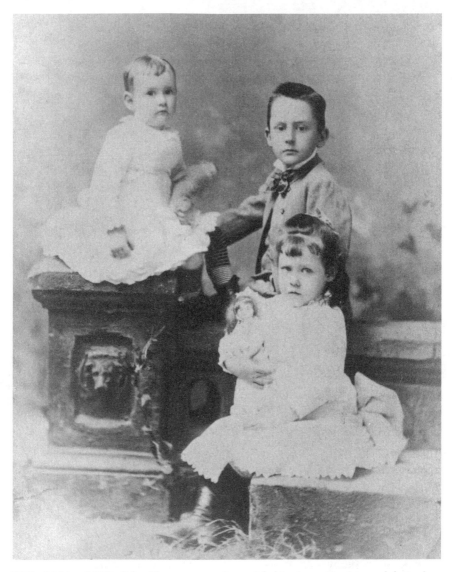

Philadelphia, 1880: John Sloan at age nine, with his sisters Marianna, left, and Elizabeth (Delaware Art Museum)

naturally talented artist of the three children, and that may well have been true. As an adult, she was a more than respectable painter and had several well-received exhibitions. Sloan insisted that his own ability came through diligent application, that it was less fluent than his sister's gift. Yet what he had in his favor, probably from the beginning (and it in fact suggests that the girls were raised very differently from their brother), was a greater energy and flexibility, an inquisitive drive, a more open approach to just about everything—to diversity of experience, work, life, friends, pleasure, religion. By adolescence Bess and Marianna were somewhat narrow young women, true products of their aunts' forbidding social codes, and in time they were to evince what Sloan regarded as a morbid, "desperate" religious fervor and a stiff-necked sense of decorum. Marianna acquired in her youth a pinched, nervous look that stayed with her for many years. When their father stopped going to church on Sundays, both girls were sternly judgmental, visibly disapproving of his waywardness. If he came home with beer on his breath at the end of a long day, they would turn up their noses at him. At such times the spirit of the house, normally pleasant or at least tolerable, would turn uncomfortable.

For James Sloan, who liked nothing better than to relax at home and tinker with his tools, dabble with his paints, or sit in the yard and read, the weight of judgment was not easy to bear. He began to show signs of depression. As time went on, the anticipated "break" that was supposed to establish his fortunes never materialized. Had anyone actually thought it would happen? The very character trait that had led to the loss of the Sloans' house in Lock Haven through the default of John Nelson Sloan's promissory note—a generosity in, or credulity about, money matters, a lack of pecuniary savvy or caution—was slowly doing in the new business James Sloan had started in 1883 after giving up his commission sales work. As the owner of a small stationery shop of his own on Arch Street, financed by his wife's family and stocked with paper, greeting cards, and books from Marcus Ward, Sloan compounded his lack of aggressive salesmanship with a propensity for extending credit beyond the bounds of caution. (This was a problem that would be passed on from father to son, with equally serious consequences for John Sloan.) On balance, then, the impression made by this troubling situation was clear enough. His father, whom he loved, John Sloan saw—accurately—as a man who cut a poor figure in the world at large. A good soul at heart, he disappointed the women in his life and felt the burden of his own weakness. The representatives of position and power in society, on the other hand, were those of his relatives who often seemed the least playful and the least emotionally responsive.

Not all of the familial images were so frustrating, though. Uncle Alexander—Alexander Priestley, who was in fact Henrietta's uncle—was a striking exception to the patterns of amiable failure and dour success that confronted John Sloan in the 1880s. For Uncle Alexander, a middle-aged widower, was that rare thing in a bourgeois American family, an able businessman (now allied to Marcus Ward & Co. as well as his own family's company) with a scholarly bent, an aesthete and bibliophile who was more intellectually motivated than profit-minded, and the visual and literary entertainments that Priestley could offer his niece's son on his visits to his house made a strong impression on the boy. Books illustrated by George Cruikshank and Gustave Doré, elephant folios of Hogarth and Rowlandson prints, copies of *Punch* and *Harper's Monthly* with drawings by George du Maurier, John Leech, and Edwin Austin Abbey—the accumulation of Uncle Alexander's elegant library on Park Avenue in Philadelphia, in a room redolent of tobacco and sherry, was a potent treasure for a twelve-year-old with an active imagination and a curious eye. There was a dark side to this fine man, though, at least in the blinkered view of the Ireland sisters. Alexander "occasionally imbibed a trifle too much," Sloan noted years later in what was probably a generous assessment of the issue, and in those times his nieces and their daughters wanted nothing to do with him. Once, in a rare display of adolescent primness, Sloan turned his great-uncle away at the door when he arrived "under the influence"—a memory that rankled even half a century later.

Still, the lines were, or seemed to be, clearly drawn at the Sloan house: talent and accomplishment were appreciated, failings of the flesh and offenses to propriety were not ever to be tolerated. That these two contraries might overlap in the same person was, apparently, never an allowable consideration. Hence the disturbing anomaly of Uncle Alexander, alternately the black sheep of the family and one of its most distinguished members.

If in the eyes of her parents and sisters there had always been precious little that was distinguished about Henrietta's husband, the Irelands were given abundant and final verification of their judgment in the spring of 1888. The unraveling of James Sloan's finances—and mental health—was at hand.

Since the age of thirteen, John Sloan had been a student at the prestigious Central High School in Philadelphia. He had missed half of one year due to an eye ailment and his mother's wish that he remain at home, but he was in a college preparatory program, like his classmates William Glackens and Albert Barnes—the future painter and the future tycoon–art collector—and he enjoyed everything about the experience, especially his classes in geometry, history, and etymology. Despite the turmoil at home when his father's stationery store had closed the year before, Sloan had every reason to expect that he would be going on to a university as a scholarship student, like many of his peers at Central. His father had been doing odd jobs, repairing bicycles and raising chickens in the backyard, and somehow making ends meet. But in April 1888 the strain became too much, and James Sloan suffered a breakdown. From that time on he would never be fully able to shake free of the sense of failure and melancholy that slowly engulfed him. A family conference involving the in-laws was held just before Easter, and it was decided that the Sloans didn't actually have much choice in the matter. After all, the Irelands could help only so far. John would have to leave school, find a full-time job, and take responsibility for maintaining the house and supporting his parents and his fifteen- and thirteen-year-old sisters. To his credit, James Sloan took it on himself to tell his son of the decision. It was an anguishing moment for both; for the younger man, the look of pain and defeat on his father's face was hard to bear and, for all his days, impossible to forget. To compound the trauma of that spring, Horatio Hastings Weld, one of Sloan's favorite great-uncles (a supportive man who, like Uncle Alexander, had a fine library that he opened to his nephew's perusal), died, leaving Sloan feeling very much alone among the women and obligations that confronted him. His family's pastor was a helpful presence in the parlor, a friendly shoulder to lean on, but in the final analysis there wasn't much to be said or done to alleviate the situation. Six months before he would have received his diploma, Sloan dropped out of school.

Certainly he was no stranger to work. All through his adolescence Sloan had supplemented the household income with summer jobs, often in a lawyer's office or, earlier, at the railroad yard, where he was a freight-car checker and sealer (a job he found somewhat formidable at thirteen). But the stark fact of full-time employment at the age of sixteen and a half had a different meaning, obviously, and a different impact. Sloan was not one to hurl accusations or bemoan his lot. Disparaging his father, especially when the man was clearly in the throes of an incapacitating depression and made no secret of his humiliation, wasn't something he was apt to do. Such frustration or anger as he must have felt at his missed opportunities took a more interesting, underground, convoluted form. It would be two decades before the famous lacerating Sloan temper would become a feature of his personality. But within a few years he was gradually to reject many of the principles—the more superficial ones, as he saw it, though society would not have agreed—on which his mother, aunts, and sisters based their family life. In his twenties, this young man from an intensely religious, politically conservative, sexually reticent, teetotaling family would remake himself into an agnostic, vaguely left-wing, hard-drinking artist whose wife's background and sexual experiences would have shocked the life out of Henrietta, Bess, or Marianna had any of them ever known the truth. Such choices constituted one kind of reaction—a fairly decisive reaction—to an early life passed in a controlling environment and to a restrained, even docile adolescence. In the spring of the year when he was forced to leave high school, though, all John Sloan could do was make the best of a bad situation.

For a while Sloan worked as an errand boy at the office of J. Morris Harding, the Ireland family lawyer, but the work was neither interesting nor (more important) lucrative enough. Porter & Coates, where he next landed a job, was a more agreeable and, as it turned out, much more purposeful place of employment. A relaxed downtown bookstore rather like Scribner's in New York, Porter & Coates offered its newest assistant cashier (on a salary of six dollars a week, or a dollar a day) shelves upon shelves of well-made books to read when there were no customers around, and a excellent print department to browse through. The work was easy, even sedentary, and the perquisites were exactly to his taste. Balzac and the French realists were the first significant intellectual discoveries of that year for Sloan; in his off-hours on the job, he enjoyed the many volumes of *La Comédie Humaine* and the novels and stories of Flaubert, Hugo, Zola, and Maupassant. The revelations that came with a study, at once unhurried and undirected, of the prose styles and subject matter of these writers had a predictably bracing effect. This, the second great reading binge of Sloan's life, constituted, ironically, a kind of education that he would not have been exposed to at home or at Central High. The world of *The Sentimental Education, Nana, L'Assomoir, Germinal, La Bête Humaine,* and *Bel-Ami* was something else, something challenging and pleasurable, an experience both more exotic and more real. And more private, as well: it was no one's concern but his if his free moments were spent pondering Flaubert's savage satire, Zola's politics, or the women of "la belle epoque." In a similarly liberating spirit, he found the Doré-illustrated edition of Rabelais that he came upon "gloriously jolly"—hardly an opinion to voice in a middle-class home in 1888—and found within himself a taste for earthy erotic humor that he would never lose.

Of the print-room bounty at Porter & Coates, Sloan was especially struck by the original John Leech drawings for *Vanity Fair* and by the stock of Rembrandt and Dürer etchings he had access to. J. E. Carr, the director of the print department, encouraged him to try his own pen-and-ink copies of the pictures he liked, and it was not long before he was equipped with a copy of Philip Gilbert Hamerton's *Etcher's Handbook,* Chattock's *Practical Notes on Etching,* and a plate, needle, and roller. Teaching himself how to etch seemed a wonderful way to pass the evening or a Sunday afternoon, and he must have surprised himself with the skill he displayed from the start—indeed, Sloan was always to show a great reluctance to credit himself with any facility at all. The earliest extant Sloan works, none of them untalented, date from this time: a copy of the head from Rembrandt's 1639 etching *Rembrandt Leaning on a Stone Sill;* a copy of a reproduction of a Turner castle that hung over the mantelpiece at home; and a portrait of Marianna, looking coy and girlish. Nan, as Marianna was called, remembered in her old age the circumstances of the etching of her. It was after a fierce snowstorm when she was thirteen that her brother set up shop in the parlor. "The sitting room was used for his experiments," she recalled. "The open old-fashioned gas flame made a good place to heat the flame, and the whole process of etching was worked out." Hamerton in particular served as an able guide: his *Etcher's Handbook* and *Etchers and Etching,* which Sloan also acquired, provided technical information, illustrations of master etchings, and reflections on the lapidary nature of the medium. The two books displayed a practical yet quietly lyrical feel for the business of "rambl[ing] on copper," as one writer quoted by their author described the art of etching.

Happily, Sloan's progress in this area did not go unrecognized at Porter & Coates. His copies of the etchings in the print department were sold in the store for five dollars apiece, providing a handsome addition to his weekly income even after the store's cut was deducted, and his hand-drawn Valentines with satirical verses went for twenty-five cents each. Better yet, before the end of Sloan's second year there, A. Edward Newton, a clerk who had left the bookstore several months before Sloan arrived, heard of the work he was turning out—probably from Carr—and enticed him away from Porter & Coates to his own new establishment. Newton's was, in the parlance of the day, a "fancy goods" business. His shop on Locust Street sold elegant stationery, cards, little books and portfolios, button and candy boxes, handkerchief cases, bookmarks, sachets, and other assorted hand-painted, decorated, or embroidered novelties, and he wanted the young man to make calendars and etchings for him and to illustrate his cards and bookmarks. When he offered him a three-dollar-a-week raise with another three to follow soon after, Newton (who was only seven years Sloan's senior but already seemed marked for success) got the novice graphic designer he was seeking.

Work at A. E. Newton's, where Sloan remained from early 1890 until the middle of 1891, had its pleasures and its drawbacks. The drawbacks included the curtailing of his reading time on the job—no more perusing art books and volumes of Balzac, no more memorizing passages from Pope and Blake perched on a stool behind the counter—and the boisterous female company in the work area of the store. Always reticent around girls, at Newton's Sloan was the only male employee among twenty-eight women of varying ages who weren't shy about making jokes and ribald remarks concerning the awkward, easily tongue-tied artist who never asked any of them out on a date. The young women painting French lovers frolicking on the lids of candy boxes could be quite caustic sometimes. "They knew I was afraid of them," Sloan said, and they took their revenge accordingly. Yet when no one was looking, he would sneak out to the cloakroom to smell the odors of perfume that lingered on their coats and jackets.

Past question, though, the good outweighed any tribulations on the job, at least at the beginning: Sloan was paid to spend the day drawing, designing, planning, fiddling with paper, "rambling on copper"—and what could be better than that? Among his more notable projects for Newton were thirteen etchings of Westminster Abbey for an illustrated booklet about that cathedral, and six based on photographs of the homes of some of the country's best-loved writers: Longfellow, Lowell, Poe, Hawthorne, Emerson, and Whittier. The latter pictures, published by Newton in 1891 in a second edition of the portfolio *Homes of the Poets,* are particularly capable work from someone who had started to etch only two years before. Newton, the person whose judgment counted most, was sufficiently impressed to offer to take his protégé to Europe to further his study of art in the great museums that America still lacked. The sudden offer was flattering, but Sloan declined for a number of reasons. One was the impossibility of leaving his family on their own; a second was the unpleasant prospect of incurring such a huge debt to his boss; and a third, of possibly equal significance with the others, was that the whole idea of such a venture seemed too complicated and frightening for a nineteen-year-old who could count on one hand the number of times he had left Philadelphia since moving there at age six. Wanderlust was not a part of John Sloan's makeup.

James Sloan evidently felt some pride in his eldest child's laudable rise in the world, such as it was. He could take pleasure in the fact that well-to-do people like A. E. Newton admired his son, and he enjoyed what he saw of the clever handiwork that John produced at his job. A firm believer in the nurturing of innate talent, in the autumn of 1890 he accompanied John to the Spring Garden Institute—Philadelphia's version of Cooper Union, as Van Wyck Brooks has described it—where the younger Sloan registered for a freehand drawing class. The night class Sloan took there was his first formal art education. If it was not especially helpful in the development of his artistic skills (the Institute tended to emphasize commercial forms of drawing), the class did enhance his sense of himself as someone moving in the right direction, a direction his father respected.

Yet for all of its pleasures and possibilities, it was something of an odd, monastic life that John Sloan found himself leading in his late teens. "Other boys my age were going out mashing, to the theater and so forth," he later commented about those days, "and I guess I just preferred to draw and to escape the problem of what to do about girls." The problem "about girls" was that Sloan was as attracted and as sexually frustrated as any celibate boy of that age would have been (those perfumes made the right impression), but he was unsure of himself and leery of the consequences of romance. He was almost desperately afraid that like his father, he would wake up one day to find himself "married and caught for life." The possibility of a looser relationship didn't seem plausible, not in his social circle. The young women of the neighborhood or those he met through Bess, when she was in high school, seemed transparent in their expectations. Everyone was in a rush to pair off, settle down, make binding commitments. Love meant an engagement and marriage; sex meant

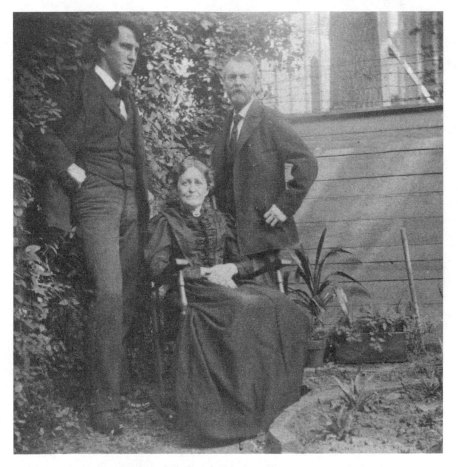

Sloan with his parents, Henrietta Ireland Sloan and James Dixon Sloan, circa 1890 (Delaware Art Museum)

pregnancy or a ruined reputation—and both of those inevitably meant marriage in the end, anyway. Drawing and etching afforded what pleasure, satisfaction, and control Sloan was able to feel in his life.

The most solid accomplishment of this period of Sloan's youth, however, had nothing to do with his drawing or etching, and was a work that Sloan himself never regarded very highly: his first self-portrait in oil. Having diligently studied John Collier's *A Manual of Oil Painting* that past winter, and feeling ready to see what he could do in his own right, he turned to the conventional subject matter of ambitious beginners—his own likeness—and the only usable flat material at hand, namely, a kitchen window shade. About the *Self-Portrait* of 1890, now in the collection of the Delaware Art Museum, Sloan was never effusive, or even objective. In 1950 he called it a "very plain piece of work[, one that] shows no facility or brilliance. The work of a plodder." In fact, the painting, though small, is a strong effort for an untutored young man not quite nineteen years old. The face is carefully modeled. The proportions are deftly managed. The shadow under the neck, the angularity of the cheeks, the glint of the eyes, and the textures of skin and cloth are all just right. Moreover, by painting himself in a black suit against a dark background, Sloan met his own challenge in a forthright way: the picture stands or falls on the detail and strength of the face and (considering the massiveness of the dapper nineties necktie) the upper torso. Here is the thin, unruddy, open countenance of a young seminarian—the Protestant minister-to-be his aunts had counted on—who seems duty-bound, ready to appear to be whatever age he has to be. But the withholding individual who hides behind the spectacles and the steady gaze is *there* nonetheless, if only in the vehemence with which he denies himself much flair—a still, undramatic figure, with the silk knot of that fat black tie obstinately, or boyishly, raked to the side.

Sloan's employment with Newton lasted for a little more than a year. Newton was not an ideal boss (though his most diligent employee never elaborated on the tenor of the relationship), and Sloan himself turned out not to be as meek or as pliable as he appeared. By the middle of 1891, as his twentieth birthday approached, he was restless and wanted to see what he could accomplish on his own. He vividly remembered the counsel his deceased Uncle Horatio Hastings Weld had given him just before he left high school: never shirk your responsibilities, but at the same time, do everything you can to keep your independence. When Newton declined his request for another raise, Sloan used the refusal as an excuse to give notice. It was time to see if the poles of his great-uncle's advice could be effectively reconciled.

A Mentor

(1891–1894)

"Youth is wholly experimental."

—Robert Louis Stevenson

Life as a freelancer had its decided advantages. The best deal in the world, Sloan thought, was to be one's own boss, answerable in success or failure only to oneself. When he took a six-by-ten-foot studio on Walnut Street, complete with a view of a brick wall and a desk that filled almost all of the space, setting himself up as a graphic-artist-for-hire, he felt a kind of cocky exuberance that nothing in his earlier experience had prepared him for. *Sole support of the family* was a role that now came with a certain thrill along with a feeling of responsibility.

Wisely, Sloan had left Newton's without severing all ties. He had earned the man's respect and maintained a sufficiently close relationship with him to get his father a part-time job at the shop for a few weeks and to complete a number of etchings on commission for his old employer. For the rest of his income, though, he was on his own as both craftsman and salesman of his wares—which included the usual potpourri of greeting and business cards, novelties, diplomas, baptismal certificates, and advertisements. For a while, Sloan remembered, business was brisk. A contract with the Bradley Coal Company for streetcar ads meant a steady if meager income and a regular supply of coal. He sold three drawings to the comic magazine *Judge;* never published, they were nonetheless paid for. Unfortunately, and not surprisingly, by late autumn expenses were exceeding revenue, a situation that Sloan knew could not last very long, and the young artist began to fear that his great venture might be

17

doomed to failure. Coming up with the six dollars a month to rent his studio and the money for the household expenses for his parents and sisters was one thing; his mother's worsening neuritis and the resulting medical bills were another.

In November he asked for, or one of his aunts provided him with, a letter of recommendation from William Ward, the Irelands' best by-marriage contact. Addressed to a Philadelphia merchant, C. W. Beck (whom Sloan obstinately declined to approach), it was strangely insightful on the part of a man who couldn't have known his nephew very well.

> As you will see [the scion of Marcus Ward & Co. wrote], my nephew has made some attempts with the etching needle. . . . He is very assiduous. . . . I feel sure he has decided talent and will get on. . . . One good trait in his character is his independence. He has got along so far entirely unassisted, and is determined to rely upon his own labour in the future, and also to help his mother. This makes the earning of some steady sum, small though it may be for a time, a necessity; and it may retard his progress in art—but with his determination to get on he is sure to succeed in the long run.

Assiduity, independence (perhaps to a fault later in life), commitment to family, slow progress, great talent and determination: no one else ever summarized John Sloan's qualities so concisely, and this in the year of his twentieth birthday.

By February, Sloan felt enough confidence in his portfolio to consider approaching a local newspaper. When he brought a selection of his drawings to the headquarters of the *Philadelphia Inquirer* on Market Street, it was with the nervous intention of applying for freelance work. He hoped that someone at the paper would think enough of his portfolio to employ him from time to time until he was better established on his own. After informing Sloan that the *Inquirer* did not use independent illustrators, the art director mentioned that his department was in fact in need of another full-time staffer. His options at the moment being rather limited, Sloan accepted the offer and so drifted, to his surprise and ultimate delight, into his first career. In return for surrendering the freedom to set his own hours and make his own pictorial choices, he was paid as much money in one week as he had been making in three on his own, and found a larger audience for his work than he had ever contemplated.

The early 1890s were dynamic, advantageous years in which to begin work as a newspaper illustrator, and the *Inquirer*—called by one historian the "most enterprising sheet in Philadelphia"—was, in its way, a good paper to join. With a circulation of eighty-five thousand, it more than held its own in a city with thirteen major dailies, not counting the foreign-language press. It was in its sixty-third year of publication and its third under a new owner, a tycoon who wanted "wide-awake" men on his large staff and saw the value in making his paper more visually stimulating in those days before mass-reproduced photography. For that matter, the *Inquirer* had always been alert to the public's desire to see newsprint interspersed with pictures and designs. As far back as the Civil War, the paper had been said to be in a class by itself; woodcuts of generals, admirals, and politicians had been featured several times a week, and its maps of Union and Confederate battlefields had been among the largest in the country.

The *Inquirer* in 1892 was also one of Philadelphia's many Republican papers, staunchly supportive of President Harrison and the local G.O.P. and sharply critical of the Democrats, those lowbrow defenders of "rum, Romanism, and rebellion." Grover Cleveland's efforts to recapture the White House were viewed as something of a national calamity. In the custom of nineties' journalism, editorial comment wasn't restricted to an inside editorial page: headlines warning that the Democrats would have to be carefully monitored at the polls, and front-page cartoons portraying Cleveland as a circus buffoon or a big-bellied pasha, weren't unheard-of under James Elverson's lively management. Not that any of this mattered to John Sloan—in his early twenties, he was as apolitical as everyone else on the art staff and, like them, scarcely read the paper at all. It was a job, it paid well, and the atmosphere in the room he shared with the other illustrators was as far removed from the oppressive feminine domain of Newton's "fancy goods" shop as it could be.

The "gang" in the art room was a diverse group, though its members were remarkably alike in their capacity for work and talk, their irreverence, their penchant for sexual bravado, and the hours they clocked propping up the bar at Greene's Hotel down the street. The paper's political cartoons came from the caustic pen of R. C. Swayze, the resident wit. Ed Davis, at twenty-four already the father of a child—two-year-old Stuart

Davis, who would become one of the country's first great abstract painters
—made feminine fashions and well-proportioned young women his specialty, an interest that some said extended beyond the paper's Sunday
supplement. Sloan also became friends with Charles Drake, Harry Ponitz,
and the affable Joe Laub, the last of whom suggested that they split a
studio of their own. It was a good match, and for no more money than he
was paying for the closet-sized space he had been renting for the past
several months, Sloan soon found himself with a more commodious after-
hours home and a like-minded pal. He was also given a tour of the city's
"cathouses" by his new associates (though if any of these was the site of
the loss of his virginity, as seems likely, Sloan was too discreet ever to
comment on it), and approvingly dubbed an easy "touch" for a loan. The
perimeters of his world, once bounded by the Camac Street house and his
solitary work experiences, were rapidly expanding. These were the equivalent of college days for him, Sloan later said—"all the fun and no examinations."

Sloan's first signed picture appeared in the edition for Tuesday, February 16, 1892. A boiler had exploded in a small local hotel that day,
killing twenty-three people and knocking out an entire side of the building. The paper's newest artist-reporter was directed to the scene for a
sketch of the carnage. What he returned with was a trifle *too* sketchy for
his editors' taste—a clear enough depiction of a damaged hotel, the street
filled with broken bricks and onlookers, but a little short on the detail the
editors liked, or any sense of gory reality. His next drawings, the following day, appeared on the front page of the paper, accompanying an article
entitled "THE AWFUL WORK OF AN EXPLOSION." An accident at the Baldwin
Locomotive Works had injured two men and blasted a third through the
roof and back down into the work area, where he had come to rest in
midair, badly burned, on a set of entwined wires. One of Sloan's drawings
shows the men at work on a huge locomotive just before the disaster, and
another portrays the unfortunate worker suspended by the wires. The
second drawing is especially skillful—the angle is dramatic, the perspective accurate—but once again, it seems to have not fully satisfied the
powers-that-be at the *Inquirer.* A month elapsed before Sloan again had a
signed illustration in the paper (this time he was sent to draw the chaos at
the liquor-license bureau at City Hall: the reporters at the *Inquirer* were
afraid that their regular watering hole was about to lose its permit), and
the gap after that was even longer. As Sloan saw the matter fifty years

later, he was just too slow for the kind of quick-sketch assignments that an "on the road" illustrator had to master. By the time he was done pondering the effect he wanted from a crowd scene, the participants had moved on.

However, there were plenty of other kinds of work for an art staffer to do on a major paper in the 1890s beyond sketching on location, and his boss knew he had a promising artist worth holding on to. Sloan was put to the task of illustrating the paper's letters to the editor, drawing decorative borders on the children's and women's pages, reproducing in pen the pictures sold to the paper by freelance photographers, and giving a visual touch-up to the copy of regular advertisers such as Lydia Pinkham's Vegetable Compound ("a woman's remedy for women's complaints"), ads that alternately featured either Miss Lydia herself as a ministering high-collared schoolmarm, or her troubled clients gazing into mirrors and studying their wrinkles.

That such work was not going to be deeply satisfying in the long run, regardless of the security and the salary it brought with it, must have been obvious to Sloan within a few months. The job had its professional compensations, to be sure: Sloan's first commission for book illustrations came his way that year as he became better known about town. (The fourteen drawings of seals, walrus hunts, and Greenland glaciers for Robert N. Keely, Jr.'s *In Arctic Seas,* published by a small Philadelphia press, were nothing very artful or remunerative.) And his old high school asked its up-and-coming almost-alumnus to design the current yearbook cover. But by that fall, he and Joe Laub had registered for a night course at the Pennsylvania Academy of the Fine Arts, suggesting that their aspirations to a different order of accomplishment were still alive.

Unhappily, Sloan entered the prestigious Academy on the corner of Cherry and North Broad Streets during a period of "unruffled academic slumber," as one writer has described this phase of the school's history. The glory days of the great Thomas Eakins were long past; working from the model, nude or otherwise—one source of a controversy that had cost Eakins his job—was not a feature of the drawing classes anymore; and charismatic instruction, or vital and inspiring teaching of any kind, was nowhere to be found. Sloan and Laub met some good men at the school—among them Maxfield Parrish, F. R. Gruger, and Sloan's old high school acquaintance William Glackens—but the tedium of sketching plaster casts in charcoal, in session after routinized session, was something of a

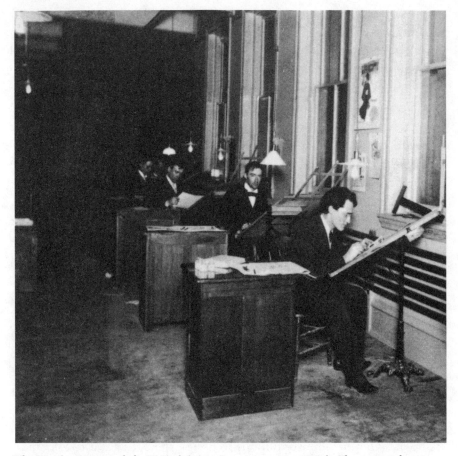

The art department of the Philadelphia Inquirer, *circa 1894; Sloan at right*
(Delaware Art Museum)

letdown to young men who spent their days in the broil of a big-city
newspaper office, an electric atmosphere at its best. Sloan in particular
had been hoping for much more, a sense of challenge and innovation.
What he got was a rigid system that mandated a long term of apprenticeship in drawing "from the antique" before one was granted admission to
the life class, where one was then able to paint a safely and thoroughly
clad living form in the prescribed style. Gone, along with Eakins's aggressive attitudes toward male and female nudity and the direct experience of anatomy, were the passion and daring that had characterized the
school in the 1880s.

The boredom among the night students gave rise to a prankish atmosphere, especially among the newsmen-artists, who liked to race down the grand staircase of the building's foyer on their drawing boards. One of the teachers, Charles Grafly, shared the playful fervor of the malcontents. Still in his twenties, Grafly had been a pupil at the Academy himself, had studied in Europe, and had finally come back to America to make a name for himself as a sculptor. He had cause to expect some success, even in a city not known for its support of the arts, as two of his busts had been exhibited in the Paris Salon of 1890, and his *Daedalus* had recently been purchased by the Pennsylvania Academy for its own collection. He also hosted some of the more exuberant low-budget social gatherings in the city, to which Sloan, Glackens, and Davis were invited, as were the paint- ers Edward Redfield, James Preston, Hugh Breckinridge, and Walter Elmer Schofield, all of whom were to make a name of sorts for themselves in American art over the next decade. More than those other occasions, though, it was his Christmas gathering that December, a raucous costume party for forty Academy alumni and students, that Sloan was always to remember. Grafly wanted his friends to enjoy a holiday revel, to outdo one another in wild, inventive attire (which they did), but he also wanted some of them to meet a special friend, an artist he had been touting that year as the great man of their circle—of the generation that was about to come into its own.

Grafly's Christmas party in 1892 changed Sloan's life in a way that Sloan himself recognized as momentous and in a fashion that sug- gests how eager he was to find an intellectual guide or mentor of the kind the newsroom had not provided. In Robert Henri, the darkly handsome twenty-seven-year-old painter and friend of Grafly's who had returned from Paris the year before, John Sloan met that evening a man he felt drawn to from their first hour together, a person who would ultimately have a profound influence—in many ways positive, in others detrimental —on his professional growth and, most significantly, on his view of him- self. With Henri's lordly appearance on the scene in Philadelphia, things changed for a number of young, unfocused artists; for Sloan, an identity and a persona, of a kind he had not been able to envision for himself, were ready to be forged.

Everything about Robert Henri was designed to awaken interest and stimulate curiosity, from the odd pronunciation of his last name

(Hen-*rye*, not French at all) to the strength of his opinions. Those opinions, and the direct conversational style in which they were expressed,
were what immediately attracted Sloan: it was as if he had been waiting
since adolescence to hear a voice as confident and insightful as Henri's. As
Henri saw it, to be an artist was to be involved in the most exciting and
meaningful of vocations, an adventure and a calling rather than a job, the
value of which was only now being appreciated in the United States. They
lived in a time, he believed, when the temptations to "sell out," to
become a crowd-pleaser—a well-paid society painter, a painter of myth
and romantic history, a secure academician like the reigning Frenchmen
Gérôme and Bouguereau—were on the rise. As everyone knew, art was a
commodity of increasing interest to the nouveaux riches in America. A
real artist had to be careful. Then, too, the snares of Aestheticism were a
problem; Henri had views on that school of thought as well. The "art for
art's sake" crowd, disciples of Whistler and Wilde, set a potential trap for
young artists who were afraid to engage the more robust spirit of their
own time. The art of the new century was going to have to be less effete,
less genteel, more energetic and inclusive of the range of modern experience, so little of which entered into the instruction offered at most art
schools and colleges—least of all in cozy, smug Philadelphia, which
seemed to Henri hopelessly provincial after his three-year stay in France
and Italy. The ideas that Henri, a fervent monologist, expressed to his
listeners were nothing that Sloan himself, limited as he was in his own
experience, could verify or dispute, but they felt right: they affirmed an
outlook he respected.

Among the other topics of conversation, one that led Sloan to feel
that he was in the presence of a kindred spirit, someone who might in
turn respond to him, was the two men's mutual interest in books, both as
readers and as collectors. Henri was immersed in Emerson and Paine at
the time, he told Sloan; Sloan was reading Molière and Ibsen and could
talk knowledgeably about Balzac, Zola, and Maupassant. Their shared
passion for Walt Whitman, deceased only ten months earlier in nearby
Camden, struck Sloan as an especially good sign. A few days after the
party, he stopped by Henri's studio at 806 Walnut Street, just a block
away from the space he and Laub had taken at 705 Walnut, to present his
new acquaintance with a better, more recent edition of *Leaves of Grass*
than the 1884 volume Henri had told Sloan he owned. The token of
friendship was warmly accepted.

Within a few weeks, by February, Sloan felt comfortable enough to approach Henri, who was busy with his own first teaching job at the Women's School of Design, to discuss his dissatisfaction with what he was learning—or rather, what he felt he *wasn't* learning—at the Pennsylvania Academy of the Fine Arts. Henri was sympathetic. Although he had studied at the Academy during the past year under the very capable Robert Vonnoh, he knew how funereal the atmosphere at the school could be, and knew, too, from the program at his own sedate place of work, how labored and unimaginative American art education often was. Part of the problem had to do with the preoccupation with technique and the love of detailed realism that had dominated American taste since the Civil War: getting every button right seemed to matter more to most painters and teachers—and art lovers—than capturing the sitter's essence or the vivid impression of the moment. The experimental approach of the Impressionists was still considered radical on this side of the Atlantic, and Americans had yet to see the work of the Post-Impressionists. A second and even larger problem, Henri indicated, was bound to American prudishness, to that ingrained fear of sensuality as symbolized by the nude model. But how else was a student to learn to paint the body and to celebrate the very physicality of his art form? The plan that Sloan and Laub had formulated to deal with their concerns—the notion of organizing a cooperative art class of their own to improve on what the Academy had to offer (especially regarding the unrestricted use of a professional model)—struck Henri as a worthy idea, and he offered to do what he could to help.

The Charcoal Club of Philadelphia lasted only from early spring to early autumn (its demise was more a result of the catastrophic recession of 1893 than of Academy displeasure), but it accomplished some good in its time, if only in reinforcing Sloan's conviction that intolerable conditions did not have to be tolerated. In their rented space at 114 North Ninth Street, an earnest, energetic group that eventually numbered thirty-eight met under a skylight and a set of gas-burning lights to sketch and paint a very uninhibited nude model three nights a week and then, on Monday evenings, to offer criticism of one another's progress. Most of the constructive comments came from Henri. At two dollars a month for membership, Henri, Sloan, and Laub charged half the Academy's rate for sessions that were considerably livelier than those at the older institution, a fact that contributed to the Club's growing popularity and eventually caused the administration at the Academy sufficient concern to sound out Henri about taking a teaching job with them in the fall. Indeed, by the time the Club's membership reached thirty-eight, that number was fully half the total enrollment of the Academy's declining student body.

The makeshift but productive experience of the Charcoal Club gave Sloan something else he was ready for. Like Laub and Glackens, Ed Davis and Frederic Gruger, and other new friends in the group—the eighteen-year-old Everett Shinn, J. Horace Rudy, Carl Lundstrom, Harry Ritter—Sloan was used to hearing art spoken of as a craft to be mastered, the goal of which was the skillful, time-honored representation of observable reality. Drawing the same plaster cast of an arm or a torso over and over and over again until one got it "right" was the plausible means to the mastery of that craft. A student would then go on to a review of composition, and later of color, rather as if a would-be writer in his adulthood were directed to concentrate on grammar, then on prosody, then on metaphor, and only later *allowed* to create a full-blown story or poem. But Henri spoke up at the Club for a wider, gutsier grasp of what they were all hoping to achieve, the newspapermen no less than the "pure" artists. As Henri's notes from the time put it, what mattered was the "subordination of so-called 'finish' to broad effects, simplicity of planes, purity and strength of color, and particularly the preservation of that impression which first delighted the sense of beauty and caused the subject to be chosen." This was the argument, rare in Philadelphia in the nineties, of a man who had seen Monet's new haystack series at Durand-Ruel, tried to make sense (not very successfully, in truth) of the van Goghs and Rousseaus at the Salon des Independents, and chafed under his teacher Bouguereau's demand for completion and detail at the expense of the "big impression." The independent painters, the controversial exhibitions, the current re-thinking of the classical ideal in Europe, the movement away from an art of "fine drawing" toward a more aggressively painterly art of color and texture—all of these things that Robert Henri talked about opened doors of thought that Sloan felt would never have been glimpsed, let alone approached, under the leadership at Cherry and North Broad Streets.

In practical ways as well as inspirationally, Henri helped Sloan. When the director of the Women's School of Design invited Beisen Kubota, a prominent Japanese newspaper artist and teacher who was in the country for the World's Columbian Exposition, to come to Philadelphia, Henri made sure that Sloan was able to witness a demonstration of Kubota's

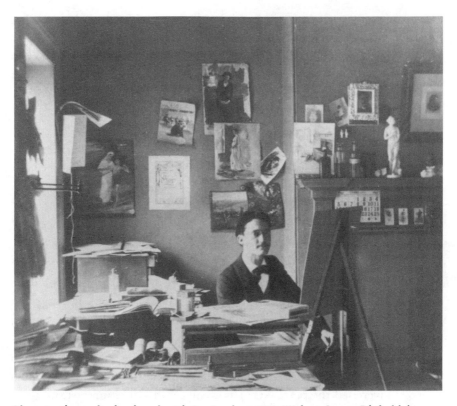

Sloan in the studio he shared with Joe Laub at 705 Walnut Street, Philadelphia, 1893 (Delaware Art Museum)

quick-sketch brush-and-ink technique. Following the big fair in Chicago, the Occidental fascination with *japonisme* was in full force in America, and it is likely that Sloan appreciated having the chance to study the simplicity and élan of Kubota's drawings even more than he valued anything Henri himself had to say about the properties of oil painting. Kubota excelled at sketches with thick outlines, done from memory and never overworked, and as Sloan at the age of twenty-two still saw himself as primarily a graphic artist, the example of a Japanese master in the field was compelling. On their outings to the Chestnut Street Opera House or to the Academy of Music later that year, Sloan and Henri would bring their bottles of Higgins ink, their sketch pads, and small brushes "à la japonese" to record the spectacle of actors, musicians, and audience.

Still and all, something was missing in the relationship, Sloan felt. Despite the goodwill that the two men had toward each other since that

first convivial winter, it seemed to John Sloan that Henri held back, that
he was one person whom it was impossible to know fully or intimately.
His assessment was not inaccurate. As Sloan was later to learn, Henri had
a peculiar family history that he needed to keep hidden, a past that didn't
allow for too much honesty or too many questions.

Sloan had been with the *Inquirer* for just over a year and was
heavily involved with the month-old Charcoal Club when a new development in the visual arts took hold in America with remarkable speed. In
April 1893, the illustrator Edward Penfield's poster for *Harper's Monthly*
appeared on newsstands and in bookshops around the country. It was not
at all unusual for magazines—or newspapers or book publishers or manu-
facturers of any kind—to advertise their products with an informative or
eye-catching poster. But Penfield's image was something different. The
drawing depicts a man in a hunter's cap and a green overcoat caught in
the rain, but the man isn't running for cover; he's reading a magazine,
oblivious to the weather around him. "HARPER'S FOR APRIL" are the only
words that appear on the whole of the poster. The starkness that so
caught the attention of the magazine-buying public achieved two purposes: it advertised the poster itself as an object of visual interest, first and
foremost (no table of contents for the issue, no cluttering language of any
sort), and it advertised the magazine as a publication quite out of the
ordinary, almost mysterious in its wordless allure.

The next month *Harper's* announced its May issue with a similar terse
drawing. Other Penfield posters followed, and eventually other magazines
and book publishers awakened to the fact that an innovative selling tool
had evolved. Moreover, hand in hand with advances in color printing and
photomechanical reproduction, a whole new attitude toward visual experience outside the boundaries of traditional "fine art" was emerging in the
last decade of the century. Dust jackets, for instance, were common before
the 1890s, but it was only in the wake of the "poster period" that they
became the norm in the industry and that their design became an important aspect of book publication. Likewise, the idea that periodicals might
employ a different cover image each month meant a departure from the
old way of doing things. It was hardly coincidental that the same artists
who were interested in the new posters—and in the study of Japanese

prints, with their flat, elemental, sometimes abstract qualities—were involved in the remaking of dust jackets, magazine covers, and newspaper illustrations. All of these breakthroughs were, in one way or another, connected to what became known as the "poster craze." Even the words "poster style" came to mean more than simply a kind of art that resulted in a poster. Although Sloan himself produced several excellent posters, recognition of his role in this movement came originally through his drawings, done with brush and pen and ink over pencil and reproduced in the Philadelphia newspaper.

In this matter, Europe was of course far ahead of America. The mania for decorative posters—*affiches illustrées,* as they were known in France—was already approaching its peak in Europe by the time of the Universale Exposition in Paris in 1889, and by the 1890s *afficheurs* were peeling posters for their collections off walls and kiosks so fast that laws had to be passed restricting the vandal-aesthetes. But in America the first organized showing of the new poster art did not take place until 1890, when the Grolier Club in New York City hosted a sumptuous display of posters by the masters Jules Cheret and Eugene Grasset and some of their American counterparts. It was only later that Americans got their first look at the poster styles of Pierre Bonnard and Henri de Toulouse-Lautrec and were able to compare the native versions of these artists—Edward Penfield, Will Bradley, Louis John Rhead—with the best Europe had produced. There were significant differences, though, between the French and American perceptions of these artistic products. One difference had to do with the very idea of public space. In a land without kiosks and in a culture that *disapproved* of posters on walls portraying women kicking up their heels and showing their slips or happily downing glasses of champagne, what Americans saw on art posters tended to be limited to bookshops and newsstands and determined by the mores of a given area. Of necessity, a Penfield, a Bradley, a Rhead, or a Sloan was not going to be the sensually provocative thing that a Cheret, a Bonnard, or a Lautrec often was.

Be that as it may, a notable cultural development was in the making, an unexpected surge that for the moment provided urbane Americans with a livelier visual landscape (all this in marked contrast to the sedentary ways of the "high art" museums), and John Sloan found himself well situated and suitably talented to take part in the process.

None of this could have been predicted, least of all by Sloan himself. Through his first year and a half with the paper, he was apparently assigned nothing more elaborate than the scut work he had been doing since the discovery of his inadequacy for on-the-spot jobs. There are very few signed Sloan drawings from 1893, and most of the unsigned images published in the *Inquirer* are in a style patently not his. Swayze, Drake, and others continued to claim the lion's share of the meaty assignments. (When the low-man-on-the-totem-pole *was* given the chance to do something on a large scale in these days, a growing sense of the mischievous often took over. In the August 6 edition of the paper, for example, Sloan's depiction of a young woman standing on the rocks of the New Jersey shore and looking out over the water is a conventional, even boring line treatment of the subject. Open at her feet, though, and partly hidden in the rocks, is a copy of Sappho's poems. Sloan probably assumed, no doubt accurately, that few readers and no one among his supervisors would catch his salacious drift about this vacationing Gibson Girl in her private moments.) Given the extent of the recession, it is possible that Sloan wasn't even working full-time during all of that year. The economy was in shambles, a state of affairs that always results in a commensurate drop in advertising and income even for big-city newspapers, and Sloan thus had ample time to continue his freelance work for A. E. Newton. Commissions from that quarter always came in handy: Sloan's ledger book records payments of over sixty dollars for five etchings intended as covers for special-edition pamphlets that Newton was bringing out, each one devoted to miscellaneous quotations from a great writer. In addition to *Dickens' Immortals, Favorites of Thackeray, Moments with George Eliot, Beauties of Emerson,* and *Golden Thoughts from Ruskin,* Sloan completed commissions for a rendering of Ben Franklin and his printing press, one of Shakespeare's house in Stratford, and a personalized invitation card for Newton.

The following year, however, saw a remarkable shift in Sloan's standing among his colleagues on the paper, and a consequent need for him to put aside for the moment his ambitions as an etcher. Sloan's related interests in the poster style, in Japanese prints, and in the Botticelli reproductions he had been collecting (with perhaps their faint echo of his childhood love, the illustrator Walter Crane) converged in 1894 in a way that altered the look of the *Philadelphia Inquirer* overnight and gave him his first taste of professional notoriety.

At the beginning of June, Sloan was assigned to do the drawings for the articles covering the ladies' lawn tennis tournament at Wissahickon Heights. What he submitted marked a departure in style from anything the paper had previously published. The drawings of June 10 and June 13 are ripe with the new influences: the players' dresses are simplified to the barest contours; large figures in the foreground occupy an especially flattened space; the sky is delineated by a series of thin vertical lines that are separate from the open, unmarked area of the clouds; and the lines on the men's jackets in one drawing and for the tennis net in both are in dramatic, self-conscious contrast to the unlined space. The striking simplicity and staginess of the new American posters and the sense of elegant pattern and abstraction found in Japanese prints meet in all the drawings Sloan worked on for the paper that summer. Avoiding the danger of a precious aestheticism, these are nonetheless "art" rather than journalistic images, even as they chronicle a concrete event or the spirit of a locale dictated by the editors. (Never good with dates, Sloan was off by more than two years when, in his seventies, he tried to date the drawing entitled *On the Court at Wissahickon Heights.* By labeling it his "first for the *Inquirer,* February 1892," he gave an incongruous sense of his development in that period. The drawing, frequently reproduced in earlier Sloan catalogues, is in fact his second in this style and appeared in the June 13, 1894, edition of the paper.)

Response to these stately, well-drawn ladies and attentive men, and to the vaguely storybook settings they occupied with their sharp contrasts of dark and light, must have been favorable because, in short order, Sloan became the paper's premier chronicler of the leisure class, or of those moments of leisure, romance, and reflection that the paper's readers longingly imagined. Women on the beach, women out for a ride, women watching men fish, couples sipping lemonade or strolling on the Atlantic City boardwalk—all of these modern portraits of pleasure were in the spirit of the new movement known as Art Nouveau, paradoxically robust and langorously decorative. They weren't aggressive or subtly threatening in the way that Aubrey Beardsley's drawings in *The Yellow Book* (available in Philadelphia that year) could be; they weren't diabolically comic, like the more madcap Paris scenes of Félix Vallotton; they weren't libidinous, like the more extreme French posters. But with their loose line and blatant two-dimensionality, they were unusual according to the standards of what appeared in American newspapers in the early nineties, and they

represented a break from the dreary textbook realism that the art staff of
the *Inquirer,* and most other papers in the country, were then running to
ground. After ages of doing busywork, Sloan suddenly experienced the
delight of seeing almost forty of his drawings reproduced in the paper
over a three-month period, placed in increasingly prominent spots and
frequently enlarged to considerable size. By mid-September, three of the
four large drawings on the first page of the Sunday supplement would be
Sloan's, and by the end of the year he would have taken his turn as
illustrator on the short-story page, a sure sign of his arrival as a major
figure in the art department.

High praise came Sloan's way when *Inland Printer,* a respected trade
journal for printers, took note of his new accomplishments and popularity
with a few sentences in its October issue: "The work of Mr. John Sloan on
the *Philadelphia Inquirer* of recent months has shown a cleanness and
strength, and a perceptiveness, that has earned from critics the prophecy
of greater things to come." His sketches, the magazine noted, were "in
the Beardsley manner but they have an individuality of their own." This
was a critical reception, Sloan knew, that offered no grounds for complaint.

Throughout 1893 and 1894, as Sloan was gradually cementing
his reputation at the *Inquirer,* a circle of men had gathered around Robert
Henri, forming the nucleus of Sloan's social life. They met regularly to
leave behind the workaday world for the pleasures of free-floating conversation and good companionship. Sloan and Glackens, who had enjoyed
some sketching expeditions together out of the city in the summer of
1893, were the most devoted members of the group. They both liked
Henri (and each other) and liked the aspirations Henri represented, which
in his way he was tendering to them as well. Grafly, Preston, Gruger,
Redfield, and Breckenridge were among the other regulars. A. Stirling
Calder (father of the sculptor Alexander Calder) and Everett Shinn were
apt to stop by, as were Laub, Davis, and George Luks, an artist who
worked with Glackens at the *Philadelphia Press.* Men who were emphatically less interested in painting than in illustration, such as Joe Laub and
Ed Davis, tended to repeat their visits at irregular intervals, while those
—including the gregarious, hard-drinking, self-confident Luks—who
found Henri egocentric and long-winded were the least frequent of visi-

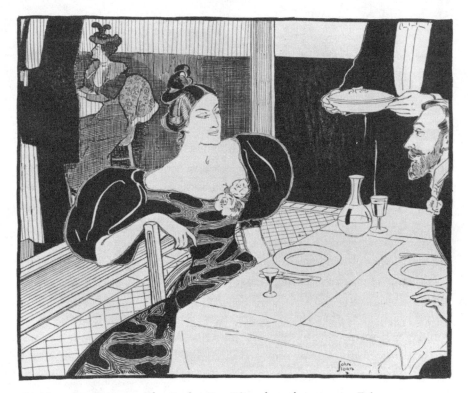

American Art Nouveau: Sloan's drawing Bliss *from the magazine* Echo,
July 1, 1895 (Delaware Art Museum)

tors. But with anywhere from four to twenty men sprawled out in his
large Walnut Street studio, which he later invited Sloan and Laub to
share, Henri was happy to play the host. At first, Thursdays were the
evenings reserved for "open house"; later the day was changed to Tuesday.
In his own version of Stéphane Mallarmé's "Tuesday evenings," an urbane
cultural institution that he had surely heard of during his time in Paris,
Henri led or initiated discussions about new books, philosophized about
art and literature, traded local gossip, arranged for dramatic readings
from anyone so inclined, and at the end of the night squired his crowd
out for a beer or over to Horn and Hardart's for some food. Interestingly,
given the intelligence of the participants, politics seems to have played
little part in these quasi-social, quasi-intellectual events, though a general
disdain for government and religion was a common thread in everyone's
remarks. In fact, Sloan credited Henri with "pull[ing] my religious
tooth"—a not-too-complex operation, one imagines, considering that

Sloan could see quite clearly how little good their churchgoing had done his devout, unhappy sisters. Reading Bakunin's *God and the State* at Henri's urging served only to clarify the doubt Sloan had long since nurtured on his own.

All hero worship tells us as much about the worshipers as about the idol, if not more, and the strange case of Robert Henri is no different in this regard. The man was a natural, witty conversationalist, physically charismatic and warmly welcoming to new acquaintances, or at least to those who appreciated his stature. He seemed better read and more cosmopolitan than he in fact was, but in that respect he was ahead of most of the other young men of Philadelphia, and that was, of course, what counted. Henri also had talent as a painter, though in 1894 no one could have known whether or not this talent would come to fruition: all of the paintings we remember him for were still several years in the future. He was then nothing more than a tentative Impressionist in a city that knew little about Impressionism. The most important characteristic he exhibited—the quality that the men drawn to him evidently needed—was a robust faith in the future, both his part in it and, by extension, the part of those who were close to him. If Philadelphia wasn't Winesburg, Ohio, it nonetheless seemed dull to a certain kind of temperament. A lifetime of paying one's bills and doing one's duty at work was a bleak prospect for someone who dreamed of a more enriched, enriching life. Henri spoke as if creativity were the means out of the trap. Not yet thirty, a product of the frontier Midwest, he gave the impression of having all the answers and no anxiety about the future. Sloan, Glackens, and Preston, all in their early twenties, were at that point in their lives where ambition and trepidation were at war, where implicit choices about career paths and identity had to be made. As Sloan succinctly put it, "Henri could make anyone want to be an artist," and the ability to instill that desire was a gift, the source of Henri's magic. When one was with Henri, such an intention seemed possible, honorable, endlessly fulfilling—all the more reason to stay with him, by his side, soaking up what one could.

About that vocation, Henri had high standards, which he impressed upon his friends. There were too many bad pictures exhibited every season at the Pennsylvania Academy of Fine Arts and the National Academy of Design in New York City, paintings brought into being solely for the purpose of finding a too-easily-satisfied buyer and catering to the most sterile aspects of contemporary art. Sloan remembered, "We came to the realistic conclusion that an artist who wanted to be independent must expect to make a living separate from the pictures painted for his own pleasure. We could attack the art academies and public taste with free-dom honestly earned." This was an easier task for Henri, whose family had a bit of money to underwrite his studies, or Glackens, who later married a woman of means, than it was for Sloan, who lived from pay-check to paycheck for many years, but it was an idea that Sloan sub-scribed to as vehemently as anyone of the Henri circle.

Two texts that were gospel to Henri at these Tuesday sessions were William Morris Hunt's aphoristic *Talks on Art* and George Moore's newly published *Modern Painting.* The latter was especially important to Sloan. George Moore, the Irish novelist, critic, and early advocate of Impression-ism, was an intellectual catalyst of the sort (not unlike Henri) that John Sloan would always relish—someone who was both sophisticated and volubly conscious of his roots as a native of a country outside the artistic mainstream. Moore's wary respect for Whistler and unbounded admira-tion for Manet and Degas as the true painters of modern life (artists whom Sloan at this point knew little or nothing about), his disdain for the tyranny of all academicians, his love for the great illustrators Leech, Keene, and Cruikshank, his defense of the artist's right to choose *any* subject matter that held his interest, and his belief in the value of an attachment to one's home ground ("We should turn our eyes from Paris and Rome and fix them on our own fields . . . making our lives mole-like, burrowing in our own parish soil")—the many and sundry opinions expressed in *Modern Painting* struck Sloan as aesthetic guidance of a high order. And how different it all was from the bone-dry lectures of the teachers at the Pennsylvania Academy, who ground the life and soul out of their subject! As Hunt observed in *Talks on Art,* the reality of a picture was too often lost in the mire of "realistic" detail, and real art too often suffocated by inflexible teacherly ideals of "beauty." Moore and Hunt argued for boldness, exploration, energy, craft allied to immediate im-pressions and intuitions, and modernity.

For all the seriousness of the time the younger men spent with Henri, there was also an element of whimsy to the whole situation. The hours given over to drinking beer and sherry, to joking and carousing, to ap-plauding one friend's ingenious card tricks or listening to another's ro-mantic woes or to George Luks's tireless anecdotes about his days in vaudeville, were something Sloan needed, too. Life away from his cronies

had a pronounced grimness to it these days. The Sloans had earlier left the
Camac Street house and relocated to Fort Washington, a suburb of Philadelphia, necessitating a longer commute to work for the one working
member of the household on the nights when he didn't sleep over at the
studio. There was no question that the move had been an advantageous
one for his parents, now prematurely aged, especially as the backyard
allowed his father more space to garden, and his mother's doubtful health
called for peace and quiet. (One of Sloan's earliest mature watercolors,
Professional Nurse of 1893, dates from this period of his mother's decline.)
Nonetheless, it made for an extreme contrast, given the enveloping gloom
of Fort Washington and the exuberance of Henri's at 806 Walnut Street.
Nor was the situation any more satisfying at the Academy, and Sloan
finally gave up his classes there early in 1894 after an altercation with his
instructor in the life class, Thomas Anshutz. The very reasons he had left
in the first place to found the breakaway Charcoal Club were still an issue.
When Anshutz, a respected painter and eminent Eakins disciple, rebuked
him for sketching his classmates rather than the prim model at the front
of the room, Sloan was furious and simply walked out.

The most raucous good times under Henri's aegis had to do with the
amateur parody-theatricals the friends staged. Even those who were dubious about attending the book-discussion sessions at the studio wanted to
be either involved in the production or to be part of the audience for these
ventures. *The Poison Gum-Drop, The Apple-Woman's Revenge,* and *The Widow
Cloonan's Curse* gave Sloan a chance to hone his histrionic skills as, along
with Henri, Glackens, Grafly, Calder, Laub, and Davis, he doubled in the
male and female parts. Their tour de force debuted on December 29,
1894, and was sufficiently talked of in local circles to merit mention in
the newspapers the men worked for (with a funny ad drawn by Ed Davis
appearing in the *Inquirer*) and to be staged in the Pennsylvania Academy's
assembly room at the invitation of the school. *Twillbe* was their own brisk
adaptation of that year's romantic best-seller, the potboiling *Trilby* by
George du Maurier. Henri made an excellent Svengali and Shinn a creditable American expatriate by the name of James McNails Whiskers, but it
was Sloan who brought down the house as the demure Twillbe herself,
falling victim to the wiles of the evil Svengali. In wig and makeup,
wearing an elaborate dress made for him by Marianna (which Sloan in his
haste put on backward) and a pair of gigantic false feet—a satiric reference to the tiny, delicate feet du Maurier's heroine was famous for—Sloan

played the part to great comic effect. His losing the two cups of his bust as he jumped onto a table in one scene only increased the audience's pleasure. With one deft kick, Henri sent the buxom padding into the wings.

Within a few months of that joyful evening, Sloan was separated from many of his friends for what would prove to be a long time. Grafly and Calder had decided to marry and were taking their brides to live abroad, and Henri, who had spent the summer of 1894 in France, was eager for another, more extended European sojourn, possibly as long as two years. William Glackens and three others of the group agreed to sail with him, lured by the prospect of cheap apartments within walking distance of the Louvre and the Luxembourg and the chance to see the Impressionists and Old Masters Henri had so often told them about. Sloan and Laub kept the Tuesday open-house ritual going at the studio, but proof of Henri's importance was readily apparent: with their mentor gone, the gang, or its remnant, was more interested in parties and in staged boxing matches than in readings from Whitman and Moore. John Sloan was once again on his own.

Philadelphia:
Journalism and Beyond

(1895–1898)

"If one is a painter {the} purest freedom must exist at the time of painting. This is as much to say that a painter may give up his hope of making his living as a painter but must make it some other way."

—ROBERT HENRI

The means of support John Sloan had settled on in 1892—newspaper illustration—was a remarkably short-lived profession, but it was nonetheless a kind of work that Sloan encountered, and enjoyed, in its prime. Prior to the early 1880s, pictures of any sort had been a rarity in the daily press in America. The technology for speedy production wasn't available. By 1897 the technique of running halftone images on rotary presses was all but perfected, the photographer was ascendant, and the days of the illustrator were obviously numbered. But in the year John Sloan started working for the *Philadelphia Inquirer,* it was estimated that over a thousand artists were employed in the United States, supplying ten thousand illustrations a week for five thousand newspapers and magazines.

Vital and appealing though such employment could be, the influence of Robert Henri, the aura of the studio, and Sloan's own belief in his nascent talent as an artist of more than journalistic potential had awakened in him a divided sense of his future. There was no question in his mind that he had to continue working full-time to support his family. Everyone he knew might be making the obligatory trip to Europe, but he was not going to abandon his parents and sisters entirely to the dubious charity of the Ireland family. Still, a self-image of more depth and sophistication than the *Inquirer* could provide was something Sloan longed for in 1895. He had been a newspaperman for less than three years, but he was already thinking (as he told Henri in a letter that December) that there had to be more to life than what he was experiencing at the moment.

His involvement with the budding Poster Movement, with the aesthetic adventurousness of the "little magazines" of the day, and with the tribulations and joys of oil on canvas pointed him, Sloan felt, in a better direction. So he was pleased when, the month after the notice in *Inland Printer, Chap-Book,* the literary magazine of the small, respected Chicago publishing house of Stone and Kimball, reproduced four of his ink drawings from the summer *Inquirer.* (The fact that *Chap-Book* had once been edited by Will Bradley, one of the biggest names in art illustration, only added to the thrill.) This exposure led to a request from *Inland Printer* for a drawing for its March issue and another for its April issue, which in turn brought Sloan to the attention of one of the key figures in the tiny but prestigious world of the American avant garde in the nineties, the critic Percival Pollard. For Pollard's elegant journal, *Echo,* also out of Chicago, Sloan completed two exceptional drawings, one a parody of *La Belle Trilby* (again with gargantuan feet) and the other a very cosmopolitan rendering of a pampered couple at an upscale restaurant, a snidely gossiping duo who might have stepped out of the pages of *La Revue blanche* or *Le Rire.* Several months later an *Echo* cover by Sloan was deemed by a writer for the *Philadelphia Ledger* to be "one of the cleverest efforts in the poster line that we have seen for many a day," and its creator surely an American poster artist of the first rank. Pollard himself was delighted with Sloan's tall, assertive woman in a floral print gown blowing on an Alpine horn, her music echoing out over the rocky cliffs beyond. Although Sloan had some trouble getting paid for his work for *Echo,* a situation he found irksome—Pollard's was a shoestring venture, like most of the little magazines in America—he took satisfaction in becoming known and appreciated outside of his hometown.

Not that Philadelphia was without its own avant-garde efforts: when two local men started a new publication with the ultimate fin de siècle title and motto *Moods: An Illustrated Quarterly for the Modern* ("a journal *intime* wherein the artist and author pleaseth himself") and appointed Sloan their art editor, he was happy to accept the underpaid challenge. For *Moods* he made three drawings, including one to accompany a story by Kate Chopin; a vigorous advertising poster; and a Symbolist-style cover image of a woman in a cape wandering through a forest of sinuous trees, a

Moods

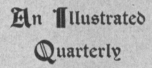

An Illustrated
Quarterly
For The Modern

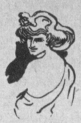

Published by

The Jenson Press

Philadelphia, U. S. A.

Whistleresque butterfly in the air just ahead of her. The magazine was short lived, having pleasethed a very small number of readers, but commercial success or even long-term survival was almost beside the point. A writer for the *New York Sun* in 1895 apparently concurred, mentioning "Cheret, Hardey, Beardsley, Bradley, Sloan, Vallotton, and the whole school [of Japanese-influenced illustrators]" as a new force on the cultural scene, one that had excited "much recent comment." Sloan's cover for *Moods* was just the sort of design to provoke such interest, printed as it was in four colors at a time when reproductions were generally restricted to one or two. That the impact of these partisans of Art Nouveau could not yet be gauged yet didn't matter. That the future of their movement and of their own careers was cloudy, especially in the wake of the Oscar Wilde scandal in London that year (with the resulting rush to brand the Aesthetes as immoral homosexuals and Symbolism as degeneracy itself), was also of little consequence. To be mentioned in the same sentence with Aubrey Beardsley and Félix Vallotton was compensation enough.

Likewise, the work Sloan did on his painting in these months was of an uncertain purpose, at least in any practical sense. Seen from another perspective, however, it served a quite useful, stimulating, and exploratory purpose. The two oils that Sloan is known to have completed in 1895 are a middling portrait of Glackens, evidence of an ongoing struggle with anatomy, and an Impressionist landscape of pink, green, and light-yellow buildings along a bank of light-blue water. American Impressionists had been prominently featured in the Pennsylvania Academy annual exhibitions for several seasons past, to the dismay of some local reviewers, so it was natural that Sloan should want to see what he could do in that vein. The year before, under Henri's influence, he had painted his second self-portrait in oil. Adopting an approach that differed radically from the more painstaking, meticulous style of the 1890 picture on the window shade, this portrait is very much in the manner of Henri's current work: edgy brushstrokes and surface dexterity, with none of the Eakins-Anshutz insistence on rigorously modeled flesh and bone. Not coincidentally, it has a generic look to it—a painting that might be by anyone and about anyone, with nothing distinctively Sloan about it.

FACING PAGE: *Sloan's cover for* Moods, *1895* (Delaware Art Museum)

In the final weeks of 1895, Sloan left the *Inquirer.* In the musical-chairs world of newspaper art departments, three to four years' employment at the same paper was neither very long nor particularly short. In the course of the 1890s, Glackens, Shinn, Luks, Davis, Gruger, and Preston all worked for more than one paper. Some worked for three or four in the span of a decade, hiring themselves out at slightly improved salaries as they became better known. But Sloan had shown no inclination for this shuttling back and forth and instead seemed content to stay put.

The offer to join the *Philadelphia Press* came at precisely the right time. The dramatic novelty of his style of sketch was wearing off, and Sloan at twenty-four was not the same self-doubting novice he had been at twenty-one. He was acutely aware of the ways in which he was different from some of his working peers. With larger spectacles and longer hair now, and sporting a cravat on occasion, he had a faint air of the dandy about him, a local version of a nineties aesthete (insofar as that role could be accommodated on a very limited budget). A young man beginning to amass his own library of art books, avidly reading about Rembrandt and studying what paintings there were to see at the Academy, in the city's galleries, and in the few private collections that were periodically opened to the public, able to quote poetry and immersed in his spare time in Voltaire and Rousseau, signing his drawings with a decorative flourish—a mannered curve—that signified both the *J* and the *S* of his first and last name: such a young man was necessarily more "arty" than a newspaper art staff was used to, especially in what might be described as the hypermasculine climate of America at century's end. His romantic nocturne for the local magazine *Gil Blas,* a heavily textured drawing in chalk and ink that the editors used for both a cover and a poster, suggests that Sloan was familiar by then with the work of Théophile Steinlen and Jean-Louis Forain. He spent time with Sadakichi Hartmann, the loquacious Japanese-German art critic (America's most full-fledged Aesthete and bona fide eccentric), whenever he was in town. He had exhibited at the Pennsylvania Academy's show of poster work that year and had been invited to send something to a December show at S. Bing's L'Art Nouveau gallery in Paris. This was the beginning of a professional résumé that might mean something. When a colleague in the office snapped at Sloan that he should get his hair cut and wouldn't let up on the point, Sloan had the first rough-and-tumble fistfight of his life. Shabby company, a narrow environment: it was time to move on.

Everett Shinn had joined the *Inquirer* staff earlier in the year—and for a time usurped Sloan's place as the principal artist for the Sunday supplement—but Ed Davis had since left. He reported favorably on life down the street at the *Press,* where he was now assistant art editor under the able and congenial Frank Crane. Sloan was never sorry he made the transition. The *Press* was just as unquestioning of the political status quo as the *Inquirer* (where the coverage of Coxey's Army and the Pullman strike debacle had been militantly, even viciously antilabor), but it had a reputation for having a more intellectual staff, fewer racist cartoons, and a less strident tone. The *Press* had been one of the first papers in the country to employ a woman as a Washington correspondent, and its editors had been savvy enough to recognize reportorial genius when they saw it in the figure of Richard Harding Davis, and literary brilliance in the form of *The Red Badge of Courage,* which had been serialized in the paper the year before. Sloan had to trade the plusher quarters of the *Inquirer*'s brand-new building on Chestnut Street for a humbler domain, but he was confident that he had made the right decision. Many years later he wrote:

> It is not hard to recall the *Press* art department: a dusty room with windows on Chestnut and Seventh Street—walls plastered with caricatures of our friends and ourselves, a worn board floor, old chairs and tables close together, "no smoking" signs and a heavy odor of tobacco, and Democrats (as the roaches were called in this Republican stronghold) crawling everywhere. But we were as happy a group as could be found.

To Henri abroad, he wrote, "I have one wheel out of the rut or at least in a shallower rut. . . . I am in better company and getting more money for which Allah be thanked and may he speed the day when I shall quit the newspaper business entirely."

In some ways, the most beneficial aspect of the move lay in the hours Sloan worked. At the *Inquirer* he had been at his desk by late morning, whereas at the *Press* he wasn't expected until midafternoon. The difference meant, if he got himself up early enough, more time for his own work in the morning, and specifically more daylight hours in which to paint. The

effect of the new schedule was immediately evident. Aside from the drawings he offered for the use of his literary acquaintances, such as the an-
guished young woman on a rooftop that appeared in *Red Letter* or the
lyrical self-portrait in *John-A-Dreams,* Sloan finished several paintings in
1896. He had the opportunity, finally, to test himself in the medium that
Henri had made sound so inviting. Most of what he did was of no distinction or even competence—any untutored gifts he had once had with
brush, oil, and canvas had vanished after several years of working on a
regular basis with pen and ink, crayon and pencil, and an etcher's tools.

Sloan's standing as an important illustrator and an up-and-coming
painter was nonetheless high enough in Philadelphia that year that Henry
Thouron, a teacher at the Pennsylvania Academy of the Fine Arts, approached him as one of thirteen former students who were being asked to
decorate the walls of the school's lecture room with mural representations
of the Arts and the Muses. Sloan was skeptical about the project from the
start, but as the Academy was not paying any of its alumni for their labor,
he felt no great need to be fastidious about the task. Throughout the
autumn of 1896 and into the winter of 1897, Sloan (as he told Henri) did
his "share in painting a band of mural villainy" about the innocent walls
of the lecture hall. *Terpsichore,* destroyed in 1968 after long since falling
into disrepair, exists today only in the form of two rudimentary oil
sketches in the collection of the Delaware Art Museum, which give little
sense of how effective or otherwise Sloan's first public commission may
have been.

In September 1897, after an absence of more than two years,
Robert Henri returned to Philadelphia. His time in Europe had been
remarkably productive, opening Henri, now in his early thirties, to new
influences of style and subject. A bicycle trip through Holland with
Glackens had given both men their first experience of Frans Hals, an
opportunity that in itself was worth the whole trip, Henri maintained. In
Paris he had lingered over the Manets in the Louvre and the Luxembourg
and profited from repeated visits to the Manet retrospective at Durand
Ruel's the winter before his departure. A trip to London to see an exhibition of Velásquez's paintings had left him greatly impressed with this art
that seemed "simple and direct, about man rather than about the little

incidents which happen to man." Inspired by the grand trio of Hals, Manet, and Velásquez, when Sloan met him again Henri was painting in a darker, more decisive, and more urban fashion than when they were last together. He had also become adept at painting *pochades,* on-the-spot oil sketches on small wood panels that were useful for recording quick impressions of the passing scene—the view from the café in Paris or, now that he was home, whatever would be the equivalent in this land of few cafés but countless interesting street scenes.

There was another change, too, for Sloan and others to take note of, a change at least as significant as the shift in artistic influences and methods. If two years earlier Henri had been a young man on the verge of achievement and recognition, he was now ready to take his place in the American art world without further delay. Soon after his arrival in Philadelphia, he requested a one-man show at the Pennsylvania Academy of Fine Arts, and a month later, on the strength of a New York review of his paintings at the Champ-de-Mars Salon in Paris and some well-placed connections at the Academy (including Henry Breckenridge, now serving as secretary to the faculty), he was given one. Sloan and Edward Redfield worked with Henri "day and night" during the four weeks he had to tend to the myriad details that the show involved and to frame the eighty-seven paintings and thirty *pochades* he was going to display. While sales for the October exhibition were nil, the reviews were positively career-making, fully everything Henri and his allies could have hoped for. Here, too, Sloan did his part, making a careful pen-and-ink drawing of one work, *A Peasant,* to accompany the *Press* coverage of the event.

One visitor to the Academy proved an unexpectedly helpful contact, offering an entree to New York circles that would otherwise have been difficult to penetrate. William Merritt Chase, one of the most respected American painters of the nineties and a teacher in Manhattan at his own Chase School of Art, requested ten of Henri's new paintings to show at the school. This fortuitous little exhibition was followed in December, the very next month, with a one-man show at the Macbeth Galleries on Fifth Avenue, an event indirectly arranged by Arthur Davies, a Macbeth artist who had seen the Henris and brought the work to the attention of his dealer. In brief, rarely has any young painter enjoyed a three-month period of public exposure of the kind that was lavished on Robert Henri in the closing months of 1897. Sloan was appropriately impressed. Seeing

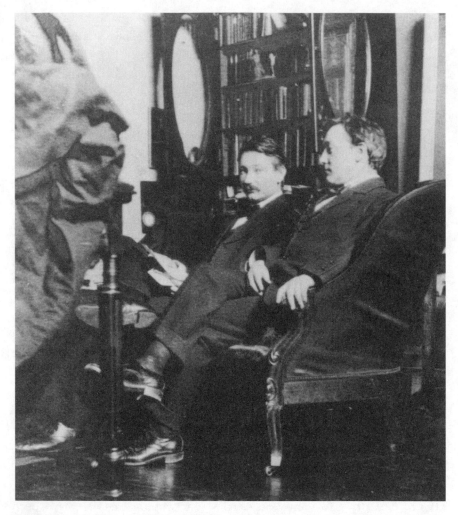

Robert Henri (left) *and William Glackens, in the 1890s* (Delaware Art Museum)

Henri hailed in the Philadelphia papers as a "prophet of the new," a vigorous antidote to academic realism, gave him a taste of the glory that awaited men of talent and nerve.

What was needed on Sloan's part, though, was more study, of both approach and technique. This he was able to acquire, slowly, through Henri's classes at 806 Walnut Street. Having relinquished his more commodious studio to Sloan and Laub in 1893 when he took quarters with Glackens, and having testified to the landlord about Sloan's "moral character and high Sunday school class average" (as he facetiously phrased it),

Henri now wanted to use the space on certain days for instruction. That was agreeable to Sloan, who then became an unpaying member of the class. He loved to watch Henri at work, to hear him talk about the desirability of a limited palette—yellow ochre, light red, blue, and black—and the need for memory development, on-site observation, and unself-conscious speed. This last point was the one issue on which Sloan could never be a true Henri disciple. His nature was too painstaking in comparison with Henri's, leading Henri to quip in frustration that *Sloan* was the past participle of *slow.*

During the few months that the class was in session, Henri urged Sloan to spend less time on his newspaper work and more on serious painting. The teacher seems never fully to have grasped the economics of his pupil's household, which ruled out the possibility of Sloan's giving full-time attention to art, but Sloan was nonetheless able to increase his output substantially in the winter and spring of 1898. When strongly motivated, he found the time. He made use of Henri's model to become slightly more skillful at facial anatomy, and before returning to portraiture, he briefly took Henri's suggestion that he look beyond the studio for his subject matter. *Philadelphia Stock Exchange; Night, Washington Square, Philadelphia;* and *Little Dark Street in Philadelphia* are not paintings of great distinction, but they show Sloan's mimicking of the muted tones of Henri's Parisian scenes, his fondness for dark or overcast skies, and his unfinicky handling of paint. No Bouguereau obsession with detail, no Gérômelike concern for "tight" drawing and elaborate composition. Even if he saw, as was likely, that he was hardly on Henri's level yet, Sloan was heartened by the advances he was making and nourished by the food for thought the classes provided.

Springtime that year brought two events with the potential to cloud any euphoria Sloan might have been feeling. One was the imminence of war. For the better part of three years, America had been following with interest—not all of it altruistic—the rebellion in Cuba against the corrupt Spanish colonial government. George Luks had been sent down to the island as early as 1895 by the *Philadelphia Evening Bulletin* to sketch some of the fighting—which he did from the safety of a Havana tavern, listening carefully to the patrons' descriptions of the conflict. Now it appeared that in the wake of the mysterious explosion of the U.S. battle-ship *Maine* in Cuban waters and the propagandizing clamor of an active "yellow journal" press, President McKinley was about to give in and ask

Congress to commit American troops. Men like William Randolph Hearst and Theodore Roosevelt were fairly chomping at the bit. Not for the first time in its history, America would go to war on foreign soil to assert its values and defend its economic interests, a thought that John Sloan found deeply dismaying. Imperialism in the guise of upholding the Monroe Doctrine was still imperialism if there was any thought of claiming Spanish territories for the United States. The apolitical artist was beginning to have opinions.

And then, on June 2, a month after the start of the war, Robert Henri surprised nearly everyone by announcing that he had married an attractive red-haired student in his class—Linda Craige, of a prominent Philadelphia family—and was leaving two days later with his bride for Paris. Whether or not Sloan was one of the few who were "in" on the secret of the whirlwind courtship is unclear. Having met Henri's parents, a "Mr. and Mrs. Lee," and his brother, "Frank Southrn," Sloan knew that there was a fair amount he was not being told about the "Henri" family saga.

What is certain is that Henri's abrupt leavetaking ended an era for the young men of Philadelphia, and Sloan no doubt suspected that his friend would not be coming back to Pennsylvania when the honeymoon was over. For artists of real ambition, everything pointed eighty miles to the north. Glackens was working in New York now, and by all accounts doing well there. *McClure's* magazine had sent him to Cuba as an artist-reporter to record the arrival and expected triumph of U.S. troops. Crane, Shinn, and Luks were in New York to stay, and James Preston was to leave for Europe two years later and then settle in Manhattan himself. Once again, the call to see the wide world or to test his mettle in the big city—the one big city that seemed to count—was not something Sloan felt he could respond to, and this sense of being left behind took a certain psychological toll. Yet in any self-evaluating that he might have done at this point in his life, Sloan ought to have given himself credit for a great deal, though he rarely seemed inclined to do that. His drawings for the *Press* over the past two years had been featured more and more prominently in the Sunday section of the paper, and he knew he was being talked about as a graphic artist whose skill surpassed that of his friends and colleagues in the business. He had five book illustrations under his belt, including a frontispiece for Percival Pollard's *Cape of Storms,* published by *Echo* in Chicago with a cover by Will Bradley; a cover design, also used as a poster, for Charles Stokes Wayne's "high society" novel, *The*

Lady and Her Tree (whose tagline promised "The American Aristocracy Graphically Depicted and Its Hollowness Exposed in the Latest and Most Interesting Novel of the Season"); and an especially fine cover and poster for William Lindsey's *Cinder-Path Tales,* produced by the prestigious Boston art publisher Copeland & Day. When Pollard brought out his collector's-item volume *Posters in Miniature* in 1898, with an introduction by Edward Penfield—himself a master illustrator of the age—Sloan was right there, in a dashing photo and represented by three of his poster drawings, with all of the other luminaries of the Poster Movement.

Still, there was one great unresolved problem that no amount of accomplishment could obscure: the problem of women and sex, of wanting the companionship of one woman whom he could trust and feel completely comfortable with. This mark of adulthood had as yet eluded John Sloan, and the loneliness was becoming harder to tolerate, especially in light of Henri's newfound happiness, his sisters' spinsterish ways, and the sexual escapades of his colleagues. Yet a few weeks before his twenty-seventh birthday, in the last week of June, John Sloan was to have an encounter that would alter his life quickly and dramatically, an unexpected meeting initiated by that most worldly and cavalier member of the newspaper crowd, Ed Davis.

The woman Sloan met at the brothel Ed Davis brought him to made an immediate impression, as Davis had probably assumed she would. She came over and sat on Sloan's lap once the introductions were made, but she didn't trigger in him any of the anxiety that such episodes usually did. She was an alert, attractive young woman, brown-haired, brown-eyed, diminutive in the extreme—almost doll-like at four foot nine—with a thin waist and a warm smile. In repose, with her features relaxed, she could look rather delicate, even somber, but she knew how to laugh and how to listen with interest. She was a month shy of her twenty-second birthday and at something of a turning point in her life. How regularly she worked as one of the girls of the house is not completely clear, for Anna Wall, unlike any of the full-time professionals, had a job during the afternoon, on the bookkeeping staff of a local department store. And she had two very good reasons for stopping by the brothel after work: first, the madam, Mrs. Dawson, was a sympathetic soul, a rare motherly figure rather than a predator to those girls (among them Anna

Wall) whose parents were dead and whose lives were in turmoil; and second—and more important—her lover had no place of his own to take her. In this safe space, part boardinghouse and part bordello and cheaper than a hotel, they could rent a room by the hour.

Yet Anna—called Dolly—also had a family history that would have made a life of prostitution a believable, even a likely, choice. By the age of three she had lost both parents and, with her two sisters, was living under the care of an older brother. John Wall was a fierce disciplinarian and a devout Catholic, while Dolly was a troubled, rebellious child in need of both firm guidance and affection. What she had to settle for under her brother's roof was an excess of the former and painfully little of the tenderness she craved. She did badly in school and more than once was caught shoplifting. Given her physical immaturity, the Wall family wondered if she would ever reach normal puberty. Adolescence did not bring much development of any kind, unfortunately, and early in her teens Dolly began to drink with her friends, not a surprising development since both of her parents had suffered from alcoholism. The brother's wife, a Quaker, was an understanding woman and did what she could to alleviate her husband's wrath when Dolly skipped school and came home inebriated, but by the time Dolly was fifteen she had been branded a hopeless case, a degenerate, by her brother. He placed her in the Convent of the Good Shepherd, a strictly supervised Catholic home for wayward girls, and told her in emphatic terms not to bother coming back. She may in fact have been pregnant at the time. From there to a low-paying clerical job, a fly-by-night lover, and a brothel was not such a great distance— rather, it was the quickly formed outline of a brutal life that was only too plausible for a young woman on her own with no money and no talents at the tag end of the "Gilded Age."

John Sloan made it clear to Dolly by the end of that first evening that he liked her as much as she seemed to like him, and that the kind of relationship he was talking about wasn't based on sex-for-hire or their meeting in a brothel. He told her that he wanted her to visit him at his studio and to get rid of her lover as quickly as possible. What Ed Davis's reaction may have been to his friend's train of thought is not hard to guess. Word got around the newsroom that Sloan had fallen for a hooker, a drunk, and however pretty the woman in question, everyone had the same response: you could have a good time with girls like Dolly Wall, but you didn't spend any real money on them, treat them like ladies, or imply that you were open to a commitment. That was socially ridiculous and more than a little eccentric, even for John Sloan. If Sloan minded, if he bristled at any looks or insinuations that came his way, he didn't show it. Used to being the odd man out, he was determined to go his own way on this matter as well, though he knew enough to make no mention of it in any of his letters to Henri.

It was an unusual, precipitous bond—one that raises some vital questions about John Sloan. *Why* was he so immediately and deeply attracted to Dolly Wall? And *why* the rush to decide that this was the woman for him? If the choice of a lover or spouse is a significant fact about any man or woman, and even if we acknowledge that it entails a measure of randomness as much as it hints at revelations about character and personal needs, a love-at-first-sight experience in a "cathouse" parlor is strange and particularly interesting. Certainly it suggests little concern with the double standard of sexual jealousy, that conventional turn-of-the-century male preoccupation. Dolly's early loss of virginity, and the potential seediness of her experience, didn't bother Sloan. If anything, those aspects must have appealed to him. He had a stronger, more ribald physical drive than his friends knew, and for him Dolly's lack of sexual innocence was refreshing rather than titillating (as it would have been for most of the brothel patrons) or disgusting (as it was, ostensibly, for society at large). He liked her sense of humor and her self-deprecation, her vulnerability and her curiosity. From the outset he also appreciated, with good cause, the fact that she wasn't a woman who would hound him to be someone other than who he was. Dolly's interest in his work and his aspirations, which he described to her that first night, felt genuine to him—as it indeed turned out to be, emphatically so—in a way that the attentions of his sisters' girlfriends never had.

But even beyond that, with this woman who was not five feet tall, who weighed a scant ninety pounds, there came an alluring blend of constancy and danger, a great gentleness and a great wildness. Sloan must have sensed this right at their first meeting, and the potent mixture carried a sexual as well as an emotional charge for him. For not only was Dolly not *of* the world of Fort Washington and Sundays at the Episcopal church; she was an *affront* to that world, a living assertion that the Sloan and Ireland families' definition of the right life was not the whole suffocating story. In thinking seriously of making Dolly Wall his common-law wife on such short acquaintance, John Sloan was taking on himself many things, one of which was the attempt to balance his belief in commitment with his yearning for sex, freedom, independence, and power. Dolly was everything Bess and Marianna weren't. He felt very much alone, and here was an oddly attractive woman who liked him, who seemed undemanding —there was no prattle of marriage, of mortgages, or of social distinction —and who would be unlikely to place him in the bind that had destroyed his father. Or so John Sloan assumed.

In later years Dolly was wont to say that she had chased Sloan. This was probably true, in its way. She knew she wanted him—so good-looking, so awkward—the minute she saw him. But there is equal reason to think that Sloan was, for once, the aggressive one. Within a few days, he had been to see Dolly's lover himself to tell him that he should leave her alone from now on (he told the man that he intended to marry her, though that was not their plan), and room had been made at 806 Walnut Street for another member of the circle.

Confusion and
Commitment

(1898–1904)

"It was lonely to be myself; but not to be myself was death in life."

—GEORGE BERNARD SHAW,
Cashel Byron's Profession

The Spanish-American War was a glorious experience for American journalists and editorial writers. The public appetite for drawings, articles, and reports from the front was fierce, and the almost universal desire to "avenge the *Maine*" and put an end to European meddling in the Western hemisphere left publishers untroubled by dissent or ambivalence. For a republic that was about to become an empire, the three-month conflict was a made-to-order event, applauded by most of the country for being precisely the short, moral, decisive, and heroic venture that congressional leaders had promised. And it wasn't only the papers of Mr. Hearst and Mr. Pulitzer that played the "liberation" of Cuba from Spanish tyranny for all it was worth: editorials in the *Press* and other papers across Pennsylvania extolled the wisdom of President McKinley, the valor of the Rough Riders, and the nobility of the American cause. Flag-waving was at the same fever pitch in Philadelphia as it was in most other cities the summer John Sloan met Dolly Wall.

For Sloan, a pacifist by nature and a skeptic by experience, none of the jingoistic claims made by his colleagues on the paper—a generally conservative group—was true or even tolerable. Sloan probably regarded Glackens's trip to Cuba as implicitly serving the cause of the War Department (all of the illustrators who followed the troops there knew what kind of drawings were expected from them), but he refrained from ever commenting to his old friend on the subject. With others he was less reserved, however, and so another wedge was driven between Sloan and the niche he had found for himself in journalism. If push came to shove, he decided, and the war escalated to the point of a draft, he would simply refuse to put on a uniform. They could drag him off to jail if they wanted to.

In this local climate of patriotic fervor and social awkwardness concerning his involvement with Dolly, Sloan welcomed a chance of escape that unexpectedly came his way that summer, initiating a move he might never have considered had his position as an outsider not been so dramatically highlighted by the war and by people's reactions to Dolly. Now he accepted the offer to move to Manhattan to work for the *New York Herald,* where Frank Crane was on staff, and he and Dolly spent an unpleasant ten weeks coping with life in a city they didn't like, sending money home to Fort Washington, and learning more about each other. Oddly, by October, just as suddenly as they had departed, they were back in Philadelphia. The *Press* was glad to have one of their best artists rejoin the fold, and Sloan was willing to overlook the five-dollar cut in salary he had to take: the *Herald* had been paying him a comfortable fifty dollars a week.

Little else was comfortable about his life at that moment. There was no question of his introducing Dolly to his family yet, a circumstance that necessitated a greater secretiveness than he was used to. When Dolly bought him a puppy, Sloan told his mother that the dog had been a gift from Edward Redfield. He was caught in the lie when Henrietta eventually met Redfield and thanked him for the pet that had become so important to the family, and Redfield confessed that he had no idea what Mrs. Sloan was talking about. Worse still, old friends of Sloan's from the Pennsylvania Academy had got wind of his tryst with a "woman of ill repute," and one young woman of a possessive temperament, Elizabeth Crooks, had dashed off a letter to Henri in Europe to warn him in vivid terms of the trap their friend had fallen into. Henri's response was predictable, and he wrote to Sloan expressing some dismay about the "scrape" he was foolishly involved in and the dangers such a situation might pose for his career. "You want to be a great artist," Henri reminded him, "and you can if you only get yourself together—and for God's sakes just give up running with the gang." Somewhat duplicitously, Sloan answered Henri by avoiding any reference whatsoever to Dolly's existence and commenting instead on his abrupt abandonment of his New York job, which Henri had also heard about. "Don't think that I have been unable to hold my own in the Metropolis," he told his mentor, "or that I have returned once more to sleep the sleep of the Philadelphian." Sloan was adamant that he had returned of his own free will to Philadelphia, where he might be a "big frog in [a] little puddle" and proceed with his career according to his own lights.

In later life Sloan never remarked on his first sojourn in Manhattan, and considering how strongly he was one day to be associated with New York life, his flight home to Pennsylvania seems all the more inexplicable. But a great deal of the trauma of that period had, no doubt, to do with Dolly. New York may have been more competitive and more expensive than Philadelphia, and his colleagues at the *Herald* less congenial than those at the *Press* (though one friendly member of the *Herald* staff that year, aside from his old boss Crane, was another Walnut Street regular, Frederic Rodrigo Gruger), but Sloan's decision to cast his fate with that of Dolly Wall entailed a great many more complications than he could have foreseen the first week they became lovers, and Dolly was by no means ready to manage outside her hometown.

What Sloan was fast learning was that his mistress was far from being in control of her life, even with the promise of emotional security that Sloan offered. Her nerves were easily shattered, her sense of self-worth was almost nonexistent on her darker days, and the demon of alcoholism was not to be put in its place as easily as either of them might have hoped. In fact, one reason that Dolly would have found a move to a new city difficult at that time was her relationship with her Philadelphia physician. Sloan met Dr. Collier Bower when they returned from New York— he painted his portrait that fall—and he could see why Dolly had grown so dependent on this gentle, caring, unjudgmental man. He had been treating her for some years, as a therapist as much as a doctor, and knew her situation well; he explained to Sloan that Dolly's need to drink was not likely ever to be conquered. The problem, on both a physical and a psychological level, was too deep. In this counsel, Bower was showing himself to be a modern, sensitive thinker. Most physicians of the day would have hectored Dolly to exhibit more willpower or character, and warned Sloan to steer clear of her.

In another piece of advice, though, Bower—at least by the standards of a later time whose knowledge of this illness is much expanded—gave the couple the worst possible counsel. He told Sloan that he might see Dolly's addiction as something in the nature of a game leg, a thing to be lived with within certain boundaries, and said it was probably for the best that she be allowed to drink in strict moderation. The belief that holds today—that a person disposed to alcoholism ought to refrain from *any* contact with liquor—was not widespread at the turn of the century, and in fact Dolly was the kind of alcoholic who could on numerous occasions restrict herself to one or two drinks without any damaging consequences. Those times when she could not control the urge, however, were frightening experiences for a man brought up in a house of teetotalers. Dolly could become angry and belligerent, a different person from the funny, soft-spoken woman she normally was. She might lie about what she had been doing or snap at Sloan to mind his own business. The ramifications of this problem would ultimately prove devastating for both John Sloan and Dolly. Yet the very fact that he stood by her after awakening to the situation he was entering into tells us much about the depth of his feeling, of his fascination with and tenderness toward a woman who was desperately troubled but responsive and loving. At this point both felt they had found the mate they wanted, drawbacks or no.

There was also something intriguing to Sloan about the possibilities of life with Dolly Wall, a kind of Pygmalion scenario. Dolly's grammar and spelling were weak, her notions of middle-class etiquette were sketchy, and her knowledge of books and art was extremely slight. She was a compulsive frequenter of the palm readers and fortune-tellers about town, and in times of stress she went to a tough neighborhood priest for confession (Sloan could hardly decide which was worse). Yet she wanted to be a more presentable and more worldly woman. There was a sort of blanket curiosity and desire to please in Dolly on her good days. She needed a teacher, and this was a role Sloan found he could enjoy. Even sexually, it seemed possible for Sloan to believe himself more experienced and capable than he usually felt. Daunted in the past by feelings of sexual inferiority in the midst of the roustabout crowd at the *Inquirer* and the *Press,* more content on group outings to cathouses to sit in the parlor and listen to the music than to take a turn upstairs, he was now connected to a woman who set him at ease in that intimate context and yet still allowed him to take the lead. As it turned out, Dolly at times exhibited a reticence about sexual matters, a sense of shame and delicacy that was perhaps not surprising in a woman from a strict Catholic background who had never wanted a permanent place in the "business," and Sloan was accordingly freed from any of the intimidation he usually experienced. In the stereotypical male role of the courtship ritual, he was finally able to be as erotically playful, humorous, and direct as he wanted to be. (Sloan's reluctance to date the "loose," insinuating women of Newton's workshop or to indulge more in brothel expeditions had been due less to any primness, moral compunction, or lack of interest on his part, he once observed, than to his sense that, once unfettered, he would be unable to stop. With Dolly, there was no need to stop—and no talk of an engagement or of "settling down.") The normal process by which a couple gradually find their way toward expressing their real sexual and sensual selves was something Sloan happily explored with Dolly in their first months together. The fears and tawdriness associated with Dolly's drinking, they discovered, could be balanced, or overshadowed, in pleasurable ways.

There was also a potentially romantic—or Romantic—aura to the studio ménage now that a woman was present. Dolly loved the whole chaotic atmosphere of 806 Walnut Street, loved the camaraderie and the intelligent, spirited work being done there. Holding on to her own small apartment but having no actual "home" of her own, she delighted in keeping the place tidy between gatherings. She sympathized with Sloan's ambition to move beyond his newspaper career. Nothing was beyond his grasp, in her view. She posed for Preston and Laub and bought Sloan his first easel, reveling in the results of her sittings for her lover. *Dolly on a Harp Chair,* the largest picture Sloan had ever painted up to that time, and one that involved some experimenting with an airy, "scumbling" technique, is an especially elegant painting that doesn't begin to hint at Dolly's minute stature or her complicated story. In this rendering she is another anonymous, attractive, self-possessed woman of the fin de siècle.

Sloan knew that he was entering what was for him emotionally uncharted territory, though this quixotic relationship promised rich rewards if all went well. He could now imagine a life in which his wants would be attended to by someone who believed in him absolutely (every artist's dream—Rembrandt with his Hendrickje, a compliant, caring, stalwart mate, more intuitive than educated?) and whose company he liked. He could even imagine that he might help her to heal the wounds of her past, to find a way out of the darkness. In the spirit of one of the young men out of his beloved Balzac, uncertain but ultimately daring, Sloan was testing social boundaries and moral codes in 1898. For that matter, Dolly

Wall herself might well have been a resident of the Maison Vauquer, unpredictable and high-spirited, protected by the doting Mrs. Dawson, hectored by pious relatives, a woman of secrets and needs.

The next three years confirmed Sloan in his faith that his arrangement with Dolly was a workable one and that he had been right to return to Philadelphia. As the careers of friends like Glackens and Shinn advanced in unexpected ways, and as word came back of Henri's successes in Europe—the Luxembourg's purchase of his painting *La Neige* in 1899 was a great coup, as so few Americans were represented in the public collections of France—Sloan could point to his own triumphs.

His first major book illustrations came out that fall, just as he was recovering from the New York experience, and the response to the zany project was favorable. *A Comic History of Greece,* written by Charles M. Snyder and published by the local firm of J. B. Lippincott, was probably modeled on the British volume *A Comic History of Rome,* with its humorous illustrations by John Leech. Sloan, Shinn, and five other artists were asked to contribute their own versions of the events and dramatis personae that Snyder was describing. Done in the same style and with the same pronounced light and dark contrasts as his newspaper drawings in ink, the twenty-six illustrations Sloan made are much more detailed and intentionally, even robustly weirder than anything he had drawn before. In the Sloan pages of Snyder's offbeat chronicle, Sappho (in an asbestos gown) clicks away on her Remington, turning out pages of poems literally sizzling with passion; Ulysses, tied to a phallically inclined mast, frantically waves to those cuties the Sirens; a grumpy Charon is captured on a busy day with a standing-room-only crowd on the barge; and a besotted Alcibiades is hauled off by a Keystone Kop. Venus as a New Woman in bicycling garb on a two-wheeler, an Olympian banquet as an Ozark debauch, a testosterone-heavy Spartan family tucking in at home: Sloan's art in *A Comic History of Greece* is in the funky mode of Leech at his most pointed. Or perhaps it can be better seen as Leech's droll artistry crossed with one side—an increasingly anarchic side—of John Sloan's temperament.

In a radically different manner, Sloan produced sixteen drawings the following year for Everett Shinn, who was now the art editor of the high-circulation magazine *Ainslee's* in New York. Adachi Kinnosuke's "Sakuma

Sukenari: The Story of a Japanese Outlaw" called for more stylized images of characters, demons, sunsets, and cranes, which Sloan produced in ink wash with thin decorative borders on each page suggesting a Japanese design. Yet a third style of representation was needed for the drawings of myriad battlefields, commanders, and soldiers illustrating Stephen Crane's *Great Battles of the World*. It was a peculiar work for an ardent pacifist to be involved with (Sloan was not happy with the resolution of Secretary Hay's "splendid little war" or the national smugness and saber-rattling that followed), and an odd, pedestrian book for the author of *Maggie* and *The Red Badge of Courage* to have written—though one of his biographers has suggested that Crane was merely a coauthor with only minimal involvement in *Great Battles*. In any event, Sloan had yet to read any Crane at all, and a job was a job. Sloan's watercolors, which unfortunately lost some of their power in reproduction, were light-years away from the Art Nouveau expertise he had already mined and more in line with Howard Pyle's brand of history painting, but everyone seemed to feel that he had done an exceedingly professional job in delineating the heroic character of Frederick the Great and Gustavus Adolphus leading their troops, and in evoking the tensions of Bunker Hill and the siege of Plevna. An especially warm review of the book in his own paper called Sloan's eight full-page drawings works of "extraordinary strength, remarkably alike for the effectiveness of the general design and the completeness of the detail." These pictures, the *Press* reviewer noted (to Sloan's great pleasure), "witness the advent of a book illustrator whose work in the higher branches of graphic art has lately attracted a good deal of admiring attention."

At the *Press* in the late nineties, Sloan was emphatically the rising star in a way that he could not have been had he remained at the *Inquirer*. In his case, technology and talent had come together in a most advantageous fashion. When he started in the business, in 1892, some of the old-timers in the office were still using the chalk-plate process, a cumbersome technique that called for the artist to coat a metal plate with a chalk compound through which he would draw his lines down to the plate. A stereotype mold would then be made from the engraved surface. Sloan had benefited from the introduction, in the early 1890s, of photomechanical reproduction, an innovation that enabled the artist to draw on paper —always better for a feeling of spontaneity—and have the image changed in scale to fit the layout of the page. Now, in 1898, the *Press* was testing

the so-called Benday process, whereby watercolor drawings could be reproduced in color. Sloan had had the opportunity to work with this
system at the *Herald* in New York and was excited by its possibilities.
The art he was able to create for the Philadelphia paper marked an even
greater milestone in newspaper illustration than had his 1894 Wissahickon and Atlantic City drawings.

Eighty of these large watercolor drawings, some enlarged to take up
two thirds of a page, appeared in the *Press* between 1899 and 1903.
Almost all of the original drawings have been lost, probably discarded
when the *Press* went out of business, but even the yellowing pages of the
newspaper that survive today give some sense of how dynamic Sloan made
the Sunday section. His snake-charmers and Indians, clowns and vagabonds, balloon vendors and serpents, storybook maidens and knights in
armor, his Mother Hubbard and Mother Goose, his Uncle Sam and William Penn—all of the characters and settings he chose to develop live
through the freedom and boldness of his line, which darts and wanders to
make a head of hair look alive with its own rolling momentum, or a wave
on the shore to fan out over the bathers like a devouring plant.

These are "rhythmic excursions" of line, as one art historian, a student of Sloan's in the thirties, has aptly described them. Fantasy images,
loose and organic, sometimes top-heavy with a morass of curves—robes,
gowns, limbs, hair, birds, plants, and flowers, none of them ever seeming
straight or stationary—they existed not to illustrate a story or article but
rather to provide the reader's eye with a respite from the columns of tight
newsprint, and to inject into the paper a note of playfulness that had been
conspicuously absent from American daily journalism up to that time.
The majority of the drawings in this style appeared on the puzzle page
(sometimes as part of the puzzle itself), an especially welcome feature of
the Sunday edition as the first solvers of the week's puzzle were offered a
munificent ten-dollar prize. Sloan's skill in selecting and arranging his
colors was more than a minor feature of the whole endeavor, and the
paper's managing editor, Alden March—later the editor of the Sunday
New York Times—let him know how delighted he and the publishers were
with his contributions.

Exhilarating as his success as a draftsman may have been, Sloan was
aware of how ephemeral even the best work done for a newspaper was
likely to be. There was an inherent gap between journalism and art,
between practical use and high aesthetic achievement, that could not be

overlooked and was often on his mind. That was why it was so important, he knew (and as Dolly, Marianna, and his friends reminded him), that he never lose sight of his other goal, of taking his place with Henri and the others who had had the benefit of time in Europe and who already identified themselves as serious artists. All things being equal, he would not have remained at the paper one more day for personal satisfaction alone. The *Press* represented a good income, in the final analysis, but not a great deal more.

Toward this larger end, Sloan continued to work hard on his portrait painting, with mixed results. *Fortune Teller's Birds, Philadelphia* of 1899 has a pleasing oddity of subject, but the birds and cage seem more effectively rendered than their owner, and the portrait of a uniformed William Wood, a friend of Sloan's on the *Press* staff who had been in Cuba during the war, is not much more than competent student work. *Girl with Grapevine* is plain silly, a last sultry gasp of the Art Nouveau influence. But when he ventured away from the human form to the urban scene—to just that subject matter which Henri had been suggesting counted now—something noteworthy began to emerge. Four paintings in particular, completed within little more than a year of each other, set Sloan firmly on the path he had been seeking.

Sloan the walker in the city, the explorer of neighborhoods near and far, the spectator of little scenes and daily dramas, ultimately came to the conclusion that it was in the streets he traveled every day, rather than in the studio or the rural areas outside the city limits, that he might find himself as an artist. Regarding his periodic Sunday trips with Glackens and other friends to search out good landscapes to sketch in the suburbs or countryside, Sloan later acknowledged that his mind-set had been all wrong, and he had known it: he had been looking, he said, "for a piece of nature that looked like someone else's picture." Hadn't that been, after all, the implicit point of the copying, all that copying from antique casts, at the Academy, where no one was ever sent out into the street to draw? He wasn't looking at life or thinking of art as a thing meant to reflect, examine, or celebrate it. His decision to paint the old Walnut Street Theater and the pedestrian square in front of Independence Hall downtown, and to see what came of those choices, served an inner purpose that immediately struck him as important.

Walnut Street Theater is a simple painting: a dark depiction of a slightly grubby building at night. Rather than selecting one of the city's grander structures, some colonial or neoclassical landmark, Sloan has here focused on an undistinguished facade dominated by a large, ugly fire escape and the glare of a gas streetlight in front of the theater's entrance. A humbler, less grandiose, more claustrophobic subject and angle would be hard to come by. *Independence Square, Philadelphia* provides the relief of some daytime sky, the revered Independence Hall, and the presence of a small group of people pondering not the majesty of Jefferson and Adams but the anomaly of flowers (a circle of tulips) in the heart of the city. *Tugs, Delaware River* reverts to the potential seediness of *Walnut Street Theater,* though Sloan has here set himself the challenge of painting an array of effects. The water, the wharf, the moving boats, the sky, and the smoke from the tugs call forth different skills with the brush—which, if Sloan could have put aside his penchant for harsh self-criticism and looked objectively at what he had done in this painting, should have struck him as a hurdle he had decisively cleared. Indeed, in *Tugs,* a random, dour, uninspiring sight becomes a locus for all that mesmerizes the true spectator of life: slow, persistent movement, water, drift, subdued color, the idea of human labor against a backdrop of nature that usually allows for reverie and idleness. Sloan has also managed here, perhaps for the first time, to convey in oil a fully credible sense of thickness, weight, and depth. He gives his art a muscular charge in the indelicate drawing and the thick brushstrokes, qualities so ample and painterly after the meagerness and confusion of the dozens of canvases that had come before that it takes an effort to realize that this is the product of the same man who was just then decorating the more frivolous pages of the *Press. The Schuykill River,* with its prominent telegraph pole off to the side, seems vaguely anticlimatic if these four paintings are to be taken as a quartet of new directions and early promise, but it is a painting that reinforces the same theme. A blue-gray sky, a mass of paint, an unlikely vista. The echoes of Sloan's mentor, now returned with Linda from Europe and teaching in New York, painting the riverside derricks and coal piers of Manhattan, are even more emphatic.

The only way to confirm his hope that he was at last painting in a way that mattered, Sloan knew, was to force himself into the next, inevitably frightening stage. If finding a suitable place to exhibit one's art at the end of the twentieth century is a process marked by long odds and ego-smashing anxiety, how much worse it was at the end of the nineteenth, when the few galleries that accepted work by living artists wanted those artists to be *European*, and when the number of major museum collections in America could be counted on two hands? Barring incredible luck with the art dealers, a cagey group even then, a painter or sculptor had only one avenue open to him (or, rarely, her): application to one of the large annual exhibitions sponsored by the more prominent big-city art institutions, namely, the Chicago Art Institute, the Carnegie Institute in Pittsburgh, the Boston Museum of Fine Arts, the Pennsylvania Academy of the Fine Arts, and the National Academy of Design in New York City. The mammoth shows hosted by these institutions were usually juried exhibitions, in which juries made up of artists with established careers would decide which artworks should be accepted. In some instances, a museum director could also extend an invitation to a particular artist to show, and herein lay the first problem. In sharp contrast to a later age when an aggressive new approach and a questioning of older methods and ideas would become a chic end in itself in curatorial circles, those with the decision-making power in 1900 wanted validation, constant and rather obsequious, of their own example and aesthetic beliefs. The artists who showed with the most regularity, then, tended to be those painters who specialized in portraits of reputable citizens and beautiful women, in genre and landscape, in historical scenes and still-life, done in acceptable native versions of Impressionism or according to the tenets of academic realism. Vulgarity, eroticism, strident political opinion, distortion of form, or sensationalism of color—in short, anything radical or *outré*—was frowned upon. Exceptions to the dictates of fashion might be made for uncategorizable geniuses, preeminently Winslow Homer, but not for untried eccentrics or rebellious students.

A second problem was the sheer volume of work exhibited. In the manner of the European salons, several hundred paintings might be hung in the galleries from floor to ceiling, meaning that those works that the jury wanted to honor (often painted by jury members themselves, their students, their imitators, or their coterie) were given pride of place "on the line," at eye level, while those that had been less enthusiastically accepted might be found over a doorway, in a dark corner, or ignominiously "skied" near the ceiling. For his part, Sloan in his first forays into the game was less concerned about where he might be positioned than about whether he would be granted admittance at all. In an art world defined at its peak by the technical dexterity of John Singer Sargent and William Merritt Chase, the earnest Impressionism of Childe Hassam and

J. Alden Weir, Tonalist atmosphere and hearty Anshutz realism, there wasn't a great deal of reason to assume that room would be made for him. Alongside the gentility of Cecilia Beaux and the moralizing sentiment of George de Forest Brush, there was something downright quirky about what Sloan was attempting.

But Sloan's luck was better than he had expected—much better. It was just the kind of luck to give a young artist a false sense of optimism about the future. His "debut in paint," as Henri termed it, came with the acceptance and hanging of *Walnut Street Theater* in the autumn 1900 exhibition at the Chicago Art Institute, followed later that same week by the hanging of *Independence Square, Philadelphia* in Pittsburgh, at the Carnegie Institute show. Closer to home, at the Pennsylvania Academy exhibition in January, *Tugs, Independence Square,* and *Walnut Street Theater* were all on view, perhaps thanks to the jury activity of Edward Redfield, the one veteran of the "Tuesday evenings" whose stature was rising as fast as Henri's. Stunned by his own impressive beginning, Sloan wrote to Henri, "You will be able to appreciate my joyful feelings all around."

More than merely appreciative, Henri was eager to see his friend acquire a New York reputation. He had arranged for a small show at the Allan Gallery in Manhattan that spring and told Sloan to send along a few choice paintings. The Independence Square scene was already scheduled to be exhibited with the Society of American Artists, but the gaslit theater and the vigorous tugs made their first New York appearance in the worthy company of works by Henri, Glackens, Alfred Maurer, Van Dearing Perrine, and two lesser-known acquaintances of Henri's, Ernest Fuhr and Willard Price. The April exhibition received little attention from the critics and yielded no sales, but Charles FitzGerald of the *Sun* observed that it was refreshing to experience the work of painters who were rarely represented at the annual "official" shows. He further noted that the "attention paid to the larger exhibitions of the year is commonly out of all proportion to their value; they are little more than repetitions of last year's." Precisely, Henri might have answered. There was a new generation primed, tested, and waiting in the wings.

With his exhibiting career under way, Sloan became more ambitious and markedly more successful. On May 1, 1901, he reported to Henri that he had "dropped [an] attempt at portrait [painting] and am now working on the City Hall doorway which I spoke of having in mind." He sent a photograph of the painting-in-progress to Henri, who promptly replied that he thought Sloan was likely to duplicate his recent success with *Independence Square, Philadelphia.* "If you get the figures below [the great arch of the building] to give as much of the eternal business of life—going in and coming out—as you get the eternal park loitering sense in the other [picture]," he wrote, then the painting would work splendidly. Not still-life nor landscape nor portraiture but rather the pursuit of the "eternal business of life" was Sloan's most bountiful inspiration now. None of the paintings done over the next three years— not the heartfelt likenesses of Sloan's parents, not Dolly's wedding portrait, not the portraits of his new friends the violinist Will Bradner and the painter George Sotter—approaches the confident complexity of *East Entrance, City Hall, Philadelphia,* the gloomy allure of *The Rathskeller,* the somber strength of color in *Wayside Station,* or the energy of *Dock Street Market.* Human interaction is slight in these paintings, but the gritty, unpastoral settings and Sloan's drive to avoid any kind of ingratiating or idealizing aura mark them for their time as curious and forceful.

When Sadakichi Hartmann published his textbook *A History of American Art* in 1901, a brief, complimentary mention of "J. Sloan of Philadelphia" represented another milestone of some consequence: a first reference to the artist in a book. Although he was listed as one of those who showed a "dash and virility very rarely met with among our younger painters," Sloan found it no easy thing to acquire a copy of the volume for his own library. At four dollars, the price of the two-volume work was a little steep, but Sloan sent the money to Hartmann anyway; on principle, it seemed a book he should have for his growing collection, which was after all his one and only financial indulgence. What followed was vintage Hartmann: Sloan received neither the book (he ended up having to buy it in a bookstore some months later) nor his money back. Instead, he was the recipient of a letter in which Hartmann narrated the travails of his own penurious life, a catch-as-catch-can existence in a country as brutal toward its writers as toward its painters, along with a request to keep the four dollars as a long-term loan. Like Sloan's colleagues at the newspaper, Hartmann had rightly surmised that John Sloan would find it impossible to refuse a friend in need, even one as melodramatic and irresponsible as Sadakichi Hartmann himself.

No matter. By the summer, Sloan had concluded that his own

finances were sufficiently in order and his emotions sufficiently clear to allow him to propose to Dolly. On August 5, 1901, they were married in the Episcopal church where Sloan had been a choirboy twenty years before, and then they moved in with the family. No one knew anything of Dolly's background, of course, with the exception of her religious history. It was distressing enough to Bess and Marianna to have a Roman Catholic in their midst, lapsed or otherwise. Apparently the Sloans never inquired too deeply into why Dolly's relatives didn't appear for the quiet ceremony or how she and their darling "Jack" had met. It seems reasonable to assume, too, that Dolly's drinking was more or less under control in the months before the wedding, leading Sloan to believe that he was safe, or as safe as he was ever likely to be, in binding his life to Dolly's and in introducing her to his scrutinizing family circle.

Dolly did quite well, under the circumstances. No woman was going to be good enough in the eyes of the Sloan sisters, who were used to waiting on their brother hand and foot (he was the household provider as well as the only son), and there was little about Dolly Wall that suggested high social aspirations or good breeding. The new bride took the situation in stride. If anything, the Sloans did not entirely measure up to Dolly's ideas of what middle-class family life should be. She was angered by what she saw as their leeching off of her husband, which had in her opinion gone on for too long; there was no reason that one of the girls—they were both well into their twenties by now—could not contribute to the family income. She set to work at once trying to convince Sloan that some limits had to be placed on his obligations. But much more than the irksome financial arrangement, she found the lack of physical affection in the house chilling and unnatural. "She loosened us up a bit," Sloan remembered. A kiss, a hug, some hand-holding: these were rare events in Henrietta and James's house, and Dolly made it clear that she was not going to live in such an austere and decorous manner. Probably for that more than for anything else, Bess and Marianna held a grudge against her. The enmity led to some absurd scenes. One night at dinner, Bess held the back of her brother's chair out and helped him to be seated. She would show Dolly who took better care of John Sloan. Dolly bounded up from her place at the table, made her husband stand up again, and reseated him with a glare that established her right to be the attentive woman. By Christmas the Sloans were in their own apartment in Philadelphia.

The first two years of their married life were an incredibly busy period for Sloan. Having his own home and freedom from the petty rancors of family life would have been essential, given the pace of work he was sustaining. Eager to continue painting in his spare time and to become a more knowledgeable student of art and art history, he was also giving the *Press* as much of himself as his employers had any right to expect. His illustrations for stories and flamboyant drawings for the puzzle page were the staples of his output at the turn of the century, but beginning in 1902, he additionally became more actively involved in the creation of some of the puzzles. His longest-running series was a sequence of "word charade" puzzles that merged his love of drawing with an affection for wordplay dating back to etymology and vocabulary classes at Central High School. These puzzles consisted of panels of ten drawings that had to be interpreted to yield a common word, phrase, city or personal name. One sequence challenged the reader to identify the reference books that the drawings illustrated, so that a man expiring on a street in front of a priest's home was decoded, charade-style, to signify "die-rectory," while a gent cutting a pile of cards in two became a visualization of a "bi-decker." Sometimes the features of the men in the puzzles would recall either Henri or Sloan himself.

Equally amusing, and even more visually elaborate, was the comic strip that Sloan briefly produced in 1902. "Paul Pallete the Practical Paintist," creation of the anagrammatic Ivan "Lanso," narrated the adventures of the trompe l'oeil painter of the series' title and his rotund sidekick, Peachy. A pair of scheming vagabonds, Paul and Peachy roam the countryside playing pranks and duping folks out of money and property by means of Paul's dazzling, eye-deceiving talent with his brush and palette. In a characteristic episode, a group of railroad tycoons gratefully bestows a reward on the two for averting a train wreck (the rocks strewn across the track are actually Paul's creations), and in another, a dopey Santa Claus is relieved of his loot by diving down Paul's fake chimneys. The victims are the gullible, the complacent, the unthinking mob, old and young alike. Each cartoon ends with Paul and Peachy being found out and brought to justice—this was the comics, after all—but not before Mr. Ivan Lanso, whose angular main character (despite the stovepipe hat and goatee) looks very familiar, gets to make and remake the same point: button-counting, every-hair-in-place naturalism in the visual arts is for rubes. *Caveat emptor,* or you get what you deserve.

Sloan's popular-culture binge of these years has the feel, somehow, of a race against time. Surely he must have seen the handwriting on the wall at the *Press.* The national interest in photography was growing, and editors and publishers were following with keen interest the changes in technology that had enabled them to make the shift three years before to illustrating all news articles with photos, thereby diminishing their dependence on draftsmen. Yet Sloan still sought to make himself almost indispensable in his office by doing more work and doing it in different, more ingenious styles. But unless he intended to become a full-time cartoonist like his friend Hugh Doyle on the *Press* staff, an alternative he did not realistically envision as part of his future, his place in the profession was not apt to last much longer.

Yet another demand on Sloan's time in 1902 and thereafter was a long-term commission that came his way courtesy of William Glackens's contacts in New York. This job was something that proved to be of particular interest to Sloan. The Frederick J. Quinby Company of Boston was planning to bring out a deluxe edition of fifty novels by Paul de

Sloan's comic strip Paul Pallete, *from the* Philadelphia Press, *1902*
(Delaware Art Museum)

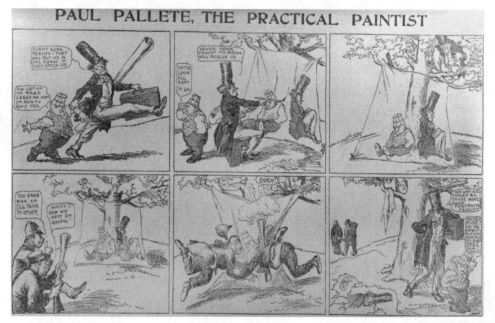

Kock, available through subscription only, with illustrations by several different artists, both drawings and etchings. De Kock was not a writer Sloan would have turned to for his own pleasure reading, but that was beside the point. A poor man's Balzac, he was a fantastically popular and prolific storyteller whose dozens of lively, sentimental novels chronicled, with no more literary flair than a Barbara Cartland of today, the marriages, affairs, duels, ambitions, joys, and tribulations of Parisians in the 1840s. Just sexy enough to be considered sophisticated and sufficiently easy to read to appeal to a mass audience—Molly Bloom, cozy in her bed on Eccles Street, is busy devouring these risqué potboilers in Dublin even as Sloan begins his drawings—the de Kock oeuvre in a collector's edition seemed a good money-making idea at the time. Publishers did quite well circa 1900 with subscription buyers eager for well-made multivolume sets of books.

Sloan's involvement with the ill-fated Quinby Company stretched out over a four-year period and eventually resulted in his completing fifty-three etchings and fifty-four drawings in crayon and ink, netting him several hundred dollars before the Quinby Company went bust and the series was discontinued. Even before he started drawing, Sloan devoted himself—as much for his own pleasure, one imagines, as for the needs of the project—to an exhaustive study of Louis-Philippe's France, the fashions and pastimes of the day, maps and histories of Paris, and the distinctive "take" on his own era of Honoré Daumier. This last, quite profitable influence was owed to Henri, who had sent Sloan a packet of lithographs by the *Charivari* satirist when he was last abroad. On the whole, Sloan was pleased with the outcome and energized by taking out the etcher's needle, plates, and acids again. The New York painter Arthur Davies, a man of no small discernment, told Robert Henri that Sloan's de Kock etchings were the best he had seen in that line, and several newspapers of 1903 and 1904 commented on the quality of the illustrations, which so deftly conveyed character traits, a sense of action and mood (Sloan seemed especially good at humor and dissipation), and the flavor of raucous, ebullient Paris. Even Dolly made an appearance in the de Kock extravaganza: hers is the funny, round face of the plump, plucky Madame Broulard falling on the dance floor, petticoats flying and wig stuck in the mouth of her inebriated partner.

To no one's surprise but his own, Sloan's life with the *Press* and the whole world of Philadelphia journalism came to an abrupt end in November 1903. In the middle of that month he received a letter from William MacGraw, the paper's new art editor, informing him that his services would no longer be required after December 3. The age of homogeneous print media was dawning: the *Press* was buying into a syndicated Sunday supplement, and because it would be doing away with its own supplement, its need for a full art-department staff would be considerably reduced. Salaried artists such as Sloan, however popular and respected, were a luxury under the new system, not a necessity. Most illustrators had long since accepted that they were going to be replaced sooner or later, and had made other arrangements. Their day was done.

Sloan was grateful when Alden March persuaded the publisher to continue the weekly "word charade" puzzles. (Although there wasn't a good enough living to be made doing four puzzles a month freelance for the paper, at an average of twenty-five dollars a puzzle, this assignment proved to be at least a regular source of income for Sloan—in fact, his steadiest income for the next seven years.) In the meantime he had to give some serious thought to the very thing he had been avoiding thinking about for the last few years: New York and the greater career possibilities it offered. A week after leaving the *Press*, he anxiously made the rounds in Manhattan, stopping at *Scribner's, Everybody's,* and the other mainstream magazines with his portfolio to see what the likelihood was of his getting story-illustration work. Newspapers may have been intent on making the switch from the one medium to the other as quickly as possible, but periodicals were still firmly committed to original drawings by quality artists; the golden age of illustration in that field would last another thirty years. At the *Century,* Sloan met with Alexander Drake, the magazine's longtime art editor, and received some vague encouragement about assignments in the near future. Tentative as it all was, it would have to do. In his heart, Sloan knew that he had to make the move and only hoped that Dolly would understand. Philadelphia was the past. For better or worse, his future was in New York.

The new year brought a taste of that "for better or worse." Henri had organized a group show at the National Arts Club in New York, which opened in January with work by Sloan, Glackens, Luks, Davies, Henri himself, and a Boston painter of his acquaintance who often spent time in Manhattan, Maurice Prendergast. The exhibition of forty-six paintings (which included *Independence Square, Philadelphia,* by now a much-traveled picture) looked "remarkably fine and satisfying," Henri told a friend. Sloan came to town to see the show and no doubt agreed with Henri's assessment. The city's newspaper reviewers, however, took a slightly different, or divided, view. Charles FitzGerald of the *Sun,* who had been one of the few critics to cover the Allan Gallery show, had some encouraging observations to make about the new realist trend in American painting (though his objectivity was open to question as he was about to become William Glackens's brother in-law), and Charles De Kay of the *Times* thought Sloan's *The Sewing Woman* indicated talent, though he speculated that the artist's fate might be the "success of esteem" rather than the "success of sales." In the main, however, critical opinion held that these paintings lacked the refinement that great art called for. In style and theme they were too plain, too dour, too roughhewn. They were idiosyncratic rather than "serious" and "inspiring." Arthur Hoeber, a prominent reviewer, wrote in the *Commercial Advertiser* that the exhibition was one where "joyousness never enters, where flesh and blood are almost at a vanishing point, and where unhealthiness prevails to an almost alarming extent." The membership of the Arts Club was acrimoniously divided about the desirability of exhibiting paintings of alcoholics like Luks's *Whiskey Bill,* or images of working-class drudgery like Sloan's *The Sewing Woman,* which Hoeber thought resembled an "animated corpse, though . . . well drawn." De Kay, writing in the *Times,* pronounced the whole spectacle alternately invigorating and "startling," even vaguely unpleasant.

No one sold anything out of the show, but that fact was hardly surprising. It would not be the last time that Henri, Sloan, and their friends would have occasion to complain about the narrowness of American taste, the difficulty of securing a broad-minded hearing in the New York press, and the uphill struggle to establish their right to paint whatever subjects they chose.

New York, 1904

(1904–1905)

*"Don't pass it by—the immediate, the real, the ours . . .
DO New York!"*

—HENRY JAMES TO EDITH WHARTON,
urging her to write about
Manhattan life (1902)

In April, feeling more than a little ambivalent, John and Dolly Sloan left Philadelphia, a city of just over a million and a place well-known to both of them, and moved north, to a city three times larger, a place self-conscious even then about its toughness and bustle, an environment infinitely more competitive, dynamic, varied, and threatening.

In his typically generous fashion, Robert Henri did his best to aid his nervous friends in the transition. He offered a loan of a thousand dollars to get them on their feet (Sloan agreed to accept five hundred) and helped them get a studio in the Sherwood Building to live in while they went apartment-hunting at their leisure. He also asked Sloan to give him some lessons in etching and took the couple on their first trips to Coney Island. This was the year, too, in which Henri extended that ultimate gesture of esteem and affection to a fellow artist by painting Sloan's portrait. The result, which Henri proudly exhibited that fall at the Carnegie Institute (and which hangs today in the permanent collection of the Corcoran Gallery in Washington, D.C.), is a perfect example of the Henri style at its best—and darkest. Tall and thin, wearing a black suit and a pince-nez, Sloan as rendered by his mentor is an intellectual and a cosmopolitan, the very things that Sloan feared he was not at this moment in his life. He looks reflective, self-confident, even a little mysterious. The plain boy of the 1890 self-portrait has grown, distinguished himself, pondered his life and his craft, and even created an aura for himself. If Henri was looking to bolster his friend's self-image even as he effected a vintage Henri portrait—all quick strokes and immediate impressions, a sensuous surface and a haunting face—he could not have done a better job.

Summer wasn't easy, as Dolly disliked staying in the crowded Sherwood Building, went on more than a few heavy drinking binges, and felt the need to retreat to Philadelphia on several occasions to see Dr. Bower and her sisters. Sloan did his best to be patient. By September, happily, he had a regular model he liked—the imposing Eugenia Stein, known as Zenka ("a great girl, so ingenuous, so paintable")—and had found an apartment and studio at 165 West Twenty-third Street. At fifty dollars a month, the new combined home-and-work-area was a bit costly (especially given the condition of the hallway and the rooms), but as a top-floor space with a skylight, it was a painter's dream. The second of the two larger rooms, facing noisy Twenty-third Street, was the living room and bedroom; a tiny, airless kitchen and a tiny, airless bathroom were squeezed in between the two principal rooms. If it was not a middle-class couple's ideal apartment, number 165 suited the family budget for the time being (Dolly didn't care so long as they could finally be alone together in a place she could make habitable) and presented, within walking distance, just the sort of street spectacle that Sloan craved. He jubilantly told Henri that he had found the "New York edition of 806 Walnut Street."

The West Twenty-third Street area that John and Dolly Sloan came to know that fall, and where they were to live for the next eight years, was a far cry from the socially desirable address it had been four decades earlier, when Edith Wharton was born two blocks to the east, just off Fifth Avenue, but that was hardly a fact to trouble the Sloans. Like all neighborhoods in Manhattan, then and now, the Chelsea district changed character—in fact, redefined itself completely—with each succeeding generation. Fashionable New York had moved uptown since the Whartons' day, shops lined both sides of what had been a residential block on Twenty-third between Fifth and Sixth avenues, and the Fifth Avenue Hotel facing Broadway and Madison Square had been rebuilt to accommodate the businessmen and tourists who were pouring into the city in staggering numbers. Even more dramatically, the brand-new boat-shaped Flatiron Building—our American Parthenon, as Alfred Stieglitz called it at the time of his famous photograph—and Stanford White's Madison Square Garden had made of Twenty-third Street in mid-island a hub of activity rather than a place for the affluent to raise their children.

It was an area, busy and colorful and robustly untidy, that soon meant a great deal to John Sloan, perfectly matching his temperament and providing the images for some of his best paintings. An avenue west of Madison Square, acting almost as a kind of north-south divider between the remnants of gentility on one side and the burgeoning seediness on the other, was the elevated train, whose roar could be heard in front of the Sloans' building at number 165. The Sixth Avenue El deposited New Yorkers in Chelsea at the northernmost point of what was left of "Ladies' Mile," the stretch from Fourteenth to Thirty-fourth Street that had housed the city's first huge department stores; a short walk from the Chelsea Hotel, an imposing redbrick emblem of the eighties; and a few blocks from several of the city's liveliest eateries, among them Mouquin's and the Café Francis. The now-shabby Grand Opera House, property of the robber barons Jim Fisk and Jay Gould, was still open on the corner of Eighth Avenue and Twenty-third Street, though its fare was nothing that uptown devotees of Verdi and Wagner would relish. Somewhat ominously, the Sloans' building—a five-story walk-up that had already seen better days—was in close proximity to the area known as the Tenderloin.

The boundaries of the Tenderloin were a trifle vague, but its spirit was not. From Twenty-fourth Street or so on up toward Forty-second, from Sixth Avenue across to Ninth, could be found the taverns, restaurants, risqué theaters, gambling dens, brothels, streetwalkers (largely but not exclusively female), cardsharps, con men, and interested spectators of the major red-light district of New York, already a definable feature of the city for more than three decades. Then as now, such turf witnessed an overlap between the reputable and the seamy. Perfectly ordinary people as well as a slightly bohemian crowd dined at Mouquin's on Sixth Avenue and Twenty-eighth Street, and at any number of Chinese restaurants that had opened north of Chinatown in the last several years. Quaint boardinghouses like Petipas on Twenty-ninth Street, run by three sisters from Brittany, offered unpretentious accommodations, a table d'hôte at reasonable prices, and dining in the backyard during the warm months. But only a block away from Petipas, the curious and the prurient flocked to Miner's Theater to watch a revue in which the female performers were clad in sheer body stockings so as to appear nude, while mere steps away from the entrance to Mouquin's, out-of-town businessmen and middle-aged husbands met available women at the dance hall known as the Haymarket, where unescorted women were admitted free of charge. (In its peak years, the Haymarket was allowed to pay the police what was considered the remarkably low protection "fee" of $250 a week, as it was such a favored hangout of the cops on that beat.) There were private cubicles there for more intimate "dancing," and even a tunnel passageway to an adjoining hotel. Other places in the area dispensed with cover charges for men altogether, on the assumption that watered-down drinks, overcharging, and the likelihood of creating some business for the lines of brownstone brothels nearby would make up the difference. The traffic in prostitution must have been astounding in this section of town, which encompassed, according to one estimate, more than two hundred brothels in a one-mile radius. Bouncers, pimps, pickpockets, patrolmen on the take, credulous tourists, neighborhood kids playing in the street, the clatter of the El, and all of this only blocks from Fifth Avenue, where the well-to-do of Manhattan still paraded by in their carriages on Sunday —in the autumn of 1904, the Sloans found themselves a world away from Fort Washington.

Outside his immediate neighborhood, there was even more to see, and Sloan confessed himself "awed" by the spectacle and the extremes of life Manhattan was home to. Walking through Greenwich Village to the south or Gramercy Park to the east, he explored the nether regions of the Bowery. Wandering up Fifth Avenue past the site of the demolished Croton Reservoir on Forty-second Street (soon to be the New York Public Library), he had his first experience of the fake palazzi, châteaux, and fortresses of the city's millionaires and the collections of the Lenox Library and the Metropolitan Museum. He was seeing the city now not as a visitor, not as the harried newspaperman of 1898 who had spent ten hours a day in the *Herald* office, but as a resident with time to look, and that made a crucial difference. A panorama that spanned the architecture of Richard Morris Hunt, the street kids of Jacob Riis's photographs, great libraries, and massive tenements—constant reminders of profitable success and abject failure, of pleasure and need—some days seemed almost too much stimulation.

New friends were a part of the excitement, too, of course, and provided a kind of emotional ballast. Through Henri and Glackens and Shinn and Preston (both of whom were married now), as well as Frank

Crane, who had married Luks's first wife and was taking care of the child Luks had abandoned, Sloan and Dolly had the opportunity of meeting a variety of interesting people in their first months in the city. The artist Jerome Myers and his wife, Ethel, were agreeable company, as were Ernest Lawson, an Impressionist painter of Upper Manhattan, and Henry Reuterdahl, a marine and landscape painter. All talented in their different ways, these people were also opinionated and conversationally engaging in a way that Sloan appreciated. William Walsh, the literary editor of the *Herald,* and Byron Stephenson, who wrote art criticism for the gossip sheet *Town Topics,* held their own with the painters in verbal and gustatory feats. At Mouquin's the Sloans made the acquaintance of Charles FitzGerald and Frederick James Gregg, the writers for the *Sun* who had done the most to tout the careers of Henri and Glackens and who would soon do their part to help Sloan. Both Dublin-born and far better educated than most American journalists, they were men with no great respect for New York's hidebound cultural institutions, and with an interest in provocative new art. FitzGerald had a waspish style and an appetite for elegant social pleasures. The versatile, scholarly Gregg—El Greggo to his colleagues—had been a schoolmate of William Butler Yeats and had been lauded in his youth by AE as Ireland's hope in poetry. Sloan found him prim and peremptory, a man too sure of himself and given to pontification, but nonetheless fascinating.

The biggest, warmest "character" of this disparate group was James Moore, owner of the Café Francis and entertainer extraordinaire. A portly, genial man, grandson of Clement (" 'Twas the night before Christmas . . .") Moore, he had an amateur's fondness for art, especially Lawson's landscapes, and a philanderer's interest in a parade of attractive younger women whom he squired about town and always introduced as long-lost daughters or nieces. He was a Manhattan type, an aging bon vivant whom it was impossible to dislike, and different from anyone Sloan had known personally in Philadelphia. The parties he hosted at his ramshackle brownstone at 450 West Twenty-third Street, only a block and a half from the Sloans', were always energizing events. The "Secret Lair Beyond the Moat," as Moore called his domain, was a place of free-flowing liquor, rich food, comfortable accommodations, and unconventional company. The walls of the basement had been decorated with virgin canvases in the interests of securing fresh work in situ from talented guests. On occasion one could catch a glimpse of the poet Edwin

Arlington Robinson walking up the stairs, silent and solitary, to the top-floor room Moore provided him with rent-free.

Another, quite separate aspect of the pleasure Sloan was able to take in his relocation was connected to his feeling that he was free at last from the overbearingly close bond to his family that had defined the first thirty-odd years of his life. Dolly had been right in her insistence that the rest of the Sloans could manage on their own, or with only minimal help from their now-married son and brother. Marianna was making some money as a dressmaker, creating copies of French fashions that were proving popular among her clients in the suburbs, and as a painter of decorative lampshades. In the autumn of 1904 she was to have her first one-woman show of her paintings at a small gallery in Philadelphia, an honor Sloan had yet to manage for himself. Freedom from guilt over abandoning his dependents accounted for a fair share of Sloan's good humor even as he dealt with the Quinby Company's failure to meet its obligations for the de Kock illustrations—he was owed six hundred dollars at that point and had to spend money on a lawyer to work out a payment schedule—and his nervousness about substituting at the New York School of Art, formerly the Chase School, where Henri was now teaching.

Sloan took over Henri's group for the opening week of the fall session while Henri stayed in Cooperstown to finish a portrait commission. "The sense of responsibility certainly seems to awe me," Sloan acknowledged to Henri. "I feel as though, should I ever teach regularly, it would be like taking holy orders in the church." The only unpleasantness of the week, a moment of rudeness that Sloan never truly forgave, came when a tall, cocky, athletic young student exhibited brash disdain toward the temporary instructor, who he apparently felt was no match for the "real" teacher he was expecting. When Sloan approached the easel of George Bellows, a twenty-two-year-old just arrived from Columbus, Ohio, Bellows turned his back on Sloan, as if to say that he had no use for a "crit" from so undistinguished a presence. Sloan, offended, said nothing.

As he must have expected she would, Dolly exacted a price from her husband for the move to New York. She was just not emotionally able to deal with the rupture in her old patterns, not yet, and the trips "home" to Philadelphia—which Sloan found hard to accept after the first few times, angrily decrying Dolly's abandonment of him—seemed to accomplish very little.

One torturous embarrassment followed another. The Sloans hadn't gone that year to William Glackens's wedding in Connecticut—where Sloan's good friend had married a vivacious Hartford heiress and art student named Edith Dimock—despite the fact that a private Pullman car had been engaged to cart a good many of the New York and Philadelphia guests there, including James Moore, Everett and Florence Shinn, James and May Preston, Ernest Fuhr, Charles FitzGerald, and, in a particularly raucous mood, George Luks. (It would be interesting to know whether the Sloans were in fact invited at all, or whether John Sloan simply thought it would be best if they didn't attend, for obvious reasons: the Dimocks were patrician New Englanders who were more than a little horrified at their daughter's wish to move in "disreputable" artistic circles.) But even when she met Edith Dimock Glackens in New York, Dolly found it hard to relax in her company. Although they would later become somewhat friendly, in 1904 Dolly could see only a figure of threatening refinement and confidence, a woman with flawless grammar and a closetful of beautiful dresses, and she suffered a torment of anxiety whenever she was expected to socialize with the new Mrs. Glackens or with Florence Shinn, May Preston, or the other artists' wives. On one occasion, while she was visiting at the Glackenses' new apartment on Washington Square, the pressure became too great, and Dolly decided that she had to leave at once and have a drink before heading home, though she had no money on her. Caught going through the purses and coats on the bed in the adjoining room, she was mortified, naturally, and confirmed for the moment in her self-doubt and self-hate. To her credit, Edith Glackens did her best to overlook the whole incident.

Sloan himself, however, could not have overlooked what was happening even if he had wanted to. What should have been a purely magical moment—an immersion in new sights and new experiences—threatened on some days to turn into a perfect nightmare. Money to drink and drinking companions can always be found in a big city by a woman still in her twenties, and Dolly was clever and maniacally enterprising when she needed to be. For a long time Sloan could not understand where the money for his wife's drink was coming from. Their own funds were carefully accounted for. Once in a while he would learn that she had borrowed from a friend on the strength of some fantastic story, and he would do his best to repay any and all loans he heard about. That Dolly was finding other means to buy her liquor became clear to Sloan when he discovered that through no activity on his part outside the home, he was suffering from a venereal discharge and had to see Dr. Bower.

For most couples, an infidelity that led to the transmission of a venereal disease from one spouse to the other would constitute the breaking-point of the marriage, or close to it. Perhaps the Sloans — or rather, John Sloan (never Dolly) — did consider separating in their first years in New York, but there is no actual evidence of that. On the one hand, Sloan seems not to have regarded Dolly's episodes with other men, of which there were several in the course of the decade, as conscious infidelities. If she set out in search of a drink in a spirit of desperate need that overshadowed any normal sense of dignity and restraint, she would return home bedraggled, self-hating, and—later that night or the next day—miserably, heartbreakingly repentant. Sloan was astounded, horror-struck, at what was happening to them, and furious with his wife, but he came to recognize (as he recounted these events years later) that she was ill and at certain times unable to control herself. Having sex with another man, either while drunk or in the hopes of gaining money to that end, had nothing to do with love, affection, or loyalty. The real tragedy of the Sloan marriage was the lack in America in the early years of this century of any program or informed counsel to deal with the affliction of alcoholism.

Sloan anxiously tried to keep the nature of Dolly's problems secret, retreating behind the quaint Victorianism of having a "sickly" wife, but certain friends were well aware of the truth, and a few even went out of their way to help. If Mrs. Crane, in Sloan's opinion, was apt to let Dolly drink too much when they were out together, Linda Henri tended to be a more supportive friend, and Sloan's cousin Eleanor, a daughter of James Dixon Sloan's younger brother, was at times a lifesaver. The only one of Sloan's relatives who really took to his wife, she came to New York frequently, loved to go shopping with Dolly, and saw her good qualities —her tenderness, her vivacity—from the first, in a way that too few other members of the family circle did. When Dolly "lapsed," Eleanor was often there for her. She was not given to moralizing about Dolly's binges. In dramatic contrast to Bess and Marianna, she wasn't easily shocked. She was never above helping Dolly sober up or talking her through a difficult moment. Sloan came to appreciate Eleanor's presence. There were too many others, he felt, who were ready to cast stones.

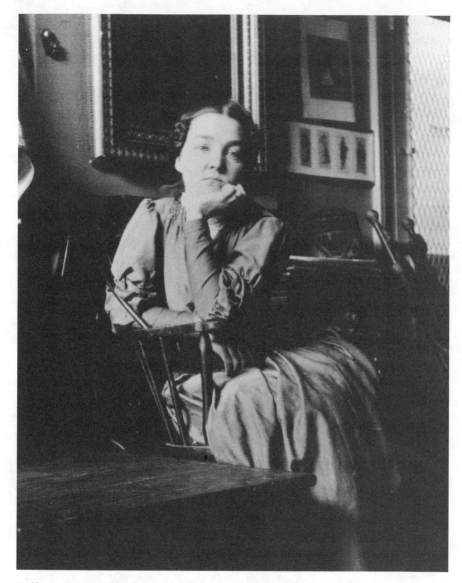

Dolly in New York City, circa 1905 (Delaware Art Museum)

What prevented Sloan from leaving Dolly was not any single element of their relationship or of his or her personality, but rather a variety of factors. One was just that quality in her husband that had so irked Dolly when it was directed toward his parents and sisters: his sense of commitment and obligation, strong to the point of obstinacy. To have brought Dolly to New York and made a life with her for seven or eight years only

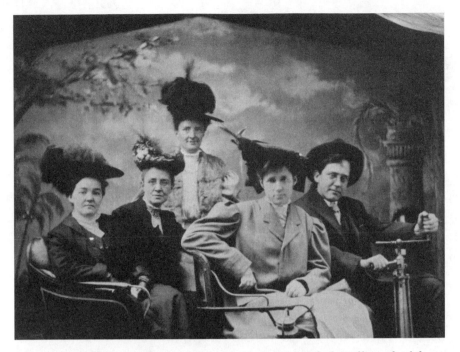

October 1906: A Coney Island outing, with Sloan at the wheel, Dolly at far left, and cousin Eleanor Sloan in front (Delaware Art Museum)

to abandon her, when he had known all along that life with this woman would involve special trials, seemed to John Sloan almost unthinkable. Then, too, there was his own anxiety about women and marriage, marital demands and satisfactions. Dolly made him feel loved, desirable, and extraordinarily talented. These were attributes of a relationship never to be minimized. No man in Sloan's family circle had ever enjoyed them, so far as he could tell. And if Henri, Glackens, Preston, and Shinn knew the pleasure of having affectionate, supportive wives, why shouldn't he? The difference was that he needed a wife who didn't want children and didn't mind that he often made less money than most of his peers. When Sloan started to drink a little more himself, feeling that it cemented his bond with Dolly even as it relieved his own tensions, he may also have decided that he was in no position to demand that Dolly be other than who she honestly was.

In any case, Dolly Sloan on her best days was a delight. She took as much pleasure in tending to the apartment and feeding and caring for her husband in their own place as she had at 806 Walnut Street. She would sometimes come over to the work area of the studio, look approvingly on Sloan's work-in-progress, and plant a kiss on his cheek before going on about her business. She had absorbed her husband's interests as her own and made no secret of how much he meant to her. She told anyone who would listen that she had married a man who would ultimately be acknowledged as a great artist. The issue of children happily never came up, as they had long since decided (whether with or without a doctor's corroboration is unclear) that Dolly was infertile. She could effect an organized, demure persona at great remove from the turmoil of her life at its worst. The woman by his side in Sloan's 1908 etching *The Copyist at the Metropolitan Museum,* which depicts the Sloans visiting the museum and observing a painter at her easel in one of the nineteenth-century galleries, is the most poised and elegant figure in the complex composition. Husband and wife are both dressed in their Sunday best (as any middle-class couple would have been on a museum outing circa 1904–1905) and might well be returning to their Gramercy Park brownstone after a stroll down Fifth Avenue. Dolly barely reaches the height of Sloan's shoulder, but she clutches his lapel as if afraid they will be separated in the crowd. They are even the subject of observation themselves: while most of the people in the room exclaim over the work of the copyist, who is getting those sheep just right—the yokels ever "taken in" by Paul Pallete—a man behind the Sloans on the left stares, with admiration or envy, right at them.

Like most men and women who perceive the work they do as a vocation rather than a job, Sloan had the ability to compartmentalize different aspects of his life, and for better or for worse, this trait represented another form of self-defense in the days of marital Sturm und Drang. (Had Sloan been unable to develop his talents as a painter, the story of his marriage might have been very different, and much shorter.) Possibly Sloan learned this resolution from Henri. No man he knew appeared more purposely divided and detached. There was Robert Henri the art star and Pied Piper from Philadelphia, with a set of friends and memories from the old days. There was Robert Henri the New York painter and teacher, who was busy cultivating the next generation of students and acolytes—among them such obviously brilliant young men as George Bellows, Guy Pène du Bois, Rockwell Kent, and Edward Hopper. Most elusively, there was Robert Henri the son of the Atlantic City real-estate tycoon "Mr. Lee," who (as Sloan was to learn years later) had been a professional gambler in the days of Henri's youth in Nebraska and had been involved in a self-defense shooting that led to the family's flight East. The young Robert Cozad had become "Robert Henri" as all the family members took different names and attempted to bury their collective past. The result was an individual whose preference it was to be ultimately enigmatic, unknowable, cut off.

So, too, on a different level, did Sloan need to block out the pain and degradation that threatened to subvert what he most wanted to accomplish. This he was able to do as, remarkably, he began to work in a much more assured, more dynamic manner upon his arrival in New York—even as he was coping with the worst of Dolly's breakdowns to date and wondering what his future with her would be like.

In painting the human figure off and on over a nine-year period, Sloan had failed more often than not. At some point, or more probably very gradually, he realized that he might have profited from a more rigorous study of anatomy in his youth, that he should not have scoffed so teasingly at the Thomas Eakins–Thomas Anshutz belief in a med-school knowledge of skeletons and muscle tissue. But that was water under the bridge for Sloan in his thirties: the Henri method called for speed, for suggestion rather than completion, for painterly flair. The only trouble, of course, was that what was easy for Henri and some of his followers was rough going for Sloan. Yet with *Stein, Profile,* he turned a corner. In what is generally considered to be the first painting Sloan completed in New York, he deals with the body of his model, Eugenia Stein, as if it were a thing of real weight and depth. There is a believable fleshiness to this picture that had eluded Sloan before. "Zenka," or "Efzenka," is seen in profile, the light hitting her round face, her neck and exposed shoulder, and her extended left forearm and hand. A section of the intricate gold braid on her dark gown reflects more of the yellow light. The rest is alluring shadow, and the result is a rapturous portrait of the kind that (like many a fine painting) says absolutely nothing in reproduction and everything in a personal encounter with this soft, girthy, dignified woman. *Stein, Profile* also serves the purpose of establishing a little distance between Sloan and Henri, who was making use of Zenka at the same time. Henri's *Young Woman in White,* a featured work in the collection of the National Gallery of Art in Washington, D.C., is less subtle and more formal, a bravura performance, a crowd-pleaser. Sloan avoided comparison and competition and, in a plausible irony, made a more resonant image.

The same confidence animates *Ferry Slip, Winter,* which Sloan painted in 1905 and continued to work on the following year—"a non-impressionistic impression of an antique friend of the commuter," as he described it—as well as his first springtime rendering of Madison Square and the Flatiron Building, and the beginning of his rooftop subjects. For the vista he wanted for the last of these, Sloan positioned Dolly by the clothesline on the roof of their building, looking west toward the Chelsea Hotel and the Hudson River and New Jersey beyond. Between the varying scale and height of the buildings of the area (the hotel on the left and the McBurney YMCA on the right are the tallest and—along with Sloan's own apartment house—the only ones in the painting still standing in the 1990s) and the presence of a person in the foreground, the street traffic below, and the expanse of dusky orange sky in the background, Sloan set himself a stiff challenge and had reason to be pleased with the outcome. Not since *East Entrance, City Hall, Philadelphia* in 1901 had he attempted a cityscape of comparable ambition. The painting was exhibited at a small show (not the main annual exhibition) at the Pennsylvania Academy in 1906, where it earned a notice in *Art News,* but curiously, Sloan decided not to send it on any of the other jury rounds that his work made over the next few years, and *Sunset, West Twenty-third Street* wasn't exhibited again until 1918.

Throughout 1904 and 1905, Sloan and Dolly's income hadn't been increased one dollar through the sale of paintings. The twenty to thirty dollars a week he was paid for the *Philadelphia Press* word-charade puzzles took care of the rent and the groceries. Though Sloan was beginning to feel that a man had only so many visual puns in him, he couldn't hope to give up that job yet. Illustrations for stories and poems in *Century, Collier's, Good Housekeeping, Leslie's Monthly Magazine, Success,* the *Saturday Evening Post, McClure's,* and *Scribner's* brought in additional income that, along with the tardy Quinby checks for the de Kock drawings, enabled the couple to manage better than they thought they might in a city with a fierce cost of living. For Sloan, the less than stirring aspects of such magazine work entailed not only his having to go hat-in-hand to the editorial offices to request work when none was forthcoming—he particularly hated approaching Howard Pyle at *McClure's*—but also the very nature of the mundane fiction he illustrated, which called for drawings less adventurous and droll than those from his "little magazine" period or for the de Kock novels.

Absorbed though Sloan was in oil painting, his love of graphic art had been reawakened by the de Kock project to an extent that he could not ignore. Violette's attempted suicide, Mademoiselle Zizi's coquettish ruses, Cherami's duels, Dodichet's histrionics, the champagne parties and the bustle of the street—everything comical, dandified, or even vaguely melancholy about de Kock's world, banal though his writing might be—suggested pictorial possibilities that led Sloan to devise illustrations surpassing their context. It was, Sloan decided, enormous fun to draw and etch for a endeavor so large and engrossing. He began to dread the thought that the Quinby Company might not be able to pay him what was owed, not only because of the professional insult that such a loss would signify but because it might mean he would have to stop work on the series.

Sloan had not been in New York long before it occurred to him that some of the extraordinary energy he was feeling, an artistic power awakening and moving in so many different directions, might also be focused on contemporary life as a subject for a skilled etcher. Early in 1905 he began what would become the New York City Life series, initially envisioned as a set of ten and then later thirteen prints that would chronicle aspects of his city and his era in a visual counterpart to de Kock's—or, better yet, Balzac's—literary chronicles of Paris in the early to middle nineteenth century. The first etching, entitled *Connoisseurs of Prints,* is dated February 1905. At an auction of prints at the American Art Galleries on East Twenty-third Street, Sloan had scanned the crowd of would-be buyers at the preview with their catalogues and magnifying glasses, their furs and their potbellies, and had played Daumier to the scene. The satire is wicked and warm, like Daumier's or Hogarth's, rather than nasty and bileful. A bit more tart is *Fifth Avenue Critics,* the print that followed. The smug old ladies in their carriage, "showing themselves and criticizing others" on their daily ride, were identifiable types before the advent of the automobile, Sloan maintained about the subject of this etching, which proved in the long run to be one of his most salable. These were the "Connoisseurs of Virtue."

Henri was enthusiastic about Sloan's work in this vein, and the two men talked about the advisability of Sloan's doing a series of prints about connoisseurs. But the "material" available to Sloan under his nose on Twenty-third Street and along Sixth Avenue was too present for him, too enticing. The "high life" as a motif had limited appeal. In succeeding weeks, the strange gentleman who wandered the side streets of Chelsea with a hand organ, a drum, and cymbals, a one-man panhandler's band oblivious to onlookers or traffic, became *Man Monkey,* just as the crowd of girls at the hand-cranked nickelodeon stand were the inspiration for *Fun, One Cent* and the adolescents gawking at corsets in Madam Ryanne's window gave life to *The Show Case.* In *The Little Bride,* newlyweds leave Saint Vincent de Paul's, descending the church steps in a shower of rice and old shoes.

The six etchings mentioned above have an innocuous quality to them. All are capable examples of the art form, and one—of the print connoisseurs—is superbly made, in the best tradition of the European satirists. Had Sloan completed his anticipated "set" with similar work, the attention paid the New York City Life prints might have been very different. As it was, urban experience as seen on the streets in the daytime was not the beginning and end of Sloan's interest. From his back window on Twenty-third Street at night, he saw a great deal more, and much of what he saw struck him as being in no way less suitable, or less usable, than his Fifth Avenue grandes dames or a model like Zenka. The fact that he was in something of a minority on this issue would not become evident until the day he first put the needle to the copper plate.

Sloan's neighbors were as poor as and usually even poorer than he was. Working-class or unemployed, laborers in shops or in the Tenderloin, they lived lives that were bereft of luxury but, Sloan strongly felt, in no way called for condescension or didactic theorizing. Accordingly, the four etchings of the first set of ten prints rigorously avoided any hint of "social conscience." The low-keyed sorrow that is a part of the shabbiness of *Flute Player* (1905), and the actual pain and grubbiness expressed in the later *Treasure Trove* (1907) and *Rag Pickers* (1913), in which destitute people are shown scrounging through the refuse of others—these had nothing to do with the spirit of these four pictures. *The Women's Page* concerns a beefy, disheveled woman in a slip or nightgown, reading the paper in her overcrowded back bedroom. Stockings and towels are everywhere; the washboard lies across the unmade bed. Her rapt attention has been caught—though it is impossible to believe that Sloan could have seen this across the wide alley from his own window—by the women's page of the paper, with its trendy fashion tips and good-housekeeping reminders. Whether invented or observed, the irony is clear enough. *Man, Wife, and Child* depicts an affectionate wrestling match between a couple (that they are married is purely the artist's supposition) in yet another jam-packed apartment, while *Roofs, Summer Night,* done after the other etchings (in February 1906), dwells on another aspect of urban congestion: the residents of one Twenty-fourth Street building have dragged their mattresses and pillows to the roof to sleep, willy-nilly by chimneys and vents, on a broiling summer night.

If there was an indecorous quality to etchings about unmade beds and mass camp-outs on dirty rooftops—themes that would never have been considered by such master American etchers as Whistler and Joseph Pennell—there was something almost lascivious according to the standards of the day about Sloan's *Turning Out the Light.* Here the artist has made no effort (fortunately) to sanitize his powerfully erotic image with reference to the lawful conjugal state of the couple pictured. A woman leans eagerly across her bed with one hand on the gas lamp and the other on the shoulder of her soon-to-be-shed nightgown or slip. In the shadow of the bed frame, a man waits beside her, hands behind his head, for the

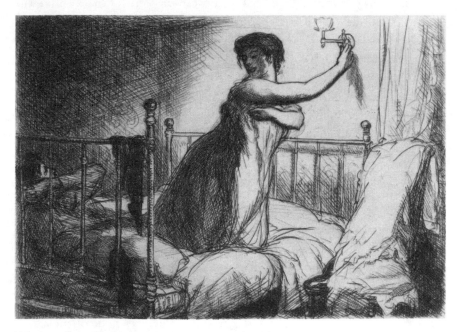

Turning Out the Light, *1905* (Kraushaar Galleries)

darkness and what will undoubtedly be a great mattress-shaking romp. Whether they have been married for ten years or been living for a short time as a common-law couple or met that evening at a bar is nobody's business. The joy of that private moment is what has been exposed to us. The skein of lines across the surface of the paper serves to shelter and enclose the couple. Sex pure and simple is an element of the New York City Life series because it is such a significant part of *any* life—cause for hurt and anxiety, as Sloan knew from his own lacerating experience, yet also the source of meaningful pleasure and potentially deeper bonds.

On one of his nightly walks through Chelsea during his first winter in New York, Sloan came upon a scene of a type long familiar to the residents of Midtown and Lower Manhattan, a city moment far removed from the warmth of *Turning Out the Light*. Several dozen cold, tired, unemployed men waited on line for a free cup of coffee near the corner of Fifth Avenue and Madison Square. The coffee, donated by one of the city's newspapers, was dispensed from the back of a horse-drawn wagon. Sloan's painting of that brutal scene, his first New York City genre work, is one of the few of his oil-on-canvas pictures that (unlike the etchings) can be said to have a purpose, implicit or otherwise, that approaches a "social comment." The dominant effect of the image in all its particulars is formidably grim: the sky is almost pitch-black, the men are no more than stabs and masses of blackish paint, even the snow is dirt-streaked and rather lurid in the glow of the few streetlights that illuminate it. *Coffee Line* is hard to take "merely" as a painting, as an arrangement of stark forms and subtle blends of dark pigments. It tends to make anyone who sees it wonder *why* so many men are in need of a handout, *why* they don't have jobs and homes and families to go to, *why* well-meant charity has to become public humiliation.

Given the ostensible concern with "good taste" that so many art exhibitions manifested in the early 1900s, and given society's penchant for turning a blind eye to critical statements about the social order—never more so than in Teddy Roosevelt's America, land of vigor and plenty, at a time when the public appetite for the naysaying of the muckrakers was peaking—one might expect *Coffee Line* to have been one of Sloan's least appreciated paintings. After all, it evinces none of the qualities that would eventually win Henri, Glackens, Luks, and Lawson a place in the important shows. But in fact, *Coffee Line* had a lively exhibition history in the first year of its existence, equaling the touring success of *Independence Square, Philadelphia*. It was accepted for display in the annual exhibitions of the Society of American Artists in New York and the Worcester Art Museum in Massachusetts, and at the end of the year for the Carnegie Institute's big show. In Pittsburgh it brought Sloan his first award—an Honorable Mention, shared with Glackens's *Chez Mouquin* (a lush painting of Moore and a new "daughter" out for a night on the town, with a bit of Charles FitzGerald visible off to the side)—as well as some notoriety. When *Art News* made mention of the picture in its December issue, Sloan was understandably excited and knew that his career was off and running, finally. In a manner of speaking, he was right. The Pennsylvania Academy of the Fine Arts wanted the picture for its show, opening in January 1906, and the Chicago Art Institute exhibited *Coffee Line* that fall. New York, Worcester, Pittsburgh, Philadelphia, Chicago: not a poor lineup for so vehemently humble a painting.

The traditional view of Sloan and the other painters who were later written about as members of "The Eight" or as participants in that great misnomer, the "Ash Can school" of American art, has portrayed them as men who were frozen out of the exhibition process. Over the years the rhetoric has played up this angle of outcasts assailing the walls of the establishment, and a fair amount of purple ink has been expended in discussing these artists. Recent scholarship questions this line, however, and with good cause. The major showcases for new work—perhaps those outside New York City even more than those in Manhattan—did, obviously, have room for art that seemed to some eyes a little gauche, a little raucous, not quite "proper" according to current notions of sound draftsmanship and brushwork. By the time they were forty, Luks, Glackens, Shinn, and Sloan were hardly unknown to people who followed the art scene. Yet before we rewrite history too dramatically, or make the climate of the time more liberal than it was, we must remember one all-important fact: the exhibition of a single painting was not in any way a commitment to a particular vision. No one was actually interested in *buying* a painting like *Coffee Line*. No museum thought it worthy of a place in its permanent collection. No collector thought it desirable for the walls of his own home or gallery. No dealer approached Sloan about taking him on. And that would continue to be the case for a very long time.

The joy of the last months of 1905 in the Sloan household, when *Coffee Line* was making its presence felt in the world and the city etchings were taking shape, was sadly overshadowed by a devastating and unexpected event. In fact, the year ended in great gloom and sorrow. Linda Henri had never been a robust woman. Since her marriage seven years before, she had suffered from bouts of pneumonia and erysipelas and, by the age of twenty-seven, needed a wig to hide the extent of her hair loss. She had also been diagnosed as tubercular and in the second half of 1905 became particularly frail. Henri worried about her as she returned to her parents' care in Pennsylvania again and again, but there seemed to be little he could do. In December, at the age of thirty, she died of gastritis. In a state of emotional collapse, Henri turned to the Sloans, who had come to regard Linda as one of their dearest friends. The grief-stricken widower moved into the apartment at 165 West Twenty-third Street for several weeks, to be fussed over by Dolly and left to rest and recover at his own pace while Sloan took over his classes at the art school.

A measure of Sloan's feeling for his friend's loss is visible in the etching *Memory,* which Sloan completed a few months later. Alternately titled *Memory of Last Year* or *Family Group,* this was a picture Sloan labored long and hard over—fittingly, it would become one of his most popular etchings—recalling one of many evenings of intimacy and good-fellowship that these two couples shared in their brief time together in New York, a moment of loving calm that was as important to the Sloans as to the Henris. Sloan's memorial image places Linda, more languid than ill, at the center of the group around the table. She is reading aloud to the others. Henri, to the left, is sketching. Dolly stares pensively into space in the middle rear of the circle. Sloan, to the right, smoking a pipe, draws on a sketch board. The activity in the room does not focus all four people on the same task or on each other; though everyone is listening to Linda's reading, Henri, Dolly, and Sloan are at the same time in their own worlds. But that, Sloan implied, was the essence of real friendship: effortless pleasure in the company of people who knew and accepted you and whom you knew and accepted. With Linda's death, it was a state of mind and heart that Sloan feared was irrevocably lost for all of them.

The "Ash Can" Myth

(1906–1907)

"The great artist is he who is most racy of his native soil. . . .
Character is everything in art. . . . A national character can
only be acquired by remaining at home and saturating ourselves in
the spirit of the land until it oozes from our pores and pencils in
every slightest work, in every slightest touch."

—GEORGE MOORE,
Modern Painting
(1893)

The move to New York, though made with some trepidation
and bringing to bear on the Sloans' marriage new stresses and a kind of
anguish that would have ended a less solid union, had been a turning
point for John Sloan. By 1906 he could see that he had found the voice
and the subject matter that were right for him, discoveries he wouldn't
have made in Philadelphia. The "spirit of the land" that his beloved
George Moore wrote about and urged artists to devote themselves to was
located, for Sloan, in the streets of New York, a terrain that he was more
than happy to saturate himself in until it influenced his "every slightest
touch."

The city he and Dolly had moved to two years earlier had at first
seemed rather threatening, but that feeling had passed. When Sloan
joined Henri, Glackens, Luks, and Lawson for a group show at a Midtown
gallery in February 1906 and basked in the praise Charles FitzGerald
directed toward his City Life etchings in the *Sun,* he knew that he was on
the right path: men of discernment understood his motives and applauded his accomplishments. The paintings of the next two years, which
include some of Sloan's most famous works—particularly *The Wake of the
Ferry, Hairdresser's Window, Sixth Avenue and Thirtieth Street,* and *The
Haymarket*—follow the pattern established by the etchings. They look

unlike any paintings that had been made before. They are not inter-changeable with, or identifiable as, anyone else's. They have the stamp of one individual's temperament, one man's view of his subject. But ironi-cally, they experienced the same muddled fate of appearing too déclassé for purchase at the time of their creation and too politically uncharged, too lacking in moral indignation, to suit Sloan's later commentators. Only a few people—and Charles FitzGerald was one of them—enjoyed them for what the artist intended them to be, which had precious little to do with the gritty term that art history has since carelessly adopted: "Ash Can realism."

Certainly the timing was right for what Sloan was interested in do-ing. A break with the Genteel Tradition and an excited attention to the urban landscape had been in the offing since the mid-nineties, when the first realist fiction had made its tentative appearance in the bookshops and on the newsstands. Yet even as the prose of Stephen Crane, Theodore Dreiser, Frank Norris, Upton Sinclair, and a score of lesser writers seemed to offer an analogous achievement to that of visual artists such as Sloan, the nature and intentions of this emerging style of literature provided an utterly false point of comparison, bound as Crane, Dreiser, Norris, and Sinclair were to the very word *realism* and to the literary idea of realism as a Zola-style chronicle of abused individualism, an examination of crush-ing social forces. In time, the "realist" slot in American cultural histories was used to accommodate a group of writers and painters who had little in common, an accommodation that served mainly (and still serves for some contemporary art writers) to devalue the painters. Indeed, even in Sloan's day the comparisons were made: references to Norris, Crane, and Maxim Gorky appear in reviews describing Sloan's urban paintings of circa 1906 and after. He never knew quite what to make of these odd, insistent allusions.

Attention to the city in all its ragtag vigor and human pain was far from a new phenomenon in 1906. Jacob Riis's revolutionary *How the Other Half Lives* had appeared in 1890, the same year that an amazed Basil March, in *A Hazard of New Fortunes,* encountered New York as an arena of grand visual opportunities neglected by America's artists. (As Luc Santé points out in his fascinating study of Manhattan squalor, appropriately entitled *Low Life: Lures and Snares of Old New York,* Riis worked hard to deny the existence of any colorful elements in the brutal urban world he depicted, while William Dean Howells's protagonist is more in line with the nineties vogue for the slum-as-exotic-locale. The two have in common, however, the shared assumption that the time had come in America to give serious attention to city life and to what we were making of it.) Throughout the 1890s and for all of the decade and a half before World War I, American novelists, journalists, painters, and photographers fairly bombarded the literate, art-conscious public with images and interpretations of the new metropolis.

In this sense, Sloan, Henri, Luks, Shinn, Bellows, Myers, et al. were not engaged in a revolutionary pursuit simply by virtue of painting poor people or dumpy barges. (Interestingly, Henri was finished with the city as a subject by the time Sloan moved to New York, and by mid-decade was specializing in portraiture and rural landscape. His most recent biographer suggests that his limited knowledge of perspective may have lain behind this decision: all of Henri's urban paintings are "straight-on" views, a method that allows for only a limited visual range.) Given the time lag between a cultural shift and widespread public awareness of it, the paintings and drawings being done by these artists in the early 1900s seemed unusual only to those who lacked a broad intellectual grasp of the era they were living in. What *was* new, though, was the implicit rejection —at least on John Sloan's part—of the earlier views as the defining ones. For Riis and Lewis Hine, for the novelists who had discovered the theme of the tenement and the prostitute, the American city was a moral nightmare, the mark of a society that had lost its soul. For painters like Childe Hassam, photographers like Alvin Langdon Coburn, or etchers like Joseph Pennell, it was an emblem of a culture come of age, with New York as a version of a European capital, a worthy subject for well-made art. Neither of these poles spoke to John Sloan's personality or experience.

For Sloan, there were as many "real" views of the city, as many authentic angles on modern urban life for a "realist" to explore, as there were individual temperaments through which that experience could be filtered. This meant that Riis's documents of pain and deprivation were true—he had seen the same children, the same slums, the same gutters and alleyways in his own walks through the city—but no more true than, say, the measured elegance of Hassam and Pennell, in its way. The inadequacy of each extreme, for him, was that neither corresponded to his own filtering view, his sense that the city encompassed squalor and exuberance *at one and the same time,* and that moments of anguish and exhilaration were not antithetical but necessarily linked, or not so much overlapping as entwined. A man who chose to make his life on the edge of the Tenderloin (there were cheaper rents and similar studios to be found elsewhere in Manhattan) was obviously drawn to the social fringe and felt its power. A man who declined to paint in the relentless spirit of *Maggie* or *The Jungle* believed that the dark underbelly could represent its own kind of lopsided myth. Or, that it was the business of the sociologist, the journalist, the activist. The city, then, could not be reduced to social commentary any more than it should be reduced to an Impressionist haze. It was too big, too elusive, too varied, too *real.* If any literary reference could come close to describing Sloan's work and state of mind in the first prolific years of his city paintings, it would probably be *Leaves of Grass,* with its paean to "many-footed Manhattan . . . superb Manhattan!" Like Whitman, Sloan disdained the pretty and the tepid in art, but when engaged in his own work, he was equally distant from anger or a determinist's gloom.

The need to immerse himself more and more in the images of the city, to take in the different aspects of life in New York some sustenance and pleasure while not allowing himself to be defeated by the worst of it, was of even greater importance to Sloan by early 1906. With *Sunset, West Twenty-third Street* and *Turning Out the Light,* he was no longer in Henri's shadow. Their professional lives were still connected, but Sloan was doing his own work—creating a kind of art that was both more ambitious and more intimate than Henri's—and he felt the thrill of the breakthrough. He was also distancing himself from the emotional mire that his father, mother, and sisters had fallen prey to, or given in to, and was instead *willing* himself to see more of the world than darkness and paralysis.

At this delicate time Sloan began to keep a diary, a record of the years 1906 through early 1913 that has been a rich tool for scholars since its publication in 1965. Its origins lay in that same wish to turn a source of pain into something potentially and plausibly beneficial. Exhausted by the emotional and physical toll of the last two years, Dolly was making more of an effort to grapple with her problem, seeing a sympathetic doctor whom Sloan found for them in New York as well as Collier Bower in Philadelphia; her "progress," however, was slow and marked by constant backsliding. Suffering from delirium tremens at the beginning of the new year, she was sometimes disoriented for hours at a time. Dr. Bower suggested that the distraught husband begin a diary and record some of his warmer, more appreciative thoughts about his wife, knowing —*expecting*—that she would look at it when he was out. Their hope was that Dolly would see that her worst fear—the one that sent her back to drinking, the fear that Sloan would leave her—was groundless. Sloan agreed to the ploy. There is something potentially disingenuous about most diaries (except those that the writer never shows to anyone and eventually destroys), and Sloan's is especially so, having as it does a central purpose other than naked self-examination and honest documentation. Yet the little department-store date books that Sloan wrote in eventually took on, as such things will, a pleasing life of their own. The result was a two-part accomplishment: a partial assuaging of Dolly's anxiety and a record of one American's intellectual life—books read, plays seen, exhibitions attended—and professional growth as he created several of the most robust paintings of the first decade of the twentieth century.

The road leading to that achievement, to those several paintings, was circuitous. First, it was necessary for Sloan to satisfy himself that he had mastered certain skills in oil that he had long been uneasy about. *Picnic Grounds* proved quite to his satisfaction that he could finally deal with groups of people in social interaction, on canvas as well as on paper. Where *The Rathskeller* of five years earlier had depicted a silent, somber couple and a lone eavesdropper at the next table, *Picnic Grounds* was inspired by a boisterous working-class gathering (the setting is a Memorial Day picnic in Bayonne, New Jersey, which Sloan attended with Frank Crane and his family, now living across the river) and shows young men and unchaperoned young women gamboling about a park and enjoying a rare weekday off from work—altogether a more active, more complex social scene than any he had attempted before. In *Dust Storm, Fifth Avenue*, begun two weeks after the Bayonne outing, the city at Twenty-third Street and Madison Square dissolves into a comic whirlwind as cartoon figures—little kids, matrons, a chauffeured couple—duck for cover, and the stately area around the Flatiron Building is transformed by clouds and gusts of dirt into a scene of mass pandemonium. *Hairdresser's Window*, of the following summer, is an even more captivating vignette that focuses on a motley Sixth Avenue crowd gathered to watch, through an open second-floor window, a woman having her hair bleached at the shop of Madam Malcomb, Hair Restorer, above the neighborhood chop suey joint.

In these paintings, Sloan was doing his best to bypass his great weakness, anatomy—the human figure as painted by Eakins, Anshutz, and Homer—by giving us so much else to look at, and thus, rightly, to capitalize on his strengths. Those strengths include a heartfelt view of the city as a messy but fascinating stage (no place for the fastidious), a growing facility with the brush as a sensuous tool, a willingness to try more complicated compositions, and a more capable feel for color. (Although *Hairdresser's Window,* at the Wadsworth Atheneum, in Hartford, has darkened considerably over the years, it was in its day—and is, falsely now, in most reproductions—a bright painting.) Sloan searched for moments of interest and worked to convey from memory an unpatronizing sense of what was pleasurable to him in those undramatic, even (to some eyes) mundane episodes.

The theme of the window frame and the very act of looking inevitably became almost a preoccupation for Sloan and led to one especially haunting painting done in 1907, a glimpse into a private moment on the order of what he had done in the City Life etchings. His "nightly vigils," as he called them, in the dark at his back window, were his version of the more artificial looking that took place in life class at art school, and they inspired his urge to move occasionally beyond the street, beyond what could be observed from the city pavement, into the tenement bedroom. *The Cot* is not anecdotal, nor is it literally a product of Sloan's observations of his neighbors (Zenka posed for the painting), but it is in spirit one and the same with the etchings. A woman undressing, her shoulders and arms exposed and one hefty naked leg over the edge of her unmade bed, occasioned some of Sloan's best, darkest, most delicate brushwork, a kind of *hommage* to the act of disrobing. Between the smutty full nudes of French artists like Paul Chabas, fashionable with American buyers of the day, and the moralists' mania for covering the body to protect the "innocent," Sloan's unclassical working woman in her slip is accorded a dignity, even an erotic reverence, that neither Chabas's affluent patrons nor the Society for the Suppression of Vice would have appreciated. She isn't a nymph or an adornment of the harem or a Sabine victim. She is just a woman, alive in 1907, getting ready for bed, and that, for Sloan, was an image of lasting beauty in itself.

Not that Sloan was an incurable romantic about the city or about life itself, oblivious to its seamy or brute sexual side, its capacity to hurt and degrade. His own homelife in 1906 and 1907 afforded him too much opportunity to reflect on the squalor. *South Beach, Bathers* and *Movies, Five Cents* and almost all of the Madison Square pictures seem relentlessly upbeat (as in fact people at the beach or at the movies or in parks often are), and the frenzied Herald Square crowd of trumpet blowers and confetti throwers in *Election Night* is a bacchanalian group—even the roar of the El above them does nothing to dampen or contain their pleasure. But the oppressive grays and browns and the isolation of the woman at the bow of the boat in *The Wake of the Ferry,* like the figures in many of the etchings made over the next few years—the ragpicker, the beggar-amputee, the streetwalkers—emerge from an acquaintance with the dark side, the "other half." *Sixth Avenue and Thirtieth Street* is especially alert to the sadness that can and does exist, almost unnoticed, at the heart of so much activity. A middle-aged woman carrying her "growler" of beer crosses a street in the Tenderloin in a state of some disarray and confusion, largely ignored or watched indifferently by the men around her and laughed at by two younger women passing by. Yet the coarseness here is evenly distributed: the intoxicated older woman has a red nose, but the two flashier girls are overly rouged themselves, and the men outside the corner brewery have no cause to feel superior to anyone around them. Male smugness—potbellied men sitting in judgment on "ruined" or available women—was a quality Sloan found annoying to no end, and the portly spectator off to the right in *Sixth Avenue and Thirtieth Street* has a demeanor not very different from the doorman/bouncer on the right in Sloan's version of *The Haymarket,* a man whose job it was to grant entree to those unescorted women of the right style and proportions to keep the clientele happy.

If there was anything that could be called a political dimension to Sloan's art in these years, it perhaps begins with—and is best embodied in—this one painting. Two overdressed women enter the famous house of sin under the eye of a fat, middle-aged man at the door. A little girl on the street looks admiringly at their outfits and the bright lights inside. Her mother, loaded down with laundry, upbraids the child for her interest. But, we are meant to wonder, who is to say the girl should aspire to her mother's drudgery rather than the sensuality of the dance hall, if those are her only alternatives? A reality of tiring, underpaid work has to compete with a veneer of fun, a rowdy escape from "respectable" labor. George Bernard Shaw understood the problem (and Sloan had by this time read *Mrs. Warren's Profession* and its landmark preface), but in America the discourse tended to be stuck at the level of racy novels about the "white slave trade" and Vice Commission reports.

Referring to *The Haymarket* and some of the later etchings, the historian Thomas J. Gilfoyle (the author of *City of Eros,* a comprehensive look at prostitution in New York City between 1790 and 1920) has described Sloan's images of "fallen women" as breaking new ground simply "by minimizing and undercutting the immorality of prostitutes, making them less marginal and more acceptable." In this view the artist was, whether intentionally or otherwise, engaged in a radical pursuit. Gilfoyle elaborates:

> [Sloan's prostitutes] are simultaneously accessible and aloof. Their sexuality was in a state of flux, a subject of debate and redefinition by themselves and by twentieth century society. Instead of depicting the prostitute in a brothel or as an offering for the supporting male, Sloan presented her as she presented herself and her neighborhood. The prostitute was, in essence, an ordinary working woman. Sloan, in effect, erased the line separating "loose" women from "good" women.

Sloan was not interested in painting the degradation that could be an aspect of life in a brothel—something he certainly knew about, as Dolly had seemed to him hell-bent on throwing her life away at the time they met—but instead chose other means to convey his scorn for the conventional view of the matter and the double standard in sex. In every oil or etching he made that included a prostitute (numbering probably eight or nine in all), the same troubling issues are raised: Who is to judge? For the impoverished woman, what does this ugly business have to do with character or morality?

Almost in inverse proportion, though, to the sensationalism of the era's vogue for brothel novels—one of which, the 1910 best-seller *The House of Bondage,* was written by a childhood friend of Sloan's, Reginald Wright Kaufmann—Sloan wanted to avoid any touch of the horrific, just as he avoided false piety. Even *The Haymarket* isn't frightening or lurid. In some respects, one of the best critical statements of what Sloan was doing

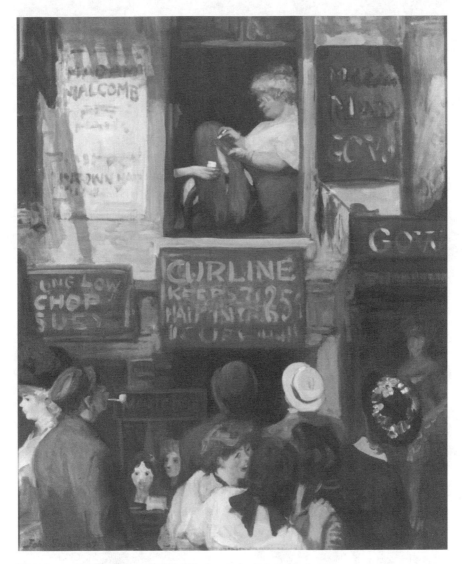

Hairdresser's Window, *1907* (Wadsworth Atheneum)

in these key paintings had been made much earlier by a friend of his. In
"A Plea for the Picturesqueness of New York," an essay published in
Camera Notes in the fall of 1900, the critic-journalist Sadakichi Hartmann
—prescient as ever—had observed that America's photographers, like her
painters and sculptors, had been embarrassingly content to deal in a
limited number of well-worn subjects and themes. "To give art the complexion of our time, boldly to express the actual," Hartmann believed,

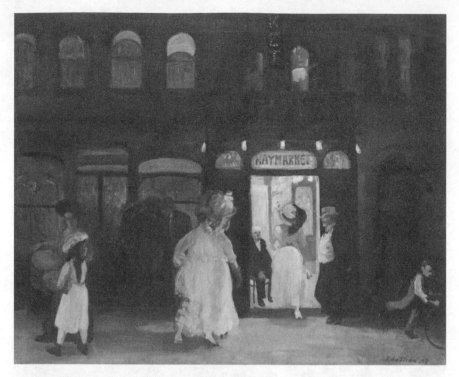

The Haymarket, *1907* (Brooklyn Museum)

Election Night, *1907* (Memorial Art Gallery of the University of Rochester)

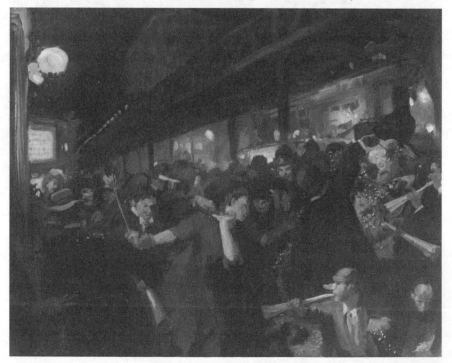

was "the thing infinitely desirable." In other words, the classic originated in the new and the timely, not in the imitation of the Old Masters. In his urgent view, America wanted a Steinlen, who could immerse himself better than Zola in the "heat, the hurry, the vexation, the lurid excitements and frivolous graces, the tragedies and comedies" of Parisian life. Such material was only waiting to be explored in New York City. But it wanted, desperately needed, artists who would see the authentic visual potential of New York City as it was, and not simply photograph or paint the metropolis as if it were Paris or London.

The subjects that the new century's young artists might look to were easily listed by Hartmann. Stand on an elevated subway platform at dawn, he directed his readers, or under the trees of Madison Square on a rainy night or on a bright afternoon when the crowd was at its height. Study the view of the Jersey City ferry as it approached Manhattan, walk the length of the Gansevoort Street Market on a Saturday morning, or enjoy the slime and the bustle of the Fulton Street Fish Market. The storage houses at Gowanus Bay, the boats at Coenties Slip, Stryker's Lane, Frog Hollow, Hester and Essex Streets, the West 110th Street entrance to Central Park and the angle it gave on the skyline, the benches of Riverside Park, the Battery, Potter's Field: the pictorial possibilities were endless and exciting, some morbid and some mesmerizingly beautiful. Most important, Hartmann felt, the resulting work would not only show the struggle of urban life and establish the basis for a truly *modern* art; almost paradoxically, it would also "teach New Yorkers to love their own city," and its visual bounty, in a way that they had yet to do. The encouragement of loving observation, vitality, and pride were also a poet's task.

Within a few years, Hartmann's desired legion of urban talent had done its duty. The photographs of Alfred Stieglitz and his Photo-Secession and the paintings of Robert Henri's circle of friends and students were precisely what the critic had had in mind. Sloan's body of work during the decade that began in 1905, for its part, was exactly concerned with what Hartmann defined, perhaps unfortunately and far too quaintly, as the "picturesque." In *Hairdresser's Window, Sixth Avenue and Thirtieth Street, The Haymarket, Election Night* and dozens of paintings to follow, Sloan created his own myth of New York—and, by extension, all of modern urban life—as a place still built to human scale, a magnet for human problems and new kinds of stimulation, a messy center of energy that affirmed life as inherently interesting and worthwhile through the very proximity of so many conflicting values and people. On Camac Street and in Fort Washington, everything difficult or real—all passions and aspirations—could be overlooked, repressed. In New York that was less possible. Life was *felt,* examined, and celebrated.

That John Sloan was not going to have an easy time of it as a breadwinner, that his vision did not coincide with what was considered marketable art in the early 1900s, was an annoying fact that became just that much clearer the more settled Sloan felt in New York. He confronted a glaring example of what he was up against when he was invited to exhibit the City Life etchings in the spring of 1906 at the American Watercolor Society's yearly show. To his astonishment, Sloan was told before the opening that only six of the ten works were to be hung, four having been deemed "too vulgar" by the committee in charge of approving the final selections. Sloan's request to meet some of these "sensitive souls," as he called them in his diary, was thwarted by Carlton Champion, the committee chairman. Champion also refused to give in to Sloan's indignant demand that all of the etchings be taken down if the whole set was not to be on view, and sent the artist a patronizing letter that said, in effect, Young man, we know best. Do remember that *we* are the connoisseurs, the experts. "Gone to seed," Glackens said of the Watercolor Society in a note to his irate friend. Sloan's attempt at sweet revenge involved displaying the pictures, both the "vulgar" and the acceptable ones, in the window of a less fastidious establishment, a bookshop on Twenty-third Street, with a little placard notifying the public that "an incomplete set was shown at the American Watercolor Society."

It distressed Sloan that none of the regular print dealers in town was interested in taking on the etchings, even on consignment, and by the end of 1906, he was ready to acknowledge that his prospects for making a living from "pure" art—uncommissioned oil painting and nonillustrational etching—were tenuous at best. Sloan's yearly income for 1904 had been in the vicinity of a healthy three thousand dollars, but that figure had been the result of the Quinby Company's de Kock money as well as fees from five popular magazines. Two years later the sum was closer to half that, even though Sloan completed story illustrations for ten magazines in 1906. Were he to give up the *Philadelphia Press* job, which was beginning to bore him but paid over a thousand dollars a year, the Sloans would slip from genteel poverty to the next rung down—a devastating thought. How infuriating it was to know that illustrators such as Howard Pyle and Frederic Remington, men whom Sloan saw as pandering to the most banal of popular tastes, were making thirty thousand dollars a year when he was lucky to see a tenth of that amount. Maxfield Parrish, an acquaintance of Sloan's from the Pennsylvania Academy in the early 1890s, was supposedly doing almost as well, and Charles Dana Gibson—creator of that female paradigm, the Gibson Girl—was known to be rewarded for his vapid artistry to the extent of an amazing sixty thousand dollars a year.

Sloan's friend Henry Reuterdahl, a painter who was a regular illustrator with *Collier's,* tried to interest his boss in the more novel style of the etchings Sloan was doing by bringing a set to the office for Robert Collier to examine. Collier told Reuterdahl that while he himself appreciated the fine qualities of something like *Rooftops, Summer Night,* such a picture couldn't possibly appear in his magazine, as "his millions of readers were not educated to that point." The reason that was the case (if indeed it was true), Sloan fumed, was that "educated idiots in droves block the path—protecting [the ordinary readers]." It was all "rot," he decided. This blinkered view of reality shouldn't have surprised him, though. Narrowness was the order of the day. That same summer, Anthony Comstock of the Society for the Suppression of Vice raided the Art Students League on West Fifty-seventh Street and confiscated all the copies he could find of a school publication that had allegedly offended community standards by reproducing paintings and drawings of nudes by League pupils. Reasonable people laughed at the famous vice crusader's excesses of prudery (the old man had been at this game since the 1870s), and "Comstockery"—Shaw's term—was a good joke in intellectual and newspaper circles, but Comstock's forces and way of thinking still had clout, even in America's largest city.

The return of Henri from a prolonged summer trip to Spain was a welcome event in October, not least because it relieved Sloan from having to cover his friend's classes at the New York School of Art. Sloan and Dolly helped Henri move from the Sherwood Building, now full of too many painful memories, to new quarters in the Beaux Arts Studios across the street from Bryant Park, where Sloan eagerly studied the evidence of a productive sojourn—Henri's small Segovia landscapes and his huge *El Matador* and *Gypsy Mother.* The selection of Goya etchings that were

Henri's gift to his untraveled comrade were as impressive to Sloan as the earlier present of Daumier lithographs had been, and as instructive as the hundreds of photographs of paintings by Goya, Velásquez, and El Greco that Henri had brought back with him. Sloan looked forward to watching his friend complete his emotional recovery, to resuming the golfing they had taken up the previous spring, and to seeing what Henri could do for all of them—himself, Glackens, Luks, the whole Philadelphia gang—now that he was about to become a major player in the august precincts of the National Academy of Design.

Robert Henri the nineties maverick as an academician: an odd notion. This development was, however, not so much a sign of the artist's accommodation to the powers-that-be as it was a product of the respect that Henri's career was winning him, and a result of a recent twist in New York art politics. Back in 1877, a group of painters, already chafing at the sterility of the National Academy of Design and what seemed to be its stranglehold on the exhibition—and, hence, patronage—process, had broken away and formed their own rival organization, the Society of American Artists. (Sloan had exhibited with them three times, in 1901, 1904, and 1905.) By 1906 this body, of which Henri was an elected member, was perceived by everyone involved as having lost its edge, and a vote was taken to rejoin the larger parent institution. So much for progressive cultural avenues in turn-of-the-century America. Shortly after the amalgamation, in May, Henri had been elected a full academician of the National Academy of Design; those who had been prominent in the now-defunct group were presumably going to be accorded some influence in the other. When it was announced that Henri had been named to the jury for the spring exhibition, Sloan was especially happy, as three of his five submissions had been rejected for the winter show. He had done well on his own by *Dust Storm, Fifth Avenue.* The eminent critic James Gibbons Huneker had called it the "best picture on view" at the Academy and deemed it fully deserving of a place on the line "beside the celebrities." But Sloan knew better than to assume that one prominent entry and one glowing review would mean much in the grand scheme of things.

The first of March, 1907, was the day on which the Academy's jury was to begin the herculean task of examining the fifteen hundred paintings that had been submitted for that season's show. For the thirty men who comprised the jury, headed by Kenyon Cox, one of the most eminent, if conservative, artists of the day, the process involved viewing each painting as it was brought by the workmen into the Vanderbilt Gallery of the Fine Arts Society building (in alphabetical order by artist), and voting it into one of four categories: numbers 1, 2, and 3—which status ranged from definite acceptance (1) to unlikeliness that nonetheless still allowed for a second, later vote (3)—and the letter R, which signifed outright rejection. It was always an exhausting experience for those involved. Henri was pleased at the start by the favorable response some of his students were receiving, especially George Bellows and Homer Boss, but by the time the jury had reached the G's and L's, Henri's elation had evaporated, as Glackens and Luks fared poorly in the balloting. When Sloan and Carl Sprinchorn, another Henri pupil, met with a similar lack of enthusiasm, Henri was furious. At the end of the day, he telephoned the Sloans to report that *Stein, Profile* had been refused and *The Picnic Grounds* accorded a 2. (This was not a good month for Sloan, as he was soon to learn that all four of his submissions to the Carnegie Institute exhibition had been rejected.)

On the second day of deliberations, Henri decided that while some of the rejections he disapproved of could be seen as inevitable but plausible differences in taste, others were callous and willful, intentional slaps at his most talented friends. Luks's *Man with Dyed Mustachios* was put on an easel for its turn in the reconsideration process and was dismissed with a loud "To hell with it!" from Kenyon Cox. As one who saw himself as doing his best to keep alive the neoclassical flame of Ingres and David, Cox could hardly have been expected to care for Luks's highly charged, undraftsmanlike style, but his pomposity and manner of rejection rankled his opponents among Henri's supporters.

The third day of the jury's session brought more trouble as Henri's own portrait *The Matador* was dropped in a revote from a 1 to a 2, while *Gypsy Mother* was likewise voted a 2. Only his more conventional *Portrait of General Perry* was given the 1 that signified its worthiness to be shown with the work of co-jurors such as Carlton Champion (of Sloan's Watercolor Society fiasco), Emil Carlsen, Samuel Isham, William Sergeant Kendall, and Frederick Dielman—not exactly legendary names in America's cultural history. Henri quickly sized up the situation: it was an intentional affront, an attempt to put him in his place after his years of speaking out to his classes and other artists against just the type of standardized work the Academy promoted. Henri requested that both of his paintings that had been voted a 2 be dropped from further consideration.

Angered even more later that week by the actions of the hanging committee, which removed Luks's *Macaws* and a street scene by Carl
Sprinchorn because they spoiled the "mural effect" of the wall they were
on, Henri did something that stunned his fellow academicians: he took
his case to the press, talking to every journalist he knew.

The articles and letters to the editors that appeared in several newspapers and magazines over the next few weeks had the desired effect. The
National Academy of Design was caricatured as a moribund force in
American art, a gathering of tired old men who were doing their utmost
to see to it that younger men with different styles and values were kept
down. The artist Albert Sterner wrote to the *New York Sun*—whose critics
FitzGerald and Gregg were happy to see the letter get printed—that he
had "often been a sufferer through the methods [Henri] decries. They
hamper seriously the newer notes or movements in American art and
prevent them from ever reaching or being taken up by the public." *Collier's,* not an audacious journal, agreed that Henri's protest was an "excellent and healthy act." Even Theodore Dreiser, editor at the time of
Broadway magazine, felt moved to write on behalf of Henri's pluck. John
Sloan was in full, not to say ecstatic, agreement.

The logical next step was arrived at quickly enough. On March 11
Sloan had William and Edith Glackens to dinner where, he noted in his
diary, the "advisability of a split exhibition" came up—not the first time
over the last year that Sloan had been present at, or initiated, a discussion
about mounting a large group show to rival the Academy's. At a second
dinner at 165 West Twenty-third Street the next week, Henri and Luks
also voiced the opinion that the time was ripe for a strategic counter-
attack. Jerome Myers told Sloan that he, too, would be interested if a
move was made in that direction. Other artists, also victims of the rigidity of the jury system, were known to be curious.

Finally, on April 4, a meeting was held at Henri's. Arthur Davies and
Ernest Lawson had been asked to join Henri, Sloan, Glackens, and Luks in
exploring the feasibility of finding either their own gallery space or a
sympathetic dealer who would be willing to exhibit a sampling of work
by those artists who saw themselves as consciously opposed to the academic tradition and the low standard of art on view at the Academy
shows. The men agreed to share whatever expenses their project entailed.
"The spirit to push the thing through seems strong," Sloan wrote jubilantly in his diary that night.

Within a month, two other artists—Everett Shinn and Maurice Prendergast—had been invited to join with the original six, and Davies had received a positive response from his dealer, William Macbeth, about the use of his Fifth Avenue gallery. Sloan was elated. Yet the thrill of these rapidly unfolding events was undercut to some extent by upheavals at home. Increasingly acrimonious battles with Dolly were followed by tender reconciliations, but the periods of calm were equally likely to be shattered by unexpected rows brought on by drinking—now, on occasion, by Sloan's drinking as well. A social gathering the day after the buoyant April 4 strategy session at Henri's took a nasty turn as the painter, angered by Dolly's intoxicated display of bile toward him in front of his cousin Eleanor and the Cranes, and in a "riotous" condition himself after mixing beer and whiskey, picked up the rocking chair next to him and threw it through a canvas he had recently finished. The painting, ironically, was *The Wake of the Ferry,* an image (of a lone woman at the bow of the boat) evoked by Sloan's sadness at Dolly's many departures from Manhattan for Philadelphia. (The damaged work was later repaired, though not before Sloan had painted a new version—hence *The Wake of the Ferry I,* owned by the Detroit Institute of Arts, and *The Wake of the Ferry II,* with a slightly different composition, owned by the Phillips Collection in Washington, D.C.) Sloan's mood at the time of this eruption was one of pure, blatant despair and rage toward his wife. He would never be a success as long as he was saddled to this woman and her demons, he felt that day, though his method of hurting Dolly was, not surprisingly, identical to hers when she wanted to hurt *him:* he was damaging his own work, and thus himself, to make his point.

However, only a short time later he was overcome with pity for the problems Dolly lived with. Walking down toward Fourteenth Street, he saw a woman, obviously an alcoholic experiencing a queasy "morning after," making her unsteady way east, and he shadowed her as far as Union Square. Nearly hit by a carriage on Fifth Avenue, "dazed and always trying to arrange [her] hair and hatpins," desperate to maintain her dignity in public, she was a wrenching sight. This, he well knew, could be Dolly, who was never going to get better as a result of any outburst of her husband's. Sloan's heart ached at the situation: an illness treated as a joke by passersby, a condition that one was told had to be accepted because it couldn't be treated, a life diminished to so vulnerable a state. Two weeks later, he began his painting *Sixth Avenue and Thirtieth Street,* simply moving the location sixteen blocks north, to an even more troubled neighborhood two blocks from the Haymarket. Coincidentally or otherwise, one of the books Sloan had been reading that spring was Thomas Hardy's classic story of a victimized woman, *Tess of the D'Urbervilles,* which he thought the most moving novel he had ever read, a "wonderful work."

Sometimes Sloan was glad when Dolly returned to Philadelphia for a while. He didn't want to know what went on while she was there, or at least not *all* of what went on, and he was able to get more work done and think more positively about her in her absence. His diary records his loneliness but also his freedom to roam and his freedom from tiring scenes. With Dolly back in Pennsylvania for a few weeks in the summer of 1907, for instance, Sloan busied himself as usual, when he wasn't working, with friends and city sights. At the Secret Lair Beyond the Moat, he and Glackens played shuffleboard with one of their host's newest female acquaintances, a dance-hall beauty who had recently been named in the trial of Harry Thaw for the murder of Stanford White ("a fattish, demi-monde looking girl with only as much sense as is absolutely necessary," as Sloan described her in a letter to Dolly). He strolled the length of Broadway from Midtown to the Village with Jerome Myers, enjoyed a good round of drinks with Frederick James Gregg and dinner chez Glackens, and one hot weekend took the subway to Coney Island alone. There, he told Dolly, awkward as it was to be on the beach by himself, he was able to act the "part of a blotter among a lot of pools of colored inks," content to " 'sop it up.' " The blanket-covered sand and choppy water, laughing bathers, boys eyeing girls, the "line of tangled hosiery and lingerie" on the Bamboo Slide in Luna Park, the rowdy crowd at the hot-dog stand, the "tawdry, gaudy, bawdy beauties" at the concert hall: this was "beautiful modern life," Sloan wrote to Dolly, "and it really is fine."

Closer to home that month, Sloan caught the aftermath of a murder on Seventh Avenue near his front door, helped rescue Jerome Myers's work and belongings when a fire broke out in the early-morning hours in his building across the street, and survived what he called the "adventure" of locking himself out of his apartment stark naked, having gone into the hall to tap on the pipes for more water for his morning bath. (After cowering briefly in the hall closet, Sloan was rescued by an amazed iceman who agreed to go through the downstairs neighbor's flat and up the fire escape to the open fifth-floor window.) The best development of midsummer, though, was Charles Caffin's visit to the studio. Caffin, a prominent British-born critic, was preparing a book—the kind of popular survey he was famous for—on American painting. An early admirer of Sloan's work, he planned to mention the young artist in *A Story of American Painting* and to include a reproduction of one of his recent works. Another cause to be hopeful, Sloan noted—another reason to assume that the tide was turning.

But the tide *wasn't* turning, not exactly, nor would Sloan's personal situation improve for quite some time. First he had to cope with the not-unexpected death of his mother in August. He and Dolly were able to visit her just before the end, immediately after she suffered a stroke, and they were at her side when she died, a few days later. Yet another tie to the old life was cut. Sloan still worried about how his father and sisters would manage, but James Dixon Sloan insisted that he didn't want his son doing without in order to send money home —a gesture much appreciated by the son, whose own finances for the fall of 1907 were looking rather grim.

Money was so tight, in fact, that Sloan accepted the offer of a teaching job that began in October. The "position," if one could call it that, entailed a one-day-a-week appearance at the Art Students League in Pittsburgh, at twenty-five dollars a week. As far as Dolly was concerned, the matter was up to Sloan; she would be the last person to tell him that he *had* to do something for the sake of income. But several friends thought it ridiculous that he should travel that distance for one day's work. As Henri pointed out, he would have to catch a Tuesday-night train to arrive in Pittsburgh Wednesday morning, and would not get back to New York until the Thursday-morning train pulled into Grand Central. That meant he would be devoting the equivalent of five days and covering four thousand miles each month for a grand total of a hundred dollars. He'd be so tired that he wouldn't be able to resume his own work for days afterward. It hardly seemed worth the time and energy. Suddenly nervous about his fluctuating financial situation, Sloan ignored the skepticism of his friends and elected to take the post of "visiting instructor."

Just as Henri had predicted, very little of the experience worked out as Sloan had hoped it would. Unlike the more established Art Students League in New York City, which shared a building on Fifty-seventh Street with the Fine Arts Society—where the National Academy of

Design shows were being held while the Academy awaited the building of its own gallery—the Art Students League in Pittsburgh was strictly a seat-of-its-pants operation. Classes were small, and talent was meager. Worse, the school was in an economic bind not much different from its new teacher's. Within a month the administration was behind in its payments to the staff, and with three weeks' salary owed to him, Sloan had to serve notice that he wouldn't be back unless he got his money. He received his seventy-five dollars, but the same problem occurred again later, and by early December Sloan had decided that he'd had enough and ended his association with the school.

There was one noteworthy aspect to Sloan's Pittsburgh expeditions, though. They registered a change in his sense of himself as a teacher, as someone who had knowledge to impart and who wanted a classroom style of his own to better enable him to have an impact on his students. With Henri's pupils—a generally confident and talented crew—Sloan was still uneasy. He drew sketches for Dolly or Henri that depicted a Lilliputian instructor before a mass of demanding Gullivers. And not only did the Henri students elicit feelings of inadequacy in the teacher, but there was, as always, the stature of Robert Henri himself to contend with. People came to study with the great man, not with John Sloan the perennial substitute, and Sloan knew it. But in Pittsburgh, he was the out-of-town celebrity whose *Coffee Line* had been singled out for notice at that city's own Carnegie Institute. He could yell, he could snarl, he could make a point as emphatically as he liked, he could speak with absolute self-assurance. He was more his own man in the "smoky city," as he called it, and felt free to cultivate a new style that included what would later be the hallmarks of the Sloan teaching manner: a tart tongue and an explosive, theatrical temper.

As it turned out, it was just as well that the Pittsburgh job lasted only a few weeks. With the National Academy's rejection for its winter show of *Gray and Brass,* Sloan's well-painted satire of the Model-T crowd bustling about the city, the need for an alternative exhibition began to seem all the more urgent. Sloan and Henri spent close to two hours that December examining every picture in the Academy show, and decided that with the exception of George Bellows's painting of the recent excavation for the new Penn Station and a scant handful of other works that were equally alive, it was the most lackluster, stultifying display of art they had seen in some time—and what was more, only a dozen people showed up to view the exhibition in the whole time they were there. New York, the art world, anyone who wanted to play a role in America's cultural life could do better—*had* to do better—than that.

Between meeting with William Macbeth to iron out the details for the group's February show, conferring with his colleagues, working on his own painting, and accepting a rush job for the *Sunday Magazine* illustrating Mark Twain's newly published autobiography, Sloan was remarkably busy in the last weeks of 1907. He and Dolly spent Christmas apart, an odd and rare occurrence for them. A letter she wrote him around that time from Philadelphia, indicating some serious news, was followed by a note about a "false alarm"; if, as the correspondence seems to hint, Dolly thought she was pregnant, it isn't hard to imagine the state of Sloan's nerves. For every imminent step forward in his life, Sloan felt, there were obstacles and detours that couldn't be predicted. But he was not going to be denied his moment in the sun, and the venture he and his colleagues were planning gave every sign of being just that.

An Event at Macbeth's

(1908)

"What a surprise straight, simple paintings about straight, simple things are to the cultured public!"

—ROBERT HENRI TO GEORGE LUKS

William Macbeth had been the right man for the group to approach. His gallery on Fifth Avenue at Fortieth Street was a stable, respected concern with a solid list of clients and an enviable sales record. More to the point in this case, the dealer in question was neither an entrenched conservative nor a bandwagon dilettante; he was that less common figure in the art world, an open-minded individual with serious interests and a willingness to gamble on a good cause.

Macbeth's business had been founded sixteen years before in the spirit of just such a gamble. At the age of forty-one, in 1892, he had left his position at the established firm of the print dealer Frederick Keppel to open his own gallery in what were, for the most part, uncharted waters. Macbeth's intentions, he was brave enough to announce, were social and art-political as well as aesthetic:

> The work of American artists [he wrote] has never received the full share of appreciation it deserves, and the time has come when an effort should be made to gain for it the favor of those who have hitherto purchased foreign pictures exclusively. As I shall exhibit only that which is thoroughly good and interesting, I hope to make this establishment known as the place where may be procured the very best our artists can produce.

As it had turned out, Macbeth's plan to sell American art works in preference to European ones had not been entirely feasible. It was an idea in advance of its market, so enthralled were American collectors before the 1910s with the imprimatur of Old World culture. A brisk business in Dutch landscapes and other "safe" stock was needed to offset the smaller interest in native talents. Still, artists like Henri and Davies were among the American painters who had reason to be grateful to Macbeth for his early, patient support. He was a professional willing to do his part to educate his clientele, as his own quarterly publication *Art Notes* suggested, and his tastes were eclectic. He had shown the watercolors of Maurice Prendergast as early as 1900, pushed Luks's *Child of the Slums* and *The Spielers* (despite the exorbitant prices Luks insisted on placing on his oils), and done his level best to sell *Dust Storm, Fifth Avenue.* His was a credo designed to strike a chord in men such as Sloan. "Instead of bewailing lost opportunities for purchasing, at trifling prices, pictures [by] artists now famous," Macbeth wrote in *Art Notes,* "let [collectors] look about them for the young artists of promise who are today repeating the struggles of great men of their days." All in all, he was a "charming" and "decent" man—Sloan's words, two adjectives he rarely applied to art dealers—and a perfectly suitable host for the kind of exhibition "The Eight" (as the press had now dubbed them) were planning.

Interestingly, some worry must have persisted among the Henri circle about their arrangement with Macbeth, as Sloan and Henri continued to scout out possible locations for the show even after they had Macbeth's word on the use of his gallery. The likeliest explanation is that they feared some interference in the selections that were to appear on the dealer's walls, some last-minute queries about whether this or that painting might not be potentially offensive to the older patrons who frequented the new gallery (Macbeth had moved in 1906 from Twenty-seventh Street to Fortieth, just across the street from the almost-completed New York Public Library). Those fears, if they did exist, were groundless, and a good thing too: taking out a lease on a space of their own, Henri and Sloan learned, would have cost two to three times the five hundred dollars Macbeth was asking as a guarantee on his involvement in the venture.

Of all the eight men, Sloan was the busiest in the matter of seeing that the show came off as planned. The stakes had risen since the idea was first announced in April, and it was important to everybody that the proper professional effect be achieved. In the several months prior to the exhibition, comment in the press gave the affair a nicely hyped military cast, describing it as a "secession" from the Academy fold, led by "men of the rebellion," as they were called by the *New York Herald*. Other papers referred to the eight artists' forming an association "in opposition" to the academicians, implying a large audience awaiting the results of a contest, a vigorous cultural clash. As they had no intention of boycotting future Academy shows, Henri and Sloan took pains to clarify their position, insisting that they didn't see themselves as antagonistically *replacing* the city's premier cultural institution. But for the journalists, who had been handed a good story by the painters for the purpose of self-publicity, these distinctions were trifling, and Sloan understood as well as anyone the advantage in this situation of having it both ways. He volunteered to photograph the paintings for the catalogue, to handle the collected funds, to oversee (with Arthur Davies) the catalogue's production, and to make sure that all was in readiness for the February 3 opening.

In readiness for what, though? "The Eight" as an entity with a discernible purpose, some thread that united these particular individuals, was not all that clear or exact. As realist painters of modern life, Henri, Sloan, Glackens, Luks, and Shinn made a unit-of-sorts. Lawson, Davies, and Prendergast, however, had nothing to do with that tie. And as for their "outcast" status, as men who weren't shown in the recognized "salons," none but Lawson could claim a truly spotty exhibition record in New York. (Sloan himself had exhibited thirty-eight different paintings in forty-seven significant shows between 1900 and the end of 1907.) Their complaint, rather, concerned three issues, all closely linked: appreciation, sales, and atmosphere, or aura. Making it into a National Academy of Design exhibition or a Carnegie or Chicago Art Institute annual was one thing; being shown "on the line," in lively company, before an educated audience that might want to buy one's paintings, was something else again. The tone of the whole business was wrong. Smothered by a style of painting they didn't approve of—from the genteel Boston crowd of Benson and Tarbell with their textbook-homey genre pictures to the overelegant portraiture of John White Alexander and Cecilia Beaux— Sloan and his friends were eager for a widening of context. A sense of energy and freedom was lacking on Fifty-seventh Street. Visitors regarded attendance at the Academy shows as a cultural duty and, like concertgoers or operagoers today, had come to expect only slight variations in the repertoire. This was a situation, all eight men knew, that was aggressively at odds with good art, serious art appreciation, and any chance for the sales they felt they deserved. In effect, then, the show organized for the Macbeth Galleries by Henri, Sloan, and Davies was dedicated to the larger purpose of opening doors, clearing the air, and endorsing pluralism seventy years before the word entered common currency—for pluralism, the group believed, was likely to benefit everyone.

Ernest Lawson, Arthur Davies, and Maurice Prendergast were the real pluralistic elements of the undertaking in relation to the other five. For if Shinn's most recent ballet scenes and theater interiors were rather genteel compared to what Sloan and Luks were doing, his earlier pastels of laundresses, dock crews, and subway riders allied him to *The Wake of the Ferry* and *Hester Street*—hardly the stuff of "Ash Can realism," but still an art with a city focus. The others, though—the non-Philadelphia men—represented an anomaly to those who were looking to Henri's "rebellion" for a cohesive movement.

Lawson seems to have been invited to join the group simply because everyone liked him and accepted that he was a very gifted painter. He had taken the most hackneyed Impressionist subjects (rowboats at the water's edge, autumn foliage, bridges and rivers, gardens and beaches) and reinvested them with unexpected power by means of an unusual technique. His color, which was alluring and lacking in the usual cotton-candy prettiness of American Impressionism (Huneker aptly and poetically called it a "palette of crushed jewels"), along with his skill with the palette knife, made of his paintings—the better ones, at least, for he was quite an uneven artist—something more solid, less marginal, than his subject matter implied. Having moved from Upper Manhattan to Greenwich Village in 1906, he was more in the swing of things by the time the idea of a separate group exhibition came about. He put in his time at Mouquin's and the Café Francis. Yet his residence in Washington Heights served him well, too: those pictures of the shore of the Harlem River and the trees of Inwood have an interesting secondary life as a document of the twilight days, the last fragments, of pastoral New York. The Cathedral of Saint John the Divine, in the 1903 Lawson of that title, is being erected in the midst of a woodland far from the noise of Sixth Avenue and Thirtieth Street.

Arthur B. Davies was the strangest member of the group in that his paintings, in their subject and style, suggest no affinity whatsoever with Henri, Sloan, or Luks. In the years before the Armory Show, when his work became more structurally self-conscious, he would create mythic landscapes of dreamlike nudes, dancing children, mountain vistas, unicorns, and waterfalls. He appealed to a taste that was rather distant from Henri's philosophy of life before art, of modern reality as the basis of all imagination. Yet he shared with Henri a skepticism toward the Academy's dictates, a record of some rejection from that quarter, and a shrewd interest in organizing the opposition. He was always more independent-minded than he at first seemed; some of those wispy landscapes have a boldly surreal rather than an academic air, and his private life was even more complicated than Henri's. (After his death, it was learned that he had been involved with two different women at the same time and raised separate families, a fact that finally accounted for his periodic disappearances and autobiographical elusiveness.) William Macbeth wasn't alone in respecting him as a seductive artist and a particularly intelligent individual, and his social contacts were known to be extensive. "Davies is a man for whom the invisible world exists," Huneker wrote of him, describing a native version of an Arnold Böcklin or a Gustave Moreau. Yet in the thin, intense, bespectacled Davies, there was also a clever art-world strategist and a most pragmatic soul.

Art historians today like to point to Maurice Prendergast—a hale forty-nine-year-old in 1908 (though going deaf and always one to look older than his years), the true eccentric of the breakaways—as the one artist of indisputable stature among "The Eight." He is sometimes treated as if he were a character who had somehow or other wandered onto the wrong stage from a different, classier play. This approach originates in the fact that Prendergast was a Modernist, not merely a man who painted some of best watercolors in American art but an artistic radical, a true Post-Impressionist who had less interest in representation or in psychology or in social realities than any of his peers. An impossible man to label or pigeonhole, really, Prendergast had used his time in Europe very differently from Henri, making himself one of the best-informed Americans about precisely those artists Henri was least alert to—Cézanne, Matisse, Gauguin—and forging a unique style of flat, patterned, glowingly colored work. There was no end to the paradoxes of the man. A shy bachelor from an impoverished background, he filled his notebooks with bracing quotations from Nietzsche and never shared Henri's concern with "art for the people." Quiet and unpretentious, he lived most of the year in Boston with his equally talented brother Charles, yet seems to have been fully aware that he was anything but the untutored "primitive" that people took him for. His subjects were often families at play at the beach or in the park (some of his best watercolors depict Madison Square in New York), but always he had more of an eye for the gorgeous, almost abstract design of the image. Sloan and Glackens found him as gracious as anyone they had ever met, and boundlessly informative to talk to.

The issue of who should be a part of the group that was going to show at Macbeth's had been more easily settled than the question of who should *not*. A fair number of painters were eager to be involved in the well-publicized exhibition, and hurt feelings were inevitable. Years later, Sloan was to speculate that they might have made a mistake in including Everett Shinn and not Jerome Myers, but at the time there was a pretty clear agreement that while the artist himself was a likable sort, some of his pictures were weak, even mawkish, in a way that would conflict with the others' work. Myers was naturally wounded by the rejection. Charles W. Hawthorne's name was mentioned (he would have been no more implausible than Lawson), but apparently Henri vetoed the suggestion. As a city realist, Eugene Higgins was another possibility, but Sloan, among others, thought his work too shallow. The venerable Albert Pinkham Ryder and the rising star of the moment, George Bellows, were much on Henri's mind. He later commented that in 1908, the one was too old and the other too young, though other factors may also have been at work in their exclusion. Bellows was hardly a casualty of the jury system—he was one of the most esteemed young artists of the day—and it is easy to imagine that Sloan might not have been overly eager to promote Henri's best protégé. The only name among Henri's followers that does not seem to have been brought up in the early discussions is that of Rockwell Kent, who was perhaps also judged too young, too brash, and too comfortably on his way to success on his own steam. Albert Sterner asked outright to be included: "You know my sympathies are with all of you," he wrote Henri, "and I want to know if you won't let me call myself one of you." Awkwardly, Henri wrote back to say that eight men had been selected already, and that that was the maximum number Macbeth's two rooms could accommodate.

By mid-January 1908, Sloan may have wondered what he had got himself into with his offer to take on as much of the preliminary work as he had. Only Henri, Davies, and Lawson brought their paintings to his studio to be photographed for the catalogue, as agreed; he was obliged to go to the others to get the job done. He found Glackens in a terrible state of mind; his wife and new baby were out of town, at his in-laws', and he had no confidence that he was getting right the pictures that he planned to include. He was "already sick of the damn exhibition," he had told his wife. Luks was in different but no better shape. With a black eye and "odoriferous breath" (as Sloan put it), he was just coming off a ferocious "bender" when Sloan arrived to photograph his entry. Luks managed to bump into the camera, breaking the lens and forcing the two men to spend part of the afternoon in search of a new one, but Sloan found it hard to consider any time passed with George Luks entirely wasted. He was so damned interesting, Sloan felt, despite his "gargantuan conceit, so huge that it is burlesque." The surprise of the day awaited him in the corner of Luks's studio, where Sloan saw an extraordinary canvas. *The Wrestlers,* a huge, raw oil of two bare-chested men in a tight, vein-throbbing grip on the mat, was as good as anything that had been seen in a National Academy of Design show in a decade. It would be the tour de force of the exhibition of "The Eight." And how like George Luks, who had imagined himself a great boxer in the days of the Walnut Street gatherings, to be caught in the clutches of alcoholism and yet to have painted a masterpiece and not told anyone about it. To his consternation, though, Sloan learned that *The Wrestlers* wouldn't be going to Macbeth's. "I'll keep it 'til I'm invited to send it to some big exhibition," Luks confided to his amazed guest. His intention, he declared, was to "show Kenyon Cox . . . and the other pink and white idiots that we know what anatomy is." The best place for such a vindication of Henri's fight for Luks before the Academy jury would have been at the Macbeth show itself, but that point was lost on the recalcitrant Luks, and Sloan knew better than to argue too strenuously. As always, Luks would do just as he wanted.

Prendergast didn't prove much steadier or more dependable. Always nervous about sending his work out into the world, he missed the agreed-upon deadline of January 28 and waited until three days before the opening to make his final selections and send them off to Macbeth. He was "working like Lucifer" right up to the end, he told a friend, and probably driving Sloan mad into the bargain. Certainly everyone had irked Sloan enough on the subject of money. Even after Macbeth generously agreed to drop his fee from five hundred to four hundred dollars, there were still complaints to be heard, especially from Shinn, about how much the gallery and the catalogue were costing them. To make matters worse, Henri

spent January in Wilkes-Barre, Pennsylvania, making money on two portrait commissions. When he returned on February 1, it was to complain
about the quality of the reproduction of his painting *Laughing Child* in
the catalogue. Sloan, depleted as well by his substitute-teaching for
Henri, bit his tongue and stoically noted in his diary, "as usual in these
affairs, one or two do the work and the rest criticize."

It was not as if Sloan didn't have his own work to attend to these
days. He was the least settled financially of the eight men (though Lawson
had his difficulties, too), and compared to Glackens, Henri, or Shinn, he
was downright poor. Although 1908 was to entail numerous activities
and preoccupations that would necessarily keep him away from his desk
and easel, that year also saw him laboring on forty-five paintings of varying sizes, the weekly puzzles for the *Press,* thirty-five illustrations for
seven different magazine stories, and a commission from Scribners—the
book publisher, not the magazine—to illustrate two Wilkie Collins
novels it was reprinting, *The Moonstone* and *The New Magdalen.* There were
days when he and Dolly didn't rise until almost noon, but that schedule
didn't imply to his friends a sluggish John Sloan. If anything, in 1908,
his afternoons and evenings, often until two or three in the morning, were
times of driven energy.

One particularly helpful person on the eve of the exhibition was the
critic and editor Mary Fanton Roberts, who wrote under the name Giles
Edgerton. In the February number of the *Craftsman,* "Edgerton" published an article (an advance copy of which she had shown to Henri, a
good friend) that treated the subject of "The Eight" from an angle that
placed the men and their art in a useful context. "The Younger American
Painters: Are They Creating Our Much-Discussed National Art?" asked a
question that had been a significant issue in American intellectual life for
more than a decade. When, Roberts wondered, would we finally have
done with copies of Corot and Burne-Jones and offer the world something
that looked to everyone like a truly *American* art, something that had an
authentic, underivative flavor and style, a way of seeing life that was *ours?*
Too many surveys of American painting, she maintained, seemed merely
weaker versions of what one saw in Europe, so that "[our] method of
mimicry suggests a quality of cheerful mental slavery about as important
to a nation's art development as the making of a tidy frock from a ten-
cent pattern." This was the problem of the "culture in effigy" that William Carlos Williams was worrying about at approximately the same

time, and a part of the search for a native musical expression that Charles Ives was pursuing in these years. These were the issues that Whitman and Eakins had been attuned to before anyone else, three or four decades earlier. What the artists at the Macbeth Galleries were going to exhibit that month, according to Roberts's essay, was the first genuine expression in the visual arts of a national coming-of-age, a separation from European-derived academic rules.

If Sloan was often skeptical—more so than Henri, who invoked the element of national feeling in his lectures—about this appeal for a close identification with one's country, smacking as it did of patriotism, he nonetheless appreciated its place in the discussion of the moment. A break from European traditions had to precede any sense of Americanness, which would in turn give way to freedom for the individual artist. Just as crucially, good reviews, eager patrons, and large, enthusiastic crowds were what was wanted for their show, and Roberts was obviously helping in that regard as much as Gregg and FitzGerald had done in their columns in the *Sun.* The *Craftsman* article was accompanied by a series of dashing photographs that Gertrude Käsebier had taken of the eight men the previous spring for publicity purposes, along with several photographs of paintings not illustrated in the catalogue. About John Sloan's work, particularly *Sixth Avenue and Thirtieth Street,* Roberts observed that the artist was showing his countrymen a "phase of sordid existence painted with that sort of fine art which Rembrandt knew long years ago."

The exhibition opened at the Macbeth Galleries on February 3, a chilly Monday. A snowfall earlier in the week that had left the streets of Manhattan full of slush did little to dampen anyone's enthusiasm. More than two thousand invitations had been mailed out, and the advance notices of the show that had appeared in so many newspapers and magazines all but guaranteed a good crowd for the opening day. From nine in the morning until six in the evening, Macbeth reported, they had just that. A steady stream of people poured into the gallery, at an estimated rate of three hundred an hour at one point. "Packed like an Academy reception," Henri crowed to a student. The supply of catalogues was quickly exhausted. Dolly went to see the show with two friends who lived nearby in Chelsea, the illustrator Rollin Kirby and his wife, and informed her husband that everything looked wonderful. Sloan, claiming that even

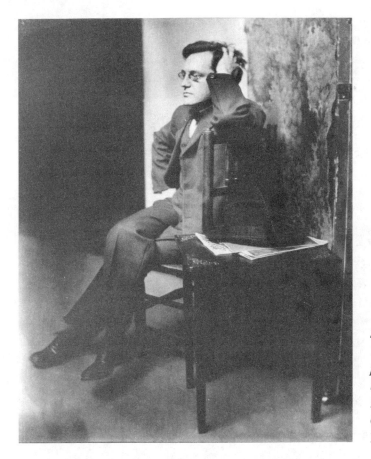

Sloan circa 1908, photographed by Gertrude Käsebier (Delaware Art Museum)

his best clothes were "not of the prosperous aspect necessary in this city," had declined to join them and instead waited at home for their report, reading *Tom Jones* and working on that week's puzzle.

Arthur Davies stopped by in the afternoon to register his impression —that the show looked "quite well," if a little crowded—and the first word of a positive press reaction arrived with Guy Pène du Bois, a young painter (and former Henri student) who was covering the exhibition for the *New York American.* Pène du Bois wanted to borrow some photographs for his article and to let Sloan know how highly he thought of all that he had seen at the gallery.

Not every reviewer was going to be as favorably inclined as Guy Pène du Bois, Sloan realized. Yet the odd fact about this exhibition, which swiftly assumed a privileged status in American art history, was that the art works themselves were so varied, so dissimilar in theme and technique, that something for every possible taste might be found, or should have been found, in one of the two small rooms. Sloan's own seven paintings—*Easter Eve; Hairdresser's Window; The Cot; Sixth Avenue at Thirtieth Street; Election Night; Nurse Girls, Spring;* and *Movies, Five Cents*—were potentially the most offensive in their lack of technical finish and their steadfastly unacademic qualities, though the gaudiness of Luks's *Feeding the Pigs* or of his street lady, *Mammy Groody,* was bound to offend those of Macbeth's older clients who had been brought up on the Hudson River School or were sympathetic to Kenyon Cox's notions of the "classical spirit." Likewise, Prendergast's Saint-Malo beach scenes would no doubt be troubling for their density and flatness, their occasional oddness of color, and the artist's obvious desire to redefine the terms of realist art. But that Glackens's *The Shoppers* (a life-size portrait of Mrs. Glackens and Mrs. Shinn) or *Chez Mouquin* (a depiction of James Moore and a sociable lady friend at table, probably the best large oil Glackens ever painted), Henri's *Dutch Soldier* or Lawson's *Floating Ice* or Shinn's painting of London's Hippodrome, should have occasioned disparaging critical comment or sarcasm is hard to fathom today, and it tells us a great deal about the damage done by the restrictive aesthetic climate maintained by conservative art schools, narrow leadership in the museums, short-sighted dealers, and the creaking edifice of the National Academy. These were paintings that had indeed escaped the "blight of imitation," as Mary Fanton Roberts termed it, yet they left many art lovers in 1908 confused or uncomfortable. "A loud chorus of disapproval . . . was heard every day" of the exhibition, Macbeth acknowledged in his next *Art Notes,* especially from the "carriage trade," those buyers with the largest funds and the least adventurous tastes. There was little question that if one purpose of the show was to stir the pot, it was happening none too soon.

Even as William Macbeth observed the displeasure that some visitors took in the efforts of "The Eight," though, he could see that his gallery was also home to a special kind of success. No one in New York City was used to such widespread public interest in art. Gallery openings and exhibitions weren't *events* in 1908. Americans argued about politics, labor strife, money, and morality, and newspapers devoted equivalent space to those topics and to sports and fashion. The show of "The Eight," in contrast, hinted at larger, younger audiences, the benefits of more attentive newspaper coverage, and the first stirrings of art as a "chic" rather than an institutional concern. The events of the next decade, from the

Independents show of 1910 to the Armory Show and beyond, would push these changes even further as the art world as we know it today began to take shape.

The sales for the two-week show were neither spectacular nor depressing, amounting to just under four thousand dollars, of which Macbeth's cut was 25 percent. The dealer pronounced himself quite pleased and was gracious enough to tell the painters that had the economy been better, he was sure the yield would have been even higher. Whether or not that was true is highly speculative; interest in owning a Sloan, a Prendergast, or a Glackens was still pretty slight at that time. Furthermore, the seven sales —two Henris, one Luks, one Lawson, one Shinn, and three works by Davies—were made to only three buyers, including Mrs. Harry Payne Whitney, who was anything but typical of her affluent set and bought four paintings. Like most other artists, Sloan knew Gertrude Vanderbilt Whitney merely as the "rich sculptress" and assumed that she was a dilettante in all matters artistic. (He would have occasion to know differently in a few years.) However, he was delighted to learn of her largesse as well as her good taste: she had acquired Henri's *Laughing Child* and Lawson's *Floating Ice,* two of the better paintings in the show. "I feel almost as glad as though I had sold some myself," Sloan wrote, commiserating more with Glackens, who needed the sales to improve his standing with his wife's Hartford relations.

From some of the papers, particularly the tabloids, "The Eight" did get the roasting they expected, while from others they received hearty encouragement, and from some the usual condescension and bafflement. "I defy you to find anyone in a healthy frame of mind . . . who wants to hang Luks' posteriors of pigs or Glackens' *Chez Mouquin* or John Sloan's *Hairdresser's Window* in his living room or gallery," blasted the anonymous writer in *Town Topics,* who then asked, "Is it fine art to exhibit our sores?" But then *Town Topics* was not anyone's idea of a highbrow publication; charges of vulgarity in the pages of Colonel Mann's gossip sheet were very much a matter of the pot's calling the kettle black. Royal Cortissoz, in the *New York Tribune,* printed what Sloan called a "sermon advis[ing] us to go and take an academic course, then come out and paint pictures," while James Townsend, writing in *Art News* that month, offered Maurice Prendergast the "palm for handing out to the art public of New York, so-called pictures that can only be the product of too much cider drunk at St. Malo in Brittany, where his crazy quilt sketches were conceived and executed." Townsend did acknowledge, though, that there was no ac-counting for fame in the long run; for all he knew, future generations might find these oddities of Prendergast's very much to their liking. "It is regrettable," Sloan observed, "that these art writers, armed with little knowledge (which is, granted, a dangerous thing) can command atten-tion. . . . I'd rather have the opinion of the newsboy." Charles de Kay, a freelance writer for both the *Times* and the *Post,* was his usual equivocal self—Sloan thought him very aptly named—and other critics took pot-shots at the want of good taste shown by *The Cot* or the willful lack of design in Lawson's brand of Impressionism or the mundane subject mat-ter of *The Shoppers* and *Mammy Groody.*

Guy Pène du Bois and Frederick James Gregg were naturally among the most vigorous defenders of the exhibition in print, and James Gib-bons Huneker (the most cultivated critical voice of the age) found a good deal to admire among the urban realists and their ethereal colleague Arthur Davies. A sometime ally rather than a propagandist, Huneker also harped most insistently on the "clashing dissonances" of the eight men's work, decrying the excessive variety that reminded him of the "jangling and booming of eight differently tuned orchestras."

Hometown reaction was lively enough, too. "A Rebellion in Art Led by Former Philadelphians" proclaimed the title of an article in the *Phila-delphia Press* on February 9, over the subheading "Henri, Glackens, Sloan, Luks, Shinn and Others Cry for an American School." The notice went on to say that "American artists everywhere are watching with deep interest" the success of "The Eight" and their battle against standardization and timidity in the visual arts. A flamboyant half-page worth of pictures of the "rebels" made for some strategically theatrical publicity. Press cover-age this calculated and dramatic had the desired effect of exciting the interest of the people who mattered outside New York City, and before the show was over Macbeth had heard from John Trask, director of the Pennsylvania Academy of the Fine Arts, who wanted the exhibition as soon as possible for his museum, and from the Rowland Galleries in Boston, for the same purpose. It seemed likely to Henri, Davies, and Sloan that offers from other museums and galleries would be forthcom-ing, and they were right. In all of this, Arthur Davies in particular "gloated in the controversy," Sloan recalled, and was sure that great things lay ahead for all of them. "We've made a success," Sloan wrote in his diary on February 18. "Davies says an *epoch.*"

Yet, strange to say, the eight men themselves never came together in a true comradely way to celebrate their triumph. In part, this may have been because it was too soon to say what they had accomplished, what they had triumphed *over*. Only in retrospect do events take on the clarity of defining moments or historical markers. So Luks kept his distance, as did Davies, who seems to have decided that he couldn't put up with Henri's assumed leadership of whatever he was involved in. The party at the Prestons' was more impromptu than not and ended with everyone's having far too much to drink, including Glackens, who rarely over-imbibed, and Prendergast, who then "lost track of things," Sloan noted. By two in the morning, the guests were sobering up in a "rather melancholy condition," and the Sloans walked home alone down Sixth Avenue. Four days later, Henri was in so touchy a mood that he lashed out at Dolly at dinner at Mouquin's—a "violent outburst," Sloan called it—devastating her and leaving her husband in an awkward, unhappy position. Sloan quickly went to see his friend the next morning to try to clear the air.

Toward the end of the month, Sloan was finally paid the $140 back salary owed him by the Pittsburgh Art Students League, which made him feel a little better. Having one's name in the paper, after all, did nothing toward alleviating mounting bills. With illustration prospects at the magazines looking "fearful" that winter and the apartment full of buckets to catch the water from the half-dozen leaks the roof had sprouted, Sloan would have had good cause to feel some envy toward the lucky five who had sold paintings from the show. Nonetheless, his good humor had reasserted itself. The thought of sending the exhibition on the road, with replacements for the seven paintings that had been purchased, was too satisfying to be spoiled. When Mrs. Luks called to say that George was "on a tear again" and that she feared the consequences of his getting the money from his sale directly from Macbeth, Sloan agreed to see to it that the check was mailed to her at home, though he found the whole business "pathetic." His tolerance for human frailty was great, but his sense of an artist's need for some dignity and discipline was even greater. At this important moment in their professional lives, Luks was skating too close to the edge.

Events in New York immediately following the show at Macbeth's were encouraging, too. The jury of the National Academy of Design accepted both of Sloan's entries for the March exhibition, and it was announced that the tradition of the hanging committee (which had always seemed to be as imperious a body as the jury itself, making last-minute rejections at its own discretion) was at an end. Henceforth one person would be asked to attend to the hanging of all the pictures that had been approved for display. Every member of "The Eight" had something in the March show, and in its most magnanimous acknowledgment of their recent triumph, the Academy grouped them all together on one wall. If some reactionaries chose to refer to it as the "freak wall," that didn't matter to Sloan and his colleagues.

Final proof that independent thinking was in the air and could no longer be contained came in the form of a hastily organized project brought off by Rockwell Kent and some fourteen other current and past Henri pupils. On March 9, they opened their own exhibition in a delapidated loft on Forty-second Street, as a "gesture of initiative," one of them wrote. The show was a chance for the men both to show their own work and, given its timing, to take another slap at the Academy's pretense of representing the best in American art. Looking over the paintings by Rockwell Kent and Guy Pène du Bois, Edward Hopper and Glenn Coleman, Arnold Friedman and Carl Sprinchorn, Sloan saw much that interested him, most of it (happily) "so different from the 'regular picture game.'" A forceful resistance to the status quo had at last been set in motion.

The Public and the Private

(1908–1909)

"It may be educational to have The Eight among us, but it certainly isn't pleasant."

—*Pittsburgh Bulletin,*
March 20, 1909

"We need someone to take an axe and hew the way.
If everyone followed the old rule, we'd have nothing new."

—GEORGE STEVENS, Director of the
Toledo Art Museum (1908)

The group's traveling exhibition, which eventually reached nine cities in the Midwest and the East (where it was shown in seven major museums and two libraries), brought out the optimist and the organizer in John Sloan. As informal "curator" of the whole enterprise, he wanted to see to it that the paintings that had made such a splash at Macbeth's reached as large and varied an audience as possible, and he knew better than to leave all the details to chance or to the gallery or museum professionals. He also hoped that the notoriety of the exhibition at home would stimulate interest in "The Eight" in other parts of the country. On the road, the paintings that had occasioned comment but few sales in New York might find buyers as well as admirers.

Despite Sloan's gut feeling that John Trask, "though affable, [didn't] really think much of the exhibition in his heart" and could stand a "little mild looking after," the Philadelphia re-creation was well installed and well attended. There was a certain lack of urgency to the reviewers' comments—outflanking the National Academy of Design mattered less in Philadelphia than it did in New York—but the *Press* wrote approvingly

127

of its former staffers, claiming that "their painting teems with the rapid fire suggestion of newspaper art work" and that it had a "vigorous feeling for character" and a "direct regard for color." The same writer advised that middle-aged or older visitors to the Pennsylvania Academy, "trained in the art of the past," would be apt to find some of what they saw unpalatable, whereas the "young art student will meet it with energetic and unstinted admiration." Oddly, the *Inquirer* and the *Public Ledger* were less enthusiastic than the *Press* (Henri, in particular, was dismissed as being dreary in his color choices), though a reporter for the *Inquirer* was encouraging in his speculation some months later that "these strong men will no doubt be the founders of the first School of American Art."

The Boston possibility fell through by early spring, in part because of the Rowland Galleries' unwillingness to assume all expenses for transporting the pictures and advertising the show (a condition Sloan felt strongly about) and in part because Sloan, at Arthur Davies's suggestion, was investigating a more prestigious alternative to the west. W. R. French, the director of the Chicago Art Institute, responded to Sloan's letter with an offer to show "The Eight" during the summer or early autumn. In conference with Davies, the decision was made to forget about Boston altogether and aim for a full circuit of the Midwest in the fall.

Even without these promising developments, Sloan would have had reason to feel cautiously hopeful in early 1908 about the exposure he was receiving. His portrait of William Walsh was on the line at the National Academy show, where *The Haymarket* had been "skied" (but at least not rejected). An invitation had come from the Cincinnati Art Museum to show *Sixth Avenue and Thirtieth Street* and *Hairdresser's Window* at their annual survey, and *Coffee Line* and *Boy with Piccolo* were on their way to a South Carolina show. All in all, Sloan thought himself lucky, though he still felt somewhat frustrated. From Henri he learned in April that, once again, he had almost won a major prize at the Carnegie Institute. In Pittsburgh, Henri and a friend, the landscape painter Walter Elmer Schofield, had served on the jury that winnowed twelve hundred submissions down to 250, setting aside fifteen of the exhibited 250 to consider for the remunerative and career-making first-, second-, and third-place awards. Despite his allies' best efforts, Sloan was not able to exceed a 4 to 5 vote on any one ballot and had to content himself with the honor of having come close. "I came near it again—near it!" he wrote in his diary. As Sadakichi Hartmann reminded him, *The Cot* was thought a beautiful

painting by those who were best qualified to know—critics such as Hartmann himself and painters such as Henri and Schofield. Sometimes a man
had to settle for that.

The price of not being established on a secure financial footing,
though, was much on Sloan's mind these days. A case in point, on a small
scale, was Sadakichi Hartmann himself, prolific and futile as ever, in one
of his needier periods. He was able to cadge some money off Sloan, who
(like everyone else) found his conversation irresistible, despite the fact
that he already owed him a few dollars. On a larger scale, there was the
failure of James Moore. Moore's financial collapse hardly came as a surprise to the Café Francis crowd or to the intimates of the Secret Lair
Beyond the Moat—he had been living on credit for some time, treating
his voluptuous "daughters" to expensive gifts and indulging every caprice
—but the reality of a friend's bankruptcy was never a pleasant sight. The
ebullient Moore lost the title to his restaurant and all of his property, the
paintings and the furniture, at both the Café Francis and his brownstone.
Sloan had tried to help him the month before, when the proprietor-
showman had asked assorted friends to buy shares in his business. The one
hundred dollars "invested" in this last-ditch effort by Moore to avoid
insolvency was money that Sloan rightly assumed he would never see
again, and could ill afford to lose, but invest he did. With Frank Crane,
he went to the auction at the Café Francis and bought back some of his
own etchings. Edith Glackens was there, along with James Preston. They
all watched Moore's beloved collection of Lawsons go for scandalously low
prices. Indeed, everyone except John Sloan walked away with one or
more.

As arrangements were made to send their art works across the
country in search of plaudits and patrons, the question of just how tight a
unit "The Eight" were, of what these individuals really meant to him,
was a fair one for Sloan to consider. It was somewhat irritating to Sloan
that whenever he and Dolly visited Luks in his studio these days, the man
was either drunk or halfway to it. Sloan could hold his own at Mouquin's
—he had become a much more accomplished drinker since those first
tentative days at the *Inquirer*—but he looked askance at the amount of
imbibing his colleague seemed to do during what should have been working hours. Then there was Shinn, who was making a complete nuisance of

himself with a ridiculous scheme to make some money off the possibility of President Roosevelt's run for a third term. His "Third Term Puzzle"—a little box with a celluloid cover over a picture of TR's face, in which the player was supposed to roll two lead balls around until they came to rest as the Rough Rider's eyes (answering the question "Can He See a Third Term?")—was harmless enough, but his statements to the press that his cohorts from the Macbeth Galleries show were in on the campaign with him, to the extent of forming a "Theodore Roosevelt III Club," were another matter. The *New York Times* headline "ARTISTS DROP WORK TO BOOM ROOSEVELT" was pure Shinn fantasy. Glackens was furious, feeling that his colleague was "making first-class idiots of the whole lot of us," while Sloan was calmer but no less dubious. He had sized Shinn up as a lightweight from the start, and he knew that the idea of John Sloan's supporting four more years in office for the San Juan Hill warmonger would seem ludicrous to anyone who knew him. (Always one to roll with the punches, Shinn was not especially disturbed either by his friends' suggestion that they had been used or by TR's refusal to run again. After the summer conventions, Shinn came up with two new puzzles, one featuring William Jennings Bryan and one for the Taft crowd.)

Henri's silence during this mini-controversy—indeed, his aloofness for several weeks past—was explained to Sloan in a note dated June 1. Henri was en route to Europe again, off with a class for a summer in Spain, and had waited until he was ready to leave before springing the unexpected news of his remarriage on his friends and relatives. The bride was Marjorie Organ, an attractive twenty-one-year-old New York newspaper cartoonist of some talent whom Henri had met at Mouquin's on the day of the opening at the Macbeth Galleries. A clandestine courtship of several weeks had ensued, Henri had painted the young woman's portrait and taken her on as a student, and the couple had been quietly married in New Jersey in May. Eager to avoid publicity, and probably just as eager to make sure that his largely female class did not lose the desire to study in Europe with their debonair instructor, Henri and his new spouse had elected to maintain absolute secrecy.

As Everett Shinn's wife, Florence, wrote to Edith Glackens:

> No one knew Henri was married until they were all on board (not even the Sloans). Think of the consternation among the twenty pupils! Wouldn't it jar you to think you were sailing with an

eligible *parti* (first having invested in a becoming steamer-rug, a seashore bag, and scented soda-mints), and then be confronted with a golden-haired bride, just as the gang-plank creaked its good-byes to the gaping crowd?

There are things even more cruel than political puzzling.

But the disappointed female pupils, who now had to endure for three months the sight of their teacher romantically attentive to a beautiful woman their own age, were not the only ones who had cause to wonder. Once again, John Sloan faced a reminder that he was not as personally close to Henri as he might have thought he was. Like his gambler father, Henri played his cards close to his chest. Even the man who was assumed to be his best friend, and certainly his closest public ally, was kept at some distance from the private side of Henri's life. Sloan and Dolly were hurt at having been excluded from the secret but pretended otherwise when talking to friends about the marriage.

With Henri in Madrid, the Glackens family off to Cape Cod for the summer, and the other members of the group engaged, it was left to Sloan to work on the arrangements for the autumn show. When the duties of shipping, insuring, confirming dates, and specifying conditions about the hanging of the pictures (*nothing* was to be hung above the line, Sloan insisted) proved too time-consuming, Sloan enlisted the aid of a friend, C. B. Lichtenstein. As the weeks went by, Lichtenstein, who was the manager of publications at the Quinby Company, assumed the role of go-between for the artists and museum directors and took a significant part of the logistical burden off his friend's shoulders. The schedule came together rather nicely, with month-long stops planned for Chicago, Toledo, Detroit, Indianapolis, Cincinnati, Pittsburgh, Bridgeport, and Newark. All of these cities either boasted reputable museums or were in the planning stages of erecting buildings commensurate with the cities' exhibition aims, with the exception of Newark and Bridgeport, whose city libraries doubled as museum space. Milwaukee, Grand Rapids, Buffalo, and the Corcoran in Washington, D.C., also expressed interest in hosting "The Eight"'s show, but nothing came of those negotiations.

Before taking his own break that summer, Sloan enjoyed an unanticipated treat when the painter Arthur Dove came to call. Dove was off to Europe for a year to work in Paris and see the sights, courtesy of his father-in-law, and offered Sloan the use of his lithographic press for that

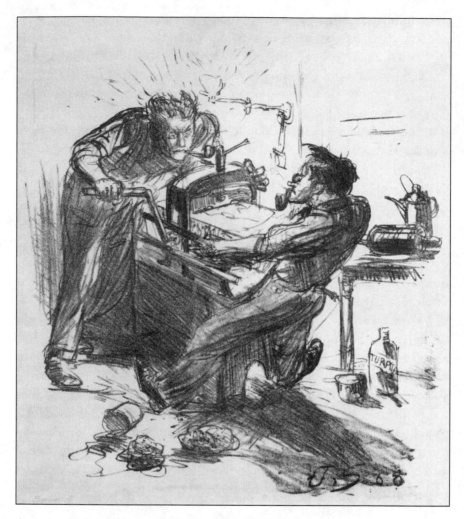

Amateur Lithographers, *1908* (Kraushaar Galleries)

time. Sloan accepted "with joy" and arranged for a carter to pick up and deliver the heavy press the next day. Over the next few weeks, with the help of a friend who was a professional lithographer, Carl Moellmann, Sloan struggled with the tools of what was for him a new medium, producing five lithographs, not without considerable frustration. One of these images is in fact a good comic rendering of the two men in the wee hours of the morning amid the mess of the studio, grappling indignantly with the stone, the press, and a lot of bad ink. Three of the other five lithographs must be judged failures—they depict a prehistoric mother and child, a street vendor, and the *Lusitania* in dock—but the fifth work, though botched in its original state and redrawn more successfully with crayon, is effective and very much a part of Sloan's body of work at this period. In it a gaudily dressed woman marches down the streets of the Tenderloin on her way to "work" at the Haymarket or any of the other nightspots of the area. The urchins of the neighborhood stare at her, especially the adolescent girls. Not in their wildest dreams can they imagine being so wonderfully attired. In their eyes and given their alternatives in life, there is something fine, something empowering, about this woman in hat, high heels, and gloves. The woman is an American version of Shaw's Mrs. Warren: alert, brassy, and unapologetic. These are her streets, and she has made the only choice that makes sense for her.

In the end, Sloan was a painter and an etcher, not a lithographer, and he completed only four other lithographs in his career. But, like most artists of real talent, he was curious about the various means of expression his peers were engaged in. In the summer of 1908, though, Sloan had no doubt, and no reason to doubt, that he was meant to be a painter. His long apprenticeship was paying off. The interesting fact about his work that summer is that his next thirty-odd paintings had nothing to do with city life and broke completely with the restrained color practice he was known for. Instead, this little-known interlude in the career of an "Ash Can realist" is exuberantly *en plein air,* freer in color and composition, unabashedly playful, and almost aggressively self-confident. Many of these pictures are small nature sketches measuring nine by eleven inches, though *City from the Palisades* is three times that size.

During the last two weeks of June and the first few days of July, the Sloans and the Laubs escaped the heat of Manhattan and stayed in the Coytesville, New Jersey, boardinghouse of a gregarious French couple, Monsieur and Madame Richard. A short walk from the boardinghouse were the cliffs of the Palisades, with a fine view of the Hudson, plenty of trees and open fields, and just a hint of the city's skyscrapers in the distance. In Coytesville and later, in August, when he spent a week in Fort Washington, Sloan energetically sketched and painted the natural world he had previously neglected. Sometimes he focused on groves of tall trees, on wind-racked clusters of leaves, or on trees as smaller elements in a vista that was wider, grander, or more tumultuous. He was drawn regularly to the cliffs themselves, to the choppy water, and on occasion to a pasture with cows or to arrange a group portrait with the Richard *filles,*

Noëlie and Aïda, playing in the hay. "I get a joy from these healthy girls that I can't describe . . . as big as life itself," Sloan wrote in his diary. That same vigorous, contented feeling is there—in the thick paint strokes as much as in the subject matter—in most of what he completed during those warm, windy weeks, particularly in the spectacle of *City from the Palisades.*

Looking over some of these works when he was back in New York that fall, Sloan commented that he felt quite the landscape painter. Always leery of the pigeonholing he believed art critics were prone to, he was glad to find that his range was broader than he himself had believed. He was glad, too, that he and Dolly had passed a pleasant summer together and painted their initials, like lovers, on a rock above the Hudson.

In September, "Paintings by Eight American Artists Resident in New York and Boston" opened at the Chicago Art Institute. The Institute's *Bulletin* referred to "The Eight" as "group of eccentric painters" and reported the next month that their pictures had "excited much attention as the work of men evidently well versed in the art of painting, who have chosen to deny themselves all conventional and classical qualities such as regularity of composition, considerations of beauty in the ordinary sense of the term, technical finish, and interest of subject." Coming from the staff of the host museum itself, these remarks struck Sloan as being of the "with friends like these . . ." variety (nor did he think much of the Institute's very proper director, Mr. French, when he met him in New York later in the year), but then one had to consider the aesthetic climate and the competition. Sloan's *Election Night* clamor and Sixth Avenue squalor, Luks's thickly painted pigs and brash birds, and Prendergast's demanding Saint-Malo studies were on view in Chicago at the same time as the paintings of Thomas Noble, the principal of Cincinnati's art school, whose pictures (the *Bulletin* primly noted) were "clearly the fruit of earnest study and clearly popular with visitors." Also at the Art Institute in September were the "very refined and carefully studied" watercolors of Charles L. A. Smith. In the matter of "regularity of composition" and "interest of subject," Noble and Smith were apparently far ahead of Henri, Sloan, et al.

With the exception of one sympathetic article in the *Chicago Record Herald,* most of the press coverage was no better. Maude Oliver in that paper described the spirit of the exhibition as "extremely vigorous, if inclined toward eccentricity," and singled out Arthur Davies's Newfoundland landscape as especially well done. She struggled with the usual uncertainty about Prendergast's "peculiar mode of expression" and quoted one visitor to the museum as having backed away from one of his pictures and observed, "Oh, it isn't nearly so bad from here as it is from over there." But the other papers, though holding their fire when it came to Davies's "poetic" images or Lawson's outdoor scenes, martialed the sharpshooters for everything else. "Bewilderment and disappointment" characterized the reaction of the critic at the *Post,* who thought Sloan's paintings to be both "as true as life, and as vulgar . . . hardly worthy of frames and a permanent place." Another reviewer speculated about the motives of these New York artists in forcing before a normal, unradical audience "things of quite such radical import." There was too much crass sensationalism in the show, he wrote, and—a line that caused Sloan to chortle —none of the "technical achievement as was witnessed the winter before last in the painting of sunlight in *Wallowing Hogs* by Heinrich Zeugel." The delicacy of Zeugel's hogs aside, there was much in the tone of the Chicago reaction to suggest that a disgruntled metropolis that too often felt itself in New York's shadow was getting some of its own back. This may pass for serious art in Manhattan, the press seemed to be saying, but we in Chicago are not so easily duped. Not surprisingly, no potential buyers emerged in the Windy City.

The smartest move that Sloan, Davies, and Lichtenstein made in planning their itinerary was to focus on some cities that were considerably smaller than Chicago and Philadelphia. After all, Sloan reasoned, there were probably plenty of intelligent art lovers in the heartland, and they might be more receptive to honest new work than the annoyingly self-conscious cognoscenti he was all too familiar with.

In Toledo the next month, that reasoning was borne out. If the reaction was not entirely appreciative, residents nonetheless showed a healthy curiosity and a desire to look and understand. ("BIG SENSATION AT THE ART MUSEUM/VISITORS THRONG MUSEUM AND JOIN IN HOT DISCUSSION," read the headline in one area paper.) Interestingly, the exhibition met with even more rigorous competition here than it had in Chicago—forty oils by the popular Hugh Breckinridge, a particular Sloan bête noire, were in an adjoining room—but it also got considerably more support from the museum's director, which made a difference. George Stevens, a painter and former actor and a man of considerable vision and energy, ran the budding Toledo Museum at the request of the wealthy Edmund Drummond Libbey, who was in the process of planning and financing a splendid new gallery for the north Ohio town. Stevens was a model of what could be achieved by someone in his position in the day and age before the generic museum professional, M.F.A.- and M.B.A.-certified, took over. He had a sense that museums needed to take risks, to challenge their audience in plausible ways. Discussing Luks's porcine extravaganza with a woman at the opening, he brought up the all-important analogy: "When Millet presented his peasants, people said, 'Why this isn't art, these dirty peasants.' . . . Everything new is laughed at." The Hudson River School represented the past, Stevens reminded his constituents. Soothing landscapes didn't speak to the times. Every age required its own reflection of the needs, drives, and issues of the moment. "We need someone to take an axe and hew the way," he told a reporter for the *Toledo Blade*. "If everyone followed the old rule, we'd have nothing new. . . . This exhibition represents movement. I don't say it's all good, I don't say it's all art, but it is *thought* and there is something in it."

Again, many people were confused by Maurice Prendergast. His pictures were said to "resemble bits of ancient tapestry" by the *Toledo News Bee* reviewer, who was in some ways even more disconcerted by Everett Shinn. "Shinn," he wrote in a vaguely guilty tone, "has struck an unusual note in portraying scraps of scenes which would never occur to anyone else as being worthy of transmission to canvas." The *Sunday Journal* looked to get in the last word with the quip, "Toledo visitors to the Art Museum [after seeing "The Eight"] are asking themselves not 'It's pretty, but is it art?' but 'As it's not pretty, can it be art?' " George Stevens had his work cut out for him, to be sure, though he obviously made some progress. The final account of the exhibition, published a week later in the *News Bee,* extolled the painters' "impressive originality" and observed that these Easterners should be seen not as rebels against the Academy— the benighted Chicago view—but as less threatening "individualists, bound together in a league of originality and unconventionality." The *Blade* critic thought Sloan's the most interesting work in the whole show and reproduced *Hairdresser's Window* in the paper, noting that this was just the sort of dynamic passing scene that a more traditional painter would have overlooked.

In Detroit, just before Christmas, the show received its most unremittingly savage press coverage yet, and not much help from the museum staff—the only city after Chicago in which that kind of uniform negative reaction was the case. The problem with the exhibition, according to the critic for the *Detroit Free Press,* one Bertha O'Brien, was its "puzzling and freakish" character: it was too defiantly a celebration of the new realism. She thought Glackens interesting, or at least acceptable, especially with *Chez Mouquin,* but found Luks and Sloan particularly offensive. *Hairdresser's Window* was vulgar in its theme (the usual, by now meaningless complaint), and *The Cot* provided a "not very alluring glimpse into the private life of a lady not disconcertingly beautiful, who is in the act of retiring for the night. One is curious," O'Brien wrote, "as to the theories of art which lie behind the execution of these pictures." Luks's gorging pigs, for their part, sent her into a near frenzy.

None of this mattered much a thousand miles to the east. Sloan was preoccupied during the weeks before and after Thanksgiving with wrangling over the fee for his puzzles for the *Philadelphia Press,* meeting and adjusting to the new Mrs. Henri, and coping with a difficult period in his relations with Dolly. The dilemma with the *Press* was resolved by a compromise. Alden March came to New York to meet with Sloan and ask him to reconsider the resignation he had just submitted. He agreed to be Sloan's go-between with the business office and was soon able to report back that his request for a raise would be honored—five months down the line, in April of the new year. Sloan accepted the offer and so managed to salvage what actually amounted to more than half of his yearly income. It had been a gamble, he told Dolly, but one he had been willing to see through to the end. She agreed that he was right. There was a limit, Sloan insisted, to how much one could allow oneself to be exploited—that was the advantage of keeping one's expenses to a minimum, of living on the edge of genteel poverty rather than in the grand style of the lord of the Secret Lair Beyond the Moat.

The unpleasantness with the Henris was less easily settled. Given the Sloans' fondness for Linda, any replacement for her was bound to take some getting used to, and not much about Marjorie Organ Henri initially struck them as appealing. She was a "conventional 'Bohemian,' " Sloan thought, an affected type he disliked, and neither overly intelligent nor overly gracious. Doing their duty as friends, he and Dolly gave a party in honor of the couple and invited Glackens, Shinn, Preston, Laub, and their respective wives. The fact that all of the other women dressed up for the occasion and Marjorie did not didn't sit well with the host, who observed, "[She] wishes to show us that she doesn't care for social affairs, in fact . . . she wishes us to dislike her. Like the princess in the fairy story, she has her wish." It was evident, too, that Marjorie knew Dolly's story: at a gathering some months later, Sloan eyed Mrs. Henri surreptitiously filling and refilling Dolly's Scotch glass at a party and felt confirmed in his view of the lady. The tight circle evoked in the etching *Memory* was not going to be re-created with a new, somewhat devious member.

Sloan must have known, though, that his marital travails were hardly a secret to any of his friends, least of all to any of the old Philadelphia crowd. He did his best to protect Dolly's dignity and their privacy, but her lapses were sometimes as much public as they were private. At a party Dolly could restrict herself to just the right number of drinks and be as jaunty and social as anyone else, but she could also lose sight of that ambiguous line and become quite "tight." Sloan's hope was that that level of behavior marked the extent of their friends' knowledge of Dolly's alcoholism; he couldn't rely on everyone to be as kindly and as tolerant as his cousin Eleanor when it came to finding Dolly on the street after a more solitary and self-destructive binge. What was more, the end of 1908 seemed to bring on a recurrence of these episodes as the pleasant, unpressured, romantic weeks in Coytesville receded further into the past.

To everyone's delight, news from the road proved more heartening just after New Year's. From January through May 1909, the exhibition of paintings by "The Eight" made its way through Indianapolis, Cincinnati, Pittsburgh, Bridgeport, Connecticut, and Newark, New Jersey. In most of these cities, the press made its usual comments about an approach to art that lacked gentility, that disdained true craftsmanship, that trafficked in subjects no one would want to look at on the wall of his home. But there were also some significant exceptions now. The critic for the *Indianapolis News* described the show as "one of the most interesting collections of pictures yet exhibited in Indianapolis, and indeed, [ever] brought together in the history of American art." W. H. Fox was sufficiently well traveled and sophisticated to know that in comparison to works he had seen in Europe the year before "by Matisse, Van Gogue, Goguin [*sic*], and others," the paintings of "The Eight" were not even all that disorienting. The group represented the future of American art, he speculated, more than did Impressionists such as Hassam, Twachtman, and their kind. William Behrens of the *Cincinnati Commercial Tribune* was equally appreciative of the anti-idealizing nature of the paintings that dealt with modern life and of the fact that "[each] of the artists has strong individuality in his work and by no chance could any of the pictures be ascribed but to the one who did it." The *Cincinnati Enquirer* pointed to Sloan's *Dust Storm, Fifth Avenue* as a "wonderfully fine arrangement of color," lauded Shinn as an "apostle of Degas," and gave Lawson some of his best notices. (In what must have seemed an amusing column back in New York, one Cincinnati writer, in commenting on *Chez Mouquin,* called Moore a well-painted "gross roué" and the young woman at his table a sad creature well on her way to dissipation and misery.)

Pittsburgh art audiences were, of course, familiar with John Sloan from his time as a teacher at the local Art Students League, though that didn't necessarily earn him any great favor. The *Pittsburgh Bulletin* pronounced spending time with the Henri circle the aesthetic equivalent of "seek[ing] diversion among bricklayers," and one wag thanked Heaven there weren't sixteen of them: eight did quite enough damage. On a more positive note, the *Pittsburgh Dispatch* critic praised this exhibition which "vibrate[d] with humanity" and had prompted some valuable discussion about new definitions of art. John Beatty, director of the Carnegie Institute, spoke up for a less Eurocentric view among Pittsburgh's art lovers and greater patronage of native art. In Bridgeport and Newark, even Maurice Prendergast, who as a true Postimpressionist was considered the most inscrutable of the group, received some good reviews. The writer for the *Newark Evening News* was aware of the growing influence of Cézanne and credited the master of Provence as a force behind Prendergast's patchwork, antirealist style.

From a vantage point eighty-five years distant, the travels of these paintings seem an event of more historical interest and significance than was noted at the time, or for a long while after. Certainly this show was not the footnote experience it has been treated as in most cultural-history texts, and it tells us much about Americans' passions and understanding of art in the years between the turn of the century and the Great War. The references to Matisse and Cézanne *by writers outside New York* indicate that many people knew something about the impending changes in the art scene and had some idea of what a profound impact these changes might have. Or as one art historian, Judith Zilczer, recently summarized the matter: "In taking their art directly to the American public, The Eight demonstrated that cultural provincialism in the United States was less pervasive than contemporary and subsequent accounts of the period have inferred." There is considerable truth to this statement; the old view of Americans—particularly those living far from New York, Boston, and Philadelphia—as existing in a cultural backwater circa 1909 is a threadbare notion. Still, one wouldn't want to make too much of the point. The revisionism must be moderate here. For Sloan, one large fact was depressingly inescapable: the paintings had toured nine cities, garnered dozens of lengthy reviews in major newspapers, been seen by tens of thousands of people in a year of travel—and yet not a single work had been sold. The prices had ranged from $3,000 for Glackens's *The Shoppers* (a large picture) to $800 for Henri's *Dutch Soldier* to $150 each for Shinn's two ballet girls, but not one private collector or museum trustee had made an offer. (Most of the Sloans were in the $750 range.) Not even any of the ten paintings marked under $300—two by Henri, two by Sloan, two by Luks, and four by Shinn—found any takers.

On June 3, 1909, Sloan made note in his diary of the return to New York of his own paintings from their long odyssey, a note that also referred to his budding political interests.

> After I came home [from shopping with Dolly] the pictures from The Eight show in Newark arrived and though the carter said he would not deliver them up four flights of stairs, and though I got mad—we afterward, through a political turn to the talk, grew more calm. I tried to convert him to Socialism but he is the contented sort. He has a little home of his own, etc. No revolt in him, and no care for his fellow workers' well being. At any rate the pictures were brought up (I carried two myself) and now the ten of them are back from their nine months and more journey through the cold, cold world "unwept, unhonored, and unsung."

As the public John Sloan made strides in all directions, sending his work out into the world (where it was, in truth, more unsold than unsung) and establishing a name that was obviously going to mean something in American art one day, the private John Sloan was facing a very different situation. His own tentative period of succès d'estime overlapped, probably not coincidentally, with a painful low point in Dolly's life, which showed no signs of abating. There were times, despite her wishes and intentions, when her husband's triumphs were just not enough for Dolly, when her need to hurt herself, and him, was over-powering.

What transpired sometime in late 1908 or 1909 (the exact date is impossible to ascertain) must on some level have seemed inevitable to the Sloans. The drinking to the point of obliterating any sense of identity and consequence, the sexual encounters with strangers, the venereal disease: there was no reason to assume that Dolly wouldn't eventually become pregnant as a result of this dark pattern. The myth of her infertility was just that. Precious little calculating was needed for Sloan to realize that he couldn't possibly be the father; his sexual relations with Dolly had been restrained for too many months prior to conception, while her relations with other men, by her own embarrassed account, had not.

The choices that confronted the Sloans in the weeks during which they had to think about it were equally terrifying. Having the baby, raising the child as their own, seemed out of the question. It was not so much a matter of shame at raising another man's child—Sloan knew about Dolly's past when he married her and was remarkably free of preju-dice that way—as an acknowledgment of the insanity of raising any child on their income, with their chaotic way of life, with Sloan's commitment to his work, with Dolly's illness. For Dolly to carry the child to term and then give it up for adoption seemed fraught with its own kind of danger. Neither of them could imagine her, when the moment came to give up the baby, actually relinquishing this life she had nurtured for nine months. If the thought of it was agonizing, the reality would be impossi-ble. Yet the third alternative was a nightmare of a different kind to a guilt-ridden woman who still considered herself, in desperate moments, a Roman Catholic, as it would have been to any woman in the early years of the century who had heard the horror stories of back-alley doctors and botched procedures.

Eventually Sloan and Dolly decided that ending the pregnancy was the only answer for them, however perilous that course of action might be. In her more lucid moments, Dolly had always known, or felt, that it would be wrong to bring this child into the world, a baby born out of confusion and anger. She had no hope, really, of controlling her alcohol-ism, no expectation that her bouts with this demon (and the sexual epi-sodes that followed) could ever be put behind her. Nor could she be sure, given her medical history, that the baby would be born healthy. In the end, Ed Davis, the best-informed man they knew in such matters, provided the medical instruments and instructions that were needed, and John Sloan performed the abortion on Dolly himself, in their apartment.

In later years, when she was in a despondent mood or had been drinking heavily, Dolly would sometimes cry out in rage and frustration and tell a bewildered visitor, "Sloan wouldn't let me have a child!" But at the time, the decision—like the torment—was mutual.

Call to Action

(1909–1911)

*"I am sure that Socialism is more apt to make one clean and decent
than religion."*

—DOLLY SLOAN, in a letter to
her husband (December 26, 1911)

How does a marriage recover from such a blow? Yet it seems
that even in the wake of the traumatic events at the end of their tenth
year together, John and Dolly Sloan never considered separating. For
Dolly, there was no life for her apart from her husband; for Sloan, affection, pity, and commitment outweighed any thoughts of what-might-
have-been. In guilt and love, they were a couple strangely, permanently,
bound to each other. Theirs was a history of pain and mutual understanding—and, as much as anything, mutual need—that had been made
deeper now by a secret they knew they couldn't share with those of their
friends who led a more settled life, a secret that served to unite rather
than to divide them in this period of their lives. The portrait of his wife
that Sloan labored over in the spring of 1909 is a testament to that
feeling, and to Sloan's desire to acknowledge all that this woman had
been through and all that she still meant to him.

Dolly with a Black Bow was the first portrait Sloan had painted of his
wife since the turn of the century, and the best of the eight he would
complete in the four decades of their marriage. In a full, high-collared
white blouse, with a large black bow at the neck and the waistband of a
black skirt visible at the bottom of the picture, Dolly in this simple
painting has an expression of great dignity and vulnerability. She is neither the strong, relaxed woman of the 1898 *Dolly in a Harp Chair* nor the
casual, homey, or quizzical figure of some of the later pictures. With a

palette limited largely to black and white, the skin of the face worked over and over for the right texture, the 1909 portrait is at one and the same time respectful, stately, and tender. By choice, it was never exhibited in Sloan's or Dolly's lifetimes.

Comforting though her husband's care and an adulatory painting might be, it was obvious that Dolly would need something more to put her life on track again. No one—not Sloan or Dolly herself, not their friends or their family—seems to have made enough of the fact that Dolly required something in her life beyond John Sloan, whether or not she could acknowledge that truth. In 1909 and 1910, that "something" gradually presented itself. Unplanned, unexpected, the new element in the Sloans' lives was ironically initiated by Sloan himself, not by Dolly, but it became in time as vitally important to her as it was to him. It was in an area in which she could, finally, be recognized and loved apart from her spouse.

As a political creature, John Sloan was a late bloomer. He claimed to have paid relatively little attention to local or national politics as a young man in Philadelphia, an indifference that was characteristic of newspaper art staffers in the nineties. The press trip to the Cleveland inauguration in March 1893 had not been especially memorable, and a friend's proselytizing interest in guild Socialism left him cold. Yet the horror of Coxey's Army's trooping through the City of Brotherly Love—where it was met with rather little goodwill from the citizenry and the conservative press— and the nightmare of the Pullman strike of the same period would have been hard to ignore entirely: the early 1890s were a vicious, dramatic time for those seeking to address the issues of labor reform and poverty in America. And Sloan knew that in those years his father had voted, once, for the Socialist party ticket, to the disgust of his female relations. By the time of his move to New York City, though, Sloan had become more politically aware, both through his increasingly wide reading and through his own observation of the direction the country seemed to be headed in. What he perceived as the idiocy of the Spanish-American War (which both major parties, with the exception of Grover Cleveland himself, had promoted in one way or another), and the resulting jingoistic thrill of America's new imperial presence on the world stage, filled him with scorn. The extent of the visible poverty in Manhattan was also troubling to him, even shocking. If Sloan on occasion romanticized in his diary the situation of the poor ("Happiness rather than misery in the whole life [of

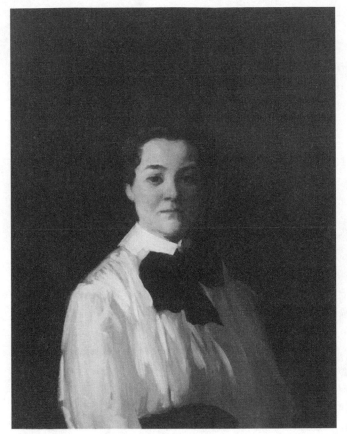

Dolly with a
Black Bow, *1909*
(Whitney
Museum of
American Art)

Lower East Side children]. Fifth Avenue faces are unhappy in comparison"
reads an odd note of February 1906), he also understood its deeper implications. Watching little girls follow streetwalkers as they struck their
deals with young men on Sixth Avenue wasn't a pleasant sight. Surely, he
remarked to Dolly, there was something wrong with a city, and a society,
in which 10 percent of the people appeared to live so comfortably and 90
percent were forced to struggle so desperately. Only the Socialists seemed
to be speaking out against the national movement toward land acquisition abroad, suppression of dissent at home, and the inequitable distribu-
tion of wealth everywhere.

New friends were doing their best to politicize Sloan. In 1908
Charles Wisner Barrell, a journalist and member of the Socialist party,
lent Sloan a copy of an interview with Eugene Debs that Lincoln Steffens
had published in *Everybody's Magazine.* What he read of Debs's beliefs

greatly impressed Sloan, particularly his insistence that Socialist politics was more than a matter of votes and governance, that it had also to do with moral and even spiritual issues. "Christianity is impossible under Capitalism," Steffens quoted Debs as saying, but under a new, less cut-throat and less competitive economic system, the charity and love advocated in the New Testament would be a more natural condition. (Sloan himself used the same idiom when he later met Debs, calling him the "most Christ-like man I have ever met.") In a year that would see the decisive electoral victory of William Howard Taft, which meant (Sloan wrote) "four more years of the cancerous growth" of Republican conservatism, Debs's idealism was appealing. William Jennings Bryan and the Democratic party hardly seemed a worthy alternative for a thinking man, especially after Debs published the text of platform the next spring. By degrees, Sloan moved toward a definite commitment.

Barrell in particular wanted to make a convert of John Sloan. An article he wrote for the *Craftsman* in February 1909, "The Real Drama of the Slums, As Told in John Sloan's Etchings," did everything but call Sloan America's great Socialist artist, whether or not the artist in question recognized that status. *Coffee Line* was saturated with political meaning, Barrell maintained; it was "as great a depiction [of] and as biting a commentary upon the social system as Stephen Crane's uncomfortable prose sketch 'The Men in the Storm' or one of Gorky's poignant little masterpieces." In this fairly unadulterated "puff piece," flattering references to Frank Norris and Jack London were thrown in for good measure. By mid-1909, Barrell had his wish. Debs's rallying cry had struck a chord. Sloan had become a regular reader of the *Call,* the Socialist daily, and over the next few months gave its editor several political drawings (under the anagrammatic name "Josh Nolan") that cleverly attacked William Randolph Hearst's gubernatorial candidacy, lampooned working-class gullibility, and scorned antipathy to radicalism. From his association with the left-wing *Call* to the next step was not a great leap.

The Sloans decided that they were ready to apply for membership in the Socialist party in December. When their cards arrived in the mail, Sloan succinctly noted in his diary on February 1, 1910, "Now we are 'Reds.' " They attended their first branch meeting a few weeks later.

For Dolly, the decision to make a political commitment proved to be even more momentous than it was for Sloan. She had no understanding of economics or social theory, Sloan later remarked (though he himself was never inclined to sit down and read Karl Marx, for that matter), but she did have a strong sense of injustice and a ready compassion for the underdog. No less significant was Dolly's need to believe in something larger than life. Even after ten years with Sloan, she had never fully weaned herself from astrology or the Catholic Church—equivalent crutches, in her husband's view. The words of the priest at confession, telling her she would burn in hell for her sexual misconduct and her shameless drinking, always hit their mark, leaving Dolly such a wreck that on one occasion Sloan went to the rectory she had been visiting to ask the priest to please stop and show his wife some pity. Socialism, then, not surprisingly took on the character of a redeeming cause for Dolly—not only as a grand idea that would make a better world, but as the source of a network of new friends, of an active, outer-directed way to occupy her time, and of a commitment to something personally transforming and ennobling. The street meetings, rallies, lectures, and party conventions she attended over the next years, before both Sloans severed their ties to the cause, opened a new world for Dolly, one that led her at last to turn her back on Philadelphia and embrace the life her husband had chosen in New York.

Immersion in politics often leads to new and intense friendships, but both John and Dolly Sloan had always had a capacity for friendship that had sustained them during their darker hours. This year Dolly was seeing more of her old piano teacher from Philadelphia, a woman of her own age named Elizabeth Hamlin. Like Sloan's cousin Eleanor, Elizabeth Hamlin found in Dolly not the unseemly neurotic whom Marjorie Henri made fun of but a lively companion and a valued confidante. When Elizabeth and her husband moved to New York a few years later, the Sloans grew to depend on them both, in different ways. But more so than anyone else they had ever met or ever were to meet, one man whom they were introduced to in the summer of 1909 made a vital difference. He was a friend to Sloan and Dolly equally, and a godsend to a marriage that he fervently, lovingly understood and wanted to see last.

John Butler Yeats, the father of the poet William Butler Yeats and the painter Jack Yeats, was sixty-nine years old when he first visited New York City with his daughter Lily in 1907. An artist himself, he was a more adventurous man than his age and thick white beard might suggest. In fact, even his family and friends back in Dublin were shocked when he

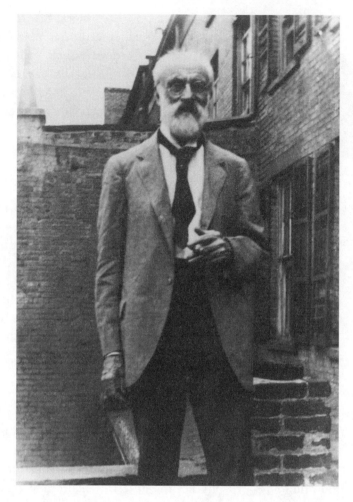

*John Butler Yeats
on the roof of
Petipas, 317 West
Twenty-ninth
Street, circa 1917*
(William M.
Murphy)

announced in 1908 that he was not going to return to Ireland with Lily when the time for their departure came round. "To leave New York," he tried to explain in a letter to his son William, "is to leave a huge fair where at any moment I might meet with some huge piece of luck." Dublin was the past, and he wanted no more of it; Manhattan was the present and the future, and Yeats—"the Pilgrim Father," as his daughter then labeled him—stuck to his guns despite much familial pressure. Over the course of the next fourteen years, he kept putting off his return, inventing new excuses to stay and claiming to be mystified that anyone could question his decision. "Why do birds migrate? Looking for food— that is why I am here," he observed. Free-thinking people, brilliant artists, warm friends, a world of opportunities: what could Dublin offer to compare with these? "All that happens in Dublin is the occasional insolvency," he wrote home again, whereas *anything* could happen in New York, where he would find his second youth, where even the "poorest has a welcome and a chance." And there was an end to the matter.

If not precisely the "poorest," John Butler Yeats was close to it, with a lack of ready cash that would have seemed to most people reason enough to head back to live in the bosom of one's family. Yet somehow Yeats always landed on his feet, writing essays for various journals, lecturing, selling his pastel sketches, accumulating debts to endlessly patient hotel proprietors, and relying on the goodwill of rich friends such as the lawyer and art collector John Quinn. Sloan thought him a remarkable man, "kindly and well informed," when they met at a restaurant one night in the company of the Henris and Mary Fanton Roberts and her husband, but he probably never suspected how close they would become before the year was out.

Yeats liked Henri and respected him as a fine artist, but he came quickly to love Sloan and to think him a great painter, the best of his generation. He was another Hogarth, he told Sloan, who didn't have much to judge the allusion by, having seen so few Hogarths in New York and Philadelphia. Yeats also endeared himself to his new acquaintances by feeling toward Dolly—and really showing her—a depth of affection and respect such as she had never known from a man other than her husband. In a year that saw Dolly requiring ever more extensive treatments from Dr. Bower and more nervous visits to a woman's specialist in New York, Yeats was just what she needed, an intellectual man who took her problems in stride, setting her at ease and separating in his own generous mind the goodness of the woman from the horror of her illness. At dinner on Twenty-third Street or sharing the table d'hôte at the Petipas boardinghouse six blocks north, where he settled in for a long, cozy stay, Yeats proved an excellent conversationalist (if somewhat prone to baroque monologues) and a font of information about European literature. Anyone who had met George Moore, Lady Gregory, and the other principals of the Irish Literary Renaissance was automatically of interest to Sloan. At a Thanksgiving dinner hosted by the Sloans—an occasion Sloan dreaded for its heavy drinking opportunities—Yeats was the star of the evening with his eloquent reading of a play by Synge, who had died that year. The person Sloan had described in his diary as "kindly and well informed" six months before was "very dear and interesting" by December, well on his way toward becoming a fixture by the couple's small fireplace.

The only real area of disagreement between the two men concerned Sloan's interest, which increased month by month during the first years Yeats knew him, in the Socialist party. Like any hardcore aesthete, Yeats found politics infinitely less important than art and philosophy, and constantly worried that his friend's energies, his better self, would be sapped by what the older man saw as the fanaticism of the left. Nor was he loath to give advice on the subject.

John Butler Yeats need not have worried on this score, however. Sloan saw his work for the party, whether at meetings or in the drawings he continued to pass on to the *Call* free of charge (increasingly clever and vitriolic efforts), as something separate from the "pure art" he was equally devoted to. He was confident that he had the time and the stamina to contribute meaningfully in each area, and he was determined—as he repeatedly told his Socialist friends—to keep propaganda out of his painting. If anything, the paintings Sloan worked on from 1909 through 1912 show a more polished technique and a growing sensitivity to the demands of the art form. A good deal of this had to do with an expanded sense of color, one of the timelier aesthetic concerns in American art after the turn of the century.

If the paintings he was best known for at the time, such as *Dust Storm, Fifth Avenue* and *Sixth Avenue and Thirtieth Street,* are not exactly riotous in color, Sloan felt comfortable enough in the work he had completed during his summer trips out of the city in 1907 and 1908 to let loose, to glory in self-consciously heavy brushstrokes and a freer, brighter choice of hues. The expanse of sky, the trees, and the water of suburban Pennsylvania and New Jersey offered an approach that the pavement and crowds of the city worked against. Yet Sloan's palette also seems to have been limited, at least to some extent, by the time it took him to get used to his new subject matter—to master the theme of the city to his satisfaction—and by his displeasure at the quality of the pigments that were available. But in the summer of 1909, Henri was full of a "scheme of color," as Sloan put it, that he wanted to impart to his friend. He brought to Sloan's apartment a new set of pigments created by a man named Hardesty Maratta, and Sloan's interest was immediately piqued. The usefulness of this range, which was based on the primary and secondary and even tertiary hues of the spectrum's providing twenty-four gradations

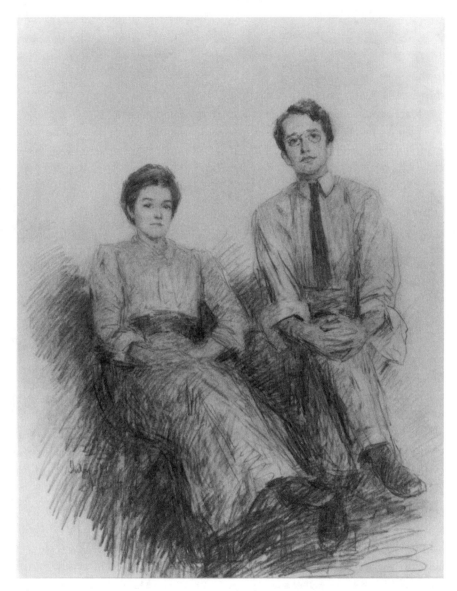

John and Dolly Sloan as sketched by John Butler Yeats, 1910
(Delaware Art Museum)

(e.g., one moved from red to orange via red-red-orange, red-orange, and red-orange-orange), was obvious. A new intensity and subtlety of color, just what Sloan was now interested in exploring, would be possible if the products themselves were sound. More than a mere manufacturer of pigments, Maratta was a Chicago painter, recently transplanted to New York, who saw himself as a color theorist. He had devised an elaborate system called the "Maratta Scales," which he equated to music, so that the twenty-four equally spaced hues corresponded to the twenty-four chords of a piano. Henri was ultimately to become a staunch partisan of the Maratta system, forcing his students to devote time to an increasingly complex and technical method of diagramming out their color harmonies, a didactic insistence that in the long run would cost him his following. Sloan likewise found the concept pleasing and was especially glad to have access to a palette that seemed better made, more exact and consistent, than what he was used to.

If Sloan never became quite as caught up in Maratta's system as did Henri, the beneficial effects of his acquaintance with the man and his ideas were nonetheless evident. His paintings of the next few years achieve effects of color that the earlier city scenes don't even aspire to. *Recruiting in Union Square* (1909) shows a young man about be conned into giving up his freedom in exchange for the right to take orders and wear a uniform, but the artist is equally concerned with the array of spectacular, competing colors that a crowded city park might present to the eye in its spectacle of dresses, hats, uniforms, ruddy noses, buildings, trees, grass, dogs, children, and billboards. *Pigeons* (1910) captures a common Chelsea sight as Sloan's portly neighbor across the backyard works on his roof with his homing pigeons, the new Penn Station looming in the distance. Yet it is easy to ignore the anecdote entirely in favor of the sumptuousness of the different shades and textures of brick in sunlight and shadow—the light on the brick having the quality of a caress, as Henri remarked. *Scrubwomen, Astor Library* (1910–1911) makes use of rich golds, green, and purple to convey the interior of the famous Astor Place Library, and *Isadora Duncan,* painted after the Sloans saw the great dancer perform for the second time, in 1911, is almost a musical study of the scale of red, pink, and orange. "God Bless the Maratta Colors," Sloan wrote in his diary after completing this strange, bright painting, full of praise for the artist-inventor's "splendidly organized 'tools.' "

Yet too much shouldn't be made of the technical advances Maratta allowed for. This was no "road to Damascus" experience for Sloan. His interest in stronger, or unusual, effects of color and light actually predated any awareness of the man or his pigments: *Three A.M.,* for example, was completed a full month before Henri brought Sloan a sampling of the new colors. In subject matter, this great painting (now in the collection of the Philadelphia Museum of Art) is of a piece with the other Tenderloin pictures, a slice of urban life. Two women chat in a dingy, gaslit kitchen in the middle of the night. One, a particularly thick-legged figure, stands at the stove in her slip preparing a meal for her heavily rouged friend or sister, who has clearly just come in from her evening's work, presumably on the street or in one of the neighborhood bars or brothels. The only sensationalistic aspect is our sense of the woman's dubious profession, emphasized by the painting's title; called *Five P.M.,* the same scene might elicit a different reaction. As it was, the image was considered offensive by the standards of the day and was exhibited only three times over the next eleven years. Yet what matters most to anyone who has actually seen the work (reproductions of *Three A.M.* are notoriously "off" in color) is the mesmerizing blue-green of the room's wall that draws us into the recesses of this space, the contrasting tones of yellow and red that enliven the "bad" creature of the night at the table, and the mass of white paint, thick and vertical like a pillar, of the slip of the "good" sister or room-mate at the stove. So much seems crude and slapdash, even ludicrous, in this vignette that Sloan has chosen (at least at first glance), and so much seems intricate and mysterious and carefully wrought: it is as if Sloan knew he was devising his own version of a sacred moment, something that could be felt only in person, in the presence of the color, the light, and the shadows that he fastidiously worked and reworked until he could at last write in his journal, "It has beauty. I'll not deny it. . . ."

On another level entirely, paintings such as *Three A.M.* also raise the intriguing question of Sloan's role as voyeur, a term that even for the artist himself had a certain limited relevance. Many of the views-from-the-back-window that Sloan created in his first decade in New York push their way into private space, ask us to be interested in what we are taught as polite people to overlook, make the private manifestly public. But after all, Sloan felt, most modern painters and novelists were in one way or another engaged in the business of studying the intimate lives of their subjects; that was what art was about, transmuting that study into some-thing significant and timeless rather than prurient. It was the spirit in which the secretive viewing was done, he argued, that mattered, that made the ultimate difference. Indeed, when some friends were visiting one night and discovered just how much the Sloans could see from the rear window at 165 West Twenty-third, they mirthfully lined up to

exclaim over what they could take in of life in the back apartments on
Twenty-fourth Street—only to be promptly and angrily rebuked by Sloan
for their jokes. He was convinced that his own looking was another order
of experience entirely, and thus so was the viewer's when he contemplated
Sloan's work. This distinction has not, of course, prevented art historians
with a psychoanalytic bent from having a Freudian field day with *Three
A.M.* and *The Cot* and *Turning Out the Light.* One writer—no master of the
language—noted in the early 1970s that the "voyeuristic concerns dominating Sloan's iconography seem to be evidence of regression to
scoptophilic impulses, the original sublimation of which must have led
Sloan to become an artist." Somehow, John Sloan as repressed scoptophile
seems to throw the baby out with the bathwater, and a good deal more
besides.

   Branch One of the Socialist Party regularly convened in the
progressive Rand School on East Nineteenth Street. There, in February
1910, while Dolly was out of town, Sloan attended his first meeting.
When Dolly returned, a week later, she joined her husband for a session
and was likewise impressed with the intelligent company. A few days she
went by herself to hear Charlotte Perkins Gilman lecture at Carnegie Hall
on Socialist principles. By summer Dolly had been appointed secretary of
the local branch, and the Sloans had participated in their first outdoor
meeting, handing out leaflets at Battery Park. "Surely," Sloan noted in
his diary, it was a better use of his time than "paint[ing] pandering
pictures to please the ignorant listless moneyed class in this U.S." Yet
engaged as Sloan's thoughts were with politics in these months, and as
productive as he was in the studio, it was unquestionably the thornier
business of *art politics* that dominated his life in the spring of 1910.

   On April 1 more than two thousand New Yorkers elbowed their way
into a vast makeshift gallery on Thirty-fifth Street just west of Fifth
Avenue. They filled the three large rooms and clogged the staircases, at
one point making entry or exit almost impossible. This art "mob," a truly
unprecedented audience in America, was on hand for the opening of the
first no-jury, no-award large-scale exhibition of American artists. As
openings go, the evening of April 1 was a landmark, and the headlines,
such as the one in the *New York Mail and Express* the next day, were a
publicist's dream: "PANIC AVERTED IN ART SHOW CROWD / SPECTATORS IN

Jam at New Exhibition / Police Preserve Order." Another five hundred visitors, according to this account, never made it inside.

The 1910 Exhibition of Independent Artists surpassed the Macbeth Galleries show of "The Eight" two years earlier in what was now an unstoppable drive to curb the prestige and end the authority of the National Academy of Design. Such goals and the tactics needed to achieve them were almost as complicated as those involved in the Socialist struggle the Sloans had recently committed themselves to. The process itself was strenuous fun, but every victory had a way of proving transitory, and the public at large could not always be counted on.

Even before the return of the paintings from their grand tour to Chicago and back, Henri and Sloan had begun discussing their options for the future. Back in March 1909, they had pondered opening a gallery of their own for a year to show their paintings and the work of another dozen or so men with whom they were in sympathy. They spent some time scouting out available sites, but in the end nothing came of the plan. Equally impractical was the grandiose if well-meant suggestion of a friend, Albert Ullman, that the painters band together and rent Madison Square Garden for an independent exhibition that would be big and splashy enough to be covered by all of the major newspapers. At a weekly rental cost of nine thousand dollars, the Garden, on Twenty-sixth Street at Madison Square, was immediately ruled out. But it did occur to Sloan a short time later that if they could pare down Ullman's scheme, find a big enough space, and charge each exhibitor a few dollars per picture, they might be able to pull it off. Henri was still of the view that renting a gallery for a year was the better plan, but now with a new twist: the rent money, he suggested, could be solicited from wealthy patrons who would have the right to choose paintings of equivalent value to their donation during the course of the year. Arthur Davies liked the idea, but to Sloan it seemed fraught with potential for trouble—those demanding patrons were a frightening prospect. Still, a meeting attended by Henri, Shinn, Luks, Sloan, Jerome Myers, and the artist Walter Pach seemed to indicate that that was the direction the group wanted to proceed in.

When nothing actually happened, as a kind of collective inertia overtook the individuals who were thus far involved, Albert Ullman piped up again. Ullman, an energetic press agent for the Royal Italian Opera Company and Sloan's downstairs neighbor on Twenty-third Street, encouraged his friend to go ahead on his own if need be. The concept of a show like this was exciting and immeasurably important, he insisted. Sloan knew Ullman was right, and he gave him a hundred dollars to use as an initial fund-raising stake. Everything took a different turn, however, when the painter Walt Kuhn joined the group and backed a plan for a big show of a few weeks' duration, funded by an investment of two hundred dollars apiece from Kuhn himself, Henri, Sloan, and Davies, with requests for donations from each exhibitor. Observing that this approach had acquired some momentum among his friends, Sloan abandoned the Ullman project altogether and joined with Henri and Kuhn in setting up what would become the 1910 Exhibition of Independent Artists. Its purpose, Henri carefully explained to a reporter, was based simply on the "fact that there are a great many good pictures painted in New York which are never exhibited. We aim to place these pictures before the public."

Not all of those unseen paintings were by unknown artists. Although Sloan had had three works accepted for the March 1909 Academy show, only his *Chinese Restaurant* made it into the December 1909 exhibition, and both of his submissions for the March 1910 show were rejected outright. *Pigeons* dealt with a militantly inelegant subject, while the idea of submitting *Three A.M.* to a traditional jury, Sloan acknowledged, was practically a joke, "like slipping a pair of men's drawers into an old maid's laundry." Still, all curt dismissals rankled, and it looked to Sloan as if, after the illusory goodwill shown him by the Academy in 1908, the Kenyon Cox men were out to "cut me from the exhibition game." No less ominously, all three of Sloan's submissions for the Carnegie Institute show the year before had also been rejected—the nasty work, Sloan was sure, of his old Philadelphia pal Edward Redfield, now a prosperous academician himself and a frequent member of the Pittsburgh jury.

Pigeons, Three A.M., and two other works, *Clown Making Up* and *Recruiting in Union Square,* thus represented Sloan on West Thirty-fifth Street instead of in the galleries of the National Academy of Design. The means by which the other contributors' art works found their way there was something of a cross between a complete open-door policy and a flexible jury system. Artists of proven ability who were known to have had a hard time in official circles and to be sympathetic to the new spirit were simply invited to join and to show whatever paintings, drawings, or sculpture they wished to exhibit. Not everyone understood the premise at first hearing. Walter Pach suggested that William Merritt Chase, J. Alden Weir, and Childe Hassam be invited to show, an idea violently opposed by Sloan as these three men were as well situated in the art world as anyone could hope to be. They were not invited. Nor were artists thought to be too concerned with safe, audience-pleasing "products," like Paul Dougherty, a marine artist who showed at Macbeth's. (Even William Macbeth himself agreed with Sloan that Dougherty was a negligible talent, but there was a market for his wares, and what was a dealer to do?) The company was meant to be youngish, progressive rather than conservative, dynamic rather than staid.

The ensuing rush to see that the 260 paintings, 219 drawings, and 20 works of sculpture sent in by the 103 invited artists were properly hung, placed, and lighted in two weeks' time made the last-minute pace of the Macbeth show look calm and orderly. (The arrangement of paintings was in strict alphabetical order, a democratic contrast to the "mural effect" of the Academy's hanging practice.) Sloan did more than his share in tending to the applications, handling the art works, setting up the huge rented lights and the draperies, overseeing the finances, dealing with conflicting egos (Kuhn had no more patience with Henri's controlling manner than Davies did, and quarreled with him), and getting the catalogue to the printer's two days before the opening. One stretch of thirty-four hours of nonstop work left Sloan reeling, but the thrill of the *vernissage* and the crowd of interested viewers more than compensated.

The all-important journalists' response to the show was as varied as Sloan, by now, had come to expect. The *New York Mail and Express* writer thought that the audacity of the undertaking "mark[ed] an epoch in the history of American art," and a few reviewers were ready to acknowledge that the traditional outlet for new painting and sculpture had long since become an old boys' club that benefited too limited a circle. The *Post* and the *Sun* were less than thrilled with the range of the art itself, while the *Times* found the drawing section (which included several of Sloan's City Life etchings and the illustrations for the Paul de Kock novels) the highpoint, "much finer than the paintings"—though *Three A.M.* was singled out as having beautiful color values and a "peculiarly classic" merit. In something of a "stretch," Sloan's allies at the *Call* were happy to praise the exhibition for its implied Socialism: the artists themselves had passed the hat, rather than waiting for some fat plutocrat or dealer to set them up, and the "number of scenes from proletarian life was noteworthy." Most annoying to Sloan was Huneker's assessment that Henri, Sloan, and their fellow organizers had staged a "vaudeville in color" produced by a troupe of paint-smearing imitators of "The Eight" who were nowhere near as avant-garde as the artists Alfred Stieglitz was then exhibiting at his gallery, "291."

That the aura of "The Eight" should have lingered about this particular exhibition is not surprising—the group had been much in the news over the past two years, and they had been responsible for the lion's share of the invitations. But a show that included paintings by the budding Modernist Morton Schamberg and the twenty-year-old Stuart Davis, Henri's *Salomé,* George Bellows's *Blue Morning* and *Club Night,* Glenn Coleman's *Under the Bridge,* Rockwell Kent's *Road Roller,* the first fruits of Edward Hopper's time in Paris, one of Glackens's best nudes, Prendergast's beach scenes, *Three A.M.,* and a John Butler Yeats self-portrait could hardly be thought dull or too homogeneous. Every time Sloan walked up to Thirty-fifth Street that month, he saw crowds of enthusiastic visitors. How different this was from Wallace Stevens's characterization of a trip to the National Academy of Design the year before. "The artists must be growing as stupid as the poets," he had written to his wife in despair. "What would one lover of color and form and the earth and men and women do to such trash?"

Long before the Independents show was ready to be taken down, though, Sloan sensed a financial disaster in the making and the consequent painful loss of his two-hundred-dollar contribution to the rent fund. Popular interest, even genuine excitement, simply didn't translate into sales. Still, no one could have anticipated quite how dismal the final result would be. Given the attendance figures, it seems utterly staggering that not one of the hundreds of paintings and sculptures on view found a buyer. Only a few drawings by Henri, Coleman, and three other exhibitors were sold, the most expensive for thirty dollars. Total receipts: seventy-five dollars. And this, Henri angrily noted in his diary, during the same month that over two million was spent in New York on Old Masters and Barbizon landscapes at the auction of the Charles Yerkes estate. Could a clearer statement have been made about New Yorkers' priorities or the place of the contemporary artist in America?

In Sloan's mind, the only thing for all of them to do was put the venture behind them and work harder. To brood about the narrowness of cultural interests in America was to waste time pondering something that was not going to change overnight. Yet another illustration of that reality came Sloan's way the following January, when the Columbus School of

Art in Ohio, now under the direction of a Henri alumnus, Julius Golz, attempted to put on a small-scale re-creation of the big Independents show. Sixty-one paintings and seventy-four drawings and prints were sent to Ohio, and Henri was invited to give a lecture. Just as he was about to depart from New York, however, he learned that a local librarian, the town's version of Anthony Comstock, Manhattan's own guardian of public morals, had ordered two of Arthur Davies's nudes removed from the show. After letting Golz know that he would not give his lecture if the pictures were excluded, Henri got his way, only to discover on his arrival in Columbus that a second purge had taken place. Now several works, including Rockwell Kent's naked wrestlers in the mythological *Men and Mountains,* a Bellows fight scene, and four Sloan etchings—among them *Turning Out the Light,* of course—had been removed from view. Henri gave his speech only after the offensive art works were reinstated, albeit placed in a separate room that barred women and minors. This pitiful resolution to the whole contretemps apparently disturbed Dolly even more than it did Sloan. She felt that Henri should have taken a firmer stand on the hanging of her husband's work, but when she raised the issue with him on his return from Ohio, an unpleasant flare-up was the result. Once again Sloan was caught in the middle, but now Dolly saw herself as John Sloan's principal advocate, and woe to anyone, even Henri, who appeared to equivocate on his behalf.

If the Sloans were displeased by the Columbus absurdity, the impetuous Rockwell Kent was livid. A talented painter (as well as a fellow Socialist) and Sloan's junior by eleven years, he was of an even more radical disposition toward anyone whom he saw as thwarting progress, particularly *his* progress. Kent's plan for a 1911 Independents show called for acceptance to be restricted to those who took an explicit, even defiant stand against anachronistic tastes and conservative authority—namely, to those artists who would agree to boycott the National Academy of Design and refuse to send any work to its juried exhibitions in the future. Sloan was ambivalent about the idea, though it was evident to him that Kent would go ahead and get the show going on his own terms anyway (Kent was a "hard liver," Sloan once noted, "in the sense that one is called a hard drinker"), but Henri was actually furious. His former pupil was presuming too much, dictating to artists where they could show their art and implying that "The Eight" hadn't made sufficient inroads against the Academy. Kent's rigid proposal went against everything Henri stood for and taught (never mind the fact that Henri would never have agreed to turn his back entirely on the Academy as long as he was still a member). In the end Sloan joined Henri, Glackens, Shinn, and Lawson in boycotting Kent's show, a decision that led to some hard feelings all round. Davies, Prendergast, and Luks, for their part, were squarely under "Kent's Tent," as the insurgent exhibition was labeled in the press.

Awkwardness between the Kents and the Sloans was especially unpleasant because the former had moved in below the latter in 1910, after Albert Ullman moved out and abandoned his wife. Sloan had always alternated in his feelings toward the younger man. To his mind, Kent was a dynamo, a strong individual with great gifts but more ego than principles. He was also a "user," only too ready to ask Sloan and Dolly to baby-sit when he and his wife wanted a night out—a wife he treated cavalierly when it suited him, as he also had a mistress and an illegitimate child. (His goal was a Shelleyesque ménage, with all of them living together, but Mrs. Kent found it too difficult to live with the mistress.) Kent's amateur flute playing wafted up through the pipes, destroying Sloan's peace and quiet, and he was known to speak disrespectfully of Henri's leadership in the art world. Those Shelley-like morals notwithstanding, this last was the major offense in Sloan's view. By the time the two couples ceased talking, Dolly had lashed out at their neighbors, presumably over Kent's criticism of her husband's unwillingness to break with Henri and boycott the Academy. She also showed signs of resenting Kathleen Kent's second pregnancy, an anger only Sloan could understand.

For true friendship, Sloan did better by the Philadelphia crowd— Henri and Glackens; Joe Laub and his wife, who had moved to New York; the Cranes; the Prestons; the Hamlins; and the Ed Davis family, whom he liked to visit at their cottage at the Jersey shore, where he and Stuart Davis and Stuart's younger brother, Wyatt, could walk the beach. A year after he met John Butler Yeats, though, it was apparent to everyone around him that a special bond exceeding all others, one that was both comradely and paternal, had been established between Sloan and the éminence grise of the West Twenty-ninth Street boardinghouse. Yeats's sketches of the Sloans, both individually and together, idealized his new friends with a warm, flattering spirit. Yeats also liked to look out for the younger man when he could, repaying him in some measure for the home-away-from-home he had found on Twenty-third Street. Introducing

Sloan to the Irish-American lawyer John Quinn was certainly part of that strategy: Quinn came close to buying *Dust Storm, Fifth Avenue,* whose qualities Yeats extolled, and did purchase a complete set of the etchings for $340, money that was much needed after Sloan ended his long, rocky career with the *Philadelphia Press* in 1910. Quinn was a useful contact, and Sloan was pleased that a man of such stature in New York seemed to enjoy his company. A memorable summer outing to Coney Island that year saw Quinn, Yeats, Sloan, and a strange poet-friend of Quinn's who was just back from Europe, by the name of Ezra Pound, flying down the Shoot-the-Chutes and exploring the pavilions before taking a brisk, exuberant car ride back to Manhattan. As Pound later wrote to Quinn, the sight of Yeats *père* on an elephant, "smiling like Elijah in the beatific vision," was a spectacle never to forget.

John Sloan in turn acknowledged his affection for Yeats—and for the whole gloriously social milieu he had willed into being—in one of his most complex paintings. The sheer ambition of *Yeats at Petipas* is proof in itself of a new Sloan, one with little in common with the tentative artist of only five years earlier. In this group portrait, reworked at odd moments over a period of three years until Sloan was satisfied with it, no fewer than nine people are arranged around a table in the backyard at Petipas while one of the hostesses, Celestine Petipas, serves the after-dinner fruit. The writer Van Wyck Brooks sits to the left of the head of the table, where Yeats is ensconced, cigar in his mouth and sketchbook in hand, drawing one of the guests. The poet Alan Seeger pensively examines Yeats's progress. Dolly, looking especially animated, shares the midpoint of the composition with Celestine; the pipe-smoking writer, Robert Sneddon; and the journalist Charles Johnston's attractive wife. To the right, the painter Eulabee Dix, the editor Fred King, and Sloan himself, in a striking red tie, complete the gathering under the canopy. Several bottles of wine have been consumed in the course of the dinner, and the talk now seems fragmented but relaxed. Like the intimates in *Memory,* these people know and like each other enough to be carried along by the rhythm of the evening. They trust Yeats to hold them together. Most remarkable of all is that each face, though coming from the brush of a painter who had always found portraiture difficult, is strongly modeled and fittingly anecdotal. Brooks the observer, dapper and alert, takes in the scene from the edge of the canvas very much like Sloan at the opposite end. Seeger is a Marchbanks, holding back, keeping himself snug by Yeats's side. Eulabee

Dix is gaily attentive to Sloan's end of the table, as indeed Dolly felt she too often was. Yeats later said that the whole tableau reminded him of Dickens. If he meant by that remark that the painting contained an element of warmhearted caricature, as he seems to have felt was the case, that quality is harder to discern today: these people look distinctive and likable to us, a group meant for anyone who savors personality and unhurried conversation. Really, *Yeats at Petipas* is Sloan's hymn to friendship and sociability. More than a chronicle of a bygone New York, more than an *hommage* to his gregarious friend, it celebrates those qualities that the artist himself considered crucial to the good life.

Like the other works produced during this two-year period of superb oil painting, *Yeats at Petipas* failed to interest any potential buyers. (It was bought by the Corcoran Gallery of Art in Washington, D.C., in 1932.) The painting was, true to the form the artist's life was taking, a labor of love. But then there was an ironic advantage to the status of marginal breadwinner, Sloan felt. One's interests were given free rein; there was never any guilt about time lost that could have been spent on big money-making projects. When he was approached late in 1910 by the Socialist writer George Kirkpatrick to illustrate a new edition of one of his books, a polemic barbarously entitled *War—What For?,* Sloan happily took on the assignment. His drawings for Kirkpatrick's book were impressive enough to warrant being reprinted in four leftist periodicals between December 1910 and mid-1911—the *Call,* the *Masses, Progressive Woman,* and *Coming Nation*—and later included, in 1913, in *The Red Portfolio: Cartoons for Socialism.* The pictures of a sorrowful Jesus looking out over a field of ammunition, the soldiers marching off to war blindfolded, or the capitalists sending off their vultures to feed on the wage earner's remains were not anything out of the ordinary, in either quality or theme, for the radical press. However, Kirkpatrick's attack on the Boy Scouts of America as a paramilitary group whose purpose was to instill authoritarian values in young men delighted Sloan and yielded an image that would have cost him his freelance niche with *Collier's* and *Good Housekeeping* had their readers ever seen it: a Boy Scout in uniform, down on his knees, lovingly kisses the boot of a soldier under the approving gaze of a businessman, beneath a sign listing the proper Boy Scout virtues of unquestioning respect and obedience.

Indeed, the gusto Sloan now brought to his political drawings occasionally—and later, very often—equaled the excitement he felt about his

painting. He had already alienated a few old friends by his tendency to
bring Socialism into every conversation, and had broken off his friendship
with Rollin Kirby because he could no longer abide either Kirby's sneer-
ing at his activism or his conservative beliefs. Most of the time, Yeats and
Henri wisely knew when to drop the subject. Those acquaintances who
didn't were quickly put in their place. Considering that Sloan had allowed his name to be put on the ballot in 1910 as a Socialist candidate for
the State Assembly (he had received a grand total of 103 votes), even
well-heeled friends like William and Edith Glackens knew that his seriousness was not to be questioned. His drawings for Kirkpatrick, or those
like his picture of Death and Capitalism triumphant over the steaming,
charred body of a Triangle fire victim, published in *Coming Nation* in
April 1911, give creative evidence of that passion, that growing indignation.

In October 1911, the Sloans finally had a chance to meet Yeats's
eminent son, who was in New York on one stop of an American tour with
the acting company of the Abbey Theater. John and Dolly eagerly attended the company's performance of *The Playboy of the Western World,*
having been long since converted by "Old Yeats" (as they called him) into
ardent Synge fans. The Sloans loved both play and production, though it
was disconcerting to sit in the Maxine Elliott Theater with a crowd of
fifty or so Irish-Americans—"brainless cowards," Sloan called them—
who had come to hiss the play as a slander on the dignity of their
homeland. A squad of policemen lingered outside the theater to see that
there was no repetition of the fiasco on opening night, when vegetables
and stink bombs had been hurled from the balcony and some of the
noisier rowdies had had to be forcibly ejected. The evening with William
Butler Yeats at Petipas was agreeable enough. The poet looked just like
his photographs, Sloan thought, and talked as interestingly as his father.

That was, presumably, Sloan's one and only encounter with the famous poet, but it was not Dolly's sole experience of the Yeats temperament and ego. On a subsequent visit to New York, William Butler Yeats
met with her briefly, and disastrously, at the Algonquin Hotel. The episode was typical of Dolly, a mixture of the generous and the maladroit.
Since the very beginning of their friendship, she had worried about the
state of John Butler Yeats's finances. She would gently pry sketches out of

him and sell them to pay his mounting bills at Petipas, or arrange readings for which a small admission charge was asked. Quinn, Yeats's
wealthiest friend, had his patience sorely tested as he annually bought the
old man's boat passage back to Ireland only to have him cash in the ticket
at the last minute on the flimsiest of pretexts (a practice Quinn would
then turn a blind eye to, arranging for Yeats to keep the money). But
when her friend's son "Willie" returned to Manhattan, again with the
Irish Players, and registered at one of the best hotels in the city—in sharp
contrast to the humble quarters at Petipas—Dolly came to the conclusion
that Yeats *fils* was a rich man himself and perhaps didn't know the truth
of his father's genteelly impoverished situation. Without telling anyone,
she took it upon herself to see Yeats and advise him that the bills at
Petipas were long overdue and his father needed his help. She was unaware of the fact that Yeats's accommodations had been provided by Lady
Gregory and that the poet himself was far from affluent. She explained her
mission to Yeats, who then rose, towering over her, and opened the door
with a contemptuous stare and an icy "Good day, Madam." Humiliated,
Dolly left. When John Butler Yeats heard of the episode, he was appalled
at his son's heartlessness. He felt that Willie should have appreciated
Dolly's intentions, however inappropriate her actions, and he told him so.
Dolly Sloan had no bravado in her, the elder Yeats later remarked, and he
understood what the visit to his son and the snub she had suffered must
have cost her. Yet there were moments, he also noted, when this tiny
woman had the "courage of the devil," and then he loved her all the
more.

Fortunately for her mental health, Dolly had an amazingly busy
schedule at this juncture of her life. She was becoming known in the
party "as a hustler," according to Sloan, and that characterization was
hardly an overstatement. Dolly was one of those in charge of promoting a
lecture by Eugene Debs in the fall of 1911 and supervised the ninety-odd
volunteers who took donations and sold pamphlets at the Carnegie Hall
event. By now, the Sloans were regulars at the uptown concert hall; they
had heard Victor Berger, the first Socialist elected to Congress, talk there,
and a short time later had attended Emma Goldman's provocative lecture
series. Dolly had recently joined the Woman's Suffrage Committee of the
party, having decided that that issue was especially important to her now,
and dutifully went to every branch and committee meeting and leapt at
every chance to distribute tracts at major street rallies. She marched that

year, without Sloan, in the funeral procession for the victims of the Triangle Waist Company fire, and was responsible for securing poll watchers for the November elections.

One of those "secured" was her husband, who, if less of a joiner than his outgoing wife, was nonetheless as fervent about the cause in late 1911 as he had been when they first joined the party, in early 1910. His name was again on the November ballot for the State Assembly, and again he garnered only a minute number of votes. Sloan's involvement with Socialism was not entirely without recompense, however. To his surprise, an unexpected source of income came his way that fall via his party connections. The effervescent Miss Jessica Finch, founder of the Finch School in Manhattan (later Finch College) and another of Branch One's unlikely members, was a woman of left-wing political sympathies and well-placed capitalist connections. When the father of one of her pupils, a wealthy brewer in Omaha, announced his desire to have his portrait done and solicited her opinion as to the choice of an artist, she replied with alacrity that she had the very man, a New York painter of considerable talent and ample experience in portraiture.

Sloan, in typical fashion, was torn in his reaction to Miss Finch's "staggering" goodwill. On the one hand, the offer was flattering and appropriately remunerative (a thousand dollars plus expenses), and there was really no question of his turning down so profitable a job. That kind of money represented for Sloan and Dolly several months' living expenses, almost equaling the *Press* income he had recently lost. But on the other hand, there was the disconcerting thought of a midwinter trip to Nebraska on his own, with Dolly left behind in New York, and the stark fear that this kind of project induced: portraiture was not, Sloan felt, his real strength. Nor was he comfortable with painting "to order," that complicated, treacherous process by which an artist attempts to remain faithful to his sense of his own creative power while—baldly put—laboring to please his customer. This was something that Henri could manage, that John Singer Sargent and William Merritt Chase were known for, but not John Sloan. So it was with a fair amount of anxiety that he packed and headed west on December 8. Dolly, Henri, and assorted friends told him that of course, he had nothing to worry about. He himself was less certain.

To be sure, Henri's method of painting his sitters, which Sloan continued to grapple with, had never yielded the results he wanted. His diary entries for the preceding years are at their most self-critical when reflecting on his efforts at speedily capturing a likeness, on his difficulty in balancing the painterly flair and vitality that Henri insisted on with the need for anatomical accuracy and attention to the individual's temperament. Despairing about his portrait of Henry Reuterdahl's wife in 1907, Sloan had written, "after a wild struggle I find that I have not got anything important . . . head in a whirl, lost in my palette; unable to really 'see' the thing I was after." Two years later, contemplating his work with a model for *Girl with Fur Hat,* he recorded "another all-day attempt to paint Miss Converse which ended in dismal failure." Later in 1909, after their friend Katherine Sehon sat for her portrait, his appraisal was just as harsh. "[Katherine] does her part splendidly," Sloan wrote in his diary on October 15. "I wish that mine were done as well." He liked the face of his journalist friend William Walsh in the likeness he did of him but thought it the exception rather than the norm for him. Other portraits elicited similar disparaging comments.

In general, Sloan was too harsh on himself, too ready to find fault. His portrait of Mrs. Reuterdahl is, whatever the trauma involved in its creation, a lively, credible work. The pictures of Miss Converse and Miss Sehon represent an obvious advance on the portraiture that preceded them. The rendering of Walsh effectively captures the man's energy, stature, and bonhomie, while *Dolly with a Black Bow* is haunting and deeply felt. Yet everyone dear to Sloan understood how hard he would find the work he was about to embark on in Nebraska, and all did their best to be encouraging. Throughout his five weeks in the heartland, in fact, Sloan was bombarded with missives from a "cheering section" in the East that included Dolly, Henri, his sister Marianna, and Yeats. ("There is nothing so improving as painting portraits," Yeats lectured from fifteen hundred miles away in what was supposed to be a heartening letter, "particularly if you meet with terrible difficulties.")

Of terrible difficulties, Sloan felt he had more than his share. The winter cold dropped at one point to eighteen degrees below zero, he was uncomfortably aware of how much he was costing his hosts on a daily basis (as they insisted on putting him up at an expensive downtown hotel), and his sitter struck him initially as being rather less enthusiastic than Miss Finch had led him to believe. This was Sinclair Lewis territory, and Sloan wanted no part of it. Yet he was intent on acquitting himself in a professional manner and in a reasonable period of time. Between feeling "abjectly defeated" and embarrassed after his first day's work on "Mr. G. Storz, the victim of all this," and elatedly applying the finishing touches a week later, Sloan thought the process an eternity of labor and emotional strain. The picture was "nothing for posterity to craze over," Sloan noted in a telegram to Dolly on December 19, but it was a decent piece of work nonetheless.

The Storz family, both parents and children, evidently decided that the painting was just fine, as they then asked Sloan to stay on to paint Mrs. Storz. Considering the great financial gain that the offer represented, Sloan agreed, even though it meant he would have to remain away over Christmas and gird himself for another ordeal with canvas and brush. That Sloan's nerves were stretched to the limit is suggested by the fact that after his first day at it ("she poses splendidly, but the work is not up to scratch"), he suffered a severe attack of diarrhea, and then, on the following day, Christmas Eve, a bout with hives, "all itching like fury."

Mrs. Storz, a true turn-of-the-century matron to judge from the painting, was sweet, though she occasionally "show[ed] her riches," Sloan told Dolly. Unfortunately, her portrait did not proceed anywhere near as smoothly or as quickly as had her husband's, and the German-American sitter had her own ideas about her appearance. ("Don't gif me too much dere in de dupple chin" was one instruction.) There were days when Sloan wondered if he would be stuck in Omaha until the spring thaw: "I'm like a poor rat in a trap," he wrote home, "[going] round and round and round and never getting out." Worse still, relations between sitter and painter reached the point of an awkward, tearful scene a few days after their first session. On entering the room one morning, Sloan noticed that the canvas had been moved and his palette table upset; Mrs. Stolz had evidently come in for a peek at the work in progress. Sloan exploded in nervous anger ("I let loose the vials of my wrath"), Mrs. Stolz wept, her husband let his displeasure be known, and Mrs. Stolz continued posing for the rest of the day with tears in her eyes. All of this tension wreaked havoc on Sloan's health and state of mind. On January 6, though, he could report to Dolly, showing both self-perception and a momentary calm, "I am beginning to see my way out of the job now. I don't really know how to draw in that way at all. The consequence is that when I don't feel a face right, I'm 'up in the air' till I get hold of it." Mrs. Storz was destined never to be entirely happy with her likeness (she wanted more aristocratic hands, Sloan told Dolly), and further aggravation must have ensued, as the artist suffered a second painful attack of hives before leaving Nebraska.

At last, at the beginning of the third week of the month, the picture was done, presumably to everyone's satisfaction (or close enough), and Sloan was two thousand dollars richer. If the Storz family was relieved to see their high-strung New York painter return to Manhattan, Sloan was even more eager to collapse into his berth for the two-day trip east. The Omaha interlude had confirmed his reservations about himself and any prestigious commissions. The money was fine, but at what cost was it attained? You sacrificed some crucial part of yourself to please another, when the motivation and measurement of success were not completely your own. Simply put, it was a matter of trading independence for cash, and that, Sloan felt, was altogether too risky a proposition.

An Independent Path

(1912–1913)

"[The Masses] had the seriousness of strong convictions
and the gaiety of great hopes."

—GRANVILLE HICKS

Sloan returned from Omaha worn out and thoroughly trauma-
tized from his struggle to be something he was not, but he was pleased to
see that Dolly had held her own while he was gone. What under other
circumstances might have been a painful separation had in fact been a
relatively stable and productive period on the homefront: Dolly had kept
in touch with Yeats and Henri, had a small group over for dinner with
the labor leader "Big Bill" Haywood when he was in town, and involved
herself with numerous party meetings. She was delighted to see her husband and was full of news and concern about the important strike taking
place in Lawrence, Massachusetts. About the only thing that had gone
wrong in Sloan's absence, apparently, happened on a Christmas visit
Dolly made to Fort Washington, where the subject had somehow got on
to the vileness of women who stooped to prostitution and the dangerous
"foreign" (i.e., Socialist) ideas that were corrupting impressionable minds
of late. Dolly considered herself a saint for keeping her mouth shut at the
table, but to Sloan she vented her anger about his two narrow, neurotic
sisters.

Once Sloan was unpacked and resettled, what transpired for him was
nothing short of remarkable. On his own ground again, he was soon
ready to walk the streets and "soak in something to paint." Rather than
experiencing any tentativeness after his prolonged and not really successful bout with Mrs. Storz of the "dupple chin," he instead felt a quickly

renewed confidence in his ability and an unrestrained joy at being back in New York. The result was one excellent oil painting after another. A walk down to Bleecker and Carmine streets yielded the idea for *The Carmine Street Theater,* a vignette in which a group of children, bundled against the chill, waits expectantly in the sun on the pavement outside a movie house for the gates to open, while a nun walks by and a dog picks for scraps from a garbage pail—Sloan's first ash can!—at the curb. Despite their suggestiveness, the three main representational elements of the picture don't actually tell much of a story, and that was as Sloan intended it. The kids' pleasure at the thought of a moving picture is his theme; like the diners in *Renganeschi's, Saturday Night,* the patrons of the all-male *McSorley's Bar* (both also painted in 1912), or the adults in *Yeats at Petipas,* these are companions come together to enjoy one of the great social pleasures of city life. *(Movies,* painted the following year, shows the same theater at night, aglow with bright lights, and the street crowded with more children, couples, and unattached men and women appraising their chances with the opposite sex—confirmation of small-town America's anxieties about both Hollywood and Gotham.) But our pleasure with *The Carmine Street Theater* goes far beyond its anecdotal or thematic interest: the picture is so phenomenally well painted, the morning light of winter striking the pavement and the theater arches so credibly rendered, the draftsmanship of the figures and the application of the color so precise, so right, that any satisfaction in this case must be almost wholly aesthetic and only marginally narrative. One of Sloan's most successful oils thus ironically followed one of his least successful, the portrait of Mrs. Storz.

Light and energy would become almost subjects in themselves as Sloan continued to explore what interested him about the city in 1912. The crowds at street level in *Six O'Clock, Winter* are nearly pressed out of the bottom edge of the canvas as the El rips across the diagonal of the picture under a dusky, cold sunset. The trees in Gramercy Park and Madison Square filter the sun or the rain for anyone out for a stroll, and a warm afternoon light floods both the bar and the back room in the two views of McSorley's that Sloan produced during this time.

This combination of contentment and activity is equally important in those of Sloan's paintings from this year and the next that exclusively portray women. The figures dry their hair or sit and gossip in the sun on rooftops, they hang their laundry out to dry on rooftop lines, they dig in

small plots of ground to plant spring flowers in their brownstone back-
yards, but they never look either tired or effete, and they exist and func-
tion in warm, healing light. The two poles in the depiction of women in
early-twentieth-century American art—represented on the one hand by
the dark, grimy street women and hard drinkers of George Luks, and on
the other by the beautiful, pampered, ethereal women of Thomas Wilmer
Dewing, Frank Benson, and Edmund Tarbell—are something that Sloan
carefully avoided, maybe more so than any of his contemporaries. These
values simply have nothing to do with Sloan's image of women or with
his needs, which have instead inspired pictures that involve work and
order, sorority and calm. Thinking of these paintings as well as the Astor
Library scrubwomen of the year before, the art historian Patricia Hills has
speculated about Sloan's underlying concern with "ritual cleansing and
renewal . . . a desire for purification, redemption, and regeneration in a
world *here and now.*" At the height of his involvement with Socialism, as
he watched a new side of his wife come to the fore, Sloan may very well
have had these thoughts in mind.

Many of these fine paintings were completed under less than perfect
physical conditions. The previous summer the Sloans had lost patience
with their landlord at Twenty-third Street—a man who had an inade-
quate sense of how many leaks or heating problems a reasonable tenant
could be expected to tolerate—and looked about for nicer quarters. Sloan
had consulted John Quinn about the feasibility of getting a mortgage on
a small house in Chelsea, but in the end he and Dolly took another rental
in a better building, at 155 East Twenty-second Street, near Henri's
apartment on Gramercy Park. Its only drawback was its size. There wasn't
enough room to set up an easel, pose a model, and step back far enough
from either to get a proper view. In May, using some of the Storz money,
Sloan treated himself to a just compensation for the Nebraska experience,
leasing a studio on the eleventh floor of 35 Sixth Avenue, a triangular
building that still stands at a main corner of the Village on West Fourth
Street. There he had not only a much higher vantage point for observing
the city than he had had in Chelsea, but also—an unthinkable luxury in
the days when he had worked in rooms where Dolly might be present
during the day—a chance to paint the nude.

The three nudes Sloan produced during his first weeks in the new
space are almost shockingly sensuous given the public image of John
Sloan, artist of the street scene and the upright clothed figure. The brush-

strokes sing the beauty of the flesh; the white sheets declare the naturalness, the rightness, of the body naked and prone. His model, Katherine Wenzel, was long-legged, buxom, and remarkably uninhibited for a fourteen-year-old. Sloan was to have few more capable models for a subject that he had never before attempted but would later devote himself to extensively, creating a body of work in that field that is still little known and little appreciated.

The trouble that had begun in Lawrence, Massachusetts, while Sloan was away and that had so interested Dolly that winter was quickly turning out to be the labor strike of the era. More than twenty thousand textile workers, most employed at a salary of ten dollars a week, had walked out of that mill town's factories to protest an intolerable wage cut. These were people of various nationalities and political beliefs with but one thing in common: they had been pushed to the limit by long hours of strenuous labor and an amazing arrogance on the part of management. Sensing fertile ground for their cause, two organizers from New York— Joe Ettor, an IWW man, and the poet Arturo Giovannitti, editor of *Il Proletario*—made their way to Lawrence to see to it that this spontaneous outburst of indignation would become an efficient and productive radical enterprise. After the pair's arrest by local authorities, who accused them of being "accessories before the fact" in a riot between strikers and police that left one young female picketer dead, Bill Haywood, Carlo Tresca, Elizabeth Gurley Flynn, and other professionals arrived to take over, whereupon, as one social historian has observed, the "strike was dramatized as only the Wobblies could dramatize it—battles between police and strikers, mass picket lines, huge mass meetings, revolutionary songs, flying banners, nationwide publicity, and appeals for support." Sloan immediately sat down to prepare a political cartoon for a special Lawrence strike edition of the *Call*.

Dolly's main interest lay with the strikers' children, who not only were suffering from their parents' inability to feed their families under the circumstances but were also living under a constant threat of retaliatory violence. She heartily approved of the controversial plan to transport the children out of Lawrence and place them with willing families in cities in the Northeast until the strike was over. Dolly took charge of a contingent of boys and girls who were sent to stay in Manhattan and

Brooklyn, meeting them at Grand Central Station, where police, journalists, and political types singing the "Marseillaise" and waving red flags at the police made a difficult episode even more chaotic than it had to be. The activist Mary Heaton Vorse was on hand and recalled a scene of utter pandemonium. The train was late, and the city permit to march the children down Lexington Avenue to the relocation center hadn't come. "Where's the man with the permit to parade?" Dolly was yelling. "He's down at the *Proletario* office reading *Salomé.* That's the matter with the radical movement. The man with the permit to parade is always off in the *Proletario* office reading *Salomé*!"

Even after the train and the permit arrived, the problems were endless. Sick children had to be taken to see doctors in local hospitals, where the staff was quick to show its stony disapproval of the whole relocation scheme; a woman complained to the Sloans that she had been asked to shelter a pickpocket, and demanded the return of her missing jewelry; the IWW—a more militant group than the Socialists—wanted to "use" the children, Dolly thought, for public-relations and tactical ends, and so gave the Socialist women a hard time throughout the ordeal. Back in Lawrence, matters took another violent turn when the city fathers, having decided that the sight of displaced children was turning public opinion against the factory owners, called on the police and the militia to halt the exodus, a move that led to the vicious beating of parents in front of their children at the railroad station.

Dolly's observation about the IWW's scorn for the ministrations of the Branch One ladies was borne out when Sloan attended a talk given by Bill Haywood in the city in early March. Haywood began by making a few snide and, Sloan felt, irrelevant comments about Branch One, which was known for its professional-class membership (it did have, it was true, a higher percentage of doctors, lawyers, and writers and fewer "workers" than other branches of the Socialist party). "I interrupted [him] to resent [his attitude] with great and I suppose unnecessary heat," Sloan later commented. After the meeting, Haywood and Sloan patched things up. Although Sloan always took umbrage at the sanctimonious attitudes of some (or many) of his fellow radicals, he found it hard to hold a grudge against one of the most earnest and effective organizers in the business. The Lawrence strike was concluded a short time later as one of the great IWW victories. Public opinion had been moved as never before to consider the plight of the immigrant underclass, and the infamous wage cut was rescinded. By the end of the month Dolly was able to accompany two hundred relieved children on the train back to Massachusetts, where they were reunited with their parents. "It is a big thing," Sloan proudly wrote in his diary on the eve of Dolly's departure for Lawrence, "but it's quite clear she is equal to it."

The opportunity to roll up her sleeves and accomplish something, particularly if it involved helping children, meant a great deal to Dolly. But she was also rather excited by the more frenetic aspects of party work and hated to miss a good street "action." The May Day rally in Union Square in 1912 was a characteristic free-for-all and suggested something of the internecine conflict that was dividing the movement at the time. The anarchists at the gathering were indignant that an American flag had been placed on the speakers' platform and demanded that it be taken down. A scuffle ensued, with five Italian Anarchists grabbing the banner, which was then "rescued" by several Socialists. Reporters who wanted an account of the affair, which their editors naturally worked up into the story of a left-wing riot, went to Dolly Sloan for a statement since she had been right there on the platform. (Dolly was getting her picture in the papers, including the *Times,* rather frequently these days, and was always ready with a few clear summarizing words.) She insisted that the incident had not been anything especially dramatic or violent—not at all what the reporters wanted to hear—and that it had been unseemly of the anarchists to attempt to rip down the flag. However, she asserted that she herself had no interest in promoting patriotism and added that it was "ridiculous for radical men and women to venerate it. We do *not* venerate any flag." In her view, the Socialists had been just as wrong to make a show of force in holding on to their precious Stars and Stripes; they were in Union Square to deal with more important questions. For his part, Sloan thought his wife acquitted herself admirably in her capacity as "publicist." A few days later Dolly marched in her first suffragette parade down Fifth Avenue, while her husband stood on the sidelines by the Flatiron Building and sketched the feminists and the chortling male spectators for an article in *Collier's.*

For several months that year, Dolly's activism in fact exceeded Sloan's, a development that pleased him mightily on two counts. First, it was encouraging, and moving, for him to observe the changes in Dolly, to see her at last coming to view herself as a person of worth and ability, an individual whom other people could respect. In these happy weeks, she always had somewhere to go when she got up in the morning, some conference to attend or fund-raising event to plan. Nothing in her background had suggested that she would ever make a place for herself in the world among serious, busy, determined people, but that was just what she was managing to do. Even Yeats, who thought his friends slightly daft about their beloved Socialist party and growing more so by the month, must have appreciated the good done her by the cause. Certainly Sloan did: in his mind, Dolly was living proof of the better life that a commitment to political change could offer. The second benefit of his wife's avocation was that Sloan was freed for long stretches from worry about what trouble she might be getting into on her own. The strength of Sloan's painting in 1912 and Dolly's own stability, momentary though it proved to be, were hardly coincidental or unrelated.

In September, as primary time neared, Sloan allowed his name to be placed on the ballot again as one of the Socialist candidates for the State Assembly. He did so with the knowledge that he would not be expected to make any speeches or kiss any babies and had no grounds to fear a victory at the polls. Indeed, his loss in the primary was timely, as October was a month of strenuous activity. Even with Sloan's studio on Sixth Avenue, the apartment on East Twenty-second Street was too small and expensive, but a plan to find a bigger apartment with George and Elizabeth Hamlin, who wanted to move from Philadelphia to New York, didn't work out. So the Sloans found their own apartment at 61 Perry Street and became Greenwich Villagers. They packed up everything they owned, just as Dolly was preparing to go upstate as one of Branch One's delegates to the state convention in Syracuse. She left proud and euphoric, but when she came home in a daze, exhausted and disoriented after a terrible drinking binge, Sloan realized that there were limits to Dolly's stamina and mental health. When expecting too much of herself, pushing herself too hard, she was apt to slide back into the old patterns. A precarious balance gave way when she became nervous or overtired. Dr. Bower had been right about one thing, Sloan sadly acknowledged: Dolly would be an alcoholic until the day she died. Nothing would change that.

On Election Day, Eugene Debs polled a staggering nine hundred thousand votes as the Socialist party's candidate for President, more than double his count of four years before. Socialist candidates for local and state offices across the country did well, and one railroad tycoon was quoted as saying that the best America could do was to stave off the inevitable for as long as possible. But the Sloans knew from firsthand experience how hard-won those victories were. Once again Dolly had organized her corps of poll-watchers, and once again Sloan took his place with the volunteers. This time, though, the scene turned ugly when a gang of thugs burst into the polling area and beat up a man who had come to vote the Socialist ticket, knocking over everyone who tried to stop them. If Sloan's drawing of the incident (reproduced in the *Masses* the next January under the title *Political Action)* is accurate in its details, as seems likely, he himself was pushed and held up against a wall during the altercation. The police simply stood by and watched. Just as infuriating, given the voters' mandate that the ideas of Debs and Haywood should at least be allowed a hearing, was the fact that Joe Ettor and Arturo Giovannitti were still being held in jail for organizing the workers of Lawrence. Their release from prison that winter provided the occasion for a further example of right-wing stubbornness—as well as a wonderful moment for Dolly Sloan.

When Ettor and Giovannitti were finally acquitted, even many conservatives having admitted that the case against them was of doubtful legality, a rally for them at Carnegie Hall seemed a logical idea. Dolly agreed to organize the women who would "pass the hat" up and down the aisles, as was the usual practice at such gatherings to help defray costs or pay legal bills. The police commissioner of New York, who was of the view that too many of these dangerous spectacles had already been allowed in his city and that the "Reds" needed to be put in their place, let it be known that his men would be out in force at Carnegie Hall; the Anarchists' statements that they were ready for bloodshed, if it came to that, were just what the commissioner wanted to hear. By way of provocation, he had forty detectives seated *on the stage* with the radical leadership that evening. Inevitably, the cry came up from the front and back of the hall that the stage should be stormed and the police dragged off the speakers' platform, but at just that instant a tiny Irish woman in a bright-red dress came onto the stage and attempted to pass the hat along the line of policemen, nudging and cajoling them relentlessly for donations. According to one party activist who was there, Ernest Poole, the resulting laughter brought down the house. With the tension defused and the hecklers calmed, the speeches and celebrations for Ettor and Giovannitti continued without incident.

Dolly had a way with Irish cops, Sloan once noted. Although she had a horror of being arrested and, when attending birth-control street rallies, would never distribute illegal leaflets if the police were nearby, she generally fared well with the men in the blue. A woman so small, so spunky, and so obviously Irish had a good deal going for her in this one unusual but crucial context.

For all of the hours that the Sloans spent among their fellow activists in the street or in the lecture halls, the consolidation of their ties to the cause of political change in America was finally effected in 1912, appropriately enough, not through direct action but by way of the image and the word. In becoming art editor of *The Masses,* today an especially revered forum in the history of left-wing political journalism, Sloan returned to his origins as a Philadelphia illustrator—but this time he was on the offensive against the powers and values he had once served.

The *Masses* that John Sloan became involved with was a reincarnation of the original publication of that name, which had expired the previous summer. The brainchild of a Dutch Socialist named Piet Vlag, who ran a restaurant in the basement of the Rand School, the magazine had been kept afloat throughout 1911 and into the summer of 1912 thanks to the silent backing of a New York Life Insurance Company vice president, Rufus Weeks (in an incongruity of the sort that was less uncommon before the war than it would be later). It aimed to provide a mixture of exposés, political commentary, and short fiction "written *for* the masses [but] not written *down to* the masses," as an early editorial put it. When circulation faltered and the Weeks subsidy ended, it seemed that the whole venture was doomed. Americans liked their monthlies to be securely middle-of-the-road. *Radical* was still a dirty word. Vlag gave up and left New York for Florida.

But the more ardent contributors were not yet ready to see their eighteen-month-old journal go under. In September, Art Young, a feisty graphic artist who had converted to Socialism after hearing Eugene Debs speak, called for a meeting at the apartment of Charles Allen Winter and his wife, Alice Beach Winter, fellow artists with *The Masses,* to see what could be done. Glenn Coleman, a Henri man and newspaper artist turned painter, was invited to join them, as were John and Dolly Sloan and a few others. As Young later recalled in his memoirs, everyone present felt that

the magazine was too important to be allowed to fade from the scene—
especially just at that moment, when great political progress seemed
imminent in the wake of the Lawrence strike and Debs's campaign for the
presidency—though all agreed that some changes were going to be necessary in its style and format. There had been, they all felt, too much
propaganda under Vlag (a particular Sloan bête noire) and not enough
playful satire or graphic skill. Europe offered plenty of examples of sophisticated political art journals with a left-wing slant, from *Simplicissimus*
in Germany and *L'Assiette au Buerre* in France (which printed drawings by
Félix Vallotton, Juan Gris, and Frantisek Kupka) to Italy's *L'Asino* and
Holland's *Notekraaker.* It was high time that English-speaking readers
had a publication that was as pointed, as independent, as un-middle-of-
the-road as those. "We wanted," Young said, "one magazine which we
could gallop around in and be free," adding that it was just like a group
of artists to want to bring out a magazine with neither a regular source of
funding nor any notion of how to acquire one or even of whether they
really wanted to bother.

The money issue was important because the group had decided that it
was central to its purpose that the magazine remain as unaffiliated and
unindebted as possible—which meant no binding ties to advertisers, no
concern for reader preferences, no payment to contributors, and no need
to follow an "official" Socialist party line, even though everyone involved
was a Socialist. The writers, among them Louis Untermeyer and Hayden
Carruth, as much as the artists like Sloan or Maurice Becker, wanted to
produce a visually impressive assemblage of high-quality drawings, cartoons, poems, stories, jokes, and political commentary that would instruct, mock, and entertain in as wide-ranging, comic, and aggressive a
fashion as its contributors dared. It was precisely that quality that Sloan
enjoyed in the plays of the British Socialist George Bernard Shaw that *The
Masses* post-Vlag would aim for: a jaunty intellectuality, a devil-may-care
marriage of levity and principle. All of this was to be accomplished in the
most democratic manner possible, with every regular contributor a member of the editorial board and everyone on the editorial board deciding
what went into each issue.

For help in doing this, they turned to the man whom one historian
has described as the "John Barrymore of American radicalism." To be
sure, Max Eastman was as romantically captivating as any film star. A
ladies' man and an intellectual, he relished the benefits of a lean, hand-

some figure and an impressive mind and earned the regard of men and women alike. Even his enemies—with the exception, years later, of the sexually touchy Ernest Hemingway, who loathed him—tended to have a hard time resisting this tall, courtly poet, litterateur, and disciple of John Dewey. When he received the odd congratulation note from Sloan and Untermeyer after the meeting at the Beaches' (a note that in its entirety read, "You are elected editor of *The Masses.* No pay"), Eastman was skeptical about getting involved for nothing in an undertaking that he knew would be time-consuming. But in short order he was seduced by the company, by the spirit of the journal, and by Art Young's offhand promise that he would receive a salary for his labors as editorial coordinator when and if the magazine began to make some money. It is likely that the Sloans and the others didn't know of Young's promise; it was their notion that if all went well, *The Masses* would acquire a large, enthusiastic audience, clear its expenses, and never turn a profit. It was crucial—in Sloan's mind, anyway—that their magazine not ape the structure, let alone the policies, of the mainstream publications that their circle already had so little respect for. In any event, during that fall that saw the preparation of the first issue of the revived *Masses,* Sloan and Dolly, who had heard Eastman lecture on Socialism the previous spring, were pleased to have this "brilliant untrammeled thinker," as Sloan termed him, in charge of seeing that each issue was properly pasted up, typeset, and printed. Dolly was made business manager, with responsibility for soliciting contributions (Eastman was expected to secure the larger sums from well-to-do patrons, Dolly the smaller donations), and Sloan was named art editor and told to spread the word of this new exciting outlet for American graphic talent.

The first issue of *The Masses,* which appeared in December, could hardly be said to foreshadow the great things to come. Not that John Sloan had any reservations about it: he eagerly hawked copies in the street as soon as the magazine arrived from the printer's, and claimed to have set the staff record of seventy-eight personal sales in one brisk evening. The cover, like that of the issue to follow, was by Charles Allen Winter, a crystal-ball scene done in the "tight," dull, detailed style Winter had long since perfected. Max Eastman inaugurated his column, "Knowledge and Revolution," while the rest of the text consisted of an interview with the German Socialist August Bebel, a story by Mary Heaton Vorse, and some tepid poems by Eastman and Untermeyer. The contributions of

John Sloan and Art Young were far and away the wittiest and most provocative, suggesting to its first readers (and rightly so) that it was in its visuals that the magazine would achieve real distinction. Sloan's *His Country's Flag* was a sketch of an old derelict paying alcoholic obeisance to a row of flags on a storefront under the El. Young's acerbic two-page spread depicted the American newspaper world as a bordello, with big advertisers handing over money to the madam, or editor, while the "girls"—the reporters and editorial writers, all shown in drag—sat in the parlor docilely waiting to be made use of. January's issue presented a story by John Reed, an essay by William English Walling, a long poem by Arturo Giovannitti, a funny Henri caricature of an Academy jury, Sloan's own *Political Action,* and the snippets of reportage that would be the staple of every number. With that issue, the *Masses'* credo was formulated and announced to the world: to be "a revolutionary and not a reform magazine . . . a free magazine; frank, arrogant, impertinent . . . a magazine whose final policy is to do as it pleases and conciliate nobody, not even its readers."

Sloan took pains to assure friends such as Yeats and John Quinn that he was not forsaking "high art" for propaganda, however much the cause might mean to him and however much fun he might be having. Writing to thank Quinn for his donation of twenty dollars to *The Masses,* Sloan felt compelled to note, "I hope to do my share toward making [the magazine] an artistic and Socialistic success, but as it is a monthly I do not fear that the work I do for it need sap my force for better things if my paintings can be called such." When, in January, Sloan finally asked Quinn what he thought of the periodical, he received a predictable response from the well-connected (if very broad-minded) corporate attorney. "I think it is too bitter in tone to make converts," Quinn replied. "Bitterness in propagandist literature may keep those already converted but it does not bring converts. . . . As a rule, the more bitter the attack, the harsher the cartooning, the more repellent the thing is and the less it attracts." By now Sloan knew to expect blunt honesty from Quinn, but his friend's opinion must have been distressing all the same: he was complaining of exactly those qualities that Sloan most wanted to avoid in *The Masses.* In the end, Quinn's perspective merely served to illuminate the essential differences between a liberal and a radical circa 1913. Sloan was quite sure that *The Masses* was a happy mixture of art and politics, and that its propaganda, if harsh, was also lively, meaningful, and persuasive.

Some who were familiar with the inner workings of the magazine wondered how any issue ever saw the light of day. "Collective editorship" could be a cumbersome process, and the personalities involved were anything but efficient by nature. After one editorial session, Mary Heaton Vorse, used to the briskness of the suffragist meetings she attended, observed in frustration how "slipshod" men were in comparison to women. In a letter to her family, she described going "ankle deep in slush" to a meeting at the *Masses* office only to be told that everyone was gathering at Sloan's studio instead. Making her way back down Sixth Avenue to Sloan's, she arrived at four-thirty to find Max Eastman and their host sitting there alone, no one else having arrived on time for the four-o'clock conference.

> So we dawdled on for an hour and a half, while John Sloan placidly made monotypes of Isadora Duncan, now and then spitting a little venom over his shoulder at the world at large. . . . I don't know how their *Masses* happens every month. It makes one believe in the stories of the little gnomes that come and do your work for you while you are in a trance.

At the same time, Vorse astutely noted, there was a paradoxical stringency and vigor to the whole enterprise. Eastman—and later Floyd Dell, who would sign on as coeditor in 1913—would slump down in a chair and read aloud the accumulated literary offerings to the assembled artists and writers, who would respond either with a terse "Chuck it!" or with laughter or hearty applause. Sloan was given to groaning when he didn't like a given article or poem, and the artist Boardman Robinson would make no pretense about the lethargy the writer's work induced in him. "Nothing more horrible can be imagined than having one's piece torn to bits by the artists at a *Masses* meeting," Vorse wrote in her memoirs, recalling that the artists were often more exacting critics than the writers themselves. Yet she also admitted that "there was no greater reward than having them stop their groans and catcalls and give close attention." In the literary circles of Greenwich Village, acceptance by the newest and most unusual magazine in the country was an honor not to be taken lightly.

Some didn't approve of the procedure of a group vote. Art Young fondly remembered a visit from Hippolyte Havel, a notorious Village anarchist, who was thunderstruck at the idea of letting majority rule determine the value of a work of art. "Bourgeois pigs!" he shouted at Eastman, Dell, Sloan, and their crowd. "Voting! Voting on poetry! Poetry is something from the soul. You can't vote on poetry!" When Floyd Dell argued that Havel and Emma Goldman must have edited their magazine, *Mother Earth,* in approximately the same way—how else, after all, would the material for the next issue be determined? *Someone* had to approve or reject submissions—Havel tartly answered, "Sure, sure. We anarchists make decisions. But we don't abide by them."

In truth, *The Masses* was not for everyone in the movement, nor did it aim to be. Climbing to a circulation of forty thousand at its peak, it still rubbed a fair number of would-be allies the wrong way. One prominent Socialist, W. J. Ghent, offered the complaint that the magazine "found no trouble in mixing Socialism, Anarchism, Communism, Sinn Feinism, Cubism, sexism, direct action, and sabotage into a more or less harmonious mess." The central problem with *The Masses,* he felt, was that it was the "product of restless metropolitan coteries who devote themselves to the cult of Something Else; who are ever seeking the bubble novelty even at the door of Bedlam." If Ghent was speaking for those who wanted the magazine to be less frolicsome and more consistently the voice of Socialism, Sloan would have had no difficulty in determining his own allegiances. There were many publications, including the *Call* and *Coming Nation,* that followed a strict political line, and Sloan gave them plenty of good drawings, but he had thrown himself heart and soul into the *Masses* because it encompassed Socialist values while refusing to be limited or exclusively defined by them. His colleagues were just as happy to reproduce his satiric effort *A Slight Attack of Third Dementia Brought On by Excessive Study of the Much-Talked-Of Cubist Pictures in the International Exhibition at New York,* a parody of the Duchamps and Picabias he had just seen at the Armory Show, as they were to make use of his drawings of a bloated simian businessman ignoring the fleabite of a corruption investigation or a well-fed pastor lecturing his congregation against the "unChristian spirit of discontent" among the working classes.

The four covers and thirty-two drawings that Sloan contributed in 1913 alone were as eclectic as the man himself. Several depicted Adam and Eve in the Garden of Eden, casting Eve as a huge Earth Mother taking care of her scrawny, hapless mate, the real source of trouble at the Forbidden Tree. Some were captionless sketches—of a young woman, probably a suffrage marcher, being manhandled by police; of a farmer in his field; of a kilt-clad Andrew Carnegie in a bandit's mask with a bag of filthy lucre. Some took aim at the rich—the cover for the March issue, entitled *The Unemployed,* showed a couple in a box at the opera—and others at radical sympathizers who were better at conversation than at confrontation. A cartoon in the September issue, for example, caught a couple lounging in their parlor and musing about a strike in progress: "Why don't those strikers do something—let a few of them get shot, and it'll look as if they meant business."

Sloan's covers, even more than his cartoons, inevitably riled the more doctrinaire members of the party. In contrast to the unvarying bite of Art Young's work, two of Sloan's first four covers were anything but political. The one for the May issue, depicting a teenage girl on a swing in Madison Square, seems—unless one wants to make something of the portly men on the benches staring at her—almost oppressively innocent, while the other, used for the July cover, is captioned *Return from Toil.* This is a theme that would have had Ghent, Goldman, Haywood, and the other leaders of the far left calling for bedraggled sweatshop girls or denizens of the Haymarket hiding their shame. Instead, Sloan perversely insists that not every young woman who works hard for a living goes home at the end of the day with her friends looking like a poster child for the IWW. His six shopgirls happen to be in a good mood and are gossiping, giggling, and linking arms as they walk down the street. November's issue offered a different sort of Sloan cover, with two nice-looking young women from a bad neighborhood swearing like sailors. The title below them reads: *Innocent Girlish Prattle—Plus Environment.* At this point in the history of the *Masses,* Sloan's art was not alone in being only intermittently political in nature. Many of the 1913 covers (six or seven of the twelve, depending on how one interprets them) had no overt political meaning.

One subject that did prompt explicitness from Sloan, and had always done so, was the link between sexual and economic oppression. *The Women's Night Court* was drawn as a two-page illustration for a one-act play by Frank Shay that *The Masses* printed in the August issue. Shay's unexceptional little drama, *The Machine,* is about the entrapment of streetwalkers and the callousness of the judicial system. Sloan's picture—the magazine's dynamic "centerfold," a full twelve by eighteen inches—

rivets us on the moment before the bar (a moment such as Sloan himself had observed during his visits to night court in the Village) when the arrested woman is confronted by her accuser. The only false note in the tense, crowded image is the delicacy of the hooker, who might just as easily be taken for a debutante. But even that dubious element of the drawing is effectively offset by the apple-pie good looks of the shockingly young undercover cop. The police have no business dragging this woman into court, Sloan and Shay imply, and despite appearances, the "officer of the law" on the stand is no more innocent than the voyeurs by the rail, the older policemen trying to look tough, or the heartless judge at the bench who will sentence the woman to the workhouse. But then, as a good Socialist, Sloan may be suggesting something in his drawing that Shay does not touch on in his prose, where the youth and good looks of the officer are not an issue—namely, that a young, conventionally educated, conventionally bigoted policeman might be as much a victim of the "machine" as any prostitute on Broadway. This is a fellow barely out of his teens, who should be at home in bed with his girlfriend or doing something to get the serious criminals off the street. He looks awkward, even ludicrous, on the stand. The "machine" makes a fool of *everyone*.

For a time, Sloan wondered if his work for a radical magazine in which he could vent his real thoughts about society might not land him in trouble with his more traditional employers in the periodical business. A few years earlier, that might have been the case. Now, in a period of heightened visual urbanity and with a greater awareness of the sophistication of their market, many publishers kept an eye on the fringe to see what could be appropriated in a watered-down state for their own pages. When Norman Hapgood took over as editor of *Harper's Weekly,* he announced his intention of making the graphics of the magazine livelier, and toward that end he employed Sloan and some of his friends rather frequently in 1913 and 1914 and again, briefly, in 1915. Most of what Sloan was called on to do for *Harper's Weekly,* of course, was not of a political nature; his covers and illustrations are in a more benign "slice of life" narrative mode. A drawing that appeared in the September 1913 issue, however, enabled him to interject some of the moral outrage of *The Woman's Night Court* into the living rooms of the middle class. *Two Readings* is a two-panel didactic perspective on the theme of justice. In the upper drawing, a prosecutor (wearing a Teddy Roosevelt monocle) points an accusing finger at a defendant on the stand and thunders that "Ignorance of the law excuses no one." The lower panel, illustrating a different notion of justice, portrays Christ on the cross forgiving those who have placed him there.

One wonders, actually, whether this drawing would have made it into *The Masses,* having successfully run that gauntlet of peer critics. But as Sloan himself admitted, "The strange thing was that if I got a good idea, I gave it to *The Masses.* If I got a second-rate one, I might sell it to *Harper's,* but I could never have the same feeling when working for pay."

Sloan received an agreeable Thanksgiving present, one concerned with that same subject of the artist as social critic and odd-man-out, with the appearance in *Harper's Weekly,* at the end of November 1913, of an affectionate essay about him by John Butler Yeats. Full of praise for the delicate light and shadows of *McSorley's Back Room* ("All painters from the time of Leonardo da Vinci have felt the charm of chiaroscuro . . . to paint chiaroscuro is to make a picture of infinity") and such city pictures as *Hairdresser's Window* and *Scrubwomen, Astor Library,* Yeats was also making an effort in his article to find common ground between himself, an essentially apolitical man, a philosopher and an aesthete, and this new Sloan who seemed ready to take on the world. Yeats was not the only friend who watched with mixed feelings as Sloan became more opinionated and more volatile in the wake of his politicization. "He engages in a war of opinion," Yeats wrote,

> and here let me make a distinction. There are those who are alive with the spirit of controversy; they are the great army of the dissuasive who convince us against our will. The true artist [e.g., Sloan] is persuasive. He enters into controversy without the spirit of controversy and we yield to him because he plays all so seductively upon our imaginative longings.

Part truth and part wishful thinking, Yeats's appraisal of his best friend would be even more sorely tested the following year in the aftermath of Sarajevo and the failure of European socialism to prevent the war, two developments that were to leave Sloan shaken and angry.

A New Vision

(1913–1915)

"The 'new movements in Art' add a lot to one's enthusiasm in work, have a rather electrifying effect on the general atmosphere, broaden one's horizon, smash moulds, and declare liberty."

—JOHN SLOAN TO JOHN QUINN
(1914)

In 1913, the legendary Armory Show introduced Americans en masse to the world of modern art; the Paterson Strike Pageant was held at Madison Square Garden to dramatize the plight of the striking silk workers of New Jersey; and the Haymarket, that relic of debaucheries past, was torn down. All three events had meaning of one kind or another for John Sloan.

Sloan's involvement with the Armory Show, which ran at the Sixty-ninth Regiment Armory in Manhattan from February 17 through March 15, was limited to working with the hanging committee and the catalogue committee and offering five of his etchings and two of his oil paintings, *McSorley's Bar* and *Sunday, Women Drying Their Hair,* for the American section of the exhibition. (His one sale, of the etching *The Picture Buyer,* brought ten dollars from the subject of the picture himself, William Macbeth.) But the impact of the experience—of America's first large-scale exposure to Post-Impressionist, Cubist, and Fauve art—was profound. Contrary to the long-established assumption that the realists of Sloan's generation were to a man threatened and unnerved by what they saw at the Armory on Lexington Avenue and Twenty-sixth Street that month, Sloan knew that he was in the presence of something significant and challenging. He told Quinn that had he known how important this show was to be, he would have involved himself in it to a greater extent.

This radical event had had a mild-mannered genesis. Walt Kuhn,

Jerome Myers, and another painter, Elmer MacRae, all exhibited at the same venue, the Madison Gallery run by Henry Fitch Taylor. They were, like most intelligent artists in New York, concerned with the quantity of good art, theirs included, that had been neglected by the official channels and was in need of more dynamic exposure. Unlike most other artists, however, they were eager to do something about the situation. In forming an organization with twenty others and calling it the Association of American Painters and Sculptors, Kuhn, Myers, MacRae, and Taylor were in effect picking up on the momentum established by the Macbeth show of "The Eight," the 1910 Independents exhibition, and "Kent's Tent" in their push for alternative showcases, a means of controlling the Academy's power. Sloan was elected to membership in this group, but he was preoccupied with his own work and later with *The Masses* and gave the Association and its doings little thought and no time. With J. Alden Weir as its president and the sculptor Gutzon Borglum as its vice president, this body didn't seem likely to do much.

At this point Arthur B. Davies entered the story. Described by the art historian Milton Brown as a man "of fastidiously aristocratic bearing, a painter of poetic sensitivity bordering on the ephemeral[, a] reticent and coolly formal person," Davies was on the surface as unlikely a candidate for leadership of an aggressive Modernist art-political cause as he was for membership in "The Eight," a largely urban realist group. But lead he did, in part by the force of his personality and intellect and in part because of his access to some of the more generous patrons of Manhattan, and by the time the dust settled, the principal goal of the Association had changed from mounting a large American exhibition to setting forth a monumental survey of American and European art, with Davies, Kuhn, and Walter Pach seizing control of the direction of the endeavor from the more tepid crowd of Myers, Weir, and Borglum. The month-long display in New York, and the stops that followed in Chicago and Boston, brought together an unprecedented collection of almost thirteen hundred art works that aimed to present a historical overview of modern art from Delacroix and Ingres through Cézanne and van Gogh to the best—meaning the most untraditional and startling—contemporary painters and sculptors.

The place of the Henri group in all of this was a little awkward. Pity poor William Glackens, head of the committee in charge of selecting the American art. When he first saw what Davies, Kuhn, and Pach were bringing back from their frantic ten-day trip to Europe, he realized at once how conservative, even stunted, most of the American section would look to the public. Francis Picabia's *Dances at the Spring* or Marcel Duchamp's *Nude Descending a Staircase* in close quarters with work by Kenneth Hayes Miller, Leon Kroll, Glenn Coleman, Henry Reuterdahl, James and May Preston? A Kandinsky "Improvisation" or Henri Matisse's *Goldfish* next to the circus paintings of Gifford Beal and George Bellows? Edvard Munch and Eugene Higgins? (And one wonders how much authority Glackens was given, anyway, and to what extent Davies had the first *and* the final say: Marsden Hartley, for instance, was invited by Davies to send something to exhibit, while Rockwell Kent was pointedly excluded, much to his fury. One feels the opinionated judgment of Davies here more than that of Glackens.) Equally incongruous, if not humiliating, was Henri's place on the committee for foreign art. It was evident from early on that the Armory Show was to be Davies's brainchild, and that for the first time in recent memory Henri would not be the leader of a significant "independent" enterprise in the art world. Deprived of a free hand in the selections, he stubbornly declined to have anything to do with making the choices. Regrettably, when the art works were being installed in the Armory, Davies and Pach went out of their way to remind Henri of how effectively he had been frozen out of the process, of how little his old leadership would count in the new order in which Picasso, Matisse, and Duchamp were the names to reckon with. Henri made a suggestion about the height of a painting that was being hung; Davies ignored him. Henri then wistfully commented to Pach that he hoped that for every European work sold from the show, an American work would likewise find a buyer. "That isn't the proportion of merit," Pach shot back, and he walked away, leaving his old teacher standing there.

At the boisterous party held at Healy's steakhouse on Columbus Avenue, for the benefit of the Association's "friends and enemies in the press" (probably the only time a large group of artists has ever treated New York's art critics to dinner), Sloan spoke to John Quinn about the shabby treatment accorded Henri by those who had conceived the exhibition. But Quinn, who had thrown himself into the organizing of the show and who loved what he had seen there, was in no mood to be charitable. He brusquely shrugged off Sloan's qualms, saying it was Henri's problem, and nobody else's. To his way of thinking, Davies and Kuhn had forged a more effective path. How remarkable, Sloan later observed to his wife, that a "silent, poetic type like Davies turned out to be a dictator at heart." And how curious, too, he noted, that a once-eminent figure like Robert Henri could so quickly lose his standing among his peers and his authority among the younger, more adventurous members of his profession. But Henri, at forty-eight, was about to experience just such an immediate and drastic devaluation in his position. Overnight he became a conservative. In the aftermath of the Armory Show, Sloan understood much better than his friend and first mentor that major changes were overtaking the art world in America and that the battle lines were about to shift.

Over the years Sloan had paid a few visits to Alfred Stieglitz's small gallery to see some of the new art—John Marin's watercolors, for example, or the the paintings Alfred Maurer had made under the influence of Matisse—but he had always been put off by Stieglitz's didactic, egocentric manner. (The lack of respect was mutual: Stieglitz's feelings toward "The Eight" were no secret.) Even for a regular at 291 Fifth Avenue, though, the Armory Show would have been a heady experience. One would have to have spent time in Europe, to have visited all of the major avant-garde shows and studios, as Walter Pach and Marsden Hartley had, to be fully prepared for the cumulative effect of this abrupt survey of Modernist aesthetics, and of course Sloan had never left the United States. It is difficult today to conceive of the impact of this first sight, all at the same time, of Renoir, Gauguin, van Gogh, Cézanne, Redon, Matisse, Vlaminck, Picasso, Gleizes, Kandinsky, Duchamp, Picabia, Delaunay, and Dufy. If anything, an unshakable smugness now afflicts us: we assume that the scoffers were benighted fools and that the smart people knew immediately what was artistically valuable and why, and we have no doubt which camp we would have been in. But no one can know how he or she would have reacted then to what we take for granted now, and in some ways the most intelligent reaction for someone of Sloan's background and generation may have been Sloan's own: curiosity, confusion, some skepticism, a vague unease and excitement, a desire to see more and learn more.

What struck Sloan as interesting (and Henri as worrisome) was that much progress had already been made in Europe toward putting to rest the academic prescriptions that Americans were still debating. Yet if the dead hand of the plaster-cast copiers was nowhere in evidence in the

Armory Show, neither to any significant degree was the concern for
"street life" or "real life" that Henri had insisted on, except of course in
the entries of Henri and his circle. Sloan was hardly so provincial or so
nervous as not to appreciate that his *Sunday, Women Drying Their Hair*
came from a different aesthetic universe than van Gogh's *Mountains at
Saint-Rémy* or Matisse's *Blue Nude,* one that might not be so easily justified in the days ahead. Similarly, as a believer in the Maratta palette and
color system, Sloan had been paying scrupulous attention to the issue of
color for some time already, but here, too, some of the fierce pigments
and unexpected combinations of color on display came as a shock to him.
The eighteen van Goghs and thirteen Gauguins especially captured his
imagination. Theirs was risk-taking on a grand scale, something that just
wasn't to be seen on this side of the Atlantic. To some extent, William
Glackens hit the nail on the head (or rather, Guy Pène du Bois did:
Glackens's remarks appeared in an interview "ghost-scripted" by Pène du
Bois the month the show opened) when he commented that Americans
were afraid of seeming ridiculous, and that one result of that fear was a
lack of audacity or bravery in their art. With this insight, Sloan had cause
to nod in vigorous agreement. About the structural "breakthroughs" he
saw in the exhibition, though—a Cubist fracturing of forms, a diminish-
ment of line—he was less comfortable. As Maurice Prendergast put it,
there was an awful lot of " 'Oh-my-God!' art" on view, and provocation
for its own sake seemed a questionable goal.

Perhaps even more striking for John Sloan than the extravaganza's
revelation of Post-Impressionist color was the jarring indifference of many
of the Armory Show artists to their subject matter. The human comedy,
the urban anecdote, personal psychology, emotional or literary meaning of
any kind—all of these seemed to play no more than a minute role in the
pictures that captured the serious attention of the public, the critics, the
dealers, and other artists. The Europeans painted *everything* with equal
relish; what counted for them was originality of expression. Moreover, it
was exclusively in the novel style and structure of their works that these
artists conveyed what they had to say about life—in contrast to Henri's
notion that theme and style must together break with academic traditions, a principle that Henri himself actually followed more closely in his
teaching than in the creation of his own art. At this moment, Sloan later
wrote, he paradoxically began to reflect on his distaste for religious and
"primitive" art. Perhaps it was no less misguided to turn away from a

"Virgin and Child" or a tribal mask because of its subject matter than it was to reject a van Gogh still-life because one wasn't really interested in pictures of apples. That sort of response began to seem silly if one accepted that formalist concerns were what sophisticated men and women should be attending to when they appreciated art. As the thirteen hundred art works made their way to Chicago and Boston (where they met with a decidedly less enthusiastic response) and finally back to their owners, Sloan knew that he had a great deal to contemplate. He also recognized that Henri, still smarting from the tone of an event that had made him look marginal, was not going to be a useful guide in this area.

Artists weren't the only ones stimulated or challenged by their shock-therapy encounter with European Modernism. Sharp dealers in New York soon noted the winds of change in the marketplace, and within a few months even the older establishments, like N. E. Montross's gallery, were exhibiting artists they would have scorned a year or two earlier. Writers, some of them, began to take heed of the new aesthetic climate, and collectors—John Quinn especially—sensed that there were great collections to be made by enterprising connoisseurs once the old blinders had been discarded. After 1913 there was no more talk of Quinn's buying a Sloan oil; his interests lay elsewhere. Luckily for Sloan, one major collector who was already knowledgeable about modern French art came to New York from Philadelphia and decided not to put his money into the new work. In typically irascible fashion, Albert C. Barnes announced that the Renoirs and Cézannes he owned were better than any in the Armory Show, and he went his own way for the time being, aided by his friend and art adviser William Glackens. By the end of the year he did, however, purchase a John Sloan to go with his Lawsons and Prendergasts. Counting the two Storz portraits and a Philadelphia friend's 1901 purchase, for fifty dollars, of a picture of a woman at a shooting gallery, this was Sloan's fourth sale. (Most of the literature on Sloan for some reason records it as his first, and certainly Sloan himself preferred that notion as he got older.) *Nude, Green Scarf* depicts a woman with her arms behind her head and her hips and legs turned toward the viewer, a piece of green drapery held between her knees and cascading onto the floor—a typical example of the kind of paint-soaked nudes Sloan was working on at the time.

Sloan and Glackens's classmate from their Central High days in the 1880s had done astonishingly well for himself in the intervening years. As the inventor of argyrol, a silver compound, he was a pharmaceutical tycoon of vast wealth and an ego to match. His invitation for John and Dolly Sloan to spend a weekend at his estate in Pennsylvania brought together a most unlikely foursome. Albert Barnes had a serious intellectual respect for art and artists that was rare among collectors of his day, but he also liked to belittle Mrs. Barnes in front of other people and was used to dominating the conversation. He had scant interest in left-wing politics, artists who didn't appreciate his stature as a collector, or women with opinions of their own. The Sloans' visit was not repeated. However, in what must have been fair compensation for any social tensions, Sloan had a chance that weekend to enjoy some remarkable art works that few people in America had yet seen, including Cézanne's *Toward Mont Sainte-Victoire,* van Gogh's *Joseph-Etienne Roulin,* Picasso's *Woman with a Cigarette,* and the excellent Daumiers, Renoirs, Bonnards, and Gauguins that Barnes had recently and proudly acquired. Small wonder that the man felt he had nothing to learn from the Armory Show.

The events of 1913 affected Sloan's approach to painting in a gradual, thoughtful way. In later years some artists would speak of their visits to the Lexington Avenue Armory with a road-to-Damascus fervor, whether real or retroactively imagined. But there was too much to assimilate, Sloan felt, to go off half-cocked on a binge of wild, possibly futile experimentation. Little by little, though, his paintings began to reflect that Modernist sense of being as much *about painting* as they were about their ostensible subject.

Part of this was due to Sloan himself. He was tired of the urban themes he was now identified with; ten years of painting the city and its inhabitants in that context was enough for him. The old Tenderloin was on its way out, but Sloan felt no need to mourn its loss. He wasn't happy with the number of automobiles taking over the city streets and was glad to be nestled in the sanctuary of Greenwich Village after the noise of Chelsea. And there was something liberating, too, though he might not have expressed it at the time, in being released from Henri's dicta. There had turned out to be a place for "art for art's sake" in the scheme of things after all, only it was Cézanne and the Post-Impressionists who were staking that claim now, not Whistler and Wilde. Two post–Armory Show views from his studio window, for instance—one looking down Jones Street toward Sheridan Square in the rain, the other capturing a

rainbow over the Metropolitan Tower on Madison Square to the north—
are sketchier and more impressionistic than most of Sloan's other city
pictures. Storytelling plays no part in their appeal. They have nothing to
say about class, women, change, friendship, or modern life. They are
made by someone who simply loves to play with shapes and color, to
move a brush across canvas to create effects of atmosphere and a sense of
space. Sloan's portraits of the Irish Socialist Patrick Quinlan (1913), the
young painter Stuart Davis (1913), and the novelist Floyd Dell (1914)
have broader, looser brushwork than many of his earlier figures, and in
the case of Dell's likeness, the palette finally gives a hint of how important Sloan's recent immersion in van Gogh's and Gauguin's color had
been. The somber colors of the Omaha burghers and the netherworld of
McSorley's Bar are gone for good. Sloan was ready to venture further afield,
to loosen a few of the old restraints—ready to have fun with his painting
in a way he had never done before.

All of this was in marked contrast to the bread-and-butter work that
paid the bills. That year Scribners had asked Sloan to do twenty-four
gouache drawings for six volumes it was bringing out by the French
mystery writer Emile Gaboriau. Naturally, the publisher wanted the illustrations for *The Count's Millions, Caught in the Net,* and the other novels
to conform to the realistic tradition of the genre, and Sloan complied for a
handsome $120 a book, or a total of $720 for the twenty-four drawings.
In the world of illustration, the Armory Show hadn't happened, and the
nineties were only yesterday. In that sense, Sloan was protected for the
moment. What with *Harper's Weekly,* the Storz portraits, Charles Scribner,
and the Barnes sale, the Sloans had had a good year financially—they had
also moved from Perry Street to a better building in the Village, at 240
West Fourth Street—and could see themselves, finally, on their way to
becoming part of the great American middle class.

But even if everything had worked out in smooth enough fashion
(which it did not), the Sloans would have been the last people to identify
with the urge toward "conspicuous consumption" or serious upward mo-
bility. They were both taken with Debs's idea of rising with the working
class as conditions changed for everybody, rather than rising *above* the
working class. Any movement in that direction, any strike or labor action, elicited their sympathy and interest. The biggest one in the year
after the Lawrence strike involved the fifty thousand textile workers of
Paterson, New Jersey. In general, northern New Jersey was seen as fertile

territory for political action. The IWW had already led a small strike in Paterson in 1907, the town had nearly elected a Socialist mayor in 1912 (nearby Haledon had succeeded in doing so), and almost half of its adult population was employed in the deplorable textile mills. An increase in workload, demanding that each worker supervise several looms at the same time, was followed by the firing of four men who were agitating for an eight-hour day; there was a walkout and then a shutdown of the whole system. A new, reactionary police commissioner illegally arrested Bill Haywood, Elizabeth Gurley Flynn, and Carlo Tresca as soon as they arrived in town, but the strike caught on nonetheless. The Sloans followed the news from New Jersey, so inadequately covered in the mainstream newspapers, through their radical contacts.

This particular strike inspired more than the usual mode of response from interested New Yorkers. John Reed, at this point in his adventurous life a journalist for the *American,* the *Metropolitan,* and the *Masses,* along with Mabel Dodge, an Armory Show sponsor and mistress of one of the city's few salons, conceived an idea for a public display of support that would also provide a chance to raise funds for the strikers in a flamboyantly didactic manner. Pageants, usually dealing with inspiring civic or religious themes, had been a popular feature of American life for the last three decades. Why not stage a pageant, Dodge suggested, that would dramatize what was happening across the Hudson River, and do it not with actors and actresses, but with the strikers themselves enacting their own stories? The idea caught fire, and in May Bill Haywood (now out of jail) presented John Reed to the strikers, billing him as the man who would direct them in the enormous undertaking that was to be held at Madison Square Garden three weeks later. Reed solicited the strikers' views on which scenes of their drama they wanted to re-create. As first blocked out, the Paterson Strike Pageant was to involve two hundred strikers who would walk the twenty-three miles to New York City, but by the week of the performance that number had grown to almost fifteen hundred, a crowd that would tax even the robust management skills of Reed and Haywood. As rehearsal time was limited and the expense of Madison Square Garden (at a rental fee of a thousand dollars a night) restricted the use of the theater to the night of the performance only, it was a miracle that Reed was able to pull the whole thing off. Several times the project was almost abandoned as being too unwieldy, but having once raised the hopes of the workers, everyone involved understood that the stakes were too high for them to back out. Reed was ably assisted by a range of Village friends, among them Rose Pastor Stokes, Hutchins Hapgood, Alexander Berkman, William English Walling, and John Sloan, who threw himself into the painting of the scenery, including a two-hundred-foot backdrop of a mill. Mabel Dodge, the most determined romantic of the group, was an equally vital source of logistical and financial support.

Sloan had ceased writing in his diary by mid-1913—his days were too full now, and the diary's original purpose vis-à-vis Dolly had been achieved—so we have maddeningly little documentation concerning his thoughts and feelings during this period. Yet it is hard to believe that he can have been anything but thrilled with the kinds of bold projects and committed people he was spending his time with. The night of June 7 saw fifteen thousand spectators gathered at the McKim, Mead, and White amphitheater at Twenty-sixth Street and Madison Avenue (one block west of the site of the Armory Show four months earlier) for an unprecedented experience. The strikers had crowded onto ferries from Hoboken to Manhattan, then marched the length of Christopher Street and up Fifth Avenue to Madison Square singing the "Marseillaise" and the "Internationale." At Madison Square Garden, beneath Augustus Saint-Gaudens's incongruously delicate *Diana* and amid a sea of red banners, they recreated their walkout from the mills, their rallies and their picketing, the relocation of their children, the arrest of the protesters, and the death of a bystander (whose family was in box seats in the audience) at the hands of the police. The audience was invited to participate in the singing, and then, in what was perhaps the most stunning stage image of this visually exhausting evening, a coffin was carried down the aisles to the stage, followed by a thousand strikers carrying red carnations that they placed on the casket in turn. Haywood, Flynn, and Tresca delivered the same speeches they had made at the dead man's funeral a few weeks earlier, appealing for support even if it meant, as Carlo Tresca cried out in Italian, "sangue per sangue"—blood for blood.

The ultimate benefits of the pageant were much debated. Some labor leaders thought it did the people of Paterson little good and dissipated energies and funds that might better have gone to the strike itself, while of course the organs of "establishment" opinion were dismayed at the whole spectacle of radicalism in action. The *New York Times* was particularly sanctimonious: "Under the direction of a destructive organization opposed in spirit and antagonistic in action to all the forces which have upbuilded [*sic*] this republic, a series of pictures in action were shown with the design of stimulating mad passion against law and order and promulgating a gospel of discontent." In that last phrase, at least, the *Times* was right. With their anger and exhilaration, the movers and shakers behind the Paterson Strike Pageant (like Reed, Dodge, Sloan, et al.) were hoping to awaken the curious and the indifferent to America's social ills.

Protest and gaiety continued to be the watchwords at *The Masses,* too. Throughout 1913 new contributors had been rounded up, artists who were ready to have their work printed for free and to join in the fun at the meetings, and Sloan was understandably happy with the talent he had helped bring to the magazine. Stuart Davis, George Bellows, Henry Glintenkamp, Glenn Coleman, Maurice Becker, Boardman Robinson, Kenneth Russell Chamberlain, Henri, and Sloan himself: the roster was impressive and set a high standard for Eastman to compete with in trying to find literary contributors of equivalent bite. (Although *The Masses* published poems by Amy Lowell and Carl Sandburg and a few of Sherwood Anderson's best stories from what was to become *Winesburg, Ohio,* it would be wrong to say that literary merit was ever its claim to fame.) The arrival of the Chicago writer Floyd Dell in New York at the end of the year was a boon, as he threw himself into the cause of the magazine's success as energetically as anyone ever did. As Malcolm Cowley noted in *Exile's Return,* as soon as *The Masses* moved its headquarters from the Wall Street area to 91 Greenwich Avenue in midyear, it became the intellectual center of the Village, a mecca for an assortment of smart, feisty, contentious men and women.

A healthy lack of respect for the individuals and institutions most Americans held sacred had pushed *The Masses* into progressively more daring positions, often with Max Eastman and Art Young at the forefront. The magazine's attacks on the Associated Press in the months before the war were among its most audacious and most useful acts, leading to the first of many rounds of litigation. An editorial in the July issue that called the AP to task for its failure to report on a coal miners' strike in West Virginia—where the news service's own correspondent had served on the military tribunal that had enforced martial law in the county during the strike—alerted the country to an appalling conflict of interest. Young's cartoon in that same issue, entitled *Poisoned at the Source,* was wickedly insightful in its depiction of an AP reporter polluting a reservoir that represented "The News" in America with his vials of "suppressed facts," "lies," and "slander." The AP's desire to put *The Masses* in its place led to a prolonged court battle in which people of the stature of Lincoln Steffens and Charlotte Perkins Gilman spoke up on behalf of Eastman and Young. Only after the AP management began to fear for its credibility were all charges dropped. At a time when too many people approached what they read in the major newspapers with little or no skepticism, it was a laudable decision for a small magazine, generally sneered at by the mainstream press, to play David to the wire-service Goliath. But that was its business, its mission, everyone on the board felt—to call the powers-that-be to account.

Yet there were some growing concerns on Sloan's part, a few nagging doubts. First there was the matter of the captions. Sloan liked the idea of running pictures, even on the cover, that didn't tie in to a specific article or make a concrete point. He liked the odd freedom that this policy (or nonpolicy) implied, the sense it gave that the magazine's images had a validity equal to or separate from that of its words. Not everyone was so tickled by this unconventional journalistic touch, however. Sometimes the drive to find a suitable caption or meaningfulness to a drawing worked out just fine, as with Stuart Davis's eye-catching cover for the July 1913 issue, a picture of two down-and-out working-class women from Hoboken. No one quite knew what to make of this grubby pair: wearing their best hats, such as they were, they were without context. There was no factory in the background, no tenement, no Tenderloin. Hence, no message. Sloan's suggestion of a fragment of dialogue—"Gee, Mag, Think of Us Bein' on a Magazine Cover!"—solved the problem and ended the debate; Davis's women became a caustic response to the sickeningly pretty cover girls of Howard Chandler Christy and James Montgomery Flagg. But not every discussion was so amicably resolved, and Sloan began to suspect that an annoying "party line" element was creeping into the proceedings. Did every drawing have to have a message or reiterate a Socialist principle? For that matter, did every drawing have to have a caption? If so, the art editor of *The Masses* had other ideas.

Then there was the matter of money. Max Eastman's very success at keeping the magazine afloat was a double-edged sword for those who thought like Sloan: it allowed their journal to thrive as an instrument of change, but it was also a measure of the left's cringing dependency on fashionable society, on the "limousine liberals" of the day. Dolly had bowed out as business manager after a few months, but everyone knew that Eastman was getting money from wealthy Manhattan sympathizers such as Amos Pinchot, E. W. Scripps, and Mrs. O. H. P. Belmont. (Where they supposed Eastman might raise the several hundred dollars needed each month to bring out the magazine, if not from rich patrons, isn't clear. No one complained when Mabel Dodge wrote out a big check to keep the Paterson Strike Pageant going, but the whole problem of a left-wing cause's needing capitalist funding to do its job of attacking capitalism was just beginning to be perceived as a thorny issue in the 1910s.) Sloan, ever sensitive to questions of money and independence, continually questioned the magazine's overhead and its reliance on its millionaire sponsors. But this was hardly fair to Eastman: the funds that came from the magazine's bookshop, from subscribers, from a few Village advertisers, and from Eastman's own lectures never covered the *Masses'* expenses.

John Butler Yeats was a man of unusual theories and a poet's view of the world. One of his theories, discussed in his correspondence with John Quinn, concerned the value of weakness and, in a world that worshiped strength, the transcendent beauty of need and vulnerability. He explained it to Quinn taking marriage as an example:

> When people marry it is not as the vulgar vainly imagine, that they may bring strength into union with strength. Marriage of that sort is not marriage at all, no tenderness on either side. *Marriage means that two people are bringing into the common stock all their weaknesses,* and there are two comparisons possible. Marriage is sometimes like two drunken men seeing each other home. Neither can reproach the other or refuse sympathy or help. The other comparison is this: Marriage is like two mortal enemies (the sexes are enemies) meeting on the scaffold and reconciled by the imminence of the great enemy of both. [Italics added]

It is tempting to glimpse in Yeats's analogies, expressed in a letter written in the fall of 1912, some reflection of his intimate knowledge of the Sloans' union. By any ordinary standard, the relationship between

John and Dolly Sloan was an emotional disaster on both sides—a talented artist saddled with an alcoholic wife of questionable fidelity, a woman bound to a man whose profession consumed most of his energy and who seemed incapable of helping her to end her several dependencies—and certainly that was how many people saw it, as they puzzled over why Sloan stayed with his wife and what happiness these two people could possibly know together.

Yeats alone saw things in a different light. Even in the spring of 1914, when Dolly was experiencing yet another period of breakdown and hard drinking and Sloan was fast running out of patience, Yeats continued to believe that this relationship had a special beauty to it, that it was worth preserving. Thirty years later, as Sloan pondered his friend's tender feelings toward Dolly and his intense interest in their marriage, he wondered if the desire to see them through their troubles—to make sure that they stayed together—hadn't been one of the key reasons Yeats had stayed on in New York long after it would have been prudent for him to return to Dublin.

This is not to suggest that Yeats thought of Dolly's problems as a desirable attribute or felt her indiscretions should be overlooked. At times he sternly chided her for her want of control, insisting that if she only would try a little harder she could prevent the drinking and blackouts and "scenes" that were again tormenting her, her husband, and her friends. Yet at other moments Yeats was ready to blame Sloan and his radical politics for Dolly's worsening condition. The strain of keeping her husband from alienating everyone he knew, Yeats felt, was hard on Dolly. "But for her, he'd talk nothing else," Yeats wrote in exasperation to his daughter. "His [verbal and emotional] violence is never in the same direction two days running."

Some visitors to Petipas couldn't imagine what Yeats saw in Dolly. Emma Bellows thought her a scandal. To the painter Leon Kroll she was a "little frump, a dreadful woman." Kroll particularly disliked her for her fund-raising mania, which left him feeling that he was being hit up for money for some left-wing cause or other every time he was in her company. Quinn, himself not a visitor at Petipas (the boardinghouse dining room was quite beneath his dignity, Yeats or no Yeats), also turned a deaf ear to any compliments expended on Dolly Sloan and, indeed, thought less of John Sloan for staying with her. "The horrible Mrs. Sloan," as he called her, was in his estimate a "pest" whose constant scurrying about on behalf

of Yeats's lecture-hall ambitions only prolonged the old man's stay in
America. To William Butler Yeats, no doubt a willing ear after the Algonquin fiasco, Quinn could be unmerciful in his comments, almost in inverse
proportion to John Butler Yeats's desire to emphasize Dolly's kindness, her
warmth and charm. (In one of Quinn's letters to the poet, she is a "damned
little sluttish nuisance." In another, written after Yeats senior's death, he
asserts that "Mrs. Sloan has a head like a foetus. When she walks, she
goose-steps, that is, she sticks up her ugly feet, as all dwarfs do. She is an
intriguing little cat.") Mercifully, John Quinn kept his more acid views
from John Butler Yeats, whose belief in the power of pain and vulnerability to call forth deeper emotions in others meant little to his friend, a
powerful lawyer enamored of toughness, discretion, and success.

To be fair, though, Dolly could be a horror to deal with in her worst
moments—though those were not moments that Kroll or Quinn would
have been privy to. That the middle of 1914 brought some sort of crisis
for the Sloans is indicated by the fact that Marianna came to stay with
Dolly when Sloan was out of town. Having decided that they could finally
afford a summer vacation out of the city, Sloan went on ahead of his wife
to see to the rental of a cottage in the little town of Gloucester, Massachusetts. The plan seemed a good one on two counts: Sloan would have a new
subject to paint and more relaxing conditions under which to work, and
Dolly would benefit from a break from the city. Marianna, a most unlikely marriage counselor, was surprisingly supportive toward her sister-
in-law, though she probably didn't know much, if anything, about the
specific difficulties that beset her brother's marriage. Nonetheless, she
could appreciate that any withdrawal of affection was devastating for
Dolly: "If only he will let his feelings show," she wrote to her in August,
"I know you will always be happy." Another sign of Dolly's quirkiness in
these ominous weeks was her application to John Quinn, of all people, for
a loan of twenty dollars. Once before she had borrowed money from him,
when her sister in Philadelphia was in need (or so she had said); this time,
apparently, no reason was given. Quinn advanced her the money but sent
her a blistering letter about the impropriety of asking a man for money
behind one's husband's back. His scorn was evident in every word he
wrote, but on these occasions Dolly was past caring about either the
witnesses to or the extent of her humiliation.

The Gloucester idea had been simmering in Sloan's mind for a while.

Charles and Alice Winter of the *Masses* staff knew of their friend's interest in spending the summer in a less urban setting and, having visited there twice before, recommended the fishing village on Cape Ann, just north of Boston, as ideal for an artist's purposes. The delights of the hometown of Fitz Hugh Lane, the great nineteenth-century Luminist, had been rediscovered by Winslow Homer and William Morris Hunt in the 1870s, and Impressionists like Childe Hassam and John Twachtman and even Maurice Prendergast had also spent contented time there. Rents were cheap, the town was picturesque, and the summer light was magnificent. Sloan talked to another painter he had met through Henri, Randall Davey, who agreed with him that they could advertise for students and perhaps even earn enough to cover their expenses. Many artists were making a lucrative experience of the summer trade; the docks of Provincetown on Cape Cod were fairly littered with the students of Charles W. Hawthorne and other clever teachers, Sloan noted. Furthermore, Sloan's own reputation as a good instructor was growing. Over the last year in New York, he had taken on several pupils who wanted to learn etching and had taught a few classes at the Art Students League on West Fifty-seventh Street. He was confident of his ability to deal with the simultaneous demands of a large class on the beach (this despite the fact that he was strictly a studio man himself) and of his own work.

But Sloan was never lucky with advertisements, to put it mildly. An ad in *The Masses* offering any two of his City Life etchings at the rock-bottom bargain price of two dollars each along with a one-dollar yearly subscription to the magazine had produced only two takers, and the ad for pupils to go to Massachusetts turned up just one pleasant young woman. (For twenty dollars a month, the fortunate Beulah Stevenson was taught for an entire day each week of the summer in Gloucester by Sloan and another day by Davey—a financial loss for the two teachers, who had hoped to make some money on the venture, but a wondrous amount of professional attention for Miss Stevenson.) Succeeding summers were a little less embarrassing, with five students in 1915 and three in 1916.

To save on expenses, Sloan took a lease on a small house—"the red cottage," as everyone referred to it—on East Main Street, just down the road from the Rocky Neck art colony. He then invited the Winters, Randall and Florence Davey, and the painter Agnes Richmond and her husband to join them. With the exception of Charles Winter's incessant use of his Victrola to send the arias of Verdi and Puccini echoing through the house—a never-ending stream of "Italian wife beaters," in Sloan's estimation—the group had sufficiently compatible habits to promise an amiable and productive summer. The setting was cozy. The two-story house had an open porch and a pleasant, sloping backyard surrounded by trees and thick lilac bushes, with a view of the water, and the trolley that stopped next door could have everyone downtown in five minutes. Dolly got along well with Florence Davey, and the professional interests of the Winters, Davey, and Sloan coincided perfectly, even to the extent of their all working with Henri and Bellows in these prewar years on a book, never completed, that was going to refine and codify the intricate benefits of the Maratta System.

The strange ways of these visiting New Yorkers were something for the locals to ponder. "Open house" at the cottage seemed to go on for days. When, in 1915, the Sloans persuaded Stuart and Wyatt Davis to stop by and to bring their mother with them, they also had the artist Paul Cornoyer and the pianist Katherine Groschke staying there, along with the Winters. The Henris would come down from Maine for the day, with Leon Kroll or some other friends in tow, and the whole group would pass the time eating and drinking, gamboling on the beach, and talking shop. Marianna visited for part of one summer, and the Daveys came back a second time. Dolly never cared which guests, or how many of them, decided to stay over. Elizabeth Oakes Colford, a neighborhood child at the time, later recalled that her parents used to marvel at how many people could squeeze into one little cottage. Once in a while there would be a sunset-to-sunrise party, beginning with a clambake and culminating with breakfast on the beach. Three or four daiquiris would last Sloan most of the night, he remembered, or he and Stuart Davis would repair to the nearest tavern to bring back some ale. There was plenty of drinking on those occasions (though it was nothing, Sloan noted, to what went on after Prohibition), and it seems as if Sloan had by this point resigned himself to his fate with Dolly, and was taking what solace he could from his own considerable social tippling.

The best part of being in Gloucester, though—what really mattered for Sloan—had to do with his painting, when friends and wife and career were left behind. In New York, Sloan realized, he had consciously searched for interesting subjects to paint. In Gloucester he was going to take a different approach, get into the "habit of working," paint outdoors

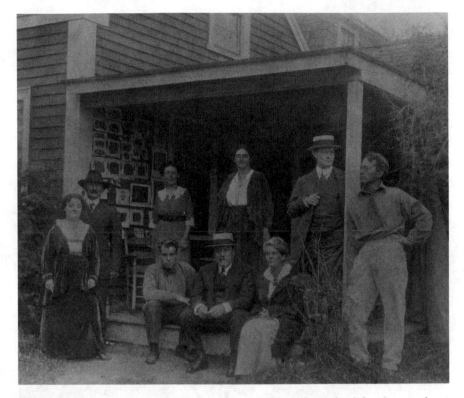

Friends and artists at the Gloucester cottage, 1915: Dolly at far left, Sloan at far right, Stuart Davis seated at left (Delaware Art Museum)

every morning regardless of inspiration, and consider his art in a more abstract, less literary way. To that end, rocks and sand and water were infinitely preferable to people or city buildings.

Intentions didn't always lead to action or fulfillment for Sloan, but in this case his intention propelled him through the most productive ten weeks of his life. During that one summer he completed sixty paintings, a figure that equaled roughly one quarter of his total output since the 1890s. Many of the Gloucester landscapes of 1914, and even a fair number of those from 1915, have an unabashedly experimental, pell-mell, even rollicking air. In his drive to complete an average of one oil a day, in his wish to let color alone do the work of line, in his break from any strict adherence to the palette of nature—in short, in his eagerness to act with the freedom of a Post-Impressionist—Sloan was becoming a young man again. At this juncture, however, he wasn't an uncertain student marking

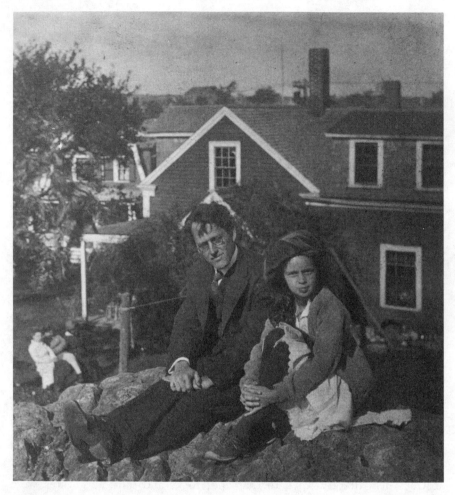

Sloan in the backyard at Gloucester with Sally Stanton, one of the neighborhood children who posed for him (Delaware Art Museum)

time in the halls of the Pennsylvania Academy, nose to the grindstone of the "classical tradition," but an invigorated admirer of van Gogh and the Fauves. He was not the average American that William Glackens had described in his Armory Show interview, afraid to seem ridiculous and accordingly reluctant to take chances. Every day, after forty-five minutes of mixing his palette, Sloan engaged in a gamble. As a result, some of that summer's sixty paintings don't add up to much. For that matter, a number of the almost three hundred landscapes he painted in his five summers on Cape Ann look slapdash rather than deftly or carefully exe-

cuted. But then Sloan wasn't considering exhibition or the reactions of
other people at that point. He was thinking instead about the value of
following his curiosity wherever it might lead him, about modifying
or altering the notions of craft and artistic purpose that he had been
living with for ten or more years. So in some of these on-site landscapes
everything takes on the fluidity of the water and the sky, the two elements of the scene that the artist was evidently enjoying the most. Rocks
don't look rock-hard, trees and hills don't always have a believable
weighted presence, and plausible anatomy has eluded Sloan in the rare
figure he has tried. Acquainted now with the flat, decorative portraits of
Matisse, like *The Red Madras Headdress* in the Armory Show, Sloan was
discovering just how difficult it was to re-create the Frenchman's startling, rhythmic, anti-realistic effects. What seemed simplest in the Modernist repertoire of techniques was sometimes the most complicated to
achieve secondhand. Sally Stanton, the twelve-year-old who posed most
frequently for Sloan when he wanted a figure in his landscape, often has
considerably less reality or presence in the painting than the tree she is
climbing or the grass she sits on.

The paintings that did succeed, which could not have existed without
the failures and false starts, were something quite new and exciting for
Sloan. *Glimpse of Gloucester Trolley* (1914) uses the Maratta triad of red-
purple, yellow-orange, and blue to create a rapturous vista of a kind Sloan
had never imagined attempting before, luring and locking in the eye at
three or four different places. *Garage on the Moors* (1915), *Path through
Rocks and Bushes* (1914), and *Sun Flowers, Rocky Neck* (1914) have that
authentic van Gogh approach to the natural world that Sloan was working toward, with the energy of the brushstrokes themselves and the intensity or unreality of the color conveying a mood, an agitated alertness,
rather than merely documenting an image. The sparkle on the water in
Glare on the Bay (1915) could be borrowed from a Vlaminck. *Stage Fort
Park* (1914) is more Mediterranean than New England shoreline. The
looseness of the forms in *Gloucester Lyric* (1915)—boats, rocks, hills, children—works in a way that earlier sketchy renderings do not, in the
abrupt, paint-jabbing mode of a Raoul Dufy. With *Red Rocks and Quiet
Sea II* (1914), Sloan managed a painting of the horizon line, the ocean, a
few waves, and a diagonal of cliff that could stand with Winslow Homer's
canvases in the great tradition of contemplative American landscape art.
If not exactly original, this is a body of work that nonetheless follows

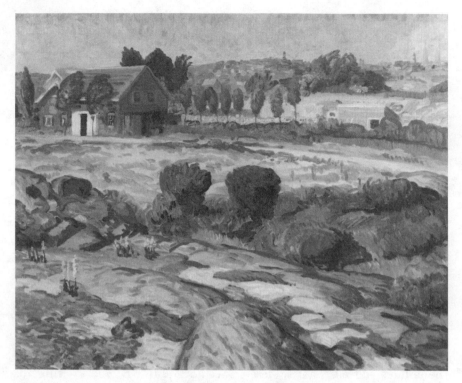

Sloan as landscape artist: Garage on the Moors, *1915* (Kraushaar Galleries)

through on its determination to liberate itself from more restrictive influences of the past.

Not surprisingly, at times Sloan even carried over this effervescence
to straight portraiture. An "Uncle Sam" portrait of 1914, oddly entitled
Old Cone, would with all its heightened colors have allied Sloan more with
the Fauves in the Armory Show than with his American colleagues had he
painted it a year or two earlier. *Miss Hart in Green* (1914) attains just the
degree of abstraction Sloan was aiming for. If *Stein, Profile,* of 1904, lives
as a real portrait of a real woman, *Miss Hart* lives as a study in shades of
green with echoes of pink and pale blue. *A study in shades of green:* that was
not an ambition he had acquired from Henri, Sloan felt. Nor was it one
that friendly critics and supporters expected from him. Gradually Sloan
came to feel that he was seeing some return on an investment of time and
energy that stimulated him but also made him somewhat nervous.

As both Leon Kroll and John Butler Yeats confirmed, Sloan had been
right to forge ahead. The best of the new work was of sound quality, as

well constructed and as fluent as the strongest of his city pictures. In spending time in what he called "one of the odd corners of America," Sloan was actually reinventing himself again: from newspaperman to urban poet to "professional modern artist." In Sloan's terms, that meant being concerned with the aesthetic issues of the time, in this instance *color expression,* and being ready to paint, more regularly now, out of love for the brush and the pigment itself.

The one jarring interruption in this creative idyll in the summer of 1914 was the news of the beginning of hostilities in western Europe. In the first week of August, the Germans marched into Belgium on their drive toward France, and England immediately declared its intention to fight Germany and Austria, developments that had seemed inevitable since the assassination of Franz Ferdinand in Sarajevo in late June, in a climate of nationalist pride and long-term militarization ("The vials of wrath were full," as Churchill phrased it only a few months before the war began). For John Sloan, the truly disappointing and infuriating aspect of the reports coming out of Europe had to do with the capitulation of the Socialist party. In an atmosphere of patriotic hysteria, an extraordinary number of Socialists and their leaders sided with their countries' governments and supported their declarations of war. Like other American Socialists, Sloan had been hoping all along that his counterparts abroad would represent a significant roadblock to the belligerent policies of the Kaiser, Franz Joseph, Lord Asquith, Poincaré, and their overeager generals. If the European Socialists remained steadfast in their refusal to fight and urged workers in their respective homelands to do the same, the major conflagration that everyone feared would be less likely to ignite, or so the theory of the moment went. Furious at this latest turn of events, Sloan was plunged into a black humor; it was 1898 and "avenge the *Maine"* all over again, but with much more serious implications. Looking ahead to the outcome of the conflict, Sloan promptly drew a sketch for the next number of *The Masses,* in which a rotund businessman who has remained safe far from the fighting welcomes home a battered, legless soldier with a cheap medal, a metaphorical pat on the back, and the words, "You've done well. Now what is left of you can go back to work."

For sharp-edged graphic art, the whole of the spring and summer of 1914 had provided Sloan with a bounty of material. The bloodred cover and the centerfold drawing in *The Masses* for April were concerned with police brutality to strikers and the homeless. The drawing in that issue

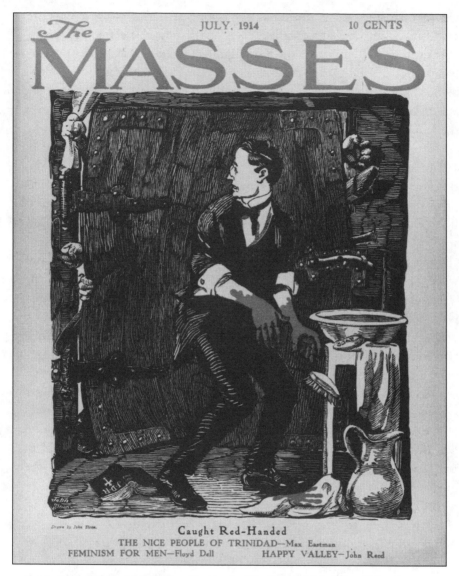

J. D. Rockefeller with blood on his hands: The July 1914 cover of The Masses
(Delaware Art Museum)

took a good swipe at the clergy as well, showing hungry crowds being
turned away from a Catholic church, with a priest looking on approvingly
as the riffraff are beaten and dispersed by the authorities. (The drawing
refers to an actual episode that year, in which the pastor of a Fifth Avenue

church called in the police to evict the homeless men who were huddled in his pews. The leader of this completely nonviolent demonstration, an eighteen-year-old activist, served a year and a half in prison for incitement to riot. The *Masses* staff helped raise funds for his defense.) The cover of the June issue, reproduced in a lurid orange and blue, showed a Ludlow, Colorado, miner firing against the troops that have killed his family in the infamous machine-gun massacre of that spring; the following month, in what was surely Sloan's most dramatic and most effective image as a political artist, the cover of *The Masses* depicted a nervous John D. Rockefeller, owner of the Ludlow mines, attempting to wash the blood from his hands as the door to his hiding place is battered down. At his feet, his personally inscribed Bible, source of moral comfort for all good Episcopalians, lies open near a soiled towel.

However frolicsome the mood at the "red cottage" may have been at the start of the summer, everyone was glad of a break from the Sloans by September. Between Dolly's "benders" and Sloan's obsession with the war (news of which he devoured every day), Randall Davey, for one, needed a respite. Writing to Bellows later, he observed that time spent with the Sloans necessarily involved too much politics, too many moods, too many emotional upheavals.

At this point in his life, one thing was clear to John Sloan: he had painted some of his best work, pictures that he felt might last, and he knew he had even better work in him yet. The Gloucester landscapes were rejuvenating him. Yet the elusive goal of recognition from others was not going to come in any burst of glory. There would be no young man's notoriety, no particularly glamorous showcasing of his talent such as Henri, Bellows, and Kent had known. Instead he might have to be satisfied, he realized, with the slow development of a solid and respectable, if rather undynamic, professional reputation.

Early in 1915 Sloan was the subject of an admiring article in *Arts and Decoration* that praised his newest work, and he was invited to participate that year in no fewer than thirteen important group shows around the country, including exhibitions in Buffalo, St. Louis, Philadelphia, Brooklyn, San Diego, and San Francisco. He won a bronze medal for his etchings at the Panama-Pacific Exposition in San Francisco (in some quarters,

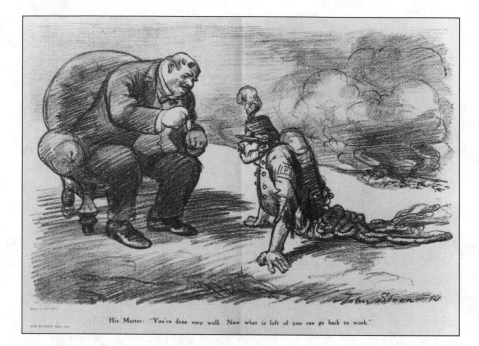

His Master: "You've done very well. Now what is left of you can go back to work."

The Master, *Sloan's illustration for* The Masses *of September 1914 that Eugene Debs kept on his cell wall during his year in prison* (Delaware Art Museum)

Sloan's reputation as an etcher exceeded his renown as a painter) and was included, as he had been for several years past, in the annual Henri-organized MacDowell Club group show, in the good company of Bellows, Davey, Kroll, Edward Hopper, and Andrew Dasburg. Still, no buyers presented themselves for either the oils or the etchings. Sloan had given up sending his paintings to the Academy shows back in 1909, and now his absence there hardly mattered since no one even took those exhibitions seriously anymore. The Armory Show had marked the definitive demise of the Academy's influence in New York, but nothing of equivalent prestige had emerged since then, no similar passageway to success. Taking matters into his own hands that spring, Sloan culled names from the latest *Who's Who* and prepared a mailing promoting sets of the City Life etchings for thirty-five dollars each. Assuming that the art world already knew about his work in that medium, he addressed his offer not only to museum curators but to a range of prominent people in other fields—writers, journalists, editors, and academics—confident that he was acting on a clever, almost foolproof idea. To his and Dolly's horror, in response to his sixteen hundred brochures, Sloan received checks from *two* interested parties. At that mortifying moment it must have seemed as if his efforts to secure the audience his work deserved were doomed to failure.

There was one promising possibility from an unlikely corner of the Village, but no one knew yet how aggressive or how fruitful that patronage was to be. Since 1907 the sculptor Gertrude Vanderbilt Whitney had been holding informal exhibitions in her studio just north of Washington Square for artists she liked, and in 1914 she took over an adjoining house at 8 West Eighth Street and converted it into a gallery. Even before she involved herself in the tricky business of exhibiting and thereby sponsoring certain artists, Mrs. Whitney had achieved a well-deserved reputation as more than just another rich dilettante. She had been the big buyer at the Macbeth Gallery show in 1908, she had contributed money for the festive Armory Show decorations, and with her generous stipends and gifts she had enabled artists as different as the Synchromist Morgan Russell and the sculptor Jo Davidson to live and study abroad. Assisted in her many projects by an imaginative, efficient, tough-minded woman in her late thirties named Juliana Force, Mrs. Whitney appeared in 1915 to be ready to move as a patron at an even more ambitious pace. Although she had yet to give any major artist a one-man exhibition, her group shows at the Whitney Studio, whether thematic or otherwise, were designed to raise funds both for good causes such as war relief and for the artists exhibited. Sloan was beginning to be recognized as a "name" in the art world when Juliana Force asked him to serve as one of Mrs. Whitney's judges for an invitational show that year on the theme "The Immigrant in America." The exhibition attracted a good deal of attention. Former President Roosevelt was one of the visitors to the show who found several works to praise and much to shake his head over, but then he admitted that in art he had (as he put it) the taste of a bull moose.

For a few months during this period Sloan was able to bask in an entirely different kind of reverence as one of his models —presumably the first but definitely not the last to do so—manifested an overpowering crush on him. Jennie Doyle began posing in late 1914 and continued into the following year. She was eighteen when they met, possibly at a Socialist party meeting, and Sloan forty-three. A working-class girl who lived with her sister and abusive brother-in-law, Jennie was almost hysterically interested in socialism and literature, thought of Zola as her literary god, and loved to hear Sloan sound off on the issues of the day. Alternately attracted to the man who was painting her and eager to hold him as a captive listener to her own thoughts and ramblings, almost forcing him into the role of her mentor, she eventually insisted on posing for free. Sloan in turn made use of Jennie not as a nude model, but for her animated face and her bright-red hair.

In one of her many long-winded letters to him, in which she poured out her heart's desire to make a name for herself and write a Gorky-style novel "that would electrify the world," Jennie called Sloan the "most disturbing and painful influence ever to come into my life." In another letter, she mentioned having to creep up the back stairs for a session at the Sloans' new apartment on Washington Place, suggesting that Dolly's ferocious jealousy was once again an issue (Dolly had a good instinct for spotting the women who would develop crushes on her husband). Yet it is not likely that Sloan was having an affair with his impetuous though not especially attractive model; that would come later, in a different phase of his life. At the time, the attentions of Jennie Doyle, a verbose and hyper-energetic young woman, were flattering—he did keep her letters, after all —but smothering. She was fundamentally a type he dreaded, well meaning but manipulative and controlling in her way. His own need for respect and attention would only be satisfied, Sloan knew, when he ceased to be the most prominent unsold artist of his generation.

1916: Opened Doors

"If I am useful as a teacher, it is because I have dug into my own work. Teaching lashes me into a state of consciousness; I find myself trying to prove in my work some of the things I dig out of my subconscious to pass on to others."

—JOHN SLOAN

In the space of eight months in 1916, John Sloan experienced three milestones in his professional life. He enjoyed his first one-man show, courtesy of Gertrude Vanderbilt Whitney and Juliana Force. He was taken on by a gallery—always a momentous day in any painter's career—and began a relationship with the Kraushaar family that would last until his death. And in a third development that was in some ways as significant as the other two, Sloan became a full-time teacher.

The path to his first exhibition, a long-overdue event in the life of a forty-five-year-old man of his experience, was a matter of both serendipity and nerve. The serendipitous part had to do with a mismailed invitation: Gertrude Whitney had decided on a show of modern masters, several American and several European, to begin the new year at the Whitney Studio. When the letters announcing her plan and extending an offer to exhibit were sent out in the fall, Sloan's went to his old West Fourth Street address, where it apparently sat, undelivered and unreturned, for some time. Sloan learned of the exhibition only after it was too late for him to participate in it. Perhaps he knew that Mrs. Whitney and Mrs. Force would be apt to feel particularly bad about the mishap: Sloan needed all the exposure he could get, and these two good women knew it. Or perhaps he felt particularly aggrieved by his bad luck. In any case, Sloan was now ready to push for himself, and he wrote to Mrs. Whitney to ask if she would consider giving him a one-man show (something he knew full well she might be reluctant to do). "The dealers in the city," he confided in frustration, "are not inclined to show more than one or two of my pictures at any one time—most of them not at all—and I feel that a collection shown together would be, at least, an artistic success and might attract considerable public notice." Mrs. Whitney evidently agreed and, giving Sloan's courage its due, changed her plan to exhibit her own work in the next slot at the Studio and told Sloan to prepare for a one-man exhibition that would run from January 26 through February 6.

In a marvelous coincidence, Sloan heard at the same time from John Weichsel that the People's Art Guild was about to offer him a one-man show that would begin at approximately the same time and end in early April. The quixotic Weichsel was the founder and director of this short-lived organization whose aim it was to bring art to the general public without the obstacles of dealer avarice and the "gallery aura," and in Sloan he knew he had an excellent artist for his purposes. From having felt left out in the cold for much of the past year, Sloan was thus suddenly transported to center stage—for a moment, anyway. It was, to be sure, a strange sensation for him to have to tell Weichsel that he would need to put off for a few days the opening of the second exhibition, which was to be held at the Hudson Guild, at 436 West Twenty-seventh Street, so that the two would not overlap. He wanted *Three A.M., Carmine Theater,* the picture of Isadora dancing, and *Gloucester Lyric* to be in both shows. At last, he and Dolly and Henri and Yeats and Davey rejoiced, a wide, eager audience would have a chance to see the scope of John Sloan's art, from the first New York pictures and etchings to the latest, most ambitious seascapes.

Of the eighty-three works Sloan selected for the walls at 8 West Eighth Street, twenty-one were paintings and the rest etchings, lithographs, monotypes, and sketches. Already trying to break the mold he had been cast in, Sloan made sure that no more than a third of those twenty-one oils were the urban works he was well known for. The calculated emphasis was on what he felt was his new strength, the radiant color of his summer portraits and paintings of the beaches and byways of Cape Ann. At the Hudson Guild, though, there was room for more of everything (the final count was fifty paintings and 150 graphic works), and *The Haymarket* and *Sixth Avenue and Thirtieth Street* shared space with the more palatable images of Sally Stanton, Rocky Neck, and Cape Ann's willow boughs and fog-covered dunes.

Most of the press notices about the two exhibitions were brief and complimentary. However, Henry McBride of the *Sun,* who was well on his way toward establishing himself as the most prominent of the new post–Armory Show critics, raised a troubling issue at the time of the Whitney Studio opening. While acknowledging that Sloan's painting showed "animation" and that "here and there" he was good at still-life (indeed, the whole review, in the vintage McBride style of High Drollery, strains to say nice things), McBride insisted on pegging—and, in a backhanded way, praising—Sloan as a satirist. As a "pure" painter, the *Sun* critic implied, Sloan didn't really measure up, but as a creator of dynamic urban satire, he was quite the American Hogarth. Even *Three A.M.,* about as satirical a picture as a Gloucester landscape, was perceived in that restrictive light: "Just what the moral lesson is I am not sure," McBride wrote, "but of course there must be one else it wouldn't be satire." It was frankly inconceivable to McBride that an artist would paint these frowzy women without having a clever "angle" on them, an ironic perspective. The noteworthy fact here is that Sloan was being patronized not by an ally of the Academy, such as Royal Cortissoz of the *Tribune,* but by an ally of the Modernists—McBride was right at the starting-gate with Cézanne, Brancusi, and Marin—who wanted to be kind and to find a way to bring him within the new, emerging critical pale. For McBride, in the end, if Sloan was not to be judged a satirist, then he was no better than any of the old-hat realists whose day (McBride and his cohorts kept insisting) had passed. This review in the *New York Sun* marked a shift, one that may not have been fully obvious at the time, in Sloan's relations with the art press and the art world. The Old Guard was no longer the problem, or the *whole* problem; it was the Young Turks, and their sophisticated forty-ish friends, whom he needed to worry about.

W. G. Bowdoin in the *Evening World* picked up on McBride's allusion to Hogarth and used it against Sloan when he covered the show at the Hudson Guild. "Without acquiescing in or combating [this] sobriquet, it may be said that [Sloan] seizes upon homely themes and exploits them broadly and modernistically . . . without regard to aestheticism." *Hanging Out Her Wash* was "exceedingly commonplace," Bowdoin wrote, lacking as it did the "redeeming quality of a careful finish." Similarly, he found *Election Night* and *Wake of the Ferry* plebeian in theme, and a good many of the others poorly executed. His sad, prissy conclusion held that "It is questionable if Mr. Sloan has the subtlety and the versatility of Hogarth."

Interestingly, this review hurt Sloan in a way that McBride's more insidious cut hadn't—so much so that he was moved to write to the *World*'s critic and question the tone of his notice, especially the pointless comparison to Hogarth. A reviewer's need for pigeonholes was something Sloan would never come to terms with, and it was a problem that would bedevil him all his life. But Bowdoin's desire for a smooth finish and elevated themes was, in the long run, going to mean less than the "Hogarthian" slotting inaugurated by the 1916 shows.

Criticism aside, the experience of seeing his works en masse and savoring the admiration of friends and strangers was every bit as gratifying as Sloan had thought it would be. When he wrote to Mrs. Whitney to express his appreciation for the opportunity she had so graciously provided, he gave her the happy news—everyone's hope, no doubt—that a dealer who had seen the two shows had offered to take him on as one of his gallery regulars, with the promise of an exhibition the following year. That the dealer was the eminent Charles Kraushaar, one of the most respected men in the business, on a par with Macbeth and Knoedler, seemed almost too good to be true. As a special thank-you to Juliana Force, whom Sloan rightly took to be as vital an ally as Mrs. Whitney herself, Sloan offered to paint her portrait. The subject obviously inspired him. In a year of more than twenty-five portraits, including three renderings of the artist himself (the sign of an improving self-image?), the picture of Mrs. Force is one of the best. Its one incongruous note, a flower-covered straw hat on the lap of a formidably stylish woman who wouldn't have been caught dead in anything so tacky, is explained by Juliana's biographer: we have seen the hat elsewhere, to the side of William Glackens's most famous, most naked, most languorous *Nude with Apple,* a joking allusion both painter and sitter enjoyed.

Disillusionment was invariably intertwined with almost every success in Sloan's life. For a time he was led to believe that the good news about Charles Kraushaar's interest was to be followed by the equally advantageous sale of some paintings. A man named Arthur Egner had met with Kraushaar and decided to purchase five works: *Movies; Six O'Clock, Winter; Old Cone;* a picture of Tammany Hall, and a Gloucester landscape. Sloan received a check for two thousand dollars, only to learn a week later, to his shock and anger, that Egner had changed his mind and was returning all of the paintings but one, *Tammany Hall, New York.* It wasn't the last time Sloan would fall victim to the ambivalence of nouveau riche patrons, "shoppers" rather than art lovers.

But if Sloan was powerless in the matter with Egner, he could take action, he decided, in other areas of his life in which he had been disappointed or riled. Being "led on" by an investment-minded businessman was one thing; being used by his Socialist colleagues was another. Just as he was getting ready to dismantle the show at the Hudson Guild, a meeting of the artists and editors of the *Masses* brought a year's worth of discontent to a head. In late March, Sloan spoke up at the request of Stuart Davis, Glenn Coleman, and Henry Glintenkamp on the touchy subject of restructuring the magazine and safeguarding the artists' right to present their work as they thought best.

To intellectual outsiders, the *Masses* seemed to be doing everything right, especially as concerned its talented artists. Only the summer before, George Bernard Shaw had volunteered the opinion that the journal's art was superior to its commentary: the prose was often good, he wrote, but the "pictures are always first rate." Its political cartoonists somehow managed to escape monotony, which he viewed as truly a "feat." The Chicago novelist Robert Herrick agreed that the *Masses'* strength was "those rude, raw drawings of Mr. Sloan and his friends, so different from the insipidities of all other magazines," and Eugene Debs was likewise known to admire the art that he saw as being "animated by the militant spirit of Socialism." But from within, the view of 1916 was a little less sanguine. New tensions and new attitudes were surfacing. The company that distributed magazines to the newsstands of New York's subway platforms was refusing to carry *The Masses* any longer, and distributors in Philadelphia and Boston were also dropping it. The magazine was barred from the mails in Canada in April, and even Columbia University got into the act, mulishly announcing the cancellation of its library subscription. Yet according to some accounts, sales were climbing, and therein lay another problem. Eastman and Dell felt the need for a more hierarchical arrangement and stricter control over the journal's contents. Success, Sloan felt, was about to corrupt a frolicsome, proudly unremunerative enterprise.

At a session attended by ten of the principal contributors, Sloan presented the artists' proposals for getting back to the original, less fettered spirit of *The Masses*. He suggested abolishment of the position of editor in chief and fund-raiser, implying that too much toadying to well-heeled uptown liberals had already gone on. The magazine now "roars as gently as a sucking dove," Sloan remarked in his least diplomatic fashion. Their brainchild should curtail its growth and expenses, he maintained; it needed to be lifted out of its status as a "charity class" drain on the purses of the rich. Under the new order, the practical business of getting out the magazine would be left to a "make-up committee" and a "make-up man" who would see that the copy arrived as desired at the printer's. But even more important, the decisions about what art and which articles would appear would be handled separately. The artists would meet on their own to choose the drawings; the writers, to select the literary contributions. No more dubious captions added to anybody's pictures without their consent, no more thought to pleasing the new benefactors or the more conservative subscribers they had been picking up. According to Dolly, who sat in on the meeting, all their troubles had begun when wealthy men like Amos Pinchot were solicited for support. "Somebody spilled the apple cart" when Pinchot and his kind were approached, she told a reporter for the *Sun*. (In moments of agitation, Dolly was queen of the mixed metaphor.)

As might be expected, Eastman was livid over Sloan's condemnation of his stewardship and offered his resignation. See if you can run this operation on your own, he challenged the artists. But no one wanted to do without Max; they all simply wanted their "leader" to be one of a team that dispensed with leaders. Floyd Dell sniped that it was Sloan and his "four fingers" (referring to the four artists backing him up) who were the real problem. When Sloan's motion was put to a vote, the result was a 5 to 5 tie, with Sloan, Davis, Coleman, Glintenkamp, and Maurice Becker on one side and Eastman, Dell, Art Young, Mary Heaton Vorse, and Kenneth Russell Chamberlain on the other.

To Art Young, it seemed astonishing that the ten of them—and everyone associated with the magazine, for that matter—couldn't see eye-to-eye at least on the subject of adding appropriate captions to the drawings. "[Men like John Sloan and Stuart Davis] want to run pictures of ash cans and girls hitching up their skirts in Horatio Street—regardless of ideas—and without title," Young complained, making the earliest known reference to an art of ash cans. But that sort of image belonged, he insisted, in a glossy art journal. A magazine like *The Masses* had to have a "policy," a program, a clear-cut intention of overthrowing the evils of the capitalist system. It shouldn't leave its readers in doubt as to where it stood on anything. "For my part," he wrote, "I do not care to be connected with a publication that does not try to point the way out of a sordid materialistic world." At the meeting he had gone so far as to yell at Sloan, "To me, this magazine exists for Socialism. That's why I give my drawings to it, and anybody who doesn't believe in a Socialist policy, so far as I go, can get out!" It would have been in vain, Sloan realized, for him to point out that while he himself was no less devoted a Socialist than Young or anyone else in the room, the magazine he had worked so hard for had *never* been the official organ of *any* party, and had been revived, after Piet Vlag, for much broader, freer purposes.

In a full balloting held a short time later, Sloan and his friends were decisively outvoted by an editorial-board tally of 11 to 6. Dell and Young, determined to see the artists' faction put down, had furiously collected proxy ballots from those members, like John Reed, who were out of town. Then, to drive home his point, Floyd Dell offered his own motion that John Sloan, Stuart Davis, Glenn Coleman, Henry Glintenkamp, and Robert Carlton Brown be expelled from the editorial board. To Eastman's relief, this provocative, vindictive move was defeated in another decisive vote, but everyone retired that night with an uneasy feeling.

At home Sloan reconsidered his position. What was the point of remaining with a group that was likely to hold a grudge against the artists for their aborted revolt and would be sure to curb their freedom in one way or another in the months ahead? Young's assertion that propaganda was as important and meaningful as art was especially troubling. Eastman, a true intellectual, was moderately sensitive to Sloan's views, but Dell and Young were furious with him and apt to make his life miserable. He wrote to Eastman the next morning, alluding to Dell's barb about him and his "four fingers": "Max, when thy right hand offendeth thee, cut it off." Sloan said that he regretted not having submitted to the amputation the day before, and that he realized, in the aftermath of their fight, that a break with *The Masses* was inevitable. Nothing could be gained by his hanging on to the past. He resigned, and Davis, Coleman, Becker, Brown, and Alice and Charles Winter followed suit. "Dear Sloan," Eastman quickly replied, "I shall regret the loss of your wit and artistic genius as much as I shall enjoy the absence of your cooperation." From the point of view of Eastman and Dell, the *Masses* had been purged of "Greenwich Villagism" and could go on to do the important work that needed to be done. From his own perspective, Sloan was reluctantly freed from what he assumed would shortly become a propaganda mill, and could get on with his life as a painter and, soon enough, a teacher.

To a reporter from the *New York Morning Telegraph* who came to the apartment for an interview, Dolly angrily (and not very logically) compared Floyd Dell to the lowest form of life she could think of, the undercover cops who testified against the streetwalkers they'd approached and then hauled into court. Eastman, whom she had always thought charming, was spared her wrath in public.

This end to the Sloans' involvement with the *Masses* did not necessarily mean an end to their participation in, or support for, radical activities in general. Politics and art made a poor match, Sloan felt, but that fact had no bearing on his life as a citizen. There was too much that was painfully, pointlessly backward about America and that demanded attention. There was far too much interference on the part of the government in matters of private life. Kudos were due those who devoted themselves to righting those wrongs.

Emma Goldman had always struck Sloan as being a little too much like those of his former colleagues on the magazine who demanded that artists wear their social consciousness on their sleeves—and in any case, his sympathies lay with the Socialists, not with the Anarchists. There was an earnestness about the woman that wore him down. Yet her pacifism and anti-capitalism were only two of the many qualities that the Sloans respected in her (Dolly's feelings were considerably warmer than her husband's), and they vehemently approved of her outspoken advocacy of birth control. This was the issue that had brought Goldman into trouble with the law once again in the eventful spring of 1916, when she was arrested for urging the dissemination of family-planning information to anyone who wanted it. On the eve of her two-week incarceration, the Sloans helped arrange a banquet in her honor at the Hotel Brevoort just north of Washington Square, a lively event that they attended with the Henris and

George and Emma Bellows. A further show of solidarity to celebrate
Goldman's release, a May 5 rally at Carnegie Hall, was organized in part
by that veteran of Carnegie Hall benefits, Dolly Sloan. In inscribing her
memoirs to them later, Goldman acknowledged the goodwill she felt
toward and from these two special people, particularly Dolly, a "fellow
fighter for justice," as she phrased it.

Gertrude Vanderbilt Whitney and Emma Goldman, John Quinn and
Max Eastman, Albert Barnes and Art Young: Sloan's circle of acquaintance had expanded to a point of stunning diversity in his middle years.
Much of it did not overlap, though. The rich and the radical, and the
artistic and the political, tended to form discrete, impenetrable categories. Partly for this reason, Juliana Force's interest in the other aspects of
Sloan's life immediately endeared her to him. A spring weekend at the
Forces' in Montclair, New Jersey, to which the Sloans had been asked to
bring John Butler Yeats, came off very well, and Juliana was only too
happy to join her new group of friends for dinner at Petipas. Like Sloan,
she came from a lower-middle-class family and was in effect making
herself up as she went along. Her rise to prominence in the New York
cultural hierarchy was an accomplishment born of naked ambition, a
lucky attachment to one of the wealthiest women in the country, and a
love of strong, original art. She had an acid tongue that Sloan enjoyed, yet
she exhibited more amused patience than most when Sloan's preoccupation with talking politics got the better of him. Most important, as the
art historian Avis Berman has observed, Juliana Force did not feel in the
least alienated or embarrassed by Dolly's problems when Sloan confided
the whole story to her. She was a woman of the world, tart when necessary
and compassionate when others were indifferent. Toward Sloan himself
she could adopt a respectful, protective manner that he was sometimes
very much in need of.

Others were less conscious of Sloan's needs. Approaching eighty,
Yeats was apt not to realize how much he depended on Sloan, who was
loath to deny his friend any service he could provide. While preparing to
depart that summer for Gloucester, where he had as usual lined up a few
private students and where he hoped to get an enormous amount of
painting done, Sloan was once again sucked into the dramatic vortex of
Yeats-as-lecturer, struggling to line up speaking engagements and then to
advertise the appearances of the man who was by now New York's most
famous and most beloved raconteur and moocher. Try though she might,

Dolly could never get Yeats to join them at the "red cottage" by the sea; nothing would budge him from his post in Manhattan. Quinn might see to it that Yeats's bills were paid (all the while railing about the old man's selfishness in remaining in America when he had family in Ireland), but it was the Sloans' lot to be the eternally understanding, affectionate friends. When Sloan finally settled down to work in Gloucester, he completed sixty-seven paintings before having to return to New York to begin a new schedule at the League.

In all of 1916 Sloan had managed to secure only one magazine-illustration assignment, a task that involved his doing seven drawings for a lackluster comic story in the *Century,* and one book-illustration job of no higher quality, for a pulp novel, *The Golden Blight,* by George Allan England. His boredom with such low-level work was palpable. If the paintings weren't going to sell—and Charles Kraushaar wasn't making any unrealistic promises, though he did sell one that year—then Sloan would have to find some other regular employment; that much was obvious. So the offer of a full-time position at the Art Students League came at just the right moment. Yet Sloan's acceptance of expanded teaching duties might be seen as more than merely a means of securing his livelihood. Curious and stimulated about where this might take him, he didn't have the affect of a man who felt trapped.

Teaching for some is an admission of defeat (the famous Shaw witticism about "those who can" cuts to the quick). For others it is a way to make some money—if never a lot—that involves minimal stress once a curriculum is established and mastered. But there is another dimension, too, to this kind of work. For the individual who approaches the profession at a moment in his life when the future is still wide open, when the past has included enough valuable experiences outside the classroom, and when energy and optimism are still to be counted on, the hours in the classroom take on a different meaning. For such a man, teaching becomes not only a way to pass on his enthusiasm and knowledge to others, but a way to explore and redefine himself *for* himself. In a year that saw him abandon *The Masses,* find a dealer, and mount two one-man exhibitions, Sloan began to discover in teaching a new forum for his ideas and personality and a further validation of his worth. Serious students, unlike magazine editors and prospective buyers of paintings, did not make good artists feel small, unneeded, marginal. Quite the contrary.

The pupils at the Art Students League appealed to Sloan for their combination of talent and energy and their lack of pretension. They were, in the main, more technically competent than the young people he had worked with at the Pittsburgh Art Students League during his weekly treks to western Pennsylvania a decade earlier, and they shared some of the excitement that was pervading the city in the wake of the Armory Show, the opening of new galleries in Midtown, and the expanding press coverage of the art scene. The arts in New York had been a sleepy business circa 1904, when John Sloan arrived from Philadelphia, but all that was changing twelve years later. Yet the fact that the League's student body comprised a range of abilities and aspirations, from those who were intent on making a career of art to those who were simply investigating a vaguely felt interest, was also fine by John Sloan. Once that lack of uniformity would have seemed a drawback; the conventional view had been that the Henri school was for serious young artists, the League for dilettantes and dullards. But Henri's school was no more (it had folded in 1915), and Sloan had revised his former acerbic attitude toward the League: the men and women before him looked promising and attentive enough. He had already revised his view of himself, for that matter. No longer the timorous substitute who had been pressed into service covering for Henri in the old days, he was more confident now of his ability to instruct, to suggest, to entertain, to criticize, and to convert.

The artist Adolph Dehn, a student in one of Sloan's earliest classes, remembered the passion, almost the maniacal fervor, of his new teacher. He recalled a man of distinctive appearance—"about 40, black hair with some grey . . . glasses and a good tan about his face"—and fiery opinions. "Oh, how he rails against institutions; how he rails at commercial artists, portrait painters, etc! . . . He can swear real handy too." Dehn was not alone in finding Sloan a refreshing change from the average instructor of more temperate demeanor and milquetoast values. Sloan understood that the young appreciated flair, definiteness, clarity of principle, and would respect the fact that their teacher actually had some principles about something—anything—and was willing to stand by those beliefs to the point of appearing eccentric or extreme. In a sense, Sloan was perpetuating the Henri doctrine that had so magnetized him in the 1890s. The idea was to offer a compelling image of the artist that had nothing to do with the mundane business of making a living or pleasing a client and that simultaneously ignored the still-current philistine notions of ethereal beings and vapid aesthetes. The great thing about being an artist, Sloan told his students, was the freedom it gave those who truly embraced the calling—freedom from the dictates of others, freedom from personal ambition, freedom from just about everything that made life seem small and crass. He loved, and polished, the interjections and asides that drove home these values. If what mattered in life was the fulfillment of your art, nothing else could touch you as deeply. In a society that too often pressured its educated young people into occupations that were either based on the exploitation of others or judged by the acquisition of goods, art asked only that you be true to your own vision and skill. Whether or not the work sold or was honored in the press or the museums, Sloan insisted, had *nothing whatsoever* to do with the art itself. That was lesson number one, a principle to underlie all others.

Surely some would-be painters sat in the classroom of the Art Students League and rolled their eyes at the belligerent idealism of their new instructor. Certain adults had had that reaction before them; George and Emma Bellows, for example, had never been overly fond of this preachy strain in John Sloan. For those who felt that they had been faithful to their vision *and* gained the approval of society, Sloan's manner smacked of sour grapes: he said these things only because he had done so badly in the marketplace, they reasoned. Students who hoped one day to become commercial artists or portrait painters would have found this irritating, high-flown talk a little hard to take. Yet Sloan occupied just that anomalous position which could validate a critical perspective on worldly success. No one at the League thought him a feeble painter, and he had been mentioned in the art magazines enough times for any student to know that he was someone important. That autumn the critic and collector Albert Gallatin had written of his work in glowing terms in the pages of his new book, *Certain Contemporaries.* If Sloan's pictures weren't selling like Sargent's or Hassam's—weren't, indeed, selling at all—then just possibly that curious situation did say something about the legitimacy of the market and the dealers as arbiters of judgment and esteem.

In this sense, Sloan was a very different kind of teacher and example from Henri. Their call for a lofty, disinterested sense of vocation was the same, but Henri's was made from a most comfortable economic base. First his father, and then his lucrative portrait commissions, had supported him, and he had been represented by a major gallery sixteen years before Sloan met Kraushaar. Sloan himself knew the cost, and let others know the cost, of following one's own bent. When Sloan said, "I have nothing to teach you that will help you to make a living," anyone who knew anything about his career understood his point and the background of the remark. There was an authenticity to Sloan that appealed to many of his students.

A further contrast with Henri and many of the other teachers of the day lay in Sloan's degree of openness toward different styles of painting. Eventually he would come to be seen as an opponent of Modernism—a narrow reading of his words at any time, but not a mistake his students would have made during his first days at the League. Like any smart instructor, Henri had spoken up for an open mind and an active eye, but when push came to shove at the Armory Show, he himself had drawn back from the challenge. Even when he urged his pupils to see what Alfred Stieglitz had on view at "291," one tends to suspect that the advice was offered out of nervousness rather than with confidence in its wisdom. But if Henri was threatened by Picasso and Cézanne, Sloan wanted his students to ponder even the work he himself had had trouble with at first, calling Cubism the "grammar of art" and hence something that could only be beneficial for everyone to study. Thomas Eakins (who had died that year and was about to have his first retrospective, which would come as a revelation to New Yorkers), John Marin, Rockwell Kent, Marsden Hartley, William Glackens, Arthur Dove, Max Weber, Severini and Matisse, van Gogh and Picasso, Prendergast and Kroll and Braque and Demuth: Sloan wanted his charges to see them all, to reject at the outset the narrowness of the Kenyon Cox approach to art, to speculate on the possibilities of an art form that was being rethought from the ground up during their lifetime.

Still, there was no mistaking John Sloan for an Arthur Davies, busy turning his delicate nymphs into Cubist dancers, or for any of the other, lesser artists who were trying to accommodate themselves too glibly to the new fashions. What Sloan wanted his students to attend to, in terms of school-taught technique, was the basic artist's tools of solid draftsmanship, composition and color, and the rudiments of anatomy and perspective. As a teacher, he was likely to look back now with a different eye to the day, twenty-five years earlier, when he had stormed out of Thomas Anshutz's class in Philadelphia. How stupid all those dull plaster casts had been, but how right Anshutz's insistence that drawing and more drawing and more drawing still was the foundation of art! In a good realist genre scene or a well-made Cubist still-life, in a Vermeer interior or a Cézanne landscape, the same sense of structure and craft applied. Nothing felt random. Everything worked toward a given effect, however subtle. For the twenty-year-old painter Elsie Driggs, who sat in on one of Sloan's early classes with a friend who had just enrolled, that was exactly the point she was ready to absorb. To her, Sloan was a fascinating blend of the traditional and the new. The compositional principles he articulated, whether in analyzing a work in progress or in holding a reproduction aloft, were insightful without being either pedantic or formulaic. He knew which arrangements of forms and figures made a painting "work" better than others, and he knew how to explain it in relatively few words. He spoke with equal regard for Old Masters and contemporary talents. "For the study of composition, whether it was Chardin or the Moderns, [Sloan] was the best," Driggs decided, and she later joined a small group for a criticism class held at his apartment.

It is curious that although Driggs (who later went on to become one of the respected Precisionist painters of the twenties) claimed to have benefited from Sloan's lessons, during her years at the League she never actually registered for his class, but instead attended sessions taught by Frank Vincent duMond, George Bridgman, George Luks, Maurice Sterne, and even Robert Henri, when he was at the school in 1920. She evidently kept a certain distance from Sloan, and even in interviews conducted some sixty years later spoke of him with an admiration tinged with caution, or awe. The persona that Sloan cultivated from the start of his teaching career was, or could be, almost too forceful; baldly put, Sloan's classes were not for the fainthearted. He could be volatile in his off-the-cuff lectures and scathing in his critiques of students' work. For Driggs, a gentle and torturously shy woman, the atmosphere in the room was simply too intense on a day-to-day basis, and she was not alone in finding Sterne and Henri less exhausting and intimidating.

Sometimes Sloan's caustic tone might have been better left in the classroom, where a captive audience of art students could take it either as they chose or as best they could. In the world beyond the League, Sloan's periodic crankiness could make bad situations worse and spoil otherwise pleasant moments. His bouts of depression, the nervous strain brought on by going anywhere with Dolly where liquor would be served (which, in 1916, seemed to be everywhere), the fear that their gradual withdrawal from party politics would have an adverse effect on her—all of this took its toll and made him ever more ready to pick a fight. Nothing provoked more bile, however, than the subject of the war in Europe.

Two days before Christmas, the Sloans and John Butler Yeats were invited to a party at the Forces' apartment in Manhattan, to celebrate both the holiday and Juliana's birthday. The hostess received a print from the artist, *Girl and Beggar,* personally inscribed, a gift she very much appreciated. Everyone seemed to be having an excellent time—any gathering at the Forces' was a festive occasion—until the unfortunate question of Germany's brutality and the Allied cause came up. Sloan's antimilitarism had been growing with each account he read from the front, and he had reached the point where he couldn't abide any talk of the moral superiority of the Allies. It was all about money and land and national honor, he insisted, and anyone who thought it mattered a damn who won the conflict was just stupid—and that included his best friend. Yeats's opinion, which invariably sent Sloan into a rage, was that all war was regrettable, but that in this instance the Germans were the aggressors and represented a menace to Western civilization that had to be stopped. At the Forces' that night, Sloan wouldn't let up. "His object," Yeats later wrote his daughter, "seemed to be to insult and humiliate everyone." Dolly sat in "indignant silence," and when asked by Mrs. Force if she was having a good time, she replied, "No, I am not," and glared at her husband. The party was pretty much ruined. Juliana Force was not above holding a grudge (far from it), but luckily for Sloan, she soon forgot—or at least forgave—the whole unpleasant incident. Those who valued Sloan's friendship were coming to see his passion and anger as an inextricable part of the whole.

Bohemia's Borders

(1917–1918)

"{In Greenwich Village} a man felt something like his raw self, though he knew well that he had been cooked to a turn by the world's conventions."

—ART YOUNG

On the wintry night of January 23, 1917, John Sloan, Marcel Duchamp, and five other friends illegally entered the side door of the Washington Square Arch at the foot of Fifth Avenue, climbed the inner spiral staircase, and proceeded through the monument's trap door to the roof for an impromptu midnight picnic. The inspiration came from Gertrude Drick, a flamboyant Village poet and student of Sloan's who was known by the name Woe ("I've always wanted to be able to say 'Woe is me' "). Having discovered that the door to the arch was not always locked and that the policemen on duty often wandered off to the other side of the park, she suggested to Sloan, Duchamp, the actor Charles Ellis, and three other hearty souls that they might take a few bottles, some food, some balloons, a supply of candles and Chinese lanterns, and a hot-water bottle or two and have a grand time. This they did, drawing up in the bibulous process a giddy document that proclaimed the secession of Greenwich Village from the America of big business and small minds and called on President Wilson to extend protection to their domain as one of the small nations. The etching Sloan made to commemorate the occasion, entitled *Arch Conspirators,* shows a lively group gathered around a small fire, with some balloons tied to the parapet and the busy city visible in the distance beyond them.

Sloan's move to the Village in 1912 had brought him—and Dolly—to the heart of a special world at just the right moment, and this nocturnal outing and the etching that celebrated it were representative of an attitude shared by many of its inhabitants. On the eve of the United States' involvement in the war in Europe, they saw themselves, these residents of Manhattan living south of Fourteenth and north of Van Dam Street, as defiantly different not only from other Americans but even from New Yorkers who lived a few miles to the north and east of them. In an area of low rents and relaxed mores, of minimal interest in conventional success and a significant amount of genuine camaraderie, Villagers perceived this as-yet-undeveloped part of the city as a "spiritual haven," in the words of one neighborhood woman of the time—a great anomaly in God's Country, "a sort of liberal/radical small town." And in many ways, such self-congratulatory happiness was justified. For men and women who had felt out of place in the industrial towns and country villages of their birth, or in even the big cities in which they had grown up but never really found a place—the would-be artists and writers (both professionals and dilettantes), the musicians and actors, the gay men and lesbians, the feminists and pacifists, the Socialists and anarchists as well as the more generally discontented, those thousands of young people who weren't sure they wanted to marry and raise children and follow in their parents' footsteps—for them, the troubled and the creative, Greenwich Village offered an alternative such as had never before been provided in America.

The possibilities for a life out of the mainstream were remarkably varied, answering every ambition from the sedentary to the high-powered. One could while away the day reading and talking at the Samovar or the Mad Hatter or any number of cheap tearooms and restaurants along Macdougal or Christopher Streets, or see the new plays of the Washington Square Players and the Provincetown Players or the new art at Robert Coady's adventurous gallery on the south side of the square. Good discussions and good browsing could be had at Albert and Charles Boni's bookstore-cum-lending-library on Macdougal between Third and Fourth Streets. One could go slumming at the Golden Swan (the "Hell Hole") on Sixth Avenue, where the toughs of the Hudson Street Dusters gang hung out in their half of the bar, or meet the most independent-minded women of the age, many of them gay, at meetings of the group called Heterodoxy. The imperious Mabel Dodge was ensconced at 23 Fifth Avenue, where her salon had become a notorious institution, the very birthplace of all radical chic. There were allies or sparring partners to be found at the new Liberal Club next to the Bonis' bookshop or, to the north, on Nineteenth Street, at the headquarters of Branch One of the Socialist party at the Rand School (where the basement restaurant, according to Louis Untermeyer, was a hectic "gathering place of all the Utopians, muckrakers, young intellectuals, and elderly malcontents south of Forty-second Street"). In such a robust world, one was spared what Mary Heaton Vorse termed the "curse of conformity." Another Village woman went even further: "I doubt if ever in America there has been a spot where art and living, intertwined for a short time, brought forth such earnestness or such good companionship." It was to take their part, such as it was, in this sustaining milieu that the Sloans moved first to 61 Perry Street, then to 240 West Fourth Street, and finally to 88 Washington Place.

Yet there were those who thought that the whole question of a "Village identity" had become more than a little self-conscious by 1916, that change was in the wind, and to some extent Sloan agreed. He and Dolly

Village frolics: Dolly dancing, en route to a costume ball (Delaware Art Museum)

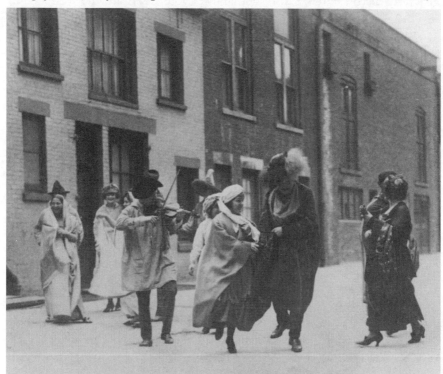

continued to attend the wild costume balls at Webster Hall (Dolly's love for playing "dress-up" grew considerably as the years went by), Dolly still liked her visits to Romany Marie's on Christopher Street, and in 1917 Sloan would do a fine etching of the "Hell Hole" (with a dapper Eugene O'Neill engaged in conversation at a corner table), but a slightly different feeling had come over him by then—just as a significant shift was about to register all over the Village and in the rest of America. It was not only that Sloan was worried about Dolly and furious about the political drift of his time. Mobilization and war would irrevocably alter the social fabric; that was inevitable. It was not only that the city fathers were preparing to extend Seventh Avenue, a main thoroughfare that prior to 1917 had ended just south of Fourteenth Street, and so destroy the West Village as an enclave of minimal traffic and noise. It was that Sloan's attitude toward the cultural scene at large, or toward that part of it symbolized by the Village, was about to broaden. Finally established as a professional with a gallery and an exhibition history, he was interested now in considering the questions of audience and accessibility, in making connections rather than severing them. Never a true "bohemian" himself, with all the antics and the isolationism that the term implies, John Sloan was ready in the winter of 1916–17 to see the boundaries of that world of difference, creativity, and struggle expand. In that light, *Arch Conspirators* seems as much elegiac record as an affirmation of a place and a rebellion, and Sloan's position so far off to the side of the group in the etching makes sense. The quaint, affectionate, closed-off experience of the outsiders was about to be reworked, transformed, by an aggressive appeal to Americans to wake up and pay attention to their artists.

Before the end of that winter, Sloan would be involved with Duchamp, Glackens, and many others in the formation of the Society of Independent Artists, an enterprise designed to make the work of "Villagers"—wherever they lived—better known to art lovers and potential buyers. It was a project that would engage his energies for the better part of the next three decades and occupy him long after most of his contemporaries had abandoned the cause.

In January Sloan had the pleasure of being included in the Whitney Studio's portrait exhibition, the second of three consecutive group shows responding to the thematic question "To Whom Should I Go for

My Portrait?" Juliana Force showed laudable (but not unexpected) goodwill in inviting Sloan to join the group, given his churlish outburst at her
birthday party the month before. She went even further, though, and
purchased his painting *Signorina Cherubino* for six hundred dollars. This
picture (now in the collection of the Delaware Art Museum) thus became
the first Sloan work to enter the Whitney collection and provided a good
omen for his upcoming venture at Kraushaar's.

Charles Kraushaar had died suddenly not long after Sloan met him,
but his brother who took over the management of the Fifth Avenue and
Twenty-ninth Street gallery was an equally clever businessman. John
Kraushaar balanced his knowledge of the family's conservative clientele
with a genuine respect for his new artist's strengths. That is to say,
Kraushaar knew he was representing a man who was as good at etching as
he was at painting; rightly assumed that the etchings would be Sloan's
financial mainstay, while the paintings would require more patient salesmanship; and understood that Sloan (like many good artists) would always be a little ahead of his audience. So if the painter was constantly
talking up his latest Gloucester landscapes or waxing ecstatic about the
bold colors and modeling of a recent portrait or nude, Kraushaar could
show a real interest in those works even as he emphasized to would-be
customers the accomplishments of the immediately preceding years. The
selection for Sloan's first one-man show at Kraushaar's, which ran from
early March to early April 1917, reflects just such a calculated approach:
visitors to the gallery saw forty-three etchings and only fifteen paintings,
the latter mainly done in the peak years of 1910–1912. The only "gritty"
oil from the days of the darker palette was *The Haymarket,* while the most
buoyant works were probably *Gloucester Harbor* and *Spring Planting, Greenwich Village* (1913), which contained some of Sloan's strongest female
figures.

Despite Kraushaar's best efforts, no oils sold that spring, but Sloan
wasn't particularly surprised. The etchings found some enthusiastic buyers, and Sloan knew that Kraushaar's commitment was for the long run.
More important, the attention he received from the New York critics,
now that he was represented by a major gallery, seemed more respectful.
Sloan's paintings and etchings "more than justify the big faith that has
been placed in him as an American artist," the reviewer for the *Evening
Mail* noted, remarking that *Clown Making Up* deserved a place in the
collection of the Metropolitan Museum if and when that august institu-

tion decided to pay closer attention to native art. McBride in the *Sun* aimed to be more agreeable after last year's testiness, and the *Times* in its *Sunday Magazine* gave Sloan an approving notice. Only that arch-conservative of newspaper critics, Royal Cortissoz of the *Tribune,* continued to hammer away at Sloan for the "prosaic and even ugly nature of his subjects," for his innate vulgarity of style and theme, for his arrogant refusal to "paint a beautiful picture." But Sloan was beyond taking Cortissoz seriously at this point. The artistic concerns of the moment were far removed from the "world of superfine emotion . . . reverie and idealism" that Cortissoz wrote about, sounding as if the calendar still read 1907, not 1917. Picasso, Matisse, and other iconoclastic thinkers such as Marcel Duchamp were raising entirely different questions.

Some of those questions, in fact, were being confronted just several blocks to the north, at the Grand Central Art Palace on Lexington Avenue and Forty-sixth Street. Three days after Sloan's show closed at Kraushaar's, he and Dolly attended the spectacular opening-night celebration for this first annual exhibition of the Society of Independent Artists. Gertrude Whitney, one of several patrons, was there to greet the artists and other visitors; a brass band played; and hundreds of guests—down-at-heels artists from the Village, the sort of black-tie crowd that was rarely seen near Washington Square, and every variation of style and persona in between—wandered the aisles and alcoves to look at over two thousand works of contemporary art, or more than half again the number seen at the Armory Show. The significance of this display of Cubists and academicians, realists and Dadaists, and of the Society that gave birth to it, was twofold. On the one hand, it was the culmination of years of effort to end the exclusivity of art exhibition in America. Going well beyond the Independents Show of 1910, the Independents of 1917 opened its walls to absolutely anyone, whether professional or amateur, who paid the initiation fee of one dollar and the organization's yearly dues of five dollars. The old rallying cry of "no jury, no prizes" had been dramatically expanded, to the point of "no restrictions whatsoever"—or so it had seemed when the Society was incorporated in 1916, with John Quinn acting as its legal counsel.

Sloan was enthusiastically in favor of the idea. With William Glackens serving as president of the Society's board and Walter Pach, Maurice Prendergast, and Prendergast's brother Charles involved (Charles, himself an unusual artist, was the board's vice president), he knew enough of the principal players to allay any uneasiness he may have felt over the role being taken by French expatriates and Armory Show stars such as Duchamp, Picabia, Albert Gleizes, and Jacques Villon. He also liked the idea—the ultimate in the democratization of the process—of selecting a letter of the alphabet at random and beginning the exhibition at that point in a strictly alphabetical order, with A following on to Z.

What Sloan was *not* prepared for was the infamous urinal. If Royal Cortissoz was still fulminating about elegant and inelegant themes in painting, about "beautiful" drawing and "refined" brushwork, Marcel Duchamp was questioning the definition of modern art itself. His *Nude Descending a Staircase,* the cause célèbre of the Armory Show, was merely a precursor of what would become a lifetime's exploration, both mischievous and nihilistic, of an art beyond "retinal pleasure," one that had nothing to do with traditional or sensuous elements of picture-making. Duchamp's submission of an actual porcelain urinal as the entry of a pseudonymous "R. Mutt" of Philadelphia predictably agitated the men and women organizing the "Big Show," as Rockwell Kent called it. Duchamp's impish test of just how open was this Society he had helped form, and how flexible a concept of art it could accommodate, elicited immediate angry reactions from most of the Americans involved. "Do you mean," Kent exclaimed, "that if a man chose to exhibit horse manure we would have to accept it?" Just so, the collector and patron Walter Arensberg felt: R. Mutt was calling his "readymade" a work of art and paying his entrance fees, and so deserved a space no less than any Sunday painter or National Academy of Design veteran who expected an uncensored showing for his own contribution. In any event, Arensberg concluded, the urinal as a sculpture or a piece of "idea art" was no more ludicrous, or incongruous, than some of the paintings they were hanging. A furious debate ensued.

Even some of Duchamp's admirers, such as the collector and abstract painter Katherine Dreier, had a hard time following their idol's reasoning. Duchamp was ready to close the books on the history of painting as a pursuit for the eye alone, to take Cézanne and the Post-Impressionists as a final chapter rather than a new beginning. But Americans—and many Europeans, for that matter—had only started to come to terms with these artists and their intentions. President Glackens didn't hesitate to express his opinion on the urinal, entitled *Fountain,* using the words "suppressed adolescence" to refer to the mind that had invented "R. Mutt" and his indecent objet trouvé. To no one's surprise, the board voted against Duchamp, whereupon Glackens, according to one account, went so far as to conclude the business by taking the urinal behind a screen at the hall and "accidentally" dropping it. Marcel Duchamp and Walter Arensberg resigned from the Society. The "no jury" notion was obviously *not* a principle of absolute freedom that their peers were ready to take literally. For his part, Sloan thought Duchamp an interesting presence in New York but felt that Glackens, Pach, Prendergast, and the other officers had spared their exhibition much ridicule in the press. Americans were finally awakening in larger numbers to an interest in contemporary art; now was the time to capture their respect, not to alienate them with frivolous ploys.

Although Sloan's two paintings in the Independents Show were anything but challenging by these extreme standards, they were just the sort of work Kraushaar had steered away from. One was a voluptuous *Blonde Nude* (1917), and the other, *Reddy in a Tree* (circa 1916), an almost garish Gloucester portrait of a little boy with a "sun-pink face and carotty hair" —another expression of Maratta ecstasy. In company with 1,234 other artists, from thirty-eight states and Europe, Sloan was free to be himself at the Grand Central Art Palace. That meant decisively moving away from his reputation as the artist of the El and the Tenderloin to be a painter of a less documentary nature. In looking at the Charles Demuths and John Marins, the Arthur Doves and Joseph Stellas, on the walls at Forty-sixth Street, and discussing them with his students, Sloan was becoming more attuned to the climate of the day. The Henri influence was now only one of many in Sloan's life.

The excitement for Sloan of the Kraushaar show and the drama of the Independents, broken urinal and all, were necessarily overshadowed, or at least colored, by other events that same week. America's entry into the morass of the war in Europe was something that many Americans had long anticipated and prepared for; indeed, as Sloan and those of his friends who shared his views knew, the whole "preparedness" movement had achieved a kind of inevitability by early 1917. The propaganda of a holy crusade to end Prussian militarism had been effectively broadcast in the press and in lecture halls around the country. Industry was geared up for production on a massive new scale. From the sinking of the *Lusitania* to the Zimmermann telegram, the affronts to American integrity had created a whirlwind effect.

The opposition had done its best, but the limits of pacifist sympathies in the United States were evident even among the Sloans' own circle. At Carnegie Hall not many months before Wilson's declaration, Helen Keller (with the aid of her teacher Annie Sullivan) had delivered one of her shockingly polemical talks on the current crisis. Her theme, which had been outraging audiences for some time, was that the "only 'preparedness' America needs is justice and well-being at home." Preparedness was just another J. P. Morgan plot to make money for already rich businessmen, she argued, and the war itself a "scheme" hatched by cranks such as Theodore Roosevelt ("His Highness of Oyster Bay") to enable little men to play soldier. In her New York speech, Keller further accused the Socialist party of being too tired and too slow-moving to do its job and prevent America from going to war. In attendance at Carnegie Hall that raucous night were the Sloans, the Henris, and the Bellowses. John and Dolly, in hearty agreement with everything they heard, applauded vigorously, but Marjorie Henri took the side of Keller's vocal adversaries and joined in the hissing. After his wife grew louder and louder, Robert Henri was forced to drag her out of the auditorium, while Dolly, now wild with joy (and no doubt glad to see Marjorie evicted), did her best to cheer Keller on and drown out the faction that continued to voice its disapproval of her "anti-Americanism." Between the "thunder" (the shouts of Dolly Sloan) and the "rain" (the hisses of Marjorie Henri), George Bellows later complained, he hadn't been able to hear much of Keller. Not that Bellows needed to hear much; he was already of the opinion that the Allied cause was just, that Germany was necessarily evil, and that the Sloans were once again—*still*—a bit daft. The president's call to arms in April simply gave everyone final cause to acknowledge the cracks that had been widening between them all for months, even years.

That George Bellows soon became an active supporter of the war, using his talents to create caricatures of Huns lopping off the hands of poor Belgian boys in *The Enemy Arrive,* was disturbing to Sloan. That Kenneth Russell Chamberlain, formerly of *The Masses,* could draw anti-German cartoons for several Philadelphia newspapers, and good Socialists such as William English Walling become Wilson supporters—that was equally hard to take. But when Stuart Davis, someone he cared about, registered for the draft in Gloucester rather than in Manhattan, Sloan was incredulous: the town's tiny population meant that the odds of his being selected were much higher than they would have been in New York City. But perhaps Davis was interested in making the world safe for democracy, Sloan acidly reflected. After all, he told Henri, Ed Davis was actually "keen for the war"—a pitiful Abraham and Isaac story in the making. Ed Davis, John Butler Yeats, and everyone else he knew who couldn't see through Wilson's rhetoric roused Sloan to the point of fury. For a man who had responded to a 1916 *Masses* survey asking "Do You Believe in Patriotism?" with the tart reply "Patriotism licks the boots of Capitalism," there was little question that the government regularly lied to its citizens, who, if they had any sense, would view all war bulletins and politicians' promises with truculent skepticism. It was unpleasant to watch draft-age friends like Randall Davey decamp to Cuba for the duration and to see Maurice Becker have to leave for Mexico. Sloan was later sad to hear of Art Young's dismissal from his job as a Washington correspondent for *Metropolitan* because of his antiwar opinions, and of the brutal treatment of *Masses* artist John Barber, forcibly sent to France as a conscientious objector and then court-martialed.

John Butler Yeats, nearing eighty, with nephews in the army fighting Germany and a deeply felt belief in the value of patriotism, was in the most awkward position of anyone close to Sloan. He couldn't bring himself to agree with his friend's ideas, but he was hurt by the increasingly frequent periods of estrangement that their differences brought about. On several occasions Sloan bluntly told him he didn't know what he was talking about. Sometimes Yeats would look to Dolly as an intermediary, writing to her of his admiration for her husband ("I love him because I find in him a rich and varied humanity, so quick in response and so fiercely tender," one letter read; "only I wish he would tie up that watchdog who sometimes does not know me when I call but treats me as a stranger"). At other times he would resort to flattery of Sloan's work, either in print or relayed by way of conversation with others. But when a principle was at stake, Sloan could be cruelly obstinate, past anything in Yeats's experience. "Unhappy . . . restless . . . quarrelsome" was Yeats's characterization of his friend's state of mind that year, a condition he could only hope would be resolved with a speedy conclusion to the conflict abroad.

Adding to the tension of this time for Sloan was the fact that Dolly was rapidly becoming a full-time concern. Ironically, her reputation in political circles for indefatigable fund-raising and intense loyalty to the cause had continued even after she and Sloan severed their ties to Branch One and *The Masses*. One New York newspaper report in May 1917, for example, complete with interview and photo, credited Dolly with a significant role in the acquittal of the labor organizer Tom Mooney, unjustly accused of murder in a San Francisco Preparedness Day bombing. "MOONEY'S CHANCE FOR LIBERTY DUE TO TINY WOMAN WITH LARGE HOBBY" ran the headline; the article below noted Mrs. Sloan's eager petitioning of every labor union in the city for contributions to a defense fund and her platform appeals for money at several rallies in New York State and New England. Yet Sloan saw the other side of the competent public image. Dolly wanted to feel needed and important, naturally, but she would come home from these outings in terrible shape. There were times, Sloan later said, when she seemed to him almost insane, a "woman of stone." Elizabeth Hamlin and Sloan's cousin Eleanor did their best to see her through her liquor-induced stupors and to keep Sloan company when his wife went missing for a day or two at a time, but the burden was ultimately his. Juliana Force arranged for Dolly to see a prominent neurologist that year and paid the bill. The report was not encouraging. Possibly, the doctor told Sloan, if Dolly was committed to a sanatorium for a period of two years, a cure could be effected, but there were, of course, no guarantees for a woman in her condition. It didn't matter. Both financially and emotionally, such a lengthy institutionalization was out of the question. Mrs. Force offered to help with the expenses of an extended treatment, but after some hesitation Sloan declined. It was unlikely in any event that Dolly would have gone willingly, and the decision to commit her would have meant a different set of problems for her husband, and a different kind of guilt. When she was in a happy or stable period, Dolly couldn't stand to be out of Sloan's company for more than a few hours, and the attention paid him by others, particularly women, would annoy her to no end. A forced rupture of a year or two was unthinkable.

Strangely enough, none of these pressures affected the caliber of Sloan's work or the fervor of his teaching in his second year at the Art Students League. Students flocked to his classes, and his paintings (the vast majority of them done in Massachusetts between June and September) reached a peak of confidence and craftsmanship. Now, when Sloan painted the "red cottage" at sunset or with its lilac bushes in full bloom, or Dolly lounging in the parlor by the front window, or horse-drawn carriages making way for touring cars on Main Street, he balanced his newly refined and invigorated sense of color with an equivalent concern for structure and composition. The neighborhood children of dubious anatomy still made the odd appearance—Dolly was forever organizing lawn parties for ever-larger groups of youngsters in Gloucester—but Sloan had found some excellent models for clothed portraits in Pearl Minor, Clara Karlin, and Amelia Rose, who brought out his strengths in dealing with the adult figure. That fall, as he painted his charismatic student and friend Gertrude Drick, the "Woe" of *Arch Conspirators* fame, Sloan showed himself just how far he had come since those nervous weeks in Omaha when he worried that he would never be able to "do" a sitter with the nuance, the living presence, that he or she demanded. Sticking to the principle of keeping his politics out of his art, Sloan focused on what appealed to his imagination in the world around him; no one could ever have guessed that any of these paintings had been made during a time of international strife and mad flag-waving. The closest he came to commenting on the martial air of America circa 1917–1918 was with the two men in khaki who waddle along on one side of *Main Street, Gloucester*, like Tweedledum and Tweedledee, while the "real life" of women talking and strolling in the sun, women being ogled, people going on about the normal business of the day, takes place on the other side of the road.

Back in New York, delighted with the view up Sixth Avenue from his fifth-floor apartment and studio on Washington Place, Sloan painted one of his most architecturally conscious works—*Jefferson Market, Sixth Avenue* expertly encompasses everything one could actually see from that vantage, from the pedestrians beneath the El to the tallest spires of the Village—as well as one of his best nudes. *Curled Nude, Red-Covered Morris Chair* is the ultimate painter's statement of what he can do: a fleshy, supple body tucked into the seat of a chair, a rich red patterned fabric, the pipe-smoking artist himself in the background quietly admiring his own handiwork, a few stabs of paint picking out his shirt and face. The goal Sloan had set himself over the better part of the past three years—to become a very different kind of painter from the one he had been when he arrived in New York—had borne fruit.

For all of his belligerence and strength of opinion, John Sloan enjoyed an unusual reputation in the American art world when he was in

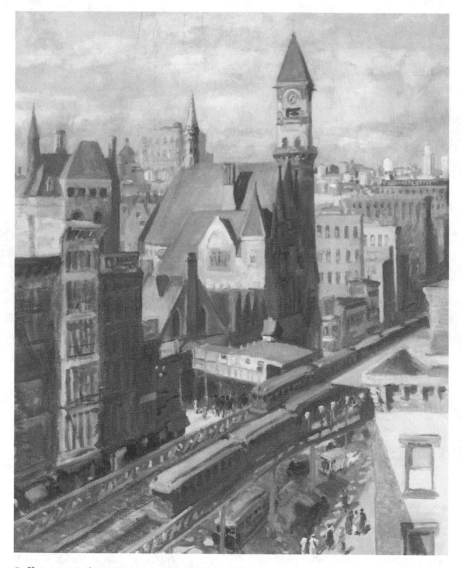

Jefferson Market, Sixth Avenue: *The northern view from Sloan's apartment at 88 Washington Place, where he moved in 1915* (Pennsylvania Academy of Fine Arts)

his late forties. Other painters made a better living, but an extraordinary number of his peers liked and respected him, while the younger generation saw him as a man worth listening to. He had a lively interest in what other artists were doing. His warm friendship with Juliana Force certainly posed no hindrance to advancement—in 1918 Sloan became a charter

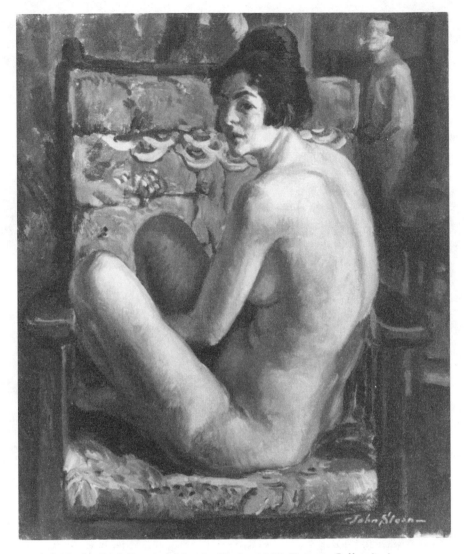

Curled Nude, Red-Covered Morris Chair, *1917* (Private Collection)

member of the Whitney Studio Club, a sort of forerunner of the consolidation of Mrs. Whitney's Eighth Street property and collection into the Whitney Museum—and any past trouble with the National Academy of Design was now seen as a badge of honor. The reviews for his second one-man show at Kraushaar's, in March (an all-paintings exhibition this time), were good and further cemented the impression that his career was finally taking off. It was hardly surprising, then, that Sloan should find himself at center stage in the Society of Independent Artists at this delicate moment in the organization's history. After the conflict over Mr. Mutt's *Fountain,* William Glackens had had more than enough of the job of heading this motley group, and the whole directorship had been dissolved later that year with the sensible idea of beginning again from scratch. An election was held, and the principal office was awarded to John Sloan. The hundreds of artists who were eager to keep the Society alive wanted a leader of creative stature and crackerjack organizational skill, a man at once unafraid of rancor and interested in bringing as many into the fold as possible, a person with experience of the group exhibition process and a combative, determined nature. They sought a true believer and a hard worker, someone perceived as neither an academician at heart nor a partisan of any of the new Modernist camps. With all of those criteria in mind, they found the right man, and Sloan was to hold the office for the next twenty-seven years.

The organization that Sloan took charge of at the end of 1917, whatever changes it was to undergo over the next three decades of its existence, was an enterprise with a broad and highly professional base of support. Duchamp's and Arensberg's departures had hardly been wounding. The other officers of the newly reconstituted Society of Independent Artists were the painter Samuel Halpert (vice president), Walter Pach (treasurer), and the art writer Hamilton Easter Field and the painter A. S. Baylinson (recording and corresponding secretaries, respectively). The Society's advisory board was something of an alumni listing of "The Eight" (with Glackens, Henri, Luks, and Prendergast), with the addition of Childe Hassam, J. Alden Weir, Arthur Dow, and Charles W. Hawthorne. The roster of "directors" spanned a healthy range from realists like Bellows and Davey to emerging Modernists such as Alfred Maurer, Abraham Walkowitz, and Max Weber. Gaston Lachaise and Glenn Coleman became active as directors soon after, while talented artists as diverse as Louis Lozowick, Jay Van Everen, Alice Morgan Wright, and George Of would run for the board in the 1920s. In other words, the Society's ranks included figurative artists and painters exploring the variations of color abstraction, Precisionists interested in the new industrial landscape and latter-day Impressionists, portrait painters, and students of Cubism—the idea, immensely satisfying to John Sloan, was that the Society of Independent Artists had room for everyone who had something to express in a recognized visual art form. While this policy bespoke a pluralism that

Alfred Stieglitz and others saw as a degraded pandering to the masses, the ultimate defeat of taste and selectivity, to Sloan and his colleagues the endeavor represented something quite different and far more important: it meant an end for all time to the closed-door policy that had kept too many artists out in the cold for too long.

In 1918 the Society had some trouble finding a venue for its annual show in wartime New York (the Grand Central Art Palace wasn't available), and the exhibition came close to being canceled during that year of austerity. But Sloan and his directors scrambled about and eventually arranged to use several storefront spaces on Forty-second Street. (By 1919 the situation had changed, and for the next ten years the Independents would convene at the Roof Garden of the Waldorf-Astoria, on Thirty-fourth Street.) The show itself—minus the Arensberg circle of Duchamp, Katherine Dreier, Joseph Stella, and John Covert, of course, as well as a few other notables such as Gifford Beal and Maurice Sterne—was smaller than its predecessor, with only 569 participants, but it was hardly less exciting. Crowds and critics alike turned out in enthusiastic numbers. Work by Picabia, Derain, and Raymond Duchamp-Villon was on view again, as were good paintings by Louis Eilshemius, Bellows, Glackens, Maurer, Kroll, Lawson, Prendergast, Walkowitz, Weber, and Marguerite and William Zorach. Theresa Bernstein, one of the very few women working in the yet-to-be-named "Ash Can" mode, exhibited here for the first time. Sloan showed *The Cot* and *The Town Steps;* Stuart Davis, his Cubist Gloucester landscapes. The inimitable Florine Stettheimer presented *The Birthday Party,* which—if it was the same 1917 group picture that was later known as *La Fête à Duchamp*—mischievously brought her friend "R. Mutt" back into the Independents, whether he liked it or not. Word was out that the Society was interested in making room for foreigners as well as for Americans, and even for those who didn't see themselves as full-time painters; the result, in 1919, was the inclusion of works by Raoul Dufy and e. e. cummings. As Theresa Bernstein later observed, for young artists worried about "breaking in," it was an altogether different game when the Independents Show opened its doors. Painters and sculptors whose work had previously been seen only by friends and colleagues in the Village now had an uptown audience of several thousand (or more) for a month out of every year. And that meant at least the *chance* of a sale, a gallery, a critical notice.

If Sloan's assumption of the presidency of the Society of Independent

Artists was in some ways a high point of his career, at approximately the same moment, in the spring of 1918, Dolly was experiencing a no less elating recognition of her worth.

Among the more distressing developments that had followed in the wake of the American mobilization against Germany was Congress's circumvention of the Bill of Rights, supported by the once-liberal Wilson. The Espionage Act of 1917 had expanded the definition of treason, and conspiracy to commit treason, not only to action but to speech and the printed word as well. Worse still, it had widened the understanding of the term "treason" to encompass any public questioning of the country's war aims, the practice of conscription, or the value of patriotism. Under these guidelines, Sloan was well out of the leadership circle of the *Masses*, as it was all he could do to keep his opinions among his friends and colleagues. But it was inevitable that the magazine would run afoul of the post office censors in any event, and indeed, in the summer of 1917 it had been declared unmailable. By the time the staff had its problems sorted out with the government, or thought it did, the *Masses* had been kept from its subscribers for so long that it was forced out of business. That didn't prevent the government, however, from filing a suit charging the magazine with conspiracy to obstruct enlistment, and in April 1918 five staff members, including Eastman, Dell, and Young, were brought to trial in New York City. One can only imagine Dolly Sloan's horror when she was called to testify in this momentous case—as a witness for the prosecution.

The *Masses* trial was a bizarre event from start to finish, "a scene," Floyd Dell noted, "out of *Alice in Wonderland* rewritten by Dostoevsky." Despite their representation by Morris Hillquit, one of the ablest lawyers in the city and a recent candidate for mayor on the Socialist ticket, the magazine's editors had ample reason to worry. Finding a jury of twelve men who didn't automatically think the worst of Socialists and pacifists was impossible. The president and the attorney general were known to be looking for a conviction, and a guilty verdict meant a mandatory jail sentence. But Dell was right: there was a Lewis Carroll dimension to the whole proceeding. Outside the courtroom a Liberty Bond drive was taking place, and every time the band struck up "The Star-Spangled Banner," everyone in the court (led by one of the defendants, the *Masses'* business manager, Merrill Rogers) felt obliged to stand, until Judge Augustus Hand finally called a halt to that disruptive display of patriotism.

Art Young, who was feisty on the stand, had a hard time staying awake otherwise, and Max Eastman did some serious backpedaling under oath in insisting that *The Masses* was by no means an antipatriotic journal. (Many radicals, expecting the trial to produce the customary martyrdom, were unhappy with Eastman's equivocations.) But Floyd Dell credited Dolly with providing some of the most crucial testimony when she was asked to discuss the workings and philosophy of the board during the period in which she and her husband had been affiliated with it. Apparently Assistant District Attorney Eric Barnes had acquired the minutes—possibly taken by Dolly herself—of the meetings in 1916 that had led to the artists' strike. He hoped to use that evidence to prove that the board was what the government said it was: a unified, anti-American, conspiratorial group. "[Dolly's] pungent testimony, however, confirmed absolutely the explanations previously made by the defense," Dell wrote in a description of the trial that summer, "and knocked Mr. Barnes' romantic surmises into a cocked hat." If there was one thing the leadership of *The Masses* had *not* been, Dolly made clear on the stand, it was a unified band of conspirators. The trouble was, they hadn't been able to agree on anything. The fights, the jabs, the sarcasm!

The jury was deadlocked with eleven for conviction and one for acquittal, and the defendants were freed. This was Dolly's shining moment, a reaffirmation of her allegiances and a very public display of her seriousness and goodwill.

The next month Sloan and Dolly left for their summer in Gloucester, the last that they were to spend there. The town was now positively overrun with artists, Sloan said; the cows were choking on the paint rags in the fields. There was an element of truth to that contention (not the part about the poor cows, of course), but only an element. The artistic population of Gloucester wasn't significantly greater in 1918 than it had been in 1914. A more plausible reason was that the Sloans had worn out their welcome on Cape Ann and felt it wise to move on. The blight of the war had not only changed life in New York but left its mark even—or especially—on the fishing villages of New England.

As fears of U-boat attacks increased in the final year of the war, particularly after the sinking of a tug and three barges off Cape Cod in July, concern about espionage and resentment toward those who weren't helping with the war effort reached a new high. Families with men in uniform overseas were openly hostile to the dissidents (and presumably some people in town knew of the Sloans' ties to *The Masses*). Gloucester eagerly joined other communities that month in enforcing new "antiloaf-ing" laws, which called for the rounding-up and questioning (in actual-ity, the harassment) of any man between the ages of eighteen and fifty who wasn't employed or in the military. The police were instructed to comb the beaches and streets for loafers—"idlers" or "slackers" in the jargon of the day—and bring them back to headquarters. If a man like Sloan, at age forty-seven within the pale of the roundup law, was sketch-ing on the rocks, he was safe because employed at his profession, even if it was a form of "work" that was looked at suspiciously by the locals in this time of national crisis. But if he was found sitting "idly" by the shore, contemplating the water or pondering the nature of life, he was fair game for the constables' queries. This couldn't sit well with John Sloan or anyone else who had originally come to Gloucester to escape the stridency and pressure of the city. When a twenty-nine-year-old New York artist, an acquaintance of the Sloans' who was staying at a nearby inn, was arrested in July 1918 because he had received what the authorities de-scribed as a "peculiar telegram," the situation must have seemed worse than ludicrous. Even after the unfortunate man was released for lack of any evidence of disloyalty, the local paper continued to refer to him as the "arrested artist" and seemed to imply some doubt about the extent of his innocence. He was, after all, neither a trusted local nor a participant in the great cause of making the world safe for democracy. The relaxed, enjoyable Gloucester of old was no more.

That there were German agents at large in Massachusetts was proba-bly a fact. Verifiable instances of sabotage were reported in many papers. It almost didn't matter, though, in this summer of Belleau Wood and the offensive on the Marne, whether the hysteria about spies was based on truth or supposition. Anyone who took a false step was subject to accusa-tion, arrest, interrogation, public humiliation. One terrifying night the earnestness of this political climate was brought home to Sloan by a visit from the local police. Dolly had been seen walking on the beach after dark with a few men who were suspected of signaling to the U-boats off the coast. No charges were being pressed at the moment; the evidence was vague. They were lucky. But Sloan knew what this meant and how far from him, and from reality, Dolly was slipping. He wept, unnerved to consider how close to disaster their lives had drifted. It was time for them to give up the "red cottage" permanently and head back to the city.

The war ended in November, and those of their friends who had fled abroad came home. Men and women who had lived in fear of arrest could relax, or so it seemed. (The "Red Scare" of 1919 and the reign of Mitchell Palmer would quickly put an end to any false hope about a blossoming of civil liberties in America.) Yeats was once more welcome at the Sloan house for long talks and leisurely dinners, and Sloan even resumed his relations with George Bellows. In discussing his situation with Randall Davey that winter, though, Sloan tried to think ahead to the following summer and to succeeding years. He and Dolly were used to escaping the city every May or June for three months or more; it was a pattern that both of them relied on now. The absence of a rural retreat was going to leave a gaping hole in their lives. Perhaps it was time for them, finally, to see another part of the country, Sloan and Davey speculated. For the past three years, since making two trips there, Robert Henri had been singing the praises of Santa Fe, a town of cheap rents, paintable landscapes and people, and pleasanter neighbors than one was apt to find in the East. This last feature probably appealed to Sloan as much as anything else after the Gloucester experience. Gertrude Whitney's purchase from Kraushaar of *Spring Rain,* one of the Madison Square paintings from 1912, provided some unexpected financial leeway. Dolly was willing, Randall Davey and his wife were agreeable to the idea, and so in the spring a decision was made. The Sloans and the Daveys would head west.

The Other America

(1919–1922)

"Why go to Greece or China? . . . {The} Southwest . . . is our own authentic wonderland—a treasure trove of romantic myth —profoundly significant and beautiful, guarded by ancient races practicing their ancient rites, in a region of incredible color and startling natural grandeur."

—Harriet Monroe, "In Texas and New Mexico," *Poetry* (September 1920)

In settling on New Mexico as the place where they would spend their summers now that Gloucester was behind them, the Sloans were exploring a part of the country that was still considered exotic to most Easterners, but they were hardly trailblazing. New Mexico had been actively campaigning for tourists and new residents since winning statehood in 1912, and Santa Fe in particular had received a much-hoped-for influx of visitors as a result of the Panama-California Exposition of 1915. People on their way to the great fair in San Diego had had a chance to see that the forty-seventh state and especially its northern towns were as attractive in climate and as culturally varied as the advertisements had promised. Willa Cather was one of those who first visited Santa Fe in 1915, while Henri and the painter Jan Matulka made their initial trips the following year. Mabel Dodge, the great patron-hostess of Greenwich Village, had come to stay in 1916, and over the next two years, Sloan's friend Leon Kroll and the artists Marsden Hartley, Andrew Dasburg, and B. J. O. Nordfeldt—men of exceptional talent and some prominence in Modernist circles—all decided to see for themselves this landscape that so many people in New York were raving about.

John and Dolly Sloan felt great seriousness and excitement about their first venture together out of the New York–New England–Philadelphia area. They trooped off to Abercrombie and Fitch and other costly stores with Randall and Florence Davey and outfitted themselves with the proper clothes, with tents and a portable stove and a small bathtub, with rain gear and edibles and travel bags. They split the expense of a used car, a 1912 chain-drive Simplex racing model that Dolly nicknamed Miss Simplex, and loaded it down with bundles tied to the back and the running boards. All four travelers professed to be eager to immerse themselves in what Henri had assured them would be some breathtaking scenery, a wonderful climate, and a fascinating culture. Dolly proudly announced that she would keep a diary of "our trip to see America."

The year just past had been a moderately productive one for Sloan, but it had not been without its disappointments, and he was ready for something new. The second exhibition of the Society of Independent Artists under his leadership had gone well, and in February the ever-dependable Mary Fanton Roberts had published a glowing account of his work in *The Touchstone,* the magazine she was now editing. (John Butler Yeats was to have written the article, but the essay he produced was not sufficiently adulatory for Mrs. Roberts's taste—which says a great deal about her faith in Sloan.) However, the annual effort to make some progress with John Kraushaar's clientele had met with the usual problems. This time Kraushaar had made the show a painting *and* drawing survey so that his artist would be able to realize some income from it, but it annoyed Sloan that the appeal of the oils continued to elude the gallery's patrons. The only sale of an oil was of *Clown Making Up,* to the Washington, D.C., collector Duncan Phillips. Reviewers praised the city pictures, of course, and reiterated the old chestnut about Sloan-as-satirist, all the while implying that Sloan as "pure" painter was still slightly off-track. A recent portrait of Dolly was singled out for criticism in both the *New York Times* and the *Sun.* All in all, Sloan couldn't wait to get on the road in June.

The Sloans and the Daveys got along very well, but if anyone in their party was expecting a pastoral idyll, he or she was quickly disabused of that quaint notion. The trip took six expensive and tiring weeks, and the car proved hardly more reliable than Dolly's intentions as a diarist (she lasted exactly four days before abandoning her journal). After resting in Syracuse, the travelers drove on to Buffalo—their second stopover without leaving New York State—at which point everything began to go downhill. If there was decent road west of Buffalo, Sloan noted, they

failed to find it. Bad tires, a faulty engine, muddy roads, confusing directions, the difficulty of getting Dolly and Florence to leave the comfortable
hotels they stayed in, and the "imminence of Prohibition"—the problems
were many and varied, as Sloan humorously remembered it. After all the
money spent at Abercrombie and Fitch, the "campers" slept a total of two
nights under the stars. They were city folks, they decided, and there was
no point in their pretending otherwise. Everyone wanted to stop when a
decent bathtub or some available liquor presented itself, though there
were definite limits to how far they would go for the latter: when a
bellboy in Ohio offered to procure a pint of whiskey for Sloan and Davey
at the astronomical cost of nine dollars, they declined. So that at least the
portable stove wouldn't go to waste, they tried to take as many of their
meals as possible by the side of the road or in open fields. By the time the
dusty foursome pulled up in front of the Art Institute of Chicago on their
first morning in the Windy City and had their photograph taken in the
baggage-laden Miss Simplex, they looked less like visiting New York
artists and their wives and more like the Joad family come to town. What
the curator of the Art Institute must have thought of his bedraggled
guests as he gave them their tour of the collection, Sloan never said.

From Chicago it was on to Omaha and then to Denver, with stops in
smaller and smaller towns along the way as the tires continued to blow
out. By mid-July Sloan would note that the rubber seemed to be almost
all gone and they were riding on the last shreds of fabric, "with three tires
ready to blow." Randall Davey was bitten by an insect, and the swelling
required treatment at a clinic in the middle of nowhere. "The girls are
heroines," Sloan wrote to Henri. Finally, with only a hundred miles to go,
Miss Simplex gave up the ghost, and the Sloans and Daveys were forced
to travel the last leg of the journey by train, leaving the car to be shipped
after them. Sloan calculated that he had managed to spend $750, or
roughly a quarter of his yearly income, in a month and a half.

Once he got to Santa Fe, though, nothing else mattered to Sloan. No
description of the light, the air, the terrain, the adobe buildings, or any
other aspect of the beauty of New Mexico could equal the reality. Everyone agreed that the difficulties of the trip paled before the keen excitement they all felt on their arrival.

While the Daveys went house hunting, the Sloans found themselves a
furnished room with a small kitchen on San Francisco Street, where Dolly
had to struggle with a wood fire and the absence of gas. Their Spanish

landlady gave them the use of the large backyard, a good place to relax in the evening, and they made the acquaintance of some of the neighborhood boys who liked to congregate there—including, Sloan noted, a six-year-old who smoked cigars. Among the first adults Sloan met in town was Marsden Hartley, an artist of the Alfred Stieglitz circle whose work he had first encountered back in 1909, when Maurice Prendergast and Arthur Davies were promoting him. Hartley's style of painting had seemed too ponderous and mystical to him then, but now he found he liked and respected this shy but amiable gay man who was experiencing the same difficulties in making a living from his art that he himself was. They set up shop in nearby studios in the newly renovated Palace of the Governors, off the town's central plaza. Soon after, Hartley introduced Sloan to a friend and patron of his, Mrs. Eva Feynes, something of a local version of Mabel Dodge (herself holding court in Taos these days). Mrs. Feynes's specialty was collecting artists' self-portraits, and Sloan obliged her by producing a sketch of himself. Whether the drawing was a gift or a sale is unclear; if, as seems likely, it was the latter, Sloan would have been entitled to see a good omen in this first week out West.

Having a suitable studio turned out to be crucial because in New Mexico, as Sloan explained to Henri, "contrary to my usual custom in Gloucester, I have made no work in the open." Santa Fe proved better for memory work of the kind that Sloan had first trained himself to do on the pavements of New York, with the amassing of intense impressions on the spot followed by the slow unfolding and reworking of those recollections at the easel. Although he would later come to feel quite comfortable working on-site out-of-doors, everything Sloan painted in the summer of 1919 was done "after the fact." Some of those paintings depicted the town itself and its inhabitants, in what was almost a transplanted version of the city genre pictures of 1904–1912. *Hotel Dance,* for instance, could really be a Manhattan painting were it not for the rustic openness of the high-ceilinged De Vargas Hotel ballroom, with its huge American flags covering the windows and its unpretentious (i.e., non-Manhattanite) revelers. *Mother and Daughter,* in contrast, acknowledges the cultural difference of this new environment in the figure of a middle-aged Hispanic mother who, wrapped in a long black shawl, escorts her daughter, in bright modern clothes, into town. But in many of the images that he created during his first weeks in Santa Fe, Sloan seems most taken with the lowness of the buildings, their simpler geometry, and their soothing,

almost abstract uniformity, all part of a network of long rectangles, gentle
verticals (posts and trees rather than skyscrapers and supports for the El),
and subtle, sun-bleached colors. Framed by the wooden pillars of the one-
story Palace of the Governors, or waiting for a midnight assignation at
the depot (an especially romantic spot), his Santa Fe figures, unlike their
New York counterparts, never seem in danger of being swallowed up by
their setting, or threatened by the great urban maw. Sky is always visible.
Clouds are a part of everyone's life, every day. Individuals fit comfortably
inside man's architecture and God's nature. These are paintings of quiet
and calm, concerned as much with composition and color as with any
kind of anecdote or idea—or, rather, content to let the composition and
the color imply the meaning, the sense of resolution, the feeling of a place
both restorative and hospitable.

At its best, the Sloans decided, Santa Fe appealed to them as a combination of two worlds. Despite the ever-growing number of summer visitors, this town of eight thousand permanent residents still felt like a
rural, roughhewn community. And that, to Sloan, meant "authentic"—in
marked contrast to New York City, which he saw as becoming too proud
of its gaudy expansion and too conscious of its wealth. The haute tourist
qualities of present-day Santa Fe, a place highly conscious of its wealth in
the 1990s, were still in the far-distant future. Then, too, the atmosphere
seemed more tolerant, more relaxed, than that of late in Gloucester: there
was no New England rectitude bearing down on them, no nosy neighbors
to make comments about "New York artists." Yet even as Santa Fe provided relief from certain aspects of the East, it had its own cosmopolitan-
ism. Edgar Hewett, the founder of the New Mexico Museum, was a
learned man with a wealth of knowledge about the Indians; he wanted to
see more artists of the stature of Sloan, Hartley, and Davey make the trip
each year, and saw to it that Sloan was comfortably set up in his new
studio. Ultimately he exerted a much greater influence on the city than a
benighted soul such as the cranky editor of the local paper, E. Dana
Johnson, who equated modern art with Bolshevism and campaigned
against both. Others whom the Sloans were to meet in the summers
ahead, including the painter Will Shuster and his wife and the poet
Witter Bynner, would prove interesting in their very different ways, and
resolutely unjudgmental. All accepted Dolly as readily as they welcomed
Sloan.

With the Daveys and their new friends, the Sloans saw as much as

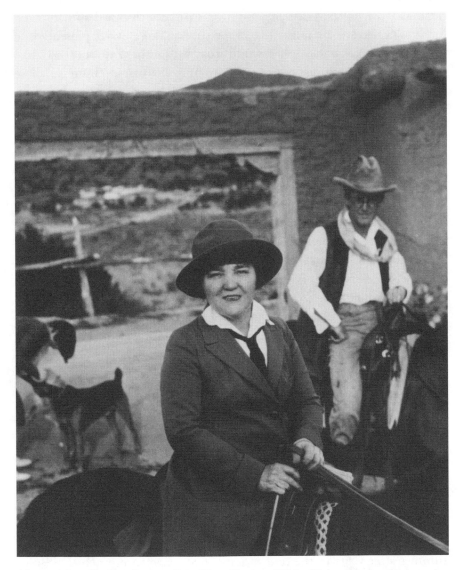

Sloan and Dolly "on the range" in New Mexico, 1920s (Delaware Art Museum)

they could outside of town, taking car trips to the major tourist sites between Santa Fe and Albuquerque to the south and up toward Taos to the north. The pictorial challenge of the arroyos, the piñon pines, the cliff caves, the vast horizon line, the spectacular sunsets, and the "desert forms, so serene and clear" served as a great impetus for Sloan; of the first forty or so paintings he completed in New Mexico, half were landscapes, and none had the tentativeness of design or structure that had so hampered his first Gloucester pictures. The other subject these drives presented, of course, was that whole other world that Sloan the Easterner had had neither contact with nor notion of. But from his first exposure to those aspects of Pueblo culture that a visitor could know—the ritual dances, the handicrafts, the art work (both ancient and contemporary), the simplicity of their way of life—he was impressed and interested, as Edgar Hewett and Marsden Hartley had assured him he would be.

The case could be made that the Pueblo Indians, as much as or more than the Western terrain or Santa Fe itself, were precisely what Sloan was looking for at this moment in his life and career. This business of painting regularly—painting anything, working with a Modernist's indiscriminate approach to content or theme—had its limitations; Sloan *did* need a good subject to provoke his best creative self, and what he observed on the Pueblo reservations was in effect co-opted for that end. His reliance on a tantalizing subject to inspire him might have separated Sloan from the Cubists or the Fauves, but it allied him to everyone else from Rembrandt and Hogarth to Eakins and Homer. The Pueblo Indians were also a group of people—"simple, unimitative, but profound," Sloan called them—who had not been extensively studied by American artists and who, almost like the residents of Chelsea, the working-class couples of the etchings and the unpretentious women of *Three A.M.,* spoke to that part of John Sloan that resisted gentrification, admired elemental values, and hated the whole aura of Protestant America and the affluent urban life. That they were to be filtered and reimagined by Sloan as much as they were "objectively" recorded goes without saying; he only hoped he wouldn't fall into the trap of sentimentalizing and trivializing them as artists like George de Forest Brush and Julius Rolshoven had done before him. *The Eagle Dance, Figures in the Dance,* and *Koshare,* painted that summer after visits to the reservations of San Ildefonso, Cochiti, Tesque, and Santo Domingo, successfully avoid that pitfall. There is a respectful plainness to Sloan's Native Americans, an absence of the corny romanticism that men like Brush and E. Irving Couse and even Henri himself fell prey to.

It was ironic that Sloan's awakening to the depth and dignity of the Native American experience should take place at just that moment when its existence was most imperiled. Among its other sorry qualities, the period of the early twenties—so often mythologized as the freedom-loving Jazz Age—was a particularly nasty time for relations between white America's government and the Indians. Artists and writers may have been busy calling attention to the aesthetic merits of what had previously been dismissed as "primitive" craft, and Indians' arts-and-crafts income may have taken a significant leap after the war, but even as the Sloans were getting settled in New Mexico, anti-Indian sentiment was on the rise. Members of Congress were charging the Office of Indian Affairs with failure to assimilate the tribes and thus to put an end to the "soft, nomad trades" of these backward peoples. Police harassment of the ceremonial dancers was recorded in 1919 in the *Santa Fe New Mexican.* By 1922 Secretary of the Interior Albert Fall, later of Teapot Dome fame, would be pushing hard for passage of the scandalous Bursum Bill to facilitate the sale of more Pueblo lands to whites, while two years after that, the Indian Oil Bill would accomplish the same goal by more devious means, and a movement to ban Indian dancing in public would find a sympathetic audience. For the Sloans and their friends, these issues were to become "causes" that mattered in much the same way that the war, socialism, censorship, and an artist's right to exhibit had mattered.

When the time came to return to New York in the early autumn, Sloan felt even more reluctant to go than he had anticipated he would. He was seeing too much that fascinated him, meeting too many lively people, having too good a time. But his life as teacher and artist in the East beckoned, and he was pleased with the knowledge that he had found a perfect substitute for Gloucester, a new home in what the Western writer Charles Lummis called the "anomaly of the Republic . . . the United States which is *not* the United States." Once again, Robert Henri's advice had been on the mark. The Daveys accompanied the Sloans by train as far as Chicago, where Randall Davey had landed a teaching job for the fall, and John and Dolly proceeded to Manhattan. Miss Simplex stayed behind.

Reaction that winter to the next Kraushaar show, in which eighteen of the twenty Sloan paintings on view were Santa Fe pictures, was decidedly mixed. Royal Cortissoz in the *New York Tribune* beat an old drum: "We have before this had occasion to allude to the want of beauty in [John Sloan's] work. Perhaps he is unconscious of it. Perhaps it is something that does not appeal to him. At all events he does not seem to

have garnered any rich imagination in the new region he has explored."
The *Brooklyn Daily Eagle* critic asserted that there was a "heaviness of
touch, a lack of spontaneity" to Sloan's art these days. But the critics for
the *Times* and the *American* agreed with the artist himself that he seemed
on the verge of an important turn in his career, that a new and revitalized
Sloan was emerging. Nothing sold during the four weeks of the exhibition, but Sloan made a present of *Koshare,* also known as *Ancestral Spirits,*
to Edgar Hewett, who immediately gave it to the Museum of Fine Arts in
Santa Fe. Thus, by the back-door route of a gift of a gift, did a Sloan oil
finally enter a museum collection.

The impact of Sloan's experience of the previous summer was also felt
at the Independents Show the following spring, where many New Yorkers
were intrigued by the inclusion of works by Native Americans of New
Mexico and Arizona, courtesy of the collections of Edgar Hewett and
Mabel Dodge. If Americans were going to lean toward a more cosmopolitan approach to art in this postwar period, whether motivated by fashion
or otherwise, Sloan wanted to see Indian artists of the Southwest such as
Fred Kabotie and Crescencio Martinez, whose watercolors he had seen in
their studios in the Palace of the Governors, get their fair share of the
attention. In the catalogue, he quoted Hewett on the theme of the "priceless inheritance" of Native American art, which white Americans had
been "blindly destroying instead of fostering"—a myopic practice that
both men hoped had come to an end. The 1920 Independents Show was
the first occasion on which Indian art was exhibited *as art,* rather than as
ethnology or archaeology, a distinction that meant a great deal in terms of
the kind and quality of interest that the work provoked. The exhibition
marked another first as well, one that was pleasing to the Society's board:
for once, when all accounts were settled, not only was there no deficit to
worry about, but the books showed a surplus of two thousand dollars (a
minor miracle, Sloan thought), ensuring the future of the project. With
attendance having exactly doubled that year and membership grown by a
fourth, the Independents had established beyond a doubt that there was a
need for this kind of unrestrictive venture.

The amount of time and energy that Sloan had to expend on the
annual shows of the Society of Independent Artists increased each time
around, or so it seemed, and the battle of conflicting principles and egos
was no small part of it. The artist and editor Hamilton Easter Field, who
had been energetically serving on three different Society committees,

caused tempers to flare that year by resigning from the publicity committee and publishing an article in the *Brooklyn Daily Eagle* charging that "old-timers" such as Robert Henri, William Glackens, George Bellows, Maurice Prendergast, Gaston Lachaise, and Walter Pach were being allowed to hog the publicity that preceded each opening, a form of favoritism that made the Independents no better—and more hypocritical—than the doddering Academy with its prize-giving and errant cronyism. As the group's main publicist, Pach came in for particular lambasting, which Sloan then felt honor-bound to defend him against. Such contretemps (and this one dragged on for almost two years, until Field indignantly quit the Society altogether) kept Sloan involved in conferences and committee meetings, some of them quite long and acrimonious, when he would have preferred to be in the studio. Between art-politics and teaching, it is small wonder that he completed only a few oils in New York during the whole of 1920, though he was particularly pleased with his two Village pieces, *Cornelia Street* and a strong portrait of the tearoom hostess Romany Marie.

His health became an issue for Sloan now, too, and some of his closest friends worried as he developed a prolonged low-grade fever and, rather than seeing a doctor, put himself on a typically fanatical diet. "Your complexion is so bad and your eyes so hectically bright," John Butler Yeats warned him in May. Henri and Bellows thought Sloan was losing his famous good looks, and told him so in hopes that an appeal to his vanity might have the effect of getting him to a doctor. However, by the time the Sloans were ready to depart New York for the summer, this time traveling all the way by train, Sloan had apparently recovered from his mysterious malady, and a pattern had been established: exhaustion by late spring, rejuvenation in the clear air and bright light of New Mexico in June, July, and August.

As it turned out, the second summer in Santa Fe was not as restful as planned. Rather than rent a room again for their three- or four-month stay, the Sloans had decided to buy property on the outskirts of town. A four-room adobe house at 134 Garcia Street with an ample backyard and plenty of privacy was available for $1,850; the owner, Madame Martin, was an old Communard of 1871—an octogenarian after Sloan's heart— who was ready to move to smaller quarters across the street. Sloan calculated that with a mortgage for $1,400, he would have enough, between his own savings and a loan of $500 from Henri, to buy the house, furnish it decently, and build an adobe studio for himself in the back. Dolly, her hair newly bobbed, was thrilled to be a homeowner at last. The apple, peach, and pear trees that filled the yard; the grape arbor; the gooseberry bushes; the rhubarb plants; the absence of trolleys or tall buildings— these more pastoral elements of their new residence were a tonic for both of them after all their years in the city and their summers in the bustling port of Gloucester. The Daveys' purchase of a little mansion on sixty acres down Canyon Road was considerably grander, but the Sloans were content, especially after their daring construction of an eight-foot observation platform atop the one-story studio. Climbing the ladder onto the studio roof and then another ladder to the platform of his tower enabled him, Sloan told Henri, to meditate at dusk on the "clouds hanging round the peaks of the Sangre de Cristo range." As the sunsets nightly soaked those mountains in red, the relevance of that Spanish term—the Blood of Christ—seemed apt to Sloan and Dolly, and hauntingly beautiful.

That something went wrong before the end of that summer is evidenced by the sudden nervous depression that overtook Dolly. For a while —several weeks, at least—she had been both even-tempered and busy, enjoying picnic outings with the Shusters and the private students her husband was working with, setting up her house, and taking part in the organization of the annual Historical Parade. Yet while Sloan was busy painting the nightly promenade on the Plaza, the Corpus Christi procession from the church orphanage, a funny satire of the absurd Julius Rolshoven posing an Indian in his studio, and some of his best landscapes in several years, his wife seemed all at once more distant than ever. Only later—two years later, to be exact—did Sloan learn the cause of her anxiety. Without telling anyone, Dolly had visited a local fortune-teller, giving in to a habit that she was never fully able to conquer and that always infuriated her husband. The cards warned of the imminence of Dolly's worst nightmare: within two years, she was told, an older man who was vitally important to her, a mainstay of her life, was going to die. Horrified by this news, Dolly chose to say nothing. She was convinced of the accuracy of the prediction and, quite sure it referred to Sloan, left to contemplate a bitter and lonely future for herself. Anxiety so intense had only one outlet for Dolly: the passage of the Volstead Act several months before had made the business of getting a drink in New York something of an expedition, but in Santa Fe she had no trouble finding sources.

The twenties began for the Sloans with high hopes and quick disillusionment. Warren Harding had his prophecies, too, but his inaugural welcome to an "era of good feelings," an enduring plateau of economic comfort, obviously didn't apply to artists, or not to *all* artists. In 1921, a Sloan painting was at last included in a major museum collection through direct acquisition when the Metropolitan Museum of Art bought *Dust Storm, Fifth Avenue* from John Kraushaar for fifteen hundred dollars, and the trend-setting magazine *Vanity Fair* featured the artist in its Hall of Fame as "one of the most vigorous of present-day American painters." But in the year he turned fifty, Sloan saw himself as more honored than fairly remunerated for his work. He was glad to have Bess and Marianna come out to New Mexico for the summer and see the house, as his two sisters treated him as the great success of the family that he surely was; new friends such as Holger Cahill, meanwhile, did their best to publicize his talents in wider circles. (Cahill wrote an essay on Sloan for a film magazine, *Shadowland*, and acted as his unofficial press agent on occasion.) All of this added up to precious little, however, in comparison to what the times promised. Everywhere, it seemed, there were indications that Americans were beginning to spend money on art in a serious way. Randall Davey, Henri, Luks, Lawson, even some of Stieglitz's "difficult" painters, not to mention the Europeans: so many artists were reaping the benefits of higher prices, more aggressive dealers, stock-market types trying their hand at collecting, and a new interest in art, either as something that mattered in a way that it hadn't before the war or as a savvy investment with its own cachet. Sloan, by contrast, found himself still having to borrow from Henri now and then, a few hundred at a time, just as he had when he first arrived in New York, nervous and unknown.

Part of Sloan's financial problem was due to the fact that he simply wasn't, and didn't want to be, the kind of man who plotted career strategies for the sake of making money, and part was due to the fact that he was becoming more generous and more impractical about money as time went on—becoming, in effect, more like his father. In November 1921 Sloan borrowed a thousand dollars against his house in Santa Fe to lend to Will Shuster, who needed to build a studio. "Shus," as his friends called him, was working hard at his painting and getting better, Sloan felt, and deserved encouragement. A few months later, Sadakichi Hartmann asked to borrow $250 toward the reprinting of one of his books, promising a quick return of the money, with interest. Although the writer had never been known to repay a loan in all his adult life, Sloan gave him a check he could ill afford and, naturally, lived to regret it: when he asked for the $250 back minus any interest at the end of 1922, hoping to deal with some pressing medical bills, Hartmann became hysterical and accused him of tactlessness and greed. (It was a ridiculous mess, but one that was typical of both men—Sadakichi Hartmann the wildly impractical prima donna, John Sloan the man under a cloud in all business or pecuniary matters.)

Of course, the medical bills were nothing Sloan could have anticipated. He required surgery for a hernia in 1922, and Dolly underwent a hysterectomy a short time later. The cost of the two hospitalizations destroyed their carefully planned budget. The real devastation of that year, however, was the death of John Butler Yeats. At eighty-three, Yeats had been slowing down for some time, but it was hard for his friends to realize that the white-bearded, garrulous, witty, gently stubborn fellow they had known for so many years as an unchanging presence in the literary life of Manhattan was nearing the end of his days. Just a few weeks before he caught the chill that forced him to take to his bed at Petipas, he had published another appreciation of his friend in the *Freeman,* extolling Sloan as a man and artist who had the "courage to be himself . . . the courage to listen to his own heart." After Yeats's quick, quiet death on February 3, who was left to speak so warmly and sincerely of Sloan, to besiege him with notes about what he was doing right and wrong in his paintings, to chide and encourage him, to understand and forgive him? James Dixon Sloan had died in 1917, but John Sloan was not exaggerating when he wrote disconsolately to Lily Yeats, "My own father's death was not so great a loss to me." Sloan senior had never been able to provide the image of strength or the kind of fervor and guidance his son needed. Henri had exuberantly filled that void for a time, but it was with John Butler Yeats that Sloan had known the only real combative, loving, paternal relationship of his life, and when he wrote on Yeats's passing that the "great warm glow has gone," he meant it. He and Dolly were emotionally crushed by their unexpected loss, the fulfillment of the Santa Fe fortune-teller's troubling prediction of two years before.

To Sloan it also seemed, sadly, that there was less and less room in America for the kind of independent spirit Yeats had been. The lover of books and paintings and conversation, the man of intellect and talent but minimal drive—that man was becoming a cruel anomaly in a land where the cost of living was on the rise and the ideals of George Babbitt and Jay Gatsby were the norm. The Village was filled with weekend sightseers, flashy cars, nighttime crowds on the prowl for the new speakeasies. The *Masses* crowd was scattered to the winds, and old friends were as apt to talk of investments as they were of belles lettres. At the time of Yeats's death, a way of life was already gone, or swiftly fading. Sloan remembered an argument of more than a decade earlier, when a friend, the illustrator Rollin Kirby, had spoken disparagingly of Yeats as a paradigm of futility, a pathetic quasi-artist who had never shown enough ambition and couldn't even pay his rent. Sloan had been furious with Kirby at the time and had told him that he was too stupid to understand Yeats's more subtle greatness of mind and spirit. But on all sides, Sloan knew, those were the terms of the world. Success, fame, prestige, money—all of these had eluded his friend, and so he would be judged a misfit, ridiculous and pitiful, by most people. Even Quinn and the great "Willie" had thought the old man a failure.

Something of this sense of modern life and the modern city as a subject at once infinitely fascinating—as it had been to Yeats—and yet treacherous and money-obsessed found its way into the painting Sloan was working on during the weeks immediately preceding and then following John Butler Yeats's death. This is *The "City" from Greenwich Village,* quite possibly Sloan's greatest work and certainly a masterpiece of American art by anyone's notion of that term. (The painting hangs today in the permanent collection of the National Gallery of Art in Washington, D.C.) Unlike most of Sloan's views of New York from his window on Washington Place at Sixth Avenue, *The "City" from Greenwich Village* is not a northerly look at the Jefferson Square Market and the buildings of Chelsea and Midtown but rather a nighttime view to the south; the "city" of the painting's title is the Wall Street area of Lower Manhattan, which rises, like the Emerald City in Oz, as a place that is splendid and distant but ultimately attainable for those who want to get there. It stretches elegantly to the top of the canvas, into the slate sky, almost an abstraction of beauty and wealth. A glowing, pink-gold light, a kind of aura, emanates from the buildings south of Canal Street and sets those blocks apart from the shadowy turf of the Village and the line of darkness that snakes its way through the middle of the picture in the form of the El. In this painting of calibrated divisions and contrasts, Sloan's most ambitious urban composition and the most dynamic study of color effects he had ever attempted, humble reality is in fact closer to the viewer, in the lower third of the picture. Despite the darkness of the rooftops and the water towers on this rainy evening, that reality has its own kind of warmth, a warmth that is all-important to the artist and arrests any viewer's attention: the headlights on the El train charging by, the streaked light reflected in the puddles on Sixth Avenue that the couples with their umbrellas have to negotiate, the storefront windows, even the bricks at the top of the building in the foreground are as gritty and homely an element in this scene as the MOONSHINE billboard ad behind Sloan's building. Radiant as it is in Sloan's canvas, the "city" of the bankers and the brokers looms in the distance as a slightly unreal place—magical, seductive, but also dangerously cut off from human lives and needs. Life, real life, or the life that matters, is in the foreground. But as the garish MOONSHINE advertisement suggests, even that is subject to change.

Indeed, the "other America" that Sloan discovered in the twenties was not only the Southwest and the great Indian culture he enjoyed each summer in New Mexico. It was more than ghost dances and arroyos. In the age of Harding and Coolidge—a time of militant "normalcy" and a stock-market boom unprecedented in American history—that new territory was also a place of avarice and chic, of slick comforts and restrictive values, in which the artist would come to feel even less at home than he had felt in the quaint Episcopalian world of his sisters and Ireland aunts.

Yearnings

(1923–1926)

"This Art Game is not a sport, it's not {a} competition; it's a mistake to give in to any such impression even momentarily."

—JOHN SLOAN to WILL SHUSTER
(1922)

At least one couple of the Sloans' acquaintance had done very well for themselves in the boom years of wartime and the early twenties. When Dolly met Elizabeth and George Otis Hamlin in Philadelphia at the turn of the century and took piano lessons with Elizabeth, the Hamlins were a middle-class couple. They proved to be loyal friends and, as George began to make money in rayon and invest it with great acumen (with sufficient success that he was able to retire from the business while still in his thirties), kept in touch with the Sloans through good times and bad. The "bad" times were certainly upon Dolly and John in 1923 as they contemplated the astronomical hospital bills they had incurred the year before and the fact that at Kraushaar's, though the etchings continued to do well, the major paintings remained unsold. With an annual salary from the League of two thousand dollars and another two thousand or so brought in each year from art sales, Sloan was getting by on an average of four thousand dollars a year in the early twenties—a decent income on the face of it, but not when one added in the expenses of models and canvas and paint, a high New York rent (a hundred dollars a month) and a Santa Fe mortgage, the cost of a cross-country trip to New Mexico every summer, and the drain of the many small loans Sloan was apt to make.

At this point George Otis Hamlin came to the rescue. A great-nephew of Hannibal Hamlin, Lincoln's first vice president, he came from a cultivated family and was as serious in his love of art as he had been in his financial dealings. Knowing of Sloan's worries, he expressed an interest in buying a block of paintings for five thousand dollars, in effect wiping out Sloan's hospital bills and other debts. The Hamlins lived in an elegant apartment on Fifth Avenue and already owned a number of their friend's etchings, which were arranged on one large wall in a kind of Sloan tableau. They periodically borrowed different oils to hang there for private exhibitions, presumably in the hope of interesting any wealthy friends or associates who came calling in the career of their favorite American artist. Sloan was agreeable to Hamlin's offer, and a deal was made. This arrangement would free him from a great deal of pressure, though it must have been obvious to all parties concerned that in the long run the Hamlins' side of the bargain was by far the better one. The twenty paintings they were acquiring for that ostensibly generous price were in reality costing them only $250 apiece. The paintings included several nudes, some Gloucester landscapes, and, preeminently, *The Cot* from 1907 and *Sunday Afternoon in Union Square,* one of the more vibrantly painted city scenes from 1912.

What John Kraushaar thought of the deal is not hard to imagine, though he left no record of his conversations with Sloan. He was in no position to argue, as he had been unable to provide his artist with the income he needed, but all dealers have to live by the art-world axiom that if a painter's work is perceived as too great a bargain, both the artist and his reputation are in trouble. And of course, who was going to buy a painting for $1,500—Sloan's average for a major work at that time—if he knew that someone else had acquired one for $250? If Kraushaar was reserved about this predicament, Sloan's newest friend, Holger Cahill, was not. With a sharp eye for the "media angle," Cahill told Sloan that under no circumstances should he let people know the facts of the Hamlin sale. On the bright side, he insisted, this was an opportunity to exploit: Businessman Buys Twenty Paintings, Whirlwind Success for Prominent Artist, good copy if ever there was any. Sloan admitted that Cahill had a point, and he let him prepare some press releases about the sale and send them out. He also gave him permission to misreport the amount of money involved, putting the "spin" they wanted on the story.

A man of initiative, energy, and a sometimes slippery sense of the truth (the facts of his origin and arrival in New York are, by his own design, a little vague), Cahill felt close to the Sloans at this point in his life. He and his wife, Katherine, had lived with John and Dolly for several months in 1921, and their new daughter, Jane, was Dolly's godchild. Sloan was not always happy about his wife's closeness to Katherine, believing that the hard-drinking Mrs. Cahill was apt to lead Dolly astray; for his part, Cahill no doubt thought it was the other way around. In any event, he wanted Sloan to become one of the big names of the decade, and he was sure his plan was a good one. "One of the most important sales of the metropolitan art season" was announced in November in newspapers across the country, with listings of the museums and private collections that were fortunate enough already to own a Sloan. At this juncture, the list didn't include many more notables than Mrs. Whitney, Duncan Phillips, and Albert Barnes, or many more institutions than the Metropolitan (*Dust Storm, Fifth Avenue*) and Brooklyn museums (*The Haymarket,* a gift from Mrs. Whitney), but the effect was nonetheless spectacular. The art magazines were happy to note a positive development for one of their own, newspapers gladly paid attention to artists when "real money" was a part of the story, and messages of congratulations for Sloan's good fortune poured in. The figure Cahill had decided on to make his client seem "hot" was twenty thousand dollars, or quadruple the actual sum. Evidently the man understood the temper of the times. The Detroit Institute of Arts soon expressed interest in *McSorley's Bar,* and the Newark Museum indicated its eagerness to acquire one or more Sloans. Happiness for Sloan must have been mixed in some quarters with envy and amazement.

The Cahill publicity blitz for the Hamlin sale had two unforeseen consequences. One was that many people naturally came to assume that Sloan had more money than he did and were reluctant to credit his later struggles during the Depression. The second was that the Internal Revenue Service, whose bureaucrats also read the papers, found it both odd and interesting that John Sloan should report on his tax return $6,020 in sales, for a total of $8,855 income for the year, when it was so widely known that he had received $20,000 from George Otis Hamlin alone. This man whose income after deductions was below the taxable limit in 1921 and 1922, this man who had never before made enough money to have to file a return at all, now found himself in the embarrassing position of having to appear for an audit before skeptical bureaucrats who were convinced he was defrauding the government. So much for the handiwork of his clever press agent, Sloan griped to his wife.

There were always other, far worse exasperations to contend with, though, than the IRS. Despite the contemporary and subsequent image-making of the postwar years as the "Roaring Twenties," a designation that suggests a relentlessly playful, high-spirited, liberal era, the decade of the flapper and the bootlegger was in fact a profoundly conservative time. Two sour episodes that occurred back-to-back in 1923 confirmed this for John Sloan. One involved censorship of the Independents; the other was a thinly veiled racist effort to curb and slander the Native American way of life. In both cases, Sloan was impelled to speak out.

Beginning in 1919, the Society of Independent Artists had rented the rooftop hall of the Waldorf-Astoria on Thirty-fourth Street for its annual exhibition. The artists and the hotel were both happy with the arrangement. On occasion the hotel's manager would have some difficulty in justifying the appearance in a public space in his building of an art work that was thought to be too erotic—even in museums in the 1920s, the contemporary nude was not as common a sight as it would be ten years later—but the directors of the Society always did their best to smooth over such awkward situations (usually by persuading the painter to submit a less controversial image) in order to ensure the renewal of their rental contract. However, during the month-long run of the spring show in 1923, a different sort of issue presented itself. The painting in question this time was challenged not on sexual grounds but for political and religious reasons, and the complainant was not the management of the Waldorf but an officer of the New York City Police Department.

The object of this concern was an unexceptional picture by J. Francis Kaufman entitled *Father, Forgive Them for They Know Not What They Do.* Of interest more for its theme than for its artistry, Kaufman's painting was a satire pitched to a nation beginning its fourth ludicrous year as a "dry" society. It depicted former Congressman Volstead, William Jennings Bryan, and William Anderson, president of the Anti-Saloon League, at Cana, preparing to arrest Christ, the original bootlegger, for turning water into wine at the wedding feast. For Sloan and his friends, Kaufman's point was a fair one: the passing of the neighborhood bar and the rise of the more expensive speakeasies were simply making criminals out of honest citizens, lining the pockets of the gangsters who owned the speakeasies, and creating a more dangerous drinking situation for all (the poor quality of the unregulated liquor often had serious consequences for unlucky patrons). Certainly Prohibition had done little to stop the intake of John and Dolly Sloan, the Shusters and other friends in Santa Fe, or old colleagues such as George Luks, whose alcoholism was now out of control. A more suitable target for an artist's wit circa 1923 would be hard to imagine.

The police department looked at the matter differently, however, and demanded that the painting be removed from the Waldorf. A. S. Baylinson, as the Society's representative in charge of accepting works for exhibition, rightly refused to take the picture down and was arrested and charged with an affront to public decency, which at that time connoted disrespect toward religion as often as it did sexual expression or vulgarity of language. With ten thousand visitors to the show that year and not one public complaint about Kaufman's sarcasm, the whole business seemed asinine to Sloan, but he dutifully appeared in court in May to testify vigorously in defense of the picture and of the Society's right to exhibit it. The judge, no friend to the artistic community, took a rather narrow view of the obscenity issue, deeming censorable any art work displayed in public that could offend any decent-minded, religious American; he thus naturally decided against Baylinson and the Society. A year after the first trial, in the fall of 1924, the state's Supreme Court Appellate Division reversed the lower court ruling, and the matter was put to rest. But it served for Sloan as a troubling indicator of how little progress had been made since the war in guaranteeing freedom of expression. Some battles were never really over.

Equally galling to Sloan at around the same time were developments in the Southwest, where right-wing Protestant groups, like the Committee on Indian Affairs of the YWCA, were working with officials in Washington and the Bureau of Catholic Missions to bring the Pueblo Indians into line. "Bringing them into line" meant calling a halt to the freedom that Native Americans had had up to that time, such as it was, to maintain their own cultural traditions; it meant initiating programs to force Native Americans into that great cozy fold of right-dressing, hardworking, churchgoing "moral" Americans. The Interior Department, not content with its Teapot Dome shenanigans, had long been trying to wrest Indian territory in New Mexico from its occupants through various quasilegal means for the sake of lucrative development by white businessmen; and in 1922 Sloan, Davey, and Henri had joined Mary Austin, Witter Bynner, Zane Grey, D. H. Lawrence, Carl Sandburg, Vachel Lindsay,

Edgar Lee Masters, and others in circulating an Artists' and Writers' Protest Petition against the land-grabbing Bursum Bill (which was ultimately defeated). But for Sloan the outer limit of decency was crossed with the YWCA's coordinated attack on Indian dances. He was horrified that the government would even consider a proposal to ban these ancient rites, which, he maintained, had their own beauty and should in no way be a concern of the white man's churches or the white man's government.

Sloan had dealt with the ritual of the Indian dances eight times in oil and once in an etching by the end of 1923. He had attended a Snake Dance in 1921 with Mabel Dodge (now married for a third time, to Tony Luhan, an Indian she met in New Mexico) and had gone with other friends to see the Eagle Dance at the San Ildefonso reservation and the Corn Dances at San Domingo and elsewhere. Sloan's attitude on these outings was always one of fascination and respect—though he was caught, once, violating the tribe's injunction against on-site drawing or photographing of the spectacle, and only reluctantly handed over his quick sketch. Beyond question, though, the charges made by those who wanted the dances stopped—that they were immoral, un-Christian displays of paganism, that they incited the participants to sexual debauchery, and

Sloan painting in New Mexico, with Dolly in the car, 1926
(Delaware Art Museum)

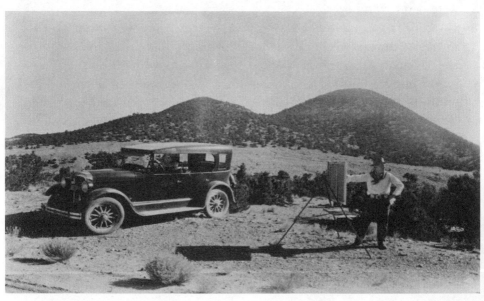

that they retarded the assimilation of the natives into the American main-stream—struck him as absurd. In fact, the shoe fit better on the other foot, he sometimes implied. In *Grotesques at San Domingo* (1923), as in his 1927 etching *Knees and Aborigines,* Sloan contrasts the intense Indians with the gawking tourists, to the detriment of the latter. "I think I am in a position to inform the reader that the grotesques in the picture are in the immediate foreground [i.e., where the Anglo spectators are gathered]," he later remarked. A pleasure-seeking society charmed by jazz, wild cabaret dancing, higher hemlines, and nudity in silent films was in no position to charge the Pueblos' religious pageants with libidinous intentions and socially destructive results. The characterization of the dances by Charles Burke, the commissioner of Indian Affairs, as "useless and harmful performances" was racism pure and simple, Sloan felt.

Sloan himself joined in the fight by taking up the pen, publishing a comprehensive essay on the debate. Though always ready to sign petitions and urge his friends and colleagues to write to Congress, he was never as comfortable with writing at any length as he was with talking or drawing, but in this case he decided that as a well-known artist, he ought to be rallying public opinion on a larger scale. The people who read the art magazines in the 1920s, for instance, tended to be just those affluent, well-connected collectors and professionals who might wield the kind of indirect influence that would make a difference. Published in the January 1924 issue of *Arts and Decoration,* "The Indian Dance from an Artist's Point of View" responded to those who wanted to portray the Native Americans as a less "civilized" people, and at the same time took a good swipe at the Puritan strain in the American temperament. "We have here in America large groups of people who would stop anything they didn't want to do," Sloan wrote. This imposition of narrow majority-rule values had to be fought on all fronts, and at the moment the front was in the Southwest. The essay reviewed and refuted the charges about the dances; questioned the incongruity of a government Indian Bureau that was supposed to protect the Native Americans yet seemed to side more frequently with their enemies; and tried to suggest something of what the dances might mean to Anglo men and women—artists—whose lives had been spent searching for beauty, mystery, authenticity, and symbolic gestures. Ultimately, Sloan wrote, the problem was ignorance, smugness, intellectual laziness, and unbridgeable divisions of culture: "I have found that very few people, even those living in their immediate vicinity, know the

Indians at all. The white races and the Indians are so fundamentally apart
that an intimacy is essentially impossible. This is true of the Chinese
people and the white race, largely true of India and the white races." Yet
ironically, Sloan felt that the Native Americans he had met were more
hospitable than their white counterparts, while too many visitors to the
reservations were "rude and unappreciative, often insulting." (If anything
was to be banned, he speculated, perhaps it ought to be the outsiders'
attendance at the dances.) "What is left of a beautiful, early civilization"
should simply be left alone, Sloan's essay concluded, "allowed to survive
with its *soul* as well as its body intact."

There were those, including some of the artist's harshest critics, who
felt that his attachment to the Southwest was itself passing beyond the
tourist stage to something deeper, more personally felt. In reviewing
Sloan's 1923 show at Kraushaar's, the exacting Henry McBride suggested
that the New Mexico paintings were more honestly realized and less self-
conscious than those of the previous years. Sloan had gone west as a "rank
tenderfoot," McBride wrote, and for the longest time had been unable to
"shed his New York eyes." As a result, the pictures he had completed
there might as well have been painted in Manhattan or Provincetown.
But as a "lover of contrasts," an artist who "requires exaggerated forms
of life in order to free his inner mental mechanism," Sloan was finally
warming to New Mexico now that the Tenderloin and the Bowery
were no more. McBride praised *Cliff Dwellings* as an "essay into the
abstract"—Sloan painted four versions of the pockmarked cliffs of the
Frijoles Canyon—and commended some of the other landscapes for
their integrity of color, their lack of anecdotal detail, their sheer painterly
skill.

There was something to McBride's point about Sloan's acclimatiza-
tion. By degrees, Sloan had settled in Santa Fe and had come to feel that
the Garcia Street house and the hills and plains outside of town were as
much his home as Greenwich Village was. In 1920 he had joined Randall
Davey, B. J. O. Nordfeldt, and other painters in organizing the Santa Fe
Art Club to sponsor exhibitions of members' work around the country,
and he had been included in group shows at the Los Angeles County
Museum (and later at the Montross Gallery in New York) in which he
was billed as a "Western painter." He was known, too, for his regular
down-home letter-to-the-editor appearances in the Santa Fe paper, de-
fending modern art and attacking stereotypes about artists. Dolly had as

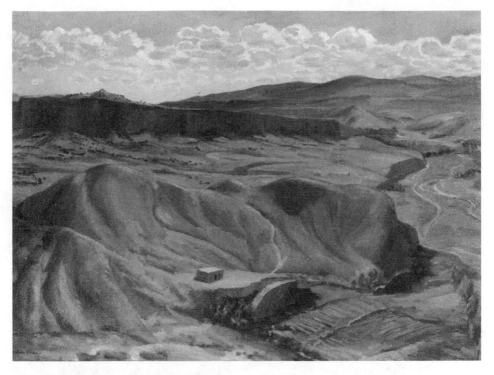

Little Ranch House, *1926* (Kraushaar Galleries)

many friends in Santa Fe as she did in New York, and Will Shuster had become Sloan's staunch companion as well as his sometime painting partner—with a much-appreciated still in his backyard. Little by little, Sloan saw himself as both a New Yorker and a New Mexican, and the two identities were, or often could be, equally satisfying.

Sloan's love of the land and the light and the whole aura of New Mexico was in marked contrast to the reactions of some of his Eastern friends. Stuart and Wyatt Davis made the trip out with the Sloans in the summer of 1923, Stuart fully expecting to fall in love with the area, just as he had with Gloucester, which he had also first visited as a guest of the Sloans. But while he painted a few fine pictures there, Davis wasn't at all pleased with the landscape in Santa Fe. It was too much, he felt, too all-pervasive, too insistent in its colors and vistas and history, not at all something that a budding abstract artist could enjoy and use for his own ends. Wyatt Davis eventually chose to settle in New Mexico, but his brother never returned for a second stay.

After eight satisfying years on the job, Sloan decided not to return to the Art Students League in 1924. There was much about the place that he enjoyed: the work still challenged him, and he was meeting any number of interesting students. His quirky young assistant Ivan Dombrowski, an impoverished Russian immigrant who had renamed himself John Graham, was obviously a painter with a future and was a delight to work with. Registration for his classes was gratifyingly high; there was even a hard core of devotees at the school who called themselves the Sloanians and looked to their middle-aged teacher as a guru, a Henri updated to the new age. They showered him with end-of-term presents, books and cuff links and Tuscan cigars. After the evening class they would walk with him the three miles or so from the League to Washington Place, where if Dolly was still awake they would be invited up the five flights for a late-night visit. But despite the good fellowship, Sloan was tired of laboring for what he saw as an unfair wage, and he called the administration's bluff over the issue of salary. The administration, in turn, accepted his resignation.

Sloan could afford the gamble—for a while, anyway. His finances were looking better thanks to the Detroit Institute's purchase of *McSorley's Bar* at the end of 1923, the sale of two paintings to the Newark Museum, and a rising tide of interest in his more recent etchings. Washington Square had replaced Madison Square as the focus of Sloan's city observations in the twenties, just as etching had replaced painting as his medium for urban themes, and his evocations of a changing New York, such as *Bandit's Cove* and *Snowstorm in the Village,* deftly captured the energy of Prohibition-era socializing and Manhattan architecture. He had also taken a job the previous fall in Baltimore, where he spent a day every three weeks critiquing student work at the Maryland Institute of Art, and that extra money nicely covered the summer rent on Washington Place (always a tricky matter when the Sloans were out of town in New Mexico). At least one student in Baltimore was grateful for the circumstances that brought this oddly flamboyant New York artist into his orbit: Lee Gatch, an important abstract painter of the 1950s, was just out of his teens when John Sloan appeared on the scene to challenge and instruct him for a few weeks. Coming from a rigid Catholic family with no respect for artists or for their son's ambitions, Gatch thought Sloan a godsend of inspiration, a cranky, not always approachable man who confirmed his feelings about how hard a life he would be choosing if he followed his bent—but how splendid a life, too. If a significant part of good teaching has to do with creating an aura about one's subject and inspiring students to want to press ahead on their own, regardless of obstacles, Sloan was a master teacher from the start. He spoke to the needy more than to the complacent, to those who saw art more as a calling than as a career choice.

The students in New York who were unhappy about Sloan's departure made their feelings known, and their teacher was back in his classroom at the League for the start of the next academic year. (How the salary issue was resolved isn't quite clear from the records, but Sloan appears to have received a raise.) Of course, none of this affection for Sloan as a teacher was due to any cultivation on his part of a more mild-mannered approach. If anything, with each year on the job, Sloan became *more* acerbic and intimidating. "Once in class I was in a terrible dilemma over painting draperies," one student remembered. "When Mr. Sloan came round, I appealed to him for help. I said I couldn't paint draperies. He exclaimed, 'Oh, oh, she can't paint draperies! That would be a wonderful epitaph! Here lies whatever-your-name-is; she couldn't paint draperies.'" Yet in recounting this moment of public abuse in a letter to a friend, the student (interestingly) did not evince any anger toward Sloan. Rather, Jennie Slaughter felt that she had understood immediately what her teacher was doing. Her problem, she thought, had been her narrow preoccupation with technique, just that state of mind that Sloan had been lecturing against. He wanted her to get beyond the idea that there was a prescribed way to do draperies, or anything else. Think of the drape as a piece of sculpture if that will help, Sloan told her later; make it out of folds and creases of paint, but don't work toward simply *imitating* the look of the drape. What she was, or should be, working toward was the *idea* of a drape, or the mental impression of one in the context of her painting, not a simple flat reproduction of a drape. *Realization,* not *realism,* was the term he was fond of. He wanted no budding academic painters in his class, but neither was he sparing of those students who didn't worry about technique because of some natural facility. Facility struck him as dangerous. Anything that mattered should come hard, should require thought and labor. To one student whose drawings seemed effortless, Sloan suggested that he use his left hand or, failing that, his feet. Resist anything that comes too easily, he warned. Resist an empty show. He liked to tell the story of the time ten years before, when

Theodore Dreiser had visited his studio looking for "atmosphere" for *The Genius,* but had left discouraged, feeling that Sloan's workplace was too serious, too mundane, too unromantic. He found what he wanted at Shinn's.

Throughout the early and middle twenties, Sloan continued to enjoy a reputation at the League for having wide-ranging interests. The Abstract Expressionist Adolph Gottlieb, a student there while still in his teens, thought that was one of Sloan's best qualities: "[He] had the most valuable influence on me because [he] was a very liberal guy for his time." Gottlieb remembered that Sloan seemed more interested in Cubism than most other instructors he knew, during a period when Cubism was still considered suspect in many quarters of America. Indeed, Sloan seemed interested "in everything that was happening in modern art," Gottlieb recalled, and that curiosity served as both a good example and a stimulus for his more inquiring students, even those who—like Gottlieb himself— would later go on to work in a vein that Sloan would find difficult to grasp. When, in 1925, *Forum* magazine asked John Sloan and several other art-world professionals to write editorials in defense of Modernism, Sloan had no trouble expressing his values. "The academic point of view is really a very modern sickness and the so-called modern movement is more nearly related to the ancient art spirit of mankind," he wrote, hinting at how great a role his enthusiasm for Native American art played in his study of Modernism. The Armory Show had had in any event effected a cure for that academic "sickness," Sloan continued, and the decrepit art "being conserved by the official and institutionalized art organizations will not long be able to resist the cure." Yet other students at the League gravitated to Sloan precisely because he hadn't thrown overboard all interest in the Old Masters in the face of the new. Easoni Martin, a student of Sloan's from 1919 to 1924, was impressed by his constant informed allusions to Rembrandt, El Greco, Goya, and Hogarth, and remembered his showing the class his Daumier lithographs and the Gericault sketch he had bought for a few dollars, unidentified, at auction. In the best work of the older artists, whether in painting or in drawing, every inch of the canvas or paper was alive with meaning, Sloan reminded his students, every section of it a work of art in itself.

The talented painter Katherine Schmidt, later the wife of the artist Yasuo Kuniyoshi, admitted that she didn't actually get much out of

Sloan's class, but she appreciated his directness and principles, his quality of mind and his view of his role as an artist and a teacher:

> I think that the people he did the most for were the people who had learned to paint in the Academy fashion . . . he would tear into their work and just put them on their feet. Nothing superficial . . . you had to be sincere. . . . And the people he loved most were the butchers and bakers and candlestick makers who came to the evening classes after working hard all day. He would work so hard over them. He loved their sincerity.

Not surprisingly, between the hours he spent at the Art Students League and the occasional weekend "crit" sessions he offered for those students who wanted or needed more attention, Sloan's own productivity declined in New York. In 1924, for instance, he painted the elegant *Grand Central Station* with its shafts of sunlight beaming through the high windows of the terminal; a portrait of the composer Edgard Varèse; a self-portrait; two nudes; a view of Washington Square from the west and one of Dolly walking in the spring rain by the carriage of a flower vendor: only seven pictures in eight months. Everything else he did that year, more than a dozen other paintings, was the product of the three or four months he spent in New Mexico. Here, Sloan feared, was the real danger of a life lived on too many fronts: there was never enough time to paint.

Chief among those other pursuits—passions or distractions, as the moment made them seem—was the growth of the Society of Independent Artists. There were those who questioned whether there was still a need for a large, open annual show now that more galleries had sprung up in New York and other cities, now that America was more "art-conscious." Writing in the *Dial* in 1924, Henry McBride worried about the "contagion of naïveté" that was spreading out from the Independents, and as always, he had a point. There *was* something incongruous about an exhibition that showed Sloan, Henri, and Glackens side by side with the most mawkish unskilled amateur, or the young Elsie Driggs or Adolph Gottlieb next to an aging Sunday painter from the hinterland. And as time went on, the contrasts were to become even more glaring: Alexander Calder, Milton Avery, Charles Burchfield, Lee Gatch, John Graham, and

Chaim Gross all exhibited with the Society in the 1920s, even as the number of nonprofessionals of stunningly little talent continued to grow. True, the public was used to the mixed-bag nature of the shows, and the professionals set prices on their works that drew a sharp distinction between them and those of amateur status offering an oil for forty dollars or a drawing for eleven-fifty, but how was one to justify the Society's annual display on the basis of seriousness and aesthetic quality?

Sloan's feelings on the matter were clear as day. Between erring on the side of an exclusivity that would admit a chosen few and keep out young or underappreciated artists—an exclusivity such as he had known and suffered when the National Academy of Design still meant some-thing—and erring on the side of a manic, slapdash democracy, Sloan would choose the latter. He had come to detest the elitist tone of the art galleries of his day, the stuffiness of most museum curators, the preten-sions of the connoisseurs who had branded his etchings vulgar some twenty years before. For Sloan, those early insults remained unforgettable, and one of his several missions in life was to see to it that no one else would have to know the experience of creating a work only to have it kept from the public by a system that narrowed and stifled expression and exposure in the name of "quality" and "fine art." These were important values, Sloan felt, but they were highly subjective ones, and the only harm in allowing every man and woman who spent time painting or sculpting or drawing a chance to exhibit was the harm done to the ego of the "professional." Most important, Sloan had no faith—he had no reason to have any faith—that the gallery system as it existed would see to it that the best and the brightest were able to thrive. A dealer was a con-servative creature, a man with a herd instinct and no special aptitude for recognizing a new style or vision. Wait for the dealers of Manhattan to find the great struggling artist of the Bronx or Omaha or Albuquerque and you might wait a long time. But the Independents, forsaking the sacrosanct aura of High Art, gave everyone a chance. "If the Society . . . only introduced to the small, appreciative audience of art lovers, *one* artist of significance a year, I would think the show worthwhile," Sloan wrote. As a reporter for the *Pittsburgh Post* summarized the situation in 1924 (to Sloan's satisfaction), "John Sloan has always been a sort of Cyrano de Bergerac of painting, taking up the battle for those less well equipped."

But even on the grounds of aesthetic quality alone, Sloan felt that the Independents had nothing to apologize for. For all of the grumbling over the years about the amateurs who turned out by the dozens at the Waldorf, the roster of artists who exhibited—many of them repeatedly—in the annual exhibitions in the 1920s (and then into the '30s and early '40s) is striking: in addition to those listed above, Reginald Marsh, Ralston Crawford, William Gropper, Jan Matulka, Stefan Hirsch, Morris Kantor, Karl Knaths, Mark Tobey, George Ault, Robert Laurent, Philip Evergood, and Raphael Soyer were all glad to participate. The mediocrity didn't obscure or diminish the flashes of genius. And where else would New Yorkers have seen the art work of Native Americans in the early twenties, Sloan argued, if not at the Independents? An invitation to Diego Rivera, David Alfaro Siqueiros, José Clemente Orozco, Rufino Tamayo, and other Mexicans to exhibit in 1923 marked a similar cultural breakthrough (at a time when Latin American painting was very little appreciated in the North), just as the organization of no-jury shows in Chicago and Buffalo that year proved that the open-door principle served a need.

By 1924, however, the financing of the show was getting to be a problem. The nine-hundred-dollar surplus of 1922 had given way to a loss the next year that mushroomed a year later to a serious two-thousand-dollar deficit. The cost of renting space at a major Midtown hotel, of printing catalogues, and of advertising the show, the aggravation of handling the correspondence and the membership paperwork and a thousand other details—all of this was proving to be a bit much for the executive skills of Sloan and his board of directors. A. S. Baylinson worked with dogged determination as the Society's secretary, and Sloan made sure that no one could accuse the administrators of wasteful spending, but still the gap remained between their bare-bones expenses and their modest income from admissions fees and the commission on any sales. Sloan's appeals to the generosity of Gertrude Vanderbilt Whitney to help the Society out of its debt, and her graciousness in meeting those appeals, became something of a spring ritual.

The squabbles that were also an inevitable and fairly regular part of the in-house business of the Society of Independent Artists were another hurdle Sloan took in stride. Glackens had been only too happy to quit the post of president in 1917; there was nothing he disliked so much as a fight. His successor, it seemed to some people, actually relished a good brawl. The energy that had once been channeled into the drama of socialism now went into coping with the divergent personalities and prejudices of New York artists. Sloan was only too happy to take on Hamilton Easter Field over Field's charges of favoritism in the Society's press coverage, and when Abraham Walkowitz lost his bid for reelection to the board and foolishly accused the president and his cohorts of anti-Semitism and of falsifying the vote, Sloan lambasted him. Sloan's tartness toward his students now carried over into other arenas. He expected his fellow directors to devote themselves to their duties with the same ardor he displayed, and he had no hesitation in turning his wit or his temper on a colleague who seemed to be slacking. Max Weber, a touchy sort under the best of circumstances, was dealt with brusquely by Sloan when he missed a number of board meetings; Sloan was embarrassed later to learn that Weber's absences had been due to the illness and subsequent death of his mother. Yet without a strong hand at the helm, a body such as the Society was sure to founder, and the membership evidently approved of his leadership, as he was reelected to his office year after year.

The makeshift, social, and uninstitutional nature of the Society of Independent Artists appealed to Sloan's personality, to his faith in artists' self-reliance and his own capacity to deal with obstacles, and when the paintings and drawings were finally on the walls every year and the sculptures arranged and tempers calmed and rivalries put to rest, John and Dolly Sloan threw themselves into the gaiety of the opening-night party or the Society's fund-raisers with the vigor of twenty-year-olds. For a time, the Society's parties were costume affairs, and Dolly—who often took charge of the events—came in a variety of Elizabethan outfits, while her husband always looked distinguished in his Navajo blanket. The Waldorf Orchestra provided the music one year, the Provincetown Players came to dance the next, and the patronage of cosmopolitan *bonhommes* such as *Vanity Fair* editor Frank Crowninshield generally ensured large crowds and abundant press coverage. As one attending artist noted, though, when the Independents opened their doors, it was always a matter of the "evening gown and the sweater . . . the diamond stud along side the flannel shirt . . . a veritable cross-section of autocracy and Bohemia"—a far remove, Sloan could reflect with pride, from the Academy receptions of old and their uniform personages, uniform paintings, uniform minds.

In this spirit of anarchic playfulness, Holger Cahill and John Sloan brought off their own little Dadaist escapade in 1924 by exhibiting an art work supposedly sent to New York by the South American Inje-Inje

tribe. According to Cahill, who served as publicist for the Society after
Hamilton Easter Field's departure, the Inje-Inje lived in a remote region
between the Amazon and the Andes; their communication was limited to
two words (*inje* and *inje*) and a great expressiveness of gesture; their
submitted "art work" consisted of a large board scraped, burned, and
scored to look like an aboriginal creation. Plans were made for a theater
evening of Inje-Inje music and a magazine with illustrations of tribal life
(Alfred Maurer, Mark Tobey, and Malcolm Cowley were ready to help),
but these aspects of the enterprise came to naught. Of interest to Sloan
and Cahill was the fact that no one in the press or among their peers not
in on the prank commented on the tribe's unusual submission to the
show. Some distance had been traveled since the days of R. Mutt and his
gleaming fountain of controversy.

The past—New York before the Great War, the heady days of
"The Eight"—seemed to recede more quickly and more emphatically in
1924 with the deaths of Maurice Prendergast (the first of the Macbeth
group to die) and John Quinn. Both had been involved with the Society
and instrumental in the success it had achieved, and Sloan felt the double
loss. (He undoubtedly never knew how low Quinn's opinion of him had
sunk; to William Butler Yeats, the lawyer spoke of Sloan as a "third-rate
painter" and erroneously implied that the Sloans had been of less help to
John Butler Yeats than they pretended.) George Bellows's death after an
appendectomy the following January was even more shocking, and Sloan
served as a pallbearer and sat on the committee that oversaw his posthumous retrospective the next year at the Metropolitan Museum. Ironically,
Bellows had come to feel a real affection for Sloan over the years, a feeling
Sloan sometimes found hard to reciprocate, given their rivalry for Henri's
affections and what he saw as Bellows's questionable values. But he had
nevertheless been a piece of Sloan's own history, a gutsy participant in
their mutual efforts to reinvent modern American art; now he was gone,
at forty-two. In the view of some critics, Luks and Glackens and Lawson
were past their prime. Everett Shinn had done well in Hollywood as an
art director and was living like the lord of the manor with his third wife
(there would be four in all) in Westport, Connecticut. Arthur B. Davies,
who spent six months of each year in Europe, was scarcely heard from
these days either. (Davies would die abroad in 1928, at which time the

story of his two families and two identities would come out.) Henri himself, teaching at the League and painting portraits of an almost generic nature, seemed less and less a figure to be reckoned with. In his midfifties, Sloan felt the press of time ever more urgently.

Yet certain things, annoyingly, never seemed to change—curators and dealers, for instance. Beginning in the middle of the decade, Sloan was invited to lecture more frequently, and he took advantage of those occasions to air some of his less diplomatic, more deeply felt opinions. Speaking to a businessmen's club in Newark early in 1925, he gave a feisty talk on the subject of art collecting in America, taking special care to ridicule the European bias that held this country back. "Most of our museums are on the wrong trail," he told his audience, "like millionaire beggars sitting hungrily around the banquet table of European art, hoping that their millions will purchase a crumb or two that will add eternal lustre to their gaping galleries." Enough of trying to establish Americans' cultural credentials by buying the "laurel-crowned masterpieces of the past," which usually (Sloan charged) turned out to be second-rate examples of an artist's work; enough of judging by the foreign name and the provenance and the textbook summaries. "The sign of the true art patron is his attitude toward the art of his own country," he observed. "Does he stimulate [the art of his time] by his interest and encourage it by supporting it?" In his own relations with art dealers, Sloan was already adopting a less patient and submissive tack: when Erwin Barrie of the Grand Central Galleries expressed interest that year in doing what he could for Sloan, the artist left some works with him. (In the twenties, arrangements with galleries were somewhat looser, so that the overlap of dealers would not have had the same significance it has today. Nevertheless, if Kraushaar had been doing better selling Sloans, it is likely that theirs would have been an exclusive arrangement after all.) Yet when Sloan heard that Barrie was playing games with the prices he quoted his clients and pretending that his commission was open to negotiation, he blasted the Grand Central Galleries director in a furious letter. At this stage in his career, Sloan wanted it known, he was not going to act grateful just because a dealer consented to look his way. He wanted fair treatment, or none at all.

One event during this period struck Sloan as a hopeful attempt to revive the best of the past, but in the end it proved short-lived and profoundly discouraging to him. In February 1925 Maurice Becker, whom Sloan had worked with on *The Masses,* and Hugo Gellert, who had arrived there after his departure, wrote to him about a plan to publish a monthly magazine of political commentary and graphic art, called *The New Masses,* under the direction of Mike Gold and Joseph Freeman. The artist Louis Lozowick had already expressed interest in joining the team, and other prominent men in the arts who were known for their left-wing sympathies, among them John Dos Passos, were being sounded out. At first Sloan was ambivalent. Gold and Freeman were active members of the Communist Party of America, a fact that didn't sit well with Sloan, who was uncomfortable with the rigidity of this organization that seemed to spout whatever line it was handed from Moscow. He was no less worried about the alternative, however: a society without any serious, lively resistance to capitalism or conservative Republican rule. Sloan had supported Robert La Follette in his third-party run for the White House in 1924, but it was obvious to anyone who had known the fervor of the Paterson Strike Pageant or the charismatic presence of Eugene Debs that the "loyal opposition" was in trouble in America. So Sloan agreed to take on a figurehead position with the new periodical. As John Dos Passos, indulging in a similar burst of optimism, wrote to Maurice Becker when he was approached by the editors, "From the list, I gather you are trying to start something like the old *Masses.* If that's so, I'm absolutely with you. . . . *The Masses* was the only magazine I ever had any use for."

When he read the first two issues of the magazine the next winter, though, Sloan realized that he was being used for his name, and in a fairly scandalous way: the masthead of this dour, party-line journal implied entirely inappropriate connections to the early freewheeling, intellectual days of Max Eastman and Jack Reed. The prose was awful, the spirit bleak and doctrinaire. Eastman himself, who had since been to Russia, was not surprised. He had long been skeptical of the new brood. Gold, Freeman, Gellert, and their friends were in his estimation the "obedient priests of the new cultural bigotry developing in the Kremlin." Sloan agreed, and in the spring of 1926, he demanded that his name be removed from the magazine immediately. "I have no intention of being used as window-dressing for the Communist Party," he told his wife. Hopeful that Russia might someday stumble its way toward a workable egalitarian society, Sloan hated to hear anyone make critical comments or predictions about Lenin's legacy, but for the Communists he knew and the party in America, he rarely had a good word.

Sloan's work from these days, a period in which his interest in etching was renewed even as he began to hit his stride again with oil painting, is full of contrasts. The solitary and the social, the single figure and the boisterously convivial group, seemed to interest him equally. Snowball fights and double-decker buses in Washington Square, windy updrafts raising skirts and eyebrows at the subway entrance, reverent crowds outside St. Francis Cathedral in Santa Fe, and yet another view in oil of the El in the Village with gangs of laughing women dodging the traffic of Sixth Avenue suggest a John Sloan at peace with himself. Yet he could also be like the lone rider by the mud-gorged river in *Chama Running Red* (1925), his imagination taken with the allure of the empty desert landscape or the pensiveness of *Dolly with Mantilla* (1925–1926). The hefty nudes he labored over in his studio don't always seem to connect with, or belong to, the world of flesh and sex and personality.

In some ways, the oddest and truest reflection of Sloan's state of mind at this time, neither here nor there, is the etching he made in the summer of 1926 for the invitation to a Santa Fe celebration of his and Dolly's twenty-fifth year together. On a rock surrounded by the breaking waves of the ocean, Sloan and Dolly lean against one another. Each steadies the other against the elements, but they don't necessarily seem to be looking at the same point on shore. His arm drapes over her shoulder and his hand hangs by her breast, yet the size and jut of the rock prevent them from pressing tightly together. *Anniversary Plate* is also known by the title *On the Rocks,* as good (and accurate) a pun as any for the situation. Of some significance in this tenuous period of the marriage, Sloan was later to acknowledge to his second wife, was Dolly's indifference to physical passion. Since her hysterectomy in 1922, Sloan said, Dolly's feeling for the conjugal side of married life had been rapidly diminishing.

That Sloan found Dolly's lack of interest in sex difficult to live with seems plausible—it would be difficult for any spouse who didn't share the lessening of desire—but there is no way to know what, if anything, he did about it (at least before meeting his student and model Gitel Kahn, with whom he was involved in the early 1930s). But the image of John Sloan in his fifties as a long-suffering, monastic, saintly man, content to let the urges of the body go while he tended to his art, seems false and a little crude. For one thing, his nature had always been more intensely sexual, even ribald, than many people knew. A favorite leisure-time book of his and Henri's in their early New York days had been Edward Fuchs's

Das Erotische Element in Der Karikatur, a German text copiously illustrated with explicit "art" pictures of copulating couples and giant winged phalluses, satyrs mounting goats, friars paddling bare-bottomed nuns, Lilliputians examining Gulliver's prodigious member, and orgies al fresco. Likewise, Sloan's own erotic art (most of it undated, alas, though the styles seem to span the decades) is extensive and not in the least restrained. In these never-exhibited drawings, little boys explore the hidden recesses between the legs of little girls; couples, nude or still partially dressed, in bed or on the ground, fuck in every possible position; and Eve plops down on Satan's ample erection beneath the real Tree of Knowledge, while Adam does his part later, in another drawing, under the watchful eye of the snake. In a drawing that probably dates from the 1920s, a man who looks a bit like the artist sprawls postcoitally in bed next to a woman, also naked (and definitely not Dolly), as each tenderly cradles the feet of the other in their hands. These sketches, a good boxful, are not the work of an inhibited or asexual man, though any statement beyond that must be pure speculation. Sloan's amorous and emotional life in the 1920s remains hidden, exactly as he wished it to be. *Girl in Ecstasy* (1927), however, would be an unusual part of any artist's canon and was surely *not* an oil that Sloan showed to Dolly: the husky model, naked, on her back, arms behind her and one leg raised on a rumpled bed, is crying out, rendered at the very moment of her orgasm.

Difficulties aside, the twenty-fifth-anniversary party in Santa Fe, held on August 5, 1926, was an occasion to emphasize all that was positive in the Sloans' union—its weird durability, if nothing else. "A very jolly affair," Sloan honestly called it, with eighty guests gathered in the garden by his studio to toast and joke and dance through the night with their hosts. The dahlias and hollyhocks, the vines and fruit trees, rejuvenated by recent showers, were brightly illuminated by electric lights, making for a "beautifully theatrical" effect, Sloan thought. There were heaps of presents, abundant "moonshine," good food, and loving friends and colleagues like Witter Bynner, Randall Davey, Edgar Hewett, the Shusters, the art collector Amelia White, the novelist Oliver La Farge, and the painters Willard Nash and Joe Bakos. These were the times, together on the metaphorical rock of the anniversary etching, when life as a couple seemed good to the Sloans, and the struggle worthwhile. Their sorrow came from the knowledge that there were too few such moments now, that the memories and the liquor had become the real bond.

Old Battles, New Resolve

(1927–1931)

> *"Some artists are tempted to compromise when the Bitch*
> *Goddess beckons . . . and one understands while not*
> *condoning the decision of an artist who has struggled*
> *with poverty for twenty years before facing this di-*
> *lemma. . . . It takes courage to be independent."*
>
> —John Sloan
> (1950)

New Year's week in 1927 saw the first transatlantic telephone call between New York and London, the beginning of the Al-Smith-for-President boom (as the future "Happy Warrior" was inaugurated on January 1 for his fourth term as governor), more big talk from Mayor Walker about urban renewal—and the spread of some disturbing rumors for the residents of the Sloans' neighborhood.

Word in the Village that month was that the city would be taking over and marking for demolition, before the end of the year, all of the buildings on both sides of Sixth Avenue between Third and Eighth streets. For John Sloan, comfortably ensconced in his apartment at 88 Washington Place for the last twelve years, the possibility that he might be forced to move was deeply disturbing. At the age of fifty-six, he had a place that suited his needs, with a barely affordable rent, a good view, and the daylight exposure he required for painting. He felt too old and too settled in his ways, and certainly too financially strapped, "to have to scuttle out like rats and hunt [for] a place to live and work and store half a thousand pictures and frames and a printing press and two thousand books and God knows what else."

Dolly finally decided to take the matter in hand and went downtown to City Hall herself to get the story, hoping to lay their worries to rest. But the news she came back with wasn't good: they'd probably have to be out by April. As Sloan told Will Shuster—happily settled in New Mexico, where nothing seemed to change—he felt unable to paint, or even to think of anything else, with such a cloud hanging over his head. Their initial investigation of comparable rents in the area only confirmed his worst fears: on their income, they might well end up moving to a smaller and darker apartment. Life in New York seemed now to offer even fewer comforts and more obstacles as time went on, a thought that threatened to plunge Sloan into depression.

Yet as was often the case, Sloan's description of his paralysis was exaggerated, and his view of his own resilience underplayed. The sense of impending loss, touching on the old anxieties about enforced change, reminding him of the tenuousness that governed life in a big city for anyone without money, was certainly crippling, at least initially. But it also, ultimately, sent him back out into the streets.

On a particularly cold night in the third week of January, Sloan took himself ("on a sudden impulse") to the corner of Fiftieth Street and Broadway and just stood, mesmerized by the light and snow, the pedestrians bundled in long coats clinging to one another, the stores, the arching lampposts, the trolley that raced by, the neon marquee. It was the kind of moment that had never ceased to enthrall him. He sketched the essentials of the scene he wanted, remaining (he told Shuster) till his ears ached with frostbite. The drawing Sloan did that night would be the genesis of one of the last of his great city pictures, *The White Way,* a painting that in its final form captured as much of his love of the metropolis as had any of the earlier urban vignettes, an image that aimed to transmute anxiety into affection and control, to fashion something timeless out of a dread of change.

Sloan worked with uncharacteristic speed and—a remarkable fact, given his usual methodical pace—finished *The White Way* in time to include it in his mid-February show at Kraushaar's. Feeling a special pride in the painting, which seemed to him (as it seems today, in the permanent collection of the Philadelphia Museum of Art) a "major" work of his career in the twenties, he no doubt anticipated some encouragement from the art-critical press. Surprisingly, none of the reviewers who covered the exhibition devoted more than a mention to Sloan's dynamic rendering of nighttime Broadway, and five days after the opening, two of the principal papers in New York weighed in with judgments that effectively curbed any elation the artist might have been feeling over his accomplishment. The *Tribune* held that most of the new works were "not so persuasive" as Sloan's earlier landscapes and city scenes, and that some were even "rather pedestrian." Worse yet, the *Times* announced that "one is apt to think of Mr. Sloan as a graphic historian first and a painter second"—torturous words to a man who saw himself as evolving in quite the opposite direction—and dismissed the New Mexico paintings as hopelessly inept. "Horace Greeley's advice about the possibilities of the West," the unsigned review observed, "never was meant for John Sloan. In New York he is at home. In New Mexico he seems a guest driven by a desire to show his appreciation of his host's beauty." *Never was meant for John Sloan:* Stick to what you can do, stick to what we are familiar with and like about your talent. We know best. You have been properly slotted. That, Sloan felt, was the subtext, patronizing and a bit dictatorial, of this vein of criticism, and he loathed it.

As Dolly and several friends told him, though, he had no cause to doubt himself, regardless of what the reviewers thought. In many of the paintings at Kraushaar's, but particularly in *The White Way,* they reminded him, he had done something strong and lasting. Indeed, the oddest thing about that painting, in this turbulent month of his life, is its spirit of unrelieved happiness, the absence of even a hint of the anxiety that motivated it. Against an agitated sky of slate gray, pink, and violet, the view of the street Sloan has chosen and developed is chaotic and exciting rather than threatening. Grime is transfigured by snow and neon. Several couples and a trio of female friends go in search of a good time after dark through a wide corridor of shops, restaurants, and a theater that reduces the darkness to a backdrop. Urban life in *The White Way* means people coming together in varied combinations, a gaudy spectacle with rich, unforeseen possibilities. As with *The "City" from Greenwich Village* of a few years earlier, Sloan draws our eye emphatically southward: Follow the trolley downtown, follow the pedestrians, follow the bend of the avenue, more pleasures await. The cavern of Broadway, tapering toward Forty-second Street, promises hidden joys. With the ebullience of *The White Way,* John Sloan put the dour "Ash Can" label behind him again, just as a generation of scholars was about to embalm him in it. It was almost as if this painting became, in its quick genesis and fruition, a self-generated reminder to the artist himself that New York had always been for him life at its best, and not, in the final analysis, a focus of oppression or injustice. The city had always offered more reasons to carry on than to give up.

The Sloans' reluctant house hunting paid off sooner than John and Dolly had expected. Within a few weeks they found an apartment and studio space in a building on Washington Square South owned by NYU, which, despite its higher rent, had the advantage of keeping them in an area they liked and providing a good fourth-floor view of the park, the Arch, and the construction of the new, taller buildings that were changing the landscape of lower Fifth Avenue. It was a "terrible shuffling ordeal," Sloan said of the business of moving thirty years' worth of possessions, but he was quite happy with the place itself ("a heavenly abode—if we can stand the racket, it can't be beat," he told Shuster) and enjoyed the uproarious housewarming attended by all of their Village and uptown friends. One of the guests was a Washington Square neighbor, Edward Hopper, who had just finished writing an article on Sloan. "John Sloan and the Philadelphians," in the April issue of the *Arts,* made just those observations that Sloan himself felt were called for at the moment and that Hopper, a rising star, was in a position to defend: it argued that there was a case to be made for the "home-staying painter" who hadn't lost his identity in slavish imitation of European Modernism; that the best figurative artists never sacrificed imagination in favor of documentation; and that artistic experimentation for its own sake might add up to very little. Sloan's was a "personal vision so strong and urgent," Hopper wrote, "as to allow no time for bypaths," and it situated him as the "inheritor of the tradition of Daumier, Gavarni, and Manet." Fresh from the glow of Hopper's praise and his and Dolly's successful move, satisfied with his work on *The White Way* and a second strong city picture, *The Lafayette Hotel,* painted the next month (which John Kraushaar thought good enough to display in his window), Sloan was excitedly talking about the imminent "dawn of better times" that spring. He was pleased with Dolly's resilience and her patience with his moods during the relocation. Kraushaar had just sold a Santa Fe landscape, *Yellow Tree by Chama,* and a few etchings. The gloom of January was behind him.

Dolly, for her part, had a different perspective on their situation—a more accurate one. The state of their bank account promised problems unless Kraushaar could sell much more work than he had sold in the last few years, and Edward Hopper's encomiums and a new, well-lighted studio weren't going to alter that sorry fact. Expenses—for models, medical bills, their summers in New Mexico—were outstripping income at an alarming rate. Sloan had had a second hernia operation the year before and was teaching only two days a week at the League in 1927, attempting to get by on fees from private pupils at home. With this dilemma in mind, Dolly had a talk with Dr. Mary Halton, a woman with a remarkably go-to-it attitude who was both the Sloans' family physician in the twenties and their personal friend. Dr. Halton regularly enlisted Dolly's help in organizing fund-raising events for a home she helped run for unwed mothers. The two women, in turn, went to see Juliana Force.

Their discussion focused on Sloan's finances and the newest of his New York paintings. The artist himself, and everyone else who saw *The Lafayette Hotel,* was charmed by its tones of yellow-brown and gold, its quiet evocation of a beloved moment and place. If this painting of a doorman and well-fed diners hailing a cab outside the popular University Place hotel (the first picture Sloan completed at 53 Washington Square South) lacks the profundity of *The "City" from Greenwich Village* or the dynamism of *The White Way,* it does a good enough job of illustrating Sloan's skills. It was a painting, Dr. Halton felt, that simply had to go to a museum. For advice on how to scale that forbidding height, Dolly and Dr. Halton had approached the right party.

Combative and manipulative with so many other people, Juliana Force was always gracious and supportive when it came to John Sloan. She wanted to help him when he needed it, without condescending to this man whom she regarded as one of the country's finest talents, and she wanted to improve the standing of American art in the museum world. (The Whitney Museum, of which Force would be the first director, was still three years away from opening its doors.) Those goals were not antithetical. Her plan was, first, to ascertain whether the Metropolitan Museum might be interested in the painting if it was offered. Curator Bryson Burroughs went to Kraushaar's and liked what he saw—indeed, if the trustees were agreeable, Burroughs said he wanted it. Next, Juliana Force approached the eminent collector Duncan Phillips and asked him to serve as titular head of a subscription committee that would seek to raise five thousand dollars to buy the painting. He said he would be glad to do so, and the business of soliciting contributions was under way. It was like the first days of the old *Masses,* with Dolly scouring the Village for the small sums and a suave Max Eastman–like figure, in this case the manager of the Whitney Studio Club, angling for the big checks. A large number of people were happy to contribute, and gifts of every denomination were dutifully recorded in Mrs. Force's ledger. Former Sloan students made five-dollar donations, and fellow artists like Charles Sheeler and Gifford Beal and old Socialist party comrades like Ernest Poole gave ten dollars each. Mrs. Force gave a hundred dollars herself, as did Dr. Halton and Mary Fanton Roberts; Duncan Phillips, Gertrude Whitney, and the Hamlins kicked in $250 each. Unfortunately, after the first passing of the hat, only fourteen hundred dollars had been collected. Some vintage Juliana Force arm-twisting was called for, along with some lobbying of the Met's notoriously cranky board of trustees (which seemed to hate the idea of including a painting by a living American artist in its collection), before Duncan Phillips could write to Sloan that the deal was done and that the "credit [for the gift] should go to the active workers on the Committee and especially to Mrs. Force."

One name that was conspicuously absent from the list of donors was Robert Henri's. When Henri, who was out of the country for much of the year, got wind of the solicitation idea, he was anything but pleased or supportive. (But then very little about Sloan was pleasing to Henri these days.) Lining up sponsors to enable the Metropolitan to acquire a contemporary painting that it could well afford to purchase on its own was not a wise move, Henri felt; it put the artist in the position of salesman and promoter doing the museum board's work of raising funds, a poor precedent to establish. The point was a fair one, but it couldn't mean much— and certainly didn't mean much to the Sloans—when the wolf was at the door. It was also just a little too easy for Henri, a man who had been financially assisted by his well-to-do father for some years, to talk about principle and precedent. When the solicitation process was completed, Sloan expressed his gratitude to everyone who had backed the plan with the gift of an etching of the same scene from a different angle on University Place. *The Lafayette Hotel* finally entered the collection of the Metropolitan Museum at the end of January 1928.

At this point, for a moment, it looked as if Sloan's "dawn of better times" was truly about to break. Not only was the artist richer by five thousand dollars—a sum that would enable him to erase all of his debts —but suddenly, quite out of the blue, enough money to see him through many years to come was dangled before him. If the deal offered by the young collector Carl Hamilton sounded too good to be true, there would prove to be good reason for skepticism. With no more acumen or luck

than his father had shown in business or financial matters, Sloan in the
spring of 1928 unwittingly tied his good name to the schemes of an
egomaniacal entrepreneur with a seductive personality and a questionable
past.

Carl Hamilton's proposition was to buy thirty-two paintings from
Sloan, including the cream of the crop (e.g., *The "City" from Greenwich
Village, Hairdresser's Window,* and *Yeats at Petipas),* for $41,200. Excited at
the prospect of a sale of such magnitude, Sloan saw to it that the paintings were put in storage right away, under bond, until the bill was paid.
What he didn't know was that he was dealing with one of the great
scandalous characters of a great gambling age, and that the likelihood of
Carl Hamilton's ever being able to pay for the paintings was pathetically
slim. By the late 1920s Hamilton, who was acquainted with Bernard
Berenson and the master dealer Joseph Duveen (both of whom he had
connived with and duped at one time or another), already had a colorful
history of living beyond his means, of ordering Old Masters for hundreds
of thousands of dollars (when he had only a fraction of that in his bank
account), and of professing his religious fervor while indulging in a taste
for teenage boys. Lest Sloan be thought too gullible, it should be noted
that the best of New York society frequented Hamilton's New York
apartment when the Berensons were in town, and most of these guests
assumed that the Renaissance art on Hamilton's walls had been paid for.
Described by one writer in the 1980s as a "strange combination of religious fanatic and unscrupulous financier[, a man who] today would be
recognized as a psychopath, for he genuinely believed his own fantasies,
one of which was that he was a millionaire," Hamilton had actually
accumulated some capital by the time Sloan met him. He certainly had
the manner and the conversational affect of an enthusiastic art lover down
pat. Mary Berenson had thought him "exhilarating, semi-intoxicating."
Sloan had no complaints.

Even before the money from *The Lafayette Hotel* sale was in hand and
before Carl Hamilton came through with his big check, Sloan emptied
his savings account to repay the debts he had accumulated to Hamlin,
Henri, and Kraushaar—how exciting it was going to be to end 1928
debt-free, such a novel sensation, he told a friend—and then used some of
what was left to treat himself and Dolly to a twenty-five-dollar Victrola
and two new paintings, one by a student and one by a friend. The pictures he bought were a small, elegant Cubist still-life by John Graham

and A. S. Baylinson's *Nude with Quilt,* a partly Cubist, partly representational work that his colleague had recently shown at the Independents. (A splendid painting, the latter is today owned by the Delaware Art Museum; it is one of the few Baylinsons in a major museum collection, as much of the artist's work was lost in a catastrophic studio fire in the 1930s.) The very fact that Sloan spent some of his hard-earned funds on art in the late twenties, rather than investing the money, makes an obvious point about his priorities; the fact that his wife likewise thought the purchases a good idea suggests that one of the original reasons Sloan had married Dolly—his hope that she would never hound him about finances and other common-sense concerns—still held. Whatever her other faults, Dolly was not going to turn cautious or mercenary on "my John Sloan," as she called him, not at this late date.

Dolly also didn't say anything about her husband's much riskier decision to advance more than seven thousand dollars to a young friend of theirs, Owen Cattell, for a business venture of his that promised a reasonable repayment with interest over a four-year period. Shades of James Dixon Sloan again: throughout 1928 and 1929, Cattell was able to meet his payments, but by 1930 (having repaid only a third of the loan) he was in trouble, and by 1931 unable to do any more. John Kraushaar had signed notes for the loan, and Sloan found himself under a mountain of new debt to his friend and dealer.

The years 1927 through 1929 marked a break in John Sloan's life at least as profound as that represented by the years 1904 through 1906, when he left behind a snug life in Philadelphia, braved the new world of Manhattan, and found his calling as a painter of the modern city. Three events in particular signaled a change. In the fall of 1927 Sloan met a new student whose devotion to him was to play a larger role in his development and career than he could have imagined at the time. In 1928 and 1929, in the wake of the realization that he was never going to enjoy contemporary success, he began to experiment with new techniques in his painting. And in the summer of 1929 Robert Henri, the last trace of the old life, died of cancer.

In the school year 1927–28, Sloan was at the crest of his popularity as a teacher. For all his harshness of tone, he was nonetheless seen as having enough practical and technical knowledge to impart to his students and a sufficiently inspiring philosophy to guarantee large, enthusiastic classes. There were some sixty students in the afternoon class when Helen Farr first attended, all drawing or painting one of two models, including the infamous Susie. (A plump blonde "with a kind of lumpy grandeur," Susie was a feature of life at the League, a once perfectly proportioned model who took no nonsense from the students. A typical anecdote about Susie concerned the time a male student left his palette on her stool, which she then sat on; the malefactor was dragged to the front of the room to clean the offending paints from her bare bottom.) Still a few months shy of her seventeenth birthday, Helen was the daughter of a Manhattan doctor. Had her life worked out as her mother wished and had her childhood not been so full of illness, she would have been bound for Bryn Mawr and very different circles from those she encountered at the Art Students League. But the Farrs had come to terms with the fact that their daughter was not interested in the path marked out for her as a pupil at Brearley, the exclusive girls' school she was attending on the East Side. At Brearley she had shown interest and talent in her art classes, to which the artist Mahonri Young came once a week to critique the students' work, and a friend of the family, the painter Guy Wiggins, recommended the League as a good alternative for Dr. Farr's daughter, who had been an able student but seemed to have a self-protective, independent streak. Indeed, Helen at this point needed to chart her own course. In 1927 she and her younger brother were living amid more than their tolerable share of marital tensions, Oedipal entanglements, and emotional aloofness. After a household in which the parents often went through periods of not speaking to each other, with Mrs. Farr frequently taking to her bed, the ambience of the League was a liberating atmosphere.

On Wiggins's advice, Helen had registered for a morning session with Boardman Robinson, another friend of the family, and an afternoon session with Maurice Sterne, the heartthrob of the League faculty. When Sterne hadn't returned from his summer in Europe by the time classes started, Helen was assigned to John Sloan's class. She knew next to nothing about him or his reputation and expected little from the class. But as soon as the artist-instructor arrived, with his full head of hair quite gray now and combed forward, wearing dark-rimmed glasses with thick lenses and dressed in a gray tweed suit and a green silk tie, Helen was struck by the man, by his grave, dapper appearance, his resonant voice, and the deference the class paid to him.

His introductory remarks seemed out of the ordinary, more about attitude than technique, and looking away from Sloan, Helen began to take notes. "I have very few things to teach you," Sloan said, "and fortunately few are new. I cannot teach you how to make a living at art. There are no formulas, no little secrets and short cuts to making art. There is no one right way to do it. There are no measurable standards of excellence." Sloan also talked about the need for the artist to think of himself as a person who was not in competition with other artists but was answerable only to himself. Eliminate any thoughts about whether or not you are making "works of art," he told his class; create paintings that interest *you,* that show some "consciousness of life"—echoes of Henri—and the rest will follow. He warned the students that his critiques would be rigorous, that they should be open to his criticism even or especially when it hurt, that they shouldn't be afraid to make mistakes. "We learn through our failures," he said. Most important, he wanted to make clear at the outset, if anyone in the room was interested in career counseling, art-market strategies, or commercial art techniques, he or she should leave now and register with another, more appropriate teacher.

At some point during that first class, Sloan noticed Helen Farr taking notes and pointedly indicated that he didn't like it. He didn't trust the note-takers, believing that "they distort what I say" and that they approached everything in too literal a fashion. Helen put aside her notepad.

What followed in the next few months, though, was a warm, slowly unfolding teacher-pupil bond between Sloan and one of his youngest new students. There wasn't anything unusual about that development: to those who could see past the demanding exterior, the showman of the classroom, and who spent some time in conversation with their instructor outside the League, especially on his walks down Broadway to the Village, Sloan could be remarkably warm and approachable. The end-of-term parties had become legendary by this time, with Sloan dancing to Ravel or doing his comic imitations of the lugubrious Woodrow Wilson. Many students shared Peggy Bacon's assessment of her favorite teacher as stimulating, tough-minded, and "oh, so amusing." He was also full of advice about which exhibitions they should see and what new artists they might profitably take note of. Even for someone like Alexander Calder, the brilliant son of Sloan's old Philadelphia friend Stirling Calder, just back from Europe that winter and beginning work on his wire sculptures, Sloan had the appeal of an oldtimer who was neither trapped in the past

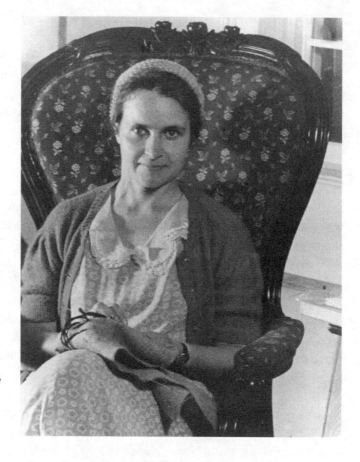

*Helen Farr at age
nineteen, 1930*
(Helen Farr
Sloan)

nor stuck in the groove of his own experience, his own way of doing things. Calder occasionally stopped by the drawing class at the League, and when he showed his *Romulus and Remus* at the 1928 Independents Show, Sloan excitedly urged his classes to see it. To Helen, too, there was something young and strange and magnetic about this painter-teacher, older than her father by a few years but more intellectually dynamic than anyone she had ever met.

Although she didn't know it at the time, Helen was encountering John Sloan at a tender moment in his life. There were tributes aplenty from the past these days. Art Young, for instance, after parting with Sloan on such bad terms back in 1916, was ready to bury the hatchet. In a volume of his memoirs published in 1928, he looked back on his fellow *Masses* artist as a "man of universal vision and understanding . . . always ready with a cryptic comment, a witticism, or a sarcastic spurt of indignation—outwardly looking like a calm professor." (Dolly's role in the movement was similarly acknowledged with praise by Young.) Max Eastman spoke well of Sloan, too, and ever since A. E. Gallatin had published the first monograph on him in 1925, the editors of the art magazines had referred to the painter in respectful tones. But this was also the roller-coaster year of the Carl Hamilton debacle, an episode that left Sloan feeling angry and humiliated.

For whatever reason and on whoever's advice (one senses the presence of the "media man" Holger Cahill here, but perhaps the decision was his own), Sloan made the grave error of announcing his good fortune before the paintings and the cash had changed hands. No doubt he reasoned that those in the art world who didn't like him—and he had made plenty of enemies in the course of running the Independents and maligning the Academy—would choke on the thought of his forty-thousand-dollar windfall, while those who did admire him would rejoice in his deserved, long-overdue financial vindication. Several art magazines broadcast the story at some length, and the newspapers in turn picked up on it. Sloan was asked to write a happy little piece for *Creative Art* entitled "My Recent Encounter"—an encounter with, presumably, the Great Lady "Success," soon enough to be the Bitch Goddess again—in which he told the world that he was far too old to be changed by his patron's generosity but was, in any event, grateful for "this splendid gesture of appreciation." Always interested in art when it had some connection to money, *Time* magazine gave space to the good news that even America's painters could attain their share of the prosperity that Herbert Hoover was describing as a permanent feature of life in the United States.

Then, only a few weeks later, Carl Hamilton announced that he had had unforeseen business reverses. (Exactly what he meant by this is unclear, as so much of his financial life was tied to speculation and credit. The only "business" that Hamilton was ever recorded as doing amounted to two ventures, the first in the Philippines, during World War I, where he oversubscribed his company many times over and then absconded with the funds when the stockholders' dividends were due, and the second in New York, where he hatched an unsuccessful plan to help Joseph Duveen sell Botticellis and Bellinis by hanging them in his apartment and pretending they were his.) As a result of Hamilton's abrupt turnabout, Sloan was stuck with his thirty-two paintings in storage, a seventy-three-hundred-dollar loan to Owen Cattell that would continue to haunt him for years, and the embarrassment of having been, for all intents and purposes, "set up." No doubt his ostensible patron liked Sloan's work, and no doubt he thought his forty thousand dollars would be a spectacular investment—as no doubt he believed he would have the forty thousand to pay for the pictures when the money came due. But Carl Hamilton's reality was not the world's, and the stinging truth that John Sloan was left to cope with was that he was probably never going to be a rich man and would always have to teach and economize and worry about bills.

Perhaps it was at this time that Kraushaar broached the subject of his marketability. He suggested, Sloan recalled, that Coney Island pictures would be the ticket; there was always an audience for New York genre scenes. That was nice to know, Sloan said, in effect. From that day on, he never went near Coney Island.

What definitely did take place at this time, though, was a pronounced shift in the direction and character of Sloan's art. He had decided to all but abandon paintings of city life and to taper off his work in landscape in order to concentrate on portraiture and the nude, but in a style that had only a slight relationship to what he had done before in those areas. The critical and popular view of the art Sloan began producing in 1928 and 1929 has never been enthusiastic, but there was no question in Sloan's mind that he was right to forge ahead as he did.

As they evolved over a period of a year or more, the technical changes Sloan focused on addressed his desire for more solid form and, in line with the ethos of the Armory Show, his wish to create images that satisfied a mental as well as, or rather than, a visual reality. Photographic realism, insofar as it had ever meant anything, he told his students, was played out. Pure "eyesight painting," as he called it, was something to avoid. But equally irrelevant, he felt, were grand painterly effects for their own sake, of the kind that Sargent and Chase were known for (and presumably of the kind he himself had created in rich color masterpieces such as *The "City" from Greenwich Village*). Looking at more Rembrandts, Goyas, Courbets, and Renoirs in the 1920s (now that there were more to be seen in American galleries and museums than there had been in the days of Sloan's youth), the painter of *Dust Storm, Fifth Avenue,* and *The White Way* wasn't as happy as he had once been with the sketchiness or airiness of much of his work. He liked what he called the "under and over" method of Renoir, which involved painting over an area of pale-gray and white

underpainting. Direct application of the oil to the canvas no longer satisfied his needs, Sloan felt. He wanted to express in his paintings the
"clinching reality . . . the plastic power" that he was able to achieve in
the wonderfully textured charcoal figure drawings he was working on
at the time, and underpainting seemed a means to that end. In this
centuries-old technique, which he learned more about in A. P. Laurie's
book *The Painter's Methods and Materials,* the figure would be rendered
first in a monochromatic underpaint as in a drawing, with the color then
being built up over layers of transparent glazes. Sloan also made the
transition to tempera, a medium better suited than oil to the creation of
the impasto he was seeking. This exacting process, this matter of underpainting and glazing, could hardly be further removed from the on-
site work Sloan had been doing in recent years in New Mexico, and that
seemed to please him, too. The young man who had ignored the details of
craft and technique in the 1890s was now devoting himself to the science
of art.

At almost the same time, Sloan began to disregard, in slight ways,
the academic principles of perspective that establish the illusion of size
and distance in a painting, foreshortening his figures, or parts of them, for
the effect he wanted. (Of course, because the changes weren't particularly
radical, as they would be in, say, a Picasso or a Max Beckmann, many
viewers saw bad drawing rather than inventive distortion, a risk Sloan was
willing to accept.) Finally, this development was in turn followed, in
1929, by the use of linework, whereby he actually covered his figure or
other parts of the picture with a skein of neutral or vaguely reddish lines.
By crosshatching his forms or, to use the term Sloan himself preferred, by
giving them a "linear texture," he felt he was strengthening their solid-
ity, modeling them even more forcefully, as in a drawing or an etching,
and helping to flatten the space they occupied. Texture, of the sort the
stitches in a tapestry might provide; reverberations of color; an interplay
of mind and eye; a work of art that represented an idea of reality rather
than a literal re-creation of it—these were the goals Sloan set himself in
cutting loose from his old moorings.

It was probably a convergence of factors that led to this critical trial-
and-error moment in Sloan's career. On the one hand, he felt that he had
come to a dead end artistically. "The nudes I painted before I started
glazing are not eyesight painting," Sloan later commented, "but they
haven't the powerful realization I have been able to get in the later

ones. . . . The more color power I wanted for realizing textural painting, the more this opaque paint obliterated the under-form painting. The
thing got choked up." His very mastery of surface color was working
against him now, he thought, and in a sense he was eager to spurn the
Henri premise according to which he had been trained, the belief that a
quick, spontaneous impression—an honest capturing of mood, a display
of deft brushwork and thick paint—was the thing to strive for. On the
other hand, the Postimpressionist and Cubist idea that a painting should
not aim to be an exact transcription of what the eye sees, but should
instead satisfy other artistic purposes, had always mattered more to Sloan
than people realized. Pure abstraction may not have interested him, but
"abstract motives," as he termed them, did: in the "low-relief" *Gypsy
Girl, Bandanna* (1928), the folds of cloth behind the woman are no less
central to the picture than are her hair, scarf, and face, while in the many
nudes of 1929 the heaps of pillows and sheets the women recline on have
the immediate billowy presence of so many thighs, arms, and breasts.
Storytelling and human incident, "Ash Can" or otherwise, is here elimi-
nated, even though identifiable figures and objects remain.

  Last of all, Sloan had to confront that feeling which motivates all
radical breaks with a comfortable past or a safe state of mind, the sense
that perhaps there is something to be gained, and certainly nothing to be
lost, in going one's own way. If his only chance of making a living on a
level with the most respected artists of his time lay in churning out
Coney Island scenes or more Washington Square vignettes, endlessly rep-
licating the spirit of *Yeats at Petipas* or *McSorley's Bar* while pinning his
hopes on the Carl Hamiltons of the world, then he would gladly turn his
back on all of it. Sloan was about to put into practice in a more literal,
more determined way than he had ever done the doctrine he preached at
the League: independence in everything, easy money and popular approval be damned.

  If Sloan had any doubts about how odd these paintings might look to
people, they were put to rest quickly enough. One of his first models was
Yosene Balfour Ker, the daughter of an artist-illustrator Sloan had been
friends with at the turn of the century, William Balfour Ker, and herself
later the mother of the actress Tuesday Weld. Yosene was new to the city
and stayed with the Sloans for a few months in 1929 as she tried to make
a life for herself in New York. She posed for Sloan in the weeks when he
was first developing his crosshatch technique. Her first reaction to the

sight of the paintings of herself gently covered in an overlay of reddish lines was to giggle uncontrollably. Sloan stiffened and grew red himself, she remembered, and finally barked in fury, "You're here to show your figure, not your ignorance."

When Sloan brought some of these new works, with their glazes and underpainting and linear textures, to show Robert Henri in the hospital that summer, the reaction was different in manner but not in effect. Henri simply turned away from the pictures without comment, implying his distaste for the paintings and his awareness that Sloan was decisively rejecting everything he himself had ever stood for as an artist and a teacher. Reaction from critics and viewers at the next Kraushaar show was no less skeptical. The general feeling seemed to be, Why should a man of fifty-eight turn his back on his own strengths and try to make something out of an elaborate system that no one else quite comprehended or believed in? Sloan's need to be contrary, to make a place for himself outside the mainstream—whether of left-wing politics or the academic tradition or the new art world—had never been so clear and jarring as it was on the eve of the Crash and the Great Depression.

Ironically, in the summer of 1929, at about the time of Henri's death, Sloan painted one of his best portraits in the new style—and then proceeded to store it in his studio, from which it was never removed for exhibition at Kraushaar's. Using a flaxseed tempera underpaint and an oil-varnish glaze on a panel, Sloan created a self-portrait that was effective on all the terms he was striving for: solid form, subtle color, a space of limited depth, the *gravitas* of an Old Master. He made himself look closer to seventy than to sixty, but the lines hint at a kind of honorable battle-weariness, and the Navajo blanket draped over his right shoulder is a clever allusion to another, older tradition of linear textures.

Throughout most of 1930 Sloan was in a restless mood. His sister Bessie had died that spring, and he worried that Marianna was in danger of succumbing completely to the tendencies she had already shown toward depression and neurotic eccentricity. ("You will be alone now," he wrote her, "and there is a weird strain in our blood that you will have to resist.") It had been satisfying for him to be included in the Nineteen Living Americans exhibition, the second show at the newly opened Museum of Modern Art, along with Charles Demuth, Edward

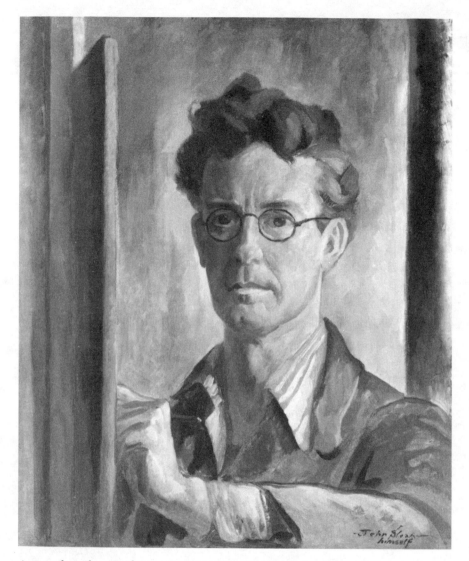

At age forty-four: Self-Portrait, *1915* (Pennsylvania Academy of Fine Arts)

Hopper, Rockwell Kent, John Marin, and Georgia O'Keeffe—an honor despite the mixed reviews—and to be invited to speak on radio on behalf of the College Art Association, about etching at the American Institute of Graphic Arts, and on "Robert Henri and His Friends" at the Detroit Institute of Arts, where he was a key part of a group show by that title. The year before he had been made a member of the National Institute of Arts and Letters, under the sponsorship of Childe Hassam, and had been the subject of a well-received two-man show with Guy Pène du Bois at the Chicago Art Institute. But art-world accolades for his older work did little to improve his frame of mind. Throughout the spring he had debated the question of whether or not to resign from the League, again over the infuriating issue of salary, and in June he was unable to meet his mortgage payment on time with the Santa Fe Bank and Loan Association. Kraushaar wasn't encouraging, *ArtNews* had criticized the spring show for being full of the new style of nudes, which seemed "born of theory, not enthusiasm," and Sloan sensed that he was, or might be, in trouble.

One relief from these aggravations could be found in the pleasures of friendship in Santa Fe. The excited talk that summer had to do with Indians and patronage. Sloan and his friends had for some time been mulling over the concept of putting on a large exhibition of Native American art to be sponsored by artists, writers, museum people, and patrons—transplanted Easterners like Witter Bynner and Oliver La Farge and regular visitors like Sloan and Amelia White—who would then return to New York, or wherever they lived, and put the creative achievements they had come to love in the Southwest, from Navajo blankets to pre-Columbian pottery, "on the map" of American culture. In the summer of 1930 that vision began to take shape as they discussed incorporating as the "Exposition of Indian Tribal Arts." Sloan also took time out from working on several Santa Fe genre pictures and one of his more ambitious temperas, *Procession to the Cross of the Martyrs,* to perform in a satirical musical revue called *Tourists Ahoy!*, which was stage-managed by Dolly and performed for the benefit of the local Red Cross.

Yet the most enjoyable, and perhaps most disconcerting, aspect of the summer for Sloan was the presence of Helen Farr. Though no longer a pupil of his now that she was studying lithography with Charles Locke and etching with Harry Wickey, Helen was still in close, regular contact with her first League teacher, and that initial fascination hadn't dimmed, a fascination that seemed mutual. She was to become recording secretary of the League that fall when Sloan became president, and in the spring she had shown her support for his new linear-textured style by buying her first Sloan oil, a nude, for five hundred dollars. Helen had come out on the train with the Sloans and was staying with a family on Garcia Street. Dolly had a good sense of which of Sloan's students were experiencing the inevitable hero worship and which of the young women were in love with her husband, and there is no reason to assume that she wasn't fully aware

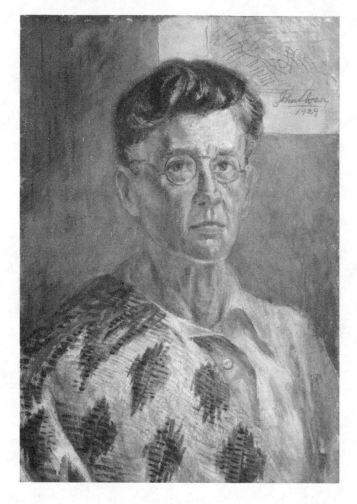

At age fifty-eight:
Self-Portrait,
1929 (National
Portrait Gallery,
Smithsonian
Institution)

of what Helen—now nineteen, with thick, dark hair, quickly bronzed by the New Mexico sun—was doing in their midst. A photo that Sloan took one afternoon in his backyard when Helen came to visit after lunch summarizes the situation with brutal clarity: seated under the trees at the table, Dolly looks ten years older than her fifty-four years, her skin puffy and lined from five decades of physical and emotional trials, while Helen looks to be as young, alert, demure, and attractive a rival as Dolly could imagine in her worst fears. In an odd way, though, Dolly understood that Helen hadn't come to Santa Fe or into their lives with the intention of seducing her husband. There was still, at this point, something reassuringly innocent to Dolly about Helen Farr.

Sloan was honest with himself about his attraction to "Pete," as Helen was called in those days. "I am more fond of you than I can help, and I trust you not to take advantage of that," he told her one day not long after their arrival. But in an alcoholic atmosphere—and sixty years later, Helen Farr would remember it as a summer of much imbibing—it was inevitable that something untoward would occur. On a car ride back from the Shusters' one night, with Randall Davey and Witter Bynner in the front seat and Sloan and Helen in the back, Sloan showed the effects of an intense night of carousing and made a fumbling romantic advance. Assuming that her former teacher wouldn't refer to, or perhaps even remember, his actions in the backseat the next morning, Helen asked Davey and Bynner to forget what they had seen. But Sloan did remember, and his way of dealing with his embarrassment the following day was to blame Helen, implying that she had been the one to make the first move. Helen let the matter pass and hoped that that would put an end to it. An account of the car ride did get back to Dolly, though, probably by way of Witter Bynner, who had now affectionately dubbed Helen the "great little virgin of Santa Fe." Dolly's comment was circumspect: "If Helen Farr won't take John Sloan," she said, "she won't take anybody." Yet Dolly had it wrong if she assumed that Helen was immune to the sexual undercurrents of the situation she found herself in; it was simply that at nineteen, she wasn't going to initiate anything that threatened to be more than she could handle, and Sloan was obviously ambivalent as well. Of her own attraction to John Sloan, however, Helen had no doubt, and when Sloan asked her to model, she obliged. *Susannah in Santa Fe* is a version of the biblical tale of Susannah among the Elders; in this case, the two voyeuristic elders peering over the wall have been added after the fact, but the nude full-bottomed Susannah lying on her stomach in the warm sun was very much present in the flesh. For the moment, those were the terms implicitly agreed upon: warm friends, mentor and disciple, artist and model.

Before returning to New York in September, Helen had a chance to see even more of the Sloans' life and the intensity and turmoil provoked by so much alcohol. *The Old Homestead,* painted that summer, documents an eerie, ostensibly convivial night out at the Shusters' cabin. Will and Helen Shuster, looking a little the worse for wear, occupy the center of the scene, next to a straw basket with a jug of corn whiskey. Sloan is positioned by himself off to the left, smoking his pipe, and Helen and

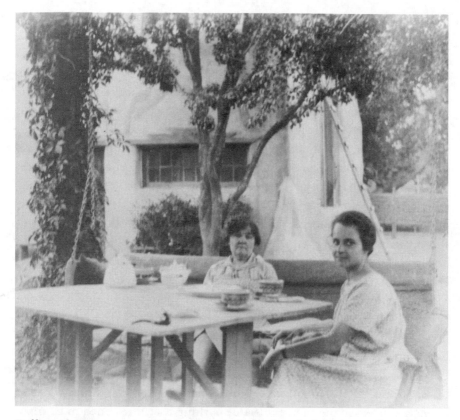

Dolly and nineteen-year-old Helen Farr in the backyard of the Garcia Street house in Santa Fe, 1930 (Delaware Art Museum)

Dolly fill the lower right-hand edge of the painting, Helen in a flapper's headband, Dolly holding a drink and a cigarette and looking more strangely "dwarfish" (to use John Quinn's word) than she does in any other rendering by her husband. Helen Farr also observed—though not having known the Sloans before this time, she wouldn't have had a point of comparison with the earlier, more socially delicate stage of their marriage—that Sloan was now at a point in his life when he was as apt to lash out at his wife as to protect her. "She's a cancer in my side," he angrily told Helen in a private moment at a party at Amelia White's. On another evening, when Dolly had humiliated him with her drinking and her own barbs, he frightened her back into control with the warning "Remember where I found you"—a comment that brought the scene to a jarring halt.

"Don't tell Pete!" was all Dolly could say. The shame of that early life, and the self-abusing comparisons between her sorry background and the refinement of Edith Glackens and the other artists' wives, were something Dolly could never overcome. The thought that her husband might act differently toward her now, if he could reinvent his past, was a kind of torture that could shock Dolly like nothing else.

Dolly took her revenge on the world through her efforts, quite frequently successful, to manipulate her husband's volatility. "Sloan is the most vituperative person in New York," she told a student, Frances Beisel, "and I can turn him against anyone I want to." She wasn't above telling old friends that Sloan didn't want to see them anymore or telling her husband that someone had made a disparaging remark about him or his work. William and Edith Glackens, for example, kept their distance these days, and soon enough Helen Farr would have that malevolent, defensive skill turned against her. At other times Dolly would take a completely different (but no less controlling) approach by insisting that she, better than anyone else, looked out for Sloan's interests and understood his greatness. When she decided, in 1931, that the Kraushaar Gallery hadn't been aggressive enough in its sales, she took the etchings away from Kraushaar without her husband's knowledge and brought them to the Grand Central Galleries. John Kraushaar and his family—he was aided now in the business by his daughter, Antoinette, and his son, Charles—were deeply hurt by the gesture, which threatened a secure fifteen-year relationship between the artist and the gallery.

The irrevocable and heartrending decline of Dolly Sloan's mental stability became even more evident when Sloan suddenly became ill in Santa Fe that same year. Stricken on the night of July 30, he was taken north to St. Mary's Hospital in Pueblo, Colorado, for emergency prostate surgery. Florence Davey, now divorced from Randall and remarried to the millionaire businessman Cyrus McCormick, knew a good doctor there and made the necessary arrangements. In her notes to Kraushaar and to various friends in the East, Dolly tried to sound positive about her husband's condition—and, indeed, the operation was successful and his recovery guaranteed. He spent his sixtieth birthday resting comfortably in the hospital, trying not to think about the new round of bills he would have to deal with. For Dolly, however, the whole experience was unendurable. Even the possibility of her husband's dying left her distraught beyond any ability to cope. In a room at the hospital one night, she intentionally took a serious overdose of Veronal and went to sleep. Father Thomas Fitzgerald, the hospital's chaplain, discovered her and summoned help in time. Sloan remarked later that his talk with Father Fitzgerald was warm and encouraging (rare praise from a staunch anti-cleric and anti-Catholic); he understood the frightening situation Sloan was in and admired his pluck. But the sensitivity of others was of limited use now, and by the time the Sloans returned to New York in the autumn, a pall had settled over their marriage that was difficult to dispel.

In a letter written to Helen Farr, of all people, just before she and Sloan left New Mexico, Dolly tried to put her wild actions in perspective and enlist Helen as her own ally. "I guess you do know," she wrote,

> that that is about all I ask of life—that people will give Sloan his due. . . . I have done things that annoyed and irritated him but I do know in spite of everything—I have given all that was best in me to and for Sloan. . . . I would not change my life with Sloan for any other life I know of. I only hope Sloan will live to see the financial return [on his work]. He asks so little and gives so much.

Although Sloan's illness in August and a subsequent infection prevented him from being as involved as he would have liked in the venture, the Exposition of Indian Tribal Arts show that opened in December at the Grand Central Galleries provided welcome relief from his own troubles. New York had seen selected examples of Native American art throughout the twenties, beginning with the 1920 Independents Show, but never before had such a concerted effort been made to alter the terms in which Americans thought of the Indians and the place they should occupy in the country's cultural histories. Now that Modernism had ended the tyranny of Kenyon Cox's worship of the "classical tradition" in American art, the time seemed right to suggest that Native Americans, with their eye for color and decorative qualities, their understanding of the power of abstraction and expressive gesture, had been misdefined as "primitives," as a people of quaint historical interest. In fact, it was the whole "curio concept" of the Indian, Sloan wrote, that he wanted to see banished—the notion of the Indians as curiosities, their art as a good tourist buy, the cost of which bore no relationship to what a collector would pay for a painting or a sculpture by a white man or woman. It could well be argued at the end of the twentieth century that Sloan's and his friends' interest in Native Americans was in itself appropriative and condescending by nature: the Indians legitimized as proto-Modernists, their products finally given meaning under an alien concept of "art," a diverse people sentimentally described as inherently creative (but at the same time in need of protection from their all-white mentors). Yet the alternatives were grim, darker than any complaint a latter-day cultural historian might want to make against the Exposition of Tribal Arts. Hollywood saw joke material and stories of evil savages in the Native American experience, politicians and businessmen saw a childlike people sitting on valuable land, and museum professionals saw objects that didn't *deserve* to be contemplated next to an oil by Manet or a statue by Rodin. The Exposition of Tribal Arts was the one force in America (as a cultural rather than a political agency) that wanted to change some of those conditions and values and had the wit and the muscle to do so.

The Exposition of Indian Tribal Arts was as artfully formed an organization as the cause required. Designed to "win aesthetic appraisal of Indian art" and to "awaken public appreciation so as to encourage the Indians to continue to create and develop their art," it flew in the face of a decade of vicious attacks on Native American rights and aimed for the most mainstream, "establishment" credentials. Originally the group had decided on twelve directors, including Amelia White, John and Dolly Sloan, Mary Austin, Oliver La Farge, and Clark Wissler of the Museum of Natural History. By 1931, though, when the dream of a big show gave promise of becoming a reality, they expanded their governing board, opened an office on Madison Avenue, and asked Sloan to serve as president and Charles Curtis, Herbert Hoover's vice president (and a man of Indian ancestry), to lend his name as honorary chairman. Charles Dawes, Coolidge's vice president; Edward Delafield, president of the Bank of America; Herbert Spinden of the Brooklyn Museum; *Vanity Fair* publisher Frank Crowninshield; and Abby Rockefeller were among the other directors, nominal or otherwise—names designed to secure choice loans (President Hoover and Jacques Cartier were lenders) and to give their exhibition the imprimatur of the best of conservative society. The complaint of the congressmen and senators who had pushed for the Bursum Bill and sought to curb the Indian dances had been that the artists and writers who supported the tribes with their annoying petitions and press releases were a kind of riffraff themselves, a fringe element in the culture. The "tony" Exposition of Indian Tribal Arts, Inc., rendered that assertion untenable by 1931.

With years of experience behind them priming the publicity pump for similar events, Sloan and his colleagues were quick to seize on every opportunity to stimulate audience expectations. Twelve Pueblo Indians and two Navajos were brought to Manhattan to meet with the press and talk about their traditions and art-making, on an itinerary prepared by Dolly. Sloan gave a radio talk on the eve of the opening (in which he put in a plug for the use of the term "Amer-Indian," insisting that the white appropriation of the term "American" was in itself part of the problem), and Walter Pach published an article in the *Times* to advertise the show. The exhibition was billed as a major educational enterprise as well, with materials sent out to area schools and invitations extended for teachers to bring their classes and buy one of the two catalogues at a discount. One of the catalogues brought out by the Brooklyn Museum contained twelve illustrated essays by various scholars on different aspects of Indian art, from its symbolism to the several techniques of weaving; the second catalogue consisted of an essay by Sloan and Oliver La Farge that sketched an overview of the subject, stressing the economic conditions and belittlement the Indian artists had to cope with and the reasons they should be seen in the same light as our Homers, our Marins, our Sloans.

At the opening, Sloan felt confirmed in his hopes. Three thousand New Yorkers turned out to celebrate the occasion and to study more than six hundred objects of the sort that Americans only a generation earlier would have rejected as "barbarous." By all accounts, it was a dazzling display, comprising huge Apache baskets and Alaskan bone carvings, Arapaho saddlebags and Chippewa pipes, Navajo rugs and blankets, Hopi pottery and dance wands, Blackfoot belts, Zuni and Iroquois masks, pre-Columbian pottery, and the contemporary watercolors and paintings of such artists as Awa Tsirch, Fred Kabotie, Otis Polelonema, Oqwa Pi, Richard Martinez, and Leo Guatoque from the reservations of New Mexico, Arizona, and Oklahoma. Limitations of time and money ruled out a comprehensive survey of Native American art from all regions of Canada and the United States, of the kind a major museum might mount today, but within its ability to gather quality objects—and the directors had been in agreement that the standards of worksmanship must be high, that nothing was to be gained by exhibiting lesser examples of a particular style or object—the Exposition fulfilled its mission to everyone's satisfaction. Alaska, Washington, California, British Columbia, the Southwest, the Great Plains: the idea was to suggest a continent of creativity, of variety, of rich experience and stunning craft.

Even conservative art critics were swayed. The usually stodgy Royal Cortissoz wrote in his column in the *Herald-Tribune* that the show was an "affair of uncommon interest" for laymen and art professionals alike. All of the art magazines provided extensive positive coverage. The reviewer for the *Nation* was sure that the Exposition would lead to an "awakened appreciation, and to renewed stimulation, of Indian art" such as "only a blind imagination" could ignore. Traces of that "blind imagination" were, of course, hard to obliterate, even—or perhaps especially—in Manhattan. The Sloans approached curators at the Metropolitan Museum about picking up the show in the wake of its glowing reviews, but there was no interest yet in exhibiting Chilkat blankets or Hopi masks in the galleries at Fifth Avenue and Eighty-second Street.

Better still than reviews were sales. The 1931 exhibition was anything but a repeat of the humiliating 1910 Independents Show with its seventy-five dollars in purchases. The appetite for art had grown considerably since those pathetic days. With five thousand dollars taken in on admissions fees and another thousand in catalogue sales, the directors were pleased to be able to cover a good portion of their expenses. But the sale of $6,595 worth of works from the show was the real source of delight. In America, Sloan felt, you knew that something was taken seriously by the fact that people paid a good price for it. Living Native Americans, used to penurious levels of income, were being given money for their work that would enable them to live and continue with that work. The Tribal Arts exhibition caused a great stir, Sloan wrote happily to Will Shuster in December, "[receiving] more publicity than any art exhibition for years past and dignified publicity at that." With pride, he observed, "The Indian as an artist has been established, I believe." Leaving New York, the show then traveled under the auspices of the College Art Association to Philadelphia, Springfield, Rochester, Buffalo, Boston, Manchester, Milwaukee, Cincinnati, Cleveland, and St. Louis, all of which reported lively, interested crowds.

From the challenge of "The Eight" and the Independents to the way in which Native American art was perceived, the issue of the widening and diversification of American culture had mattered to Sloan almost as much as his own painting, and at the end of 1931, amid a sea of personal woes, he had reason to feel some satisfaction in the task. The show sponsored by the Exposition of Tribal Arts was also the last big project that brought together in close collaboration the event-loving, media-rousing organizational skills of John Sloan and his troubled, mercurial wife.

Fear Itself

(1932–1936)

ANNOUNCEMENT TO DIRECTORS OF ART MUSEUMS: *John Sloan, the well-known artist, will die sometime in the next few years (he is now sixty-two). In the event of his passing, is it likely that the trustees of your museum would consider it desirable to acquire one of his pictures? . . . After a painter of repute dies, the prices of his works are at once more than doubled. John Sloan is alive and hereby offers these works at one-half the prices asked during the last five years. . . . Yours, full of life—and a modicum of hope, John Sloan.*

—Letter sent to sixty American
museums in 1933

In remembering the worst of the Depression, the artist Moses Soyer once remarked, "Who can describe the hopelessness that its victims knew? Perhaps no one better than the artist taking his work to the galleries. [The galleries] were at a standstill. The misery of the artist was acute. There was nothing he could do."

In this treacherous climate, not at all exaggerated by Soyer, John Sloan considered the drift of his life in the early 1930s and decided that he wanted to quit his job at the Art Students League—his one regular source of income then—and divorce Dolly so that he might have children and a life with a woman less troubled, steadier, more inspiring and sustaining. The fantasy of leaving Dolly he soon recognized as being just that; he knew he would never be able to live with himself if their separation led to the consequences he was sure would follow. Dolly's overdose in Colorado had convinced him of that: she was serious when she said that she'd rather die than live without "her John Sloan." The idea of severing ties with the League, however, was harder for him to shake.

The frustrations connected to the League and to Sloan's own sense of how difficult and marginal life was for an artist in America—these were not problems of the kind that could be simply resolved. Government and business had little interest in nurturing the arts in comparison to the patronage Europeans enjoyed, he bitterly reminded a College Art Association meeting in New York in the winter of 1932, and it was no wonder that in a society that disdained aesthetic experience, the artist felt useless and young people couldn't tell the difference between real art and the newest bandwagon. However valid Sloan's complaint about his country's lack of interest in art, there was an element of personal grievance in his analysis as well. Even before 1932, with his class size on the decline, Sloan had started to note a lessening of the appreciation or adulation he was used to receiving from his younger students. They certainly weren't interested in hearing about the battles of an earlier day; to them, "The Eight" and the National Academy of Design were equally distant, historical, almost nineteenth-century concerns. Many of them gravitated now toward the younger instructors with more obvious Modernist sympathies, or else enrolled in the more conservative classes of Kenneth Hayes Miller, whom Sloan had always regarded as his principal rival at the League. Some of them didn't see the point of mastering representational drawing —as Sloan insisted his students do—when they were intending to go on to work in a nonrepresentational style. The twenty-year-old Jackson Pollock, for instance, found that most of the League teachers he studied with let him slide by in the matter of his abysmal drawing skills, but not Sloan. His impatience with Sloan's expectations led him to drop his drawing class after only a few weeks.

In a sense, the potentially embarrassing issue of dwindling enrollment in Sloan's classes had been forestalled by his election to the presidency of the Art Students League in 1931. As president, instead of teaching, Sloan helped to determine policy at the school, which was feeling the pinch of the Depression, like every other cultural institution at the time. Yet very little about the League, once he was out of the classroom and on the board, appealed to him anymore. Although the school enjoyed a reputation as the one place where a would-be artist could oversee his own education, with no curriculum demands and complete freedom to choose his courses, Sloan felt that the student body was not always being well served by what was offered. Over the past decade and a half, artists such as Henri, Luks, Lawson, Bellows, Kent, Guy Pène du Bois, Thomas Hart Benton, and Stuart Davis had served as part-time or full-time instructors, but in Sloan's estimation most of the rest of the faculty was decidedly second-rate. It was at heart an inbred place, he complained, with students of Kenneth Hayes Miller and other lesser lights coming back in later years as teachers to repeat the same tired lessons. He found the board too hesitant for his tastes and decried the air of stagnation that was settling over the school. In the middle of March 1932, Sloan finally brought matters to a head over the issue of soliciting the new blood he thought so necessary.

In that month Sloan had heard that George Grosz, one of the best graphic artists of Weimar Germany, was coming to the United States in the fall. He told the board that he wanted to hire Grosz, that the League desperately needed someone of Grosz's strong academic background and modern vision. He was a vivid satirist and a cosmopolitan, and Sloan felt he would add the kind of stature and cachet the school was lacking. Two obstacles to the suggestion arose at once. One was that the hiring of the faculty for the next year had already been completed by the time Sloan spoke up, and allegedly no extra funds were available to finance a new position. The second problem was that some of the board members were uneasy about the wisdom of hiring a foreign artist when so many Americans were out of work—and a foreign *Communist* at that. Neither reservation meant much to the League's president, however, and he lobbied to have his way.

On the night the board met to decide the issue, Sloan was in high dudgeon. The League was a "sinking ship," he informed his colleagues, and the proposition he was advocating was the only chance it had to stay afloat. He wanted the school to dip into its reserves, a healthy hundred thousand dollars in the bank, and make some dramatic changes in the place. It was time to stop acting "like an old hen with a bunch of eggs under her . . . sitting there fondly tucking them in, keeping them warm." Not surprisingly, Sloan's aggressive style didn't win him any converts. Even before this discussion, in fact, several people had concluded that his manner was getting out of hand. The artist Jonas Lie was particularly adamant that Grosz, a flamboyantly ribald talent, would not be a "healthy influence for the progress of American youth." According to one source, Sloan referred to those board members who disagreed with him as a crowd of "boobs" and "art politicians." These were the tactics of man "past reason," the board decided, and Jonas Lie's side carried the vote. Sloan then resigned the presidency of the League, which resignation was accepted by a vote of 4 to 3. Seemingly, he was about to have his wish: an end to his affiliation with the school.

But the matter didn't end there. Given Sloan's overheated response to the issue, it does not seem wildly speculative to conclude that more was at stake for him than the hiring of one new instructor, even someone as notable and interesting as George Grosz. A host of resentments were coming to the surface, and the board of the League was both an actual as well as a symbolic target for Sloan. What he wanted was a fiery public vindication that he was right about Grosz, that his view of the world was the more dynamic one, that the young understood he was on their side, and that he hadn't become a tired, irrelevant old man, like so many of his colleagues on the staff. It was an impossibly tall order. But how else to take the fact that no sooner had Sloan resigned from an institution he claimed to be sick of, than he announced that he would run for reelection the next month, with the all-school balloting to serve as a referendum on the hiring of Grosz? And about that election, he was cocky and defiant in the extreme: "I'll win it in a walk or not at all," he said publicly.

The election was a nightmare of invective and hyperbole on all sides. Yet Sloan seemed invigorated by the challenge and confident of the outcome; in any event, he had been spoiling for a fight for long enough. At the boisterous gathering of the student body on the night of the balloting in April, each camp stated its case without equivocation. Sloan acidly referred to his detractors on the board as the "hen committee" and denounced the budgetary conservatism of the school, whereby funds could not be found to hire a brilliant man like Grosz, and its practice of judging classes and teachers by how much money they brought in. Under that kind of leadership, Sloan argued, the League was as good as dead. The board was a sarcophagus—"and I was an ornament on the sarcophagus"—and most of the instructors those old fogeys were bringing in were "not particularly strong or fitting." The supporters of the board's candidate for the presidency, the respected painter Henry Schnakenberg, insisted that the recent events had nothing to do with Grosz or with his Communist politics—that there had in fact been an effort to get him to come to America to teach at the League a few years earlier. The real question was what kind of leadership the school should have, a matter of choosing between the calm, liberal, humane approach Schnakenberg would offer and more of Sloan's "dictatorship" and know-it-all belligerence. The word *dictator* was bandied about a good deal, which seemed ludicrous to

Sloan, but he had no idea how many people he had alienated by this time. Even painter-friends such as Gifford Beal and Allen Tucker were backing Schnakenberg. The artist Homer Boss was the most vocal among those who had come to see Sloan as a rabid publicity hound. While Sloan had been filling his scrapbooks with clippings, Boss declared, the League had been paying for it with disruption and bitterness. When someone then asked if the reporters in the room should be allowed to remain during the discussion and election, and Sloan answered that he welcomed their presence, a student on Boss's side called out, "You would!"

Although it seemed as if, amid the wild applause and the heckling of speakers, Sloan's followers were in the majority at the meeting, the election proved the opposite to be the case: 165 students present voted for Sloan, and 187 for Schnakenberg. When the proxy ballots were tallied, the final count was Sloan 311, Schnakenberg 420. So Sloan was out. He was repudiated by a clear margin, and more than a little surprised. Worse yet, some art critics in town, among them Helen Appleton Read of the *Brooklyn Eagle,* reported the outcome as a vindication of the League's good sense in the face of a demagogue's antics. Forbes Watson, long a Sloan ally, thought Henry Schnakenberg a progressive choice for the students to make and said so in print. The day after the election, Schnakenberg, hoping that he and his colleague might still remain on good terms, sent Sloan a gracious, conciliatory letter. It was A. S. Baylinson, however, who wrote what his friend wanted to hear: "The Art Students League is defeated and not John Sloan."

Professing to be glad to have done with a job that took him away from his real work, his art, Sloan was in a strange position, then, in the second half of 1932. Even as he continued to work on his new technique of underpainting, glazing, and "cross-hatching," which proved to be an almost impossible sell for John Kraushaar (who very much wished his best artist would return to straight oil painting on canvas), Sloan was in the midst of his most sustained period of highly accomplished etching. Beginning with a superb portrait of Henri that he completed in January 1931, just before his old friend's memorial retrospective at the Metropolitan Museum, he did some of the best work of his career in this medium over the next two years. It is almost as if the uncertainty that inevitably came with his abandonment of direct oil painting was balanced, or compensated for, by the absolute confidence he felt in taking up the etcher's needle once again. From 1931 through 1933, he produced a series of nudes using various models, some in languorous poses and others in more intricate, demanding positions, but all with the graphic force, technical delicacy, and solid presence he was still straining to achieve in his work in tempera. But of course the market for nudes in any form in America was limited, and the prices brought by etchings were a great deal lower than those for paintings. (In the early 1930s, Sloan's current etchings were priced in the eighty-dollar range, while the average price for one of his city oil paintings was two thousand dollars.) Even to undertake the trip to Santa Fe in 1932 meant a financial stretch.

One person who was in Santa Fe that summer offered the hope of raising Sloan's spirits and reviving his reputation as a teacher: Helen Farr. The indefatigable note-taker of 1927 had had in mind for some time the idea of putting together a book of Sloan's comments about art—technical information, attitudes, and philosophy—on the order of Henri's *The Art Spirit,* published to acclaim ten years earlier. She had written to as many of Sloan's former students as she could locate, asking them to share with her their recollections of his lectures and "asides" at the League. The proposed book was not an entirely pedagogical or altruistic art-historical enterprise; by this time, Helen's feelings were apparent to several people. She was completely in love with Sloan. Sloan, however, was feeling something very different at the moment.

The most important of those who had decided that Helen was attracted to John Sloan in more than a passing way was Dolly, and she had been extremely effective in turning her husband against his former student. With her usual ferocity, Dolly had naturally followed every twist and turn of recent events at the League, taking careful note of who supported Sloan and to what degree, wild with anger at what she perceived as the lack of respect shown him. She had managed to convince Sloan that Helen had been a less vigorous ally than she seemed, and that her jealousy of his friendships with other women at the League was becoming a subject of talk there. In dismay, Sloan had returned to Helen the down payment she had lately made toward the purchase of another painting, along with a note suggesting that perhaps they might be friends again someday, but not at present. When Helen stopped by the house on Garcia Street one afternoon in the summer when she knew Dolly would be out, she experienced firsthand the extent of the tension and estrangement

Sloan's wife had wrought. Sloan was still interested in *Remarks on Art,* as it was to be called—the idea of such a book was of course flattering and useful—but he was cool toward her and could make no promises about when they might meet again. Dolly let it be known that she regarded this notion of a book as a presumption on Helen's part, an undertaking that should properly be left to the artist's wife, not a twenty-one-year-old former student.

Sloan's decision to give back Helen's money rather than sell her the painting she wanted was a good indication of how serious the breach between them really was. With payments due on the house and car in Santa Fe, and Kraushaar suggesting that another Sloan show would best be put off for a year or two, Sloan had more to fear than "fear itself," in the phrase the new president was using to reassure the country. Foreclosure was a daunting possibility, and bills were accumulating. Some much-needed good news came later that year, just before Christmas, when the Corcoran Gallery in Washington, D.C., announced that it would be holding an exhibition of Sloan's etchings the following spring and, that month, was buying the great *Yeats at Petipas* for its permanent collection. The money for the painting, which came to fifteen hundred dollars after Kraushaar's commission, arrived none too soon. The League had asked Sloan to come back as a substitute teacher, and the Archipenko School, a shoestring operation across the road on West Fifty-seventh Street, had taken him on full-time, but the salary from the one school was so small, and that from the other so nearly impossible to collect (he gave up trying to secure his back pay and left the Archipenko School after two months), that he realized he and Dolly would probably not be able to go back to New Mexico in the foreseeable future.

One irritation seemed to follow another. The IRS was again on Sloan's trail, to his annoyance, questioning him about a five-hundred-dollar donation he had made to the Tribal Arts Exposition for the big show two years before. To the agent in charge of Sloan's 1933 audit, it seemed unfathomable that a man who claimed to make as little money as Sloan did would contribute such a hefty sum to a cultural organization. The suspicion, natural enough under the circumstances, was that Sloan was a prodigious underreporter of income, and no doubt his IRS file included a clipping about the Carl Hamilton offer of forty thousand dollars. Dolly, in one of her periodic bursts of Sloan career-promotion, took it upon herself to send three of his new paintings to the Milwaukee

Art Institute, to no avail. Even flagrant self-advertisement led only to
more frustration: the half-humorous, half-desperate letter Sloan circulated
to sixty museum directors offering his paintings at half price yielded only
one feeler, from the Boston Museum of Fine Arts, whose board would
take two years to come up with the funds to buy *Pigeons* for its permanent
collection. Through these months of uncertainty, Sloan was surprisingly
uncomplaining, if only because he was far from alone in feeling the
crunch of the Depression at its worst in 1933. Of equal concern to him
was the situation of the Society of Independent Artists, which was grappling with a life-threatening deficit and nearly had to cancel its annual
show. Now that Mrs. Whitney had a museum of her own to manage and
finance, a once-steady source of funding was gone, and likewise Mrs.
Rockefeller's generosity had been tapped to the limit. (Some Society
members wrote Sloan and Baylinson the most heartrending letters in
these dark days: if cash was hard to come by, they said, they would gladly
barter their paintings at the annual show for winter coats, dresses, secondhand furniture, anything usable. Baylinson himself traded a painting for a
suit of clothes.) The 1933 show was to include six Native American
murals and fifteen paintings by inmates of the Clinton Prison in Dannemora, New York, and for those reasons alone, Sloan was glad that the
money to hold the show was finally found.

The one bright spot of the year—a quirky offer, to be sure—was an
invitation from Moscow to show in the American section of an exhibition
of the International Bureau of Revolutionary Artists, and to attend the
gala affair. The invitation was flattering to Sloan and duly noted by the
zealous file-keepers at Mr. Hoover's FBI. Unfortunately, even if Sloan had
been inclined to go, all artists were expected to pay their own way to the
border of Russia, at which point they would become guests of the state.
As it turned out, the Sloans didn't have the money even to go to Santa Fe
for the summer, so there was no question of their taking a trip to enjoy
Stalin's hospitality. Thus was posterity deprived of the memorable if
incongruous image of John and Dolly Sloan in Moscow, toasted by the
commissars.

Uneasy though Sloan was about the direction modern art—or
"ultramodern art," as he and others called it—had been taking since the
early twenties, there were certain of his contemporaries whom he recog-

nized as being indisputably great. Diego Rivera was in this category. If many of the Europeans championed through the thirties by the new Museum of Modern Art and its director, Alfred H. Barr, Jr., struck Sloan as dubious talents (in this category were Klee, Mondrian, Pavel Tchelitchew, the Futurists, Dali, and most of the other Surrealists), he harbored no reservations about the art being produced south of the border. The Mexican triumvirate of Rivera, Orozco, and Siqueiros was, for Sloan, an example of the power that nonabstract art still retained, and Rivera the paradigm of an artist who had profited by his study of Cubism yet moved on to even more distinctive accomplishments. The infamous "Battle of Rockefeller Center," in which Rivera the Communist found himself at loggerheads with Nelson Rockefeller the art patron and scion of a great capitalist family, elicited Sloan's unequivocal sympathy. Rivera had included the head of Lenin in the large mural he had been commissioned to paint for the elevator bank of the new RCA Building, and when Rockefeller protested this aspect of the work his family was paying for, he stood by his right as an artist to keep to the design as he had originally conceived it. The cause célèbre that followed had predictable results: Rivera's dismissal, noisy demonstrations outside Rockefeller Center, charges and countercharges from every direction, and the removal and ultimate destruction of the offending mural, despite promises that it would be kept intact. Sloan and friends such as Baylinson, Bynner, Pach, and Van Wyck Brooks circulated petitions to save the art work in what they all must have known would be a losing battle between the irreconcilable values of left-wing artists and their financial backers. The principle of art-before-money mattered, Sloan felt, and he was happy to take part in organizing an evening of peer celebration for the beleaguered painter.

The party held at the Algonquin Hotel in honor of Diego Rivera in October 1933 gave Sloan an opportunity to meet Rivera and Frida Kahlo, to affirm his solidarity with the painter's cause, and to spend time with some of the other guests whose company he had most enjoyed in the past and whom he saw too infrequently now—William Glackens and Ernest Lawson of "The Eight," for instance, and preeminently Max Eastman. Ironically, of all the old radicals, Eastman (who had been to Russia in the 1920s) was fast becoming the most knowledgeable about and critical of the workers' paradise as it had evolved under Lenin's successors. With typical contrariness, Sloan was honest enough to admit that he would rather not hear too much about the failings of the Bolshevik dream. With

strident Communists such as Gold and Freeman of the *New Masses,* Sloan
tended to dismiss the whole movement as impossibly rigid, but with
those who wanted to criticize the USSR, he took the opposite tack: a
noble experiment had to be given its due. The Depression and unemploy-
ment rates of 30 percent were proof enough that capitalism was a bankrupt system. Rockefeller's defensiveness about the inclusion of a portrait
of Lenin in a tableau on the theme "Man at the Crossroads . . ." only
underscored the point.

A few weeks after the Rivera banquet, Sloan was saddened to learn of
the death of an erstwhile colleague who hadn't been at the dinner, had
never wanted to have anything to do with politics or causes, and in his
last years had railed against the Modernists with more bile than the most
hidebound academician. George Luks was found dead in the early-
morning hours in a doorway on Sixth Avenue. Rumor had it that his
death was the result of yet another barroom brawl, but whatever the
cause, a distinguished if erratic career was ended, and one of the more
boisterous personalities in the art world gone. Luks also left behind him
his own small art school on East Twenty-second Street and a group of
students who didn't want to disband. They approached Sloan about taking over the ramshackle Luks School, and he agreed to give it a try. As
Sloan mused to a reporter from *Time,* "Mine has been a quiet life. George
was just the opposite. He painted on his impulses. I painted after long
thought. In fact, I think I have been thinking too much lately." He
wanted to make it clear at the outset, though, that the "supreme con-
tempt" Luks had demonstrated toward all modern art was not something
he would perpetuate at the school. Painting had been "sick" for a long
time, Sloan said—"getting sicker and sicker for over a hundred years"—
and had barely survived the blight of academic realism. The best of
Modernism was the cure, the shot in the arm, that the art form
needed.

As might have been expected, Sloan's experience at the Luks School
was not much different from his experience at the Archipenko School.
Helen Farr, who went there to study with him, remembered the place as a
"fire trap," a few dusty rooms with superb light and unreliable heating in
the winter. The manager of the space, Nick Magne, also lived there, and
wasn't sober very often; the result was that his drinking money tended to
be the same money he collected for tuition, which meant, once again,
trouble for Sloan when it came time to collect his salary. It was evident

that Sloan stayed, Helen noted, "because he liked the place, liked teaching, missed the League." But after a few months, he gave up.

The strangest development of this financially pressed time was Dolly's emergence as a breadwinner. Amelia White—"Miss Amelia White," as everyone seemed to call her—had been, on her own lesser level, the Gertrude Whitney or the Abby Rockefeller of the Native American arts movement. She was a principal backer of the Tribal Arts Exposition show and an active member of its board, equally ready to write a check or to offer an opinion about policy and strategy. According to Oliver La Farge, she and Dolly weren't getting along particularly well at this time (Dolly, rightly, saw herself as deserving an equal say in the Exposition's plans to continue promoting its cause), but that didn't prevent Miss White from doing the Sloans a good turn. When she opened the Gallery of American Indian Art on Madison Avenue, she hired Dolly as one of three women to run it and offered her the munificent salary of five hundred dollars a month. This sum was reduced each year as the Depression took its toll on the White fortunes—Dolly was paid two hundred dollars a month in 1937, the year the gallery closed—but as both a gesture and a practical help, White's bounty was much appreciated. It was, Sloan thought, absolutely typical of the woman, who was at once opinionated and pragmatic and lovingly concerned.

Dolly took to her job with great enthusiasm. It was a reason to get up in the morning, to dress up, to look and feel productive. Her husband felt that she was actually becoming quite knowledgeable about different aspects of Native American art and adept at explaining its qualities to potential buyers. She certainly had no qualms about writing (repeatedly) to the curators of the Metropolitan Museum to advise them of the need for an exhibition of the work there. There were enough occasions on which Dolly returned home in the early evening unsteady on her feet for Sloan to adopt a policy of seeing that she had cab money to get her to Midtown and directly back to the Village; left on her own, en route to the subway or the bus, she was apt to stop at various bars, with the inevitable consequences. Still, the gallery was a stabilizing influence at a time when Dolly's alcoholism was putting a strain on almost all of her relationships, even those with Dr. Mary Halton and Elizabeth Hamlin.

The job's best perquisite was a new friendship. The wife and mother-in-law of the young painter Philip Evergood also worked in the gallery, and John and Dolly Sloan quickly became good friends with the family.

The beefy, ebullient Evergood was a young man after Sloan's heart—active in left-wing circles yet not insufferably doctrinaire, committed to a modern version of figurative art, rowdy, affectionate, and energetic. An introduction to Juliana Force, arranged soon after the two painters met, established Evergood as a Whitney regular, and Dolly always seemed to be coming by with one present or another, a bracelet for Julia or a lavish, expensive art book for Philip. So warmly did John Sloan feel toward Philip Evergood that as soon as the money from the sale of *Pigeons* arrived from the Boston Museum of Fine Arts, he spent some of it to buy one of Evergood's oils, *The Old Wharf,* which he then donated to the Brooklyn Museum in hopes that it might hang near *The Haymarket* and Glackens's *Nude with Apple.* Sloan's purchase of Evergood's painting, like his earlier acquisition of works by Baylinson and John Graham, touches on a striking theme in this period of his life: a quiet generosity, a desire to help other artists, was set against a quiet rage at his own condition and the impatience with which he found himself waiting for someone to show a similar interest in the *one thousand* canvases he now had stored in his studio. Yet a splendid thing about the Evergoods, for Sloan, was that in their presence he could forget the daily aggravations and the professional indignities. Despite the thirty years' difference in their ages, they made a festive foursome, and when interviewed in later years Julia Evergood would recall one particular gathering at which both couples, in the course of a raucous evening, shed their clothes to dance. Partying with the Evergoods was an uninhibited affair.

The good times for John Sloan tended more and more to be in company and under the influence of significant drinking. For real or quiet intimacy, he had to look elsewhere now. At least one involvement in the early 1930s provided that respite. Gitel Kahn was an attractive former student who was modeling for Sloan at the time; slender and dark-haired, she was a lithe, personable model with a "warm brown torso" (Sloan later wrote) and the calm confidence of a woman who knew she had good reason to be open and relaxed about her body. She also made no secret of her sexual interest in Sloan.

Gitel was an effective muse for Sloan. He found that she inspired him in all the different modes he was working in at the moment. *Nude and Breakfast Tray* is one of the most successful etchings of that time of abundant printmaking, with Gitel sprawling across the unmade bed in feline contentment, a perfectly realized, solid, "linear-textured" figure. As an example of the new linework on canvas, she works better than many of Sloan's other women, whether clothed, as in *Girl, Back to the Piano,* or otherwise, as in *Nude on Navajo Blanket.* And as for his formidable painting of her striding down the staircase in the apartment, one hand over her head to hold back a curtain and the other on the banister, Sloan confessed that he "rated it with anything in the nude line that had been done for a hundred years." On the rare occasions when he left off experimenting with linework and went back to painting the figure without the cross-hatch marks, she is there as well, a body that Sloan knows well and respects, a person more individual and less abstract than many others of the same years. (The un-lineworked *Model in Dressing Room* of 1933 treats a theme that is somewhat rare in American art. Gitel stands in profile, nude, before the sink and mirror in an alcove, readying herself for a session, her dress, slip, and shoes on a chair beside her. The pretense that the nude model isn't a real woman who will later put on her underwear and other clothes and go out into the street is here violated; the convention of the "timeless nude" is itself stripped, under the glare of a lightbulb overhead, a ticking clock on the adjoining wall.) In *Gitel with Little Book,* she nestles in the corner of the couch with a sense of belonging to the space and to the gaze of the man observing her. It was, in fact, just that too-easy sense of her having settled in that ended Sloan's productive tryst with his model, friend, and bedmate. Dolly arrived home from work early one day to come upon Gitel Kahn wearing one of her—Dolly's—favorite kimonos, looking a bit too comfortably like the new mistress of the house. Dolly was irate, Gitel was sent on her way, and Sloan was made to feel the full weight of his wife's displeasure over the next weeks and months.

On the whole, it was an embarrassing time in many ways. There were public as well as private humiliations aplenty to cope with. In January 1934, Sloan had an exhibition of paintings and etchings at the Montross Gallery instead of at Kraushaar's. The show spanned almost thirty years of his career but resulted in the sale of only one oil, the early, satiric *Gray and Brass,* which netted Sloan $1,250. (Most of that money had to go to Kraushaar, as had some of the money for the sale of *Yeats at Petipas* in 1932: Sloan was still paying off the notes the dealer had signed for at the time of the 1928 loan to Owen Cattell, a huge debt that Cattell himself had since defaulted on.) Knocking classics such as *Three A.M.* down to $2,500 or wonderful paintings such as *Moving Picture Theatre* to $800 didn't help, either. A few etchings sold, but people hardly looked at the recent pictures, even when they were priced as low as $450 or $600. There were several respectful reviews and a few slamming notices that hurt: *ArtNews* called the whole enterprise of cross-hatching an "alarming procedure . . . an almost aesthetically disturbing mannerism." Most of Sloan's peers agreed.

Sloan lost another opportunity to show his work the following month, when he felt obliged to withdraw from the exhibition opening the RCA Building as a protest against the destruction of Diego Rivera's mural. In March he had to contend with yet more awkwardness when an "exposé" in the *New York Herald-Tribune* suggested that he was one of a few men who were profiting unfairly or illegally from government aid intended for indigent artists. The Public Works of Art Project (PWAP) fracas was a potential powderkeg, and Sloan wanted to extricate himself from it as quickly as possible. He had been accepting the allotted $38.25 a week from the PWAP for several weeks, as had hundreds of other artists across the country, after being assured by Juliana Force, who was administering the emergency relief program in the New York area, that he was both qualified and entitled. He had faithfully handed over two new paintings to the government, a view of Fourteenth Street in the snow and a rendering of the old Tammany Hall, and was sure he had discharged his part of the bargain. The point of contention, once the anti–New Deal *Herald-Tribune* editors got wind of the story, was Sloan's signed statement —signed at Juliana Force's direction—asserting that he was barely able to support himself as a painter and that any outside income he received from teaching or other sources did not exceed sixty dollars a month. Plenty of poverty-stricken artists had the impression that Sloan, given his immense reputation and the fact that several museums owned his work, was well-heeled, and they loudly objected to his being given any share at all of the welfare pie. What about those lucrative Hamlin and Hamilton sales from the twenties that everyone had heard about? What kind of cronyism was Mrs. Force practicing, subsidizing affluent friends like Sloan, William Zorach, and A. Stirling Calder with taxpayers' money when other artists were on the verge of starvation or eviction? The nastiness threatened to get out of hand as Mrs. Force was picketed at the Whitney for her alleged mismanagement of an important government program and Sloan and the other artists were harassed by indignant callers.

Interviewed by a reporter from the paper, Sloan was at pains to clarify his situation. He was irate that anyone would think he would take money in a time of crisis that more properly belonged to others. The fact, he tried to make clear, was that he had never been able to make a living by his art alone—there it was, out in the open now—and would have had to declare bankruptcy long ago were it not for his teaching and illustrating income. Furthermore, Sloan felt, the two paintings he had handed over as the work done on this $153-a-month stipend were more than just compensation. The patronage of *his* art, he suggested, was as important to the nation as the propping up of the rank amateurs who were a part of the PWAP. Sloan then showed his guest the vast stock of paintings he had on hand—90 percent of his life's output—and announced that he would be happy to give them, and anything else he painted in the years ahead, to any patron who would guarantee him a hundred dollars a week for life. So much for hidden bank accounts and high living. Several weeks later, the paper printed a retraction of its inflammatory charges against Sloan, Zorach, and Calder.

Sloan cannot have taken any more pleasure in the retraction than he had in the original article. The indignity of his having to go out of his way in public to establish his lack of financial success—to insist that unlike the work of Homer, Sargent, Chase, Hassam, Henri, Luks, Bellows, Marin, Demuth, O'Keeffe, and so on, *his* art was not avidly collected or prized in the only terms Americans understood—simply dramatized how strange a position John Sloan found himself in during the nightmare of the Depression.

The kimono episode on Washington Square South had meant an abrupt end to Gitel Kahn, though not, of course, to Sloan's need for the company of a woman who might love him in a less desperate way than his wife, who enjoyed his company when she was completely sober, and who could experience with him the sexual pleasure he wasn't ready at sixty-three to consider over and done with. It was probably inevitable that Helen Farr would reenter Sloan's life at some point in the capacity they had approached and skirted four years earlier, in the summer of *Susannah in Santa Fe,* and that is exactly what happened in 1934. The disagreements that Dolly had fabricated had long since been cleared up, and Sloan felt free to acknowledge to "Pete" that he was as interested in her as she so evidently was in him. What mattered was discretion and honest feeling. Neither Sloan nor Helen wanted Dolly to know, if that could be avoided, and no promises for the future were being made on either side. It was time, simply, to enjoy the moment. For the next two years they had exactly what they wanted: afternoons, when Dolly was at Miss White's gallery, to talk and make love, to paint and pose, to feel connected and mutually appreciated.

At some point, however, Dolly did begin to suspect that her husband and Helen were romantically involved, and gradually, in bitter silence, that suspicion became a certainty. If Sloan in turn suspected that Dolly knew the truth, his uneasiness may account for the periods of depression and even heavier drinking that plagued him the following year and whenever else he was away from Helen for too long, especially in New Mexico. Proximity to the Shusters, who were on the verge of divorce and caught up in their own cycle of more-than-social drinking, aggravated an already delicate situation. Dolly dealt with her hopelessness in her own way. In New York one afternoon in 1935, Sloan was overcome by fumes from a leak in the gas stove while preparing his dinner in the apartment on Washington Square. Dolly arrived home from work, late and a little drunk, just as he was being revived and tended to by their doctor. Her tone now held an uncharacteristic harshness: he was always trying to get attention, she snapped at her husband, and this was simply another ploy. "You're doing this just to create a scene!" Dolly yelled.

Yet in the oddest twist to the emotional ménage that was developing among Sloan, Dolly, and Helen, Dolly knew that she could look to Helen for support or reassurance in a crisis in a way that she couldn't with anyone else. Arriving home from Santa Fe before her husband in the autumn of 1935, Dolly was the first to read the letter informing them that NYU, which owned their building, was evicting all tenants and tearing down the property as part of its expansion program. Distraught at the idea of moving again, she asked Helen to stay with her until Sloan got back and found out what could be done. The answer to the latter question, as it turned out, was nothing. Sloan offered to give some free lectures at the university if the administration would rent him and his wife housing, or to enroll as a student to qualify for rooms on the Village campus. Neither gambit worked, and the scramble for affordable lodging was on again. The duplex studio and apartment that the Sloans moved

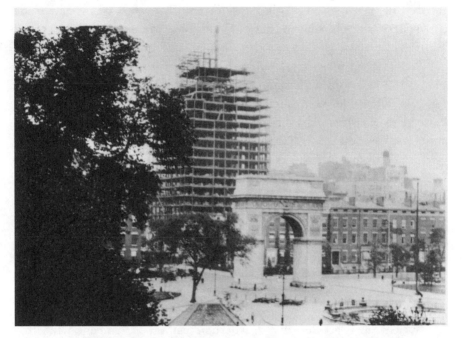

The changing city: the view from the Sloans' Washington Square South apartment, where they lived from 1927 to 1935 (Delaware Art Museum)

into that October, on the top floor of the Chelsea Hotel, was to be their final home in New York City, and once they were unpacked and able to calm down, they could even appreciate the symmetry of their wanderings. The old residence hotel was only a few steps down the block from 165 West Twenty-third Street, where their life in Manhattan had started.

To the few private students who came to his rooms at the Chelsea, all of whom represented a source of much-needed extra income, Sloan appeared to be in his element. Mary Regensberg, then in her early twenties, remembered that he seemed something of a "character." She had studied profitably with him at the Archipenko and the Luks School when she was eighteen and now wanted more one-on-one instruction. Frequently there was music playing on the radio in the studio, and Sloan was forever preaching the benefits of some radical new diet he was trying for his digestive troubles. He had the almost comical air of one who carried the parsimony of a Scotsman to new heights. Clothes that had been stylish in the twenties were still in the closet, ready to be worn. The last dab of paint on the palette, the last bit of ink in the pen, the last shred of tobacco in the pipe—all of these were carefully accounted for and made use of. It wasn't by being wasteful, Sloan liked to point out, that he and Dolly had managed as well as they had.

Neither had Sloan lost any of the nonchalance he could bring into play in his relations with younger people. Age and stature hadn't made for any "grand old man" aura; rather, Sloan dreaded the image of gray-haired decorum or stodgy eminence. His annual guest lecture that fall to the students of the League was entitled "Is It Possible to Make a Living at Art?" The answer, delivered in a feisty and jocular tone, was of course not, and you were a little slow in the head if you didn't know that. When Mary Regensberg decided to spend the summer of 1936 in New Mexico, that was fine with John and Dolly, who easily incorporated her into their life there, treating her like a daughter or a niece. Mary was necessarily unaware—which was as the Sloans wanted it—of the climatic point they had reached in their marriage, and of how far gone Dolly was in her alcoholism. A good deal was kept hidden from pupils and younger friends.

When Sloan accidentally drove their car off an embankment that summer, he and Mary were unhurt, but Dolly suffered a cracked vertebra. With Mary and others who visited her in the sling she was propped up in at the house, Dolly was a cheerful, talkative convalescent, but Sloan was privy to the other side of her confinement, a releasing of pent-up hurt over his affair with Helen and anguish at his having lost all feeling for her. Sitting by the makeshift hospital bed in the house on Garcia Street, Sloan listened to his wife sob out her pain about their life and his relationship with Helen. She had known for some time and was tormented by the truth, which he finally acknowledged. So a union that had been forged thirty-six years earlier against the advice of all of Sloan's friends, a bond of need and commitment on both sides, was tested one last time. Sloan's sense of duty was again the important factor. With trepidation at the prospect of the loneliness he was consigning himself to, but with a strong feeling for what he owed Dolly, Sloan comforted his wife and agreed to end the affair. He would keep his word.

It was a promise kept at a high cost. It was easy for Sloan, in his more despairing moments, to feel that all his life entailed now was exhaustion and frustration. Exhaustion and frustration, yes, but also work. No matter what was happening with Dolly or Helen, at the League or in the art world (where very little was in fact happening for Sloan), the painter continued to paint. In the summer of 1936, Sloan finally, determinedly returned to the theme of the Southwestern landscape. "I believe that . . . someone who is a writer is not simply doing his work in his books," the French philosopher Michel Foucault once commented, "but that his major work is, in the end, *himself in the process of writing his books. . . .* The work includes the whole life as well as the text." In this special sense, it matters not at all what his critics—or anyone—thinks of Sloan's linear-textured nudes or portraits or late landscapes. By now he had turned his back on several notions that were still current: the idea of the quick impression and the surface likeness, the idea of the masterpiece (there would be no more striving for another *"City" from Greenwich Village),* the idea of "representing one's time," the self-conscious idea of novelty and radical progress in aesthetic endeavors. The image Sloan presents us with in the thirties is of a man oppressed by the circumstances of his life but proud, lonely, furious, obstinate, and, by his own lights, free in his art.

Art: *Gist* and Struggle

(1936–1943)

"It is an artist's job to find some order in life and leave a record of what interested him—not what he thinks he ought to be interested in."

—JOHN SLOAN

In the late 1930s, there were fewer buyers for John Sloan's work than at any time since the Macbeth Galleries show. As John Kraushaar's health declined and the directorship of the firm passed into the hands of his children, principally his daughter, the situation only worsened. Antoinette Kraushaar did her best and managed a steady sale of the etchings and drawings, but sometimes it seemed as if her customers were interested in anything *but* a new Sloan oil. Never one to look away from an unpleasant truth, Sloan didn't waste time questioning the Kraushaars, but instead strengthened his resolve. Everyone else was wrong, he was right, and the indifference of the marketplace would mean to him now the same thing it had when he was younger: liberation from any expectations other than his own. The crosshatching of figures and the underpainting and glazing continued.

What Sloan was not liberated from, what no man in his position could be, was the historicizing process. Unlike Henri or Davies, he was living to see himself made into a historical figure, catalogued and pigeonholed in such a way that he might as well have been dead already as far as the art historians and the textbook writers were concerned. Some of the attention was pleasing. Lewis Mumford had described him in *The Brown Decades* as fusing "Eakins' strong realism with Homer's quick eye for incident" and proclaimed him one of the first artists to "acclimate to our minds the atmosphere . . . of the Brown Decades themselves [1880–

1910]." He had also, Mumford attested, "turned illustration from passive commentary to a more vital social activity." Thomas Craven, as influential a writer as Mumford at the time, had flatly stated in *Men of Art* that as an etcher, Sloan "had no rivals worthy of notice." The historian Susan LaFollette also situated him prominently in the modern hierarchy, calling him "one of the most deeply thoughtful of contemporary artists . . . perhaps the most complete artist in America." But what rankled was the tidy designation of him as social realist, as Ash Can chronicler of urban life, which cropped up with unceasing regularity and pretended to tell the whole story. Sloan felt he was being mummified in that cozy role, as if his several hundred New Jersey, Gloucester, and Santa Fe landscapes didn't exist, as if his work as a painter and etcher of the nude meant nothing, as if his portraits—of Floyd Dell and Stuart Davis, of Romany Marie and Edgard Varèse, of Dolly and "Woe" and countless models— were negligible achievements. It meant that when the Museum of Modern Art asked for a painting to send to Paris for a traveling survey exhibition of American art, the curators were careful to explain that what they wanted was an early city picture, preferably *McSorley's Bar,* and not anything recent. Sloan was hurt by the choice and by the reminder that no one thought of him as a vital contemporary painter. "I hate that painting," he remarked, referring to the popular McSorley scene. But there was also a certain disingenuousness in the respect for Sloan the Ash Can realist, and in any alleged interest in city images rather than linear-textured nudes. *Three A.M., Hairdresser's Window, Carmine Street Theater, The White Way,* and *The "City" from Greenwich Village,* among other gems, still sat in the closet at Kraushaar's or at the Chelsea Hotel. Curators and collectors weren't making offers on Sloans, even early ones, in the age of Grant Wood's American Scene, Surrealism, geometric abstraction, and the frantic rush to collect the School of Paris while there were still Dufys and Derains to be had.

Sloan was known to have strong opinions on all this—on everything, in fact, that had to do with art, museums, or cultural life—and he found himself, in his late sixties, in demand as a speaker. There was an element of sweet revenge for him in the status of lecturer. Whether it was at the Corcoran or NYU, at the League or the New Rochelle Art Association or any of the other art clubs he addressed, often for the purpose of fund-raising, Sloan could be counted on to be amusing, sarcastic, and indelicate. He had always deplored the American tendency to venerate

European art at the expense of native efforts, but by 1937 he wanted to lash out at a knee-jerk reaction from the opposite direction. The Regionalism of Thomas Hart Benton, Grant Wood, and John Steuart Curry was merely another "facet of Fascism," Sloan told one audience; it was idiotic that Americans hadn't yet moved beyond nationalism and patriotic motives in art. Waving the flag over a painting sickened him. And for that matter, why was an Iowa farmhouse considered more representative of the American Scene than a Canadian or a Mexican house or a pueblo in the Southwest? We had appropriated the term "American" from a whole continent. Sloan was no less ready to lambast the "mausoleum of Modernism" on West Fifty-third Street, which made no distinction between a fine Picasso still-life and the vacuity of a Salvador Dali fantasy or the facetious work of Duchamp's followers. It galled him that the new thinking among students, collectors, writers, and the younger curators implied that a Mondrian, a Klee, an Ernst was *necessarily* superior to any Sloan—or any Hopper, Marsh, Burchfield, Glackens, Evergood, or Soyer. Judgments, Sloan felt, were being made not on the worth of individual paintings but rather on the basis of a bandwagon effect: Modernism in any of its forms was inherently good; figurative art was necessarily retrograde, limited, of slight intellectual value. Léger's jubilant cry "We have destroyed subject matter in art!" was the new guide in modern aesthetics, a bias that left the circle of artists promoted by Gertrude Whitney and Juliana Force out in the cold, while Alfred Barr's tastes at the Modern were seen as holy writ. Not that Sloan couldn't appreciate the diabolical irony: he had fought against a monolithic Academy promoting a narrow, genteel realism in the first decade of the century, only to confront in his later years what he saw as a monolithic, equally doctrinaire Academy of the "ultramodern."

Sloan now registered his doubts about pure abstraction and where it might lead—especially as it took young artists away from their proper apprenticeship at drawing—with the same fervor he had once directed against the National Academy of Design. (The new, dangerous drift was "from the abstract to the abstruse to the absurd," Sloan liked to say). In other addresses, letting loose a "gentle rain of malice," Sloan attacked the art on view at the 1939 World's Fair or scorned the brutal scale of the new Rockefeller Center or caricatured the community of art critics as so many "art punchers"—like "cow punchers," branding the herd with readily identifiable labels—or, in a rare positive moment, defended his beloved Society of Independent Artists and the principle that any artist in the United States who wished to should be allowed a chance to exhibit freed from the decrees of juries and curators. When it wasn't being expressed in a speech, Sloan's activism took the old form of committee membership or petition-signing. He, Stieglitz, O'Keeffe, Hartley, and four other artists formed Living Art, Inc., at the end of 1936 to demand that artists be paid royalties on reproductions of their work—a cause, obviously, that went nowhere.

Sloan's staunchest ally in these days of his questionable significance in the art world was still Juliana Force. The power of the Whitney Museum, both financial and otherwise, had always lagged behind that of the Modern and the Metropolitan, but whenever possible, Juliana aided Sloan's cause. In December 1936, after a battle with Mrs. Whitney's financial adviser, who was urging the family to curb expenses (and doing his best to put the museum's director in her place), she had marched over to Kraushaar's to buy *Backyard, Greenwich Village* and *Sixth Avenue El at Third Street.* For Juliana, two goals were thus achieved in one deft stroke: she asserted her authority in museum budgetary matters and she helped the Sloans, just as Dolly was about to lose her job. (Financially pressed herself, Miss White had to close the Gallery of American Indian Art in 1937.)

New York Realists: 1900–1914, one of the first exhibitions at the Whitney in 1937, was a similar gesture of solidarity with a troubled group. Following on the heels of two well-received shows of his etchings, at Kraushaar's and at the Carnegie Institute, Sloan should have been able to bask in the glow of reviews acknowledging his early talent in its widest context. Certainly that was Juliana Force's intention. Henri, Sloan, Luks, Glackens, Lawson, and Shinn—the six of "The Eight" with the clearest link to what might be meant by "realism"—were represented by key examples of their pre-1915 work, along with some excellent paintings by George Bellows, Guy Pène du Bois, and Glenn Coleman. What many visitors to 8 West Eighth Street experienced, though, was something less than the excitement Mrs. Force and Mrs. Whitney felt when they looked at these pictures. To a generation for whom the important names were Hans Hofmann, Arshile Gorky, and Stuart Davis, *Chez Mouquin, Stag at Sharkey's,* and *Yeats at Petipas* might as well have been Victorian parlor scenes: they had no relevance to current issues and conflicts. It was a rare Modernist who, like John Graham, could pursue an adventurous, productive study of abstraction and still appreciate his former teacher's work on its own, very different terms. Many critics didn't bother to try. "Dust Gathers at the Whitney Museum," the *Brooklyn Daily Eagle* review was headlined. When William Glackens and the impoverished Ernest Lawson died in 1938 and 1939, respectively (Lawson in a possible suicide), their stock was at an all-time low. "Each literary generation fashions its own blinkers and then insists that they allow unimpeded vision," the critic Irving Howe once wrote, pondering the odd disdain felt for Zola in the 1930s. The same might be said for each generation interested in the visual arts. At the time of the New York Realists show at the Whitney, the Henri circle was smugly taken to be a quaint or at best "picturesque" group. Even a sympathetic critic such as Margaret Breuning felt obliged to acknowledge that anything to do with 1908 now seemed "remote," while Forbes Watson was alone in arguing the case for "Realism Undefeated" in the pages of *Parnassus.*

In the academic year 1937–38 another chapter was closed as Sloan taught his last class at the Art Students League. There were only four students in the room. One of them was David Scott, who was taking time off from Harvard to study painting and would later become a prominent art historian and curator in Washington, D.C. (and the co-organizer of the 1970 Sloan retrospective at the National Gallery of Art). Scott recalled that Sloan looked older than his years, frail and sickly, though he was still a thought-provoking teacher—and as snappish as the young man had been led to expect. At her wedding that year, Mary Regensberg thought the Sloans both seemed tired and a little lost at the reception, and she remembered that they left early. (Sloan's desire to get Dolly out of the hall before the serious drinking started always meant an unexplained, premature departure for them.) With his double vision bothering him more and more, Sloan generally found himself in need of a rest by late afternoon. There was even speculation in some quarters that the artist's gradually deteriorating eyesight was responsible for what was perceived as the growing strangeness of his art, and in a narrow sense, that idea may have had some truth to it: what Sloan saw when he looked at the linework of his figures wasn't necessarily, or exactly, what others saw. But the larger facts—that the cross-hatching predated any serious eye trouble; that he was able to work again on long-distance landscapes as of 1936; that his style didn't change after corrective eye surgery in the 1940s— indicate that there was more than literal vision to be considered.

Small satisfactions were sometimes the most reliable now. A valuable new friend had come into the Sloans' life when Ruth Martin worked with Dolly on the Exposition of Indian Tribal Arts show and subsequently started her own collection of modern paintings. Martin was an art lover of the kind Sloan most respected, a woman completely out of the common mold. In her thirties, she was employed as an assistant to a corporate executive and had no family trust fund or extra income to back her interest in owning original works of art. And best of all, to Sloan's thinking, she didn't make her choices based on fashion or status. She simply wanted to live with good paintings on her walls, and Sloan's work afforded her, she said, a "walloping experience." Her small down payments, with the balance paid out over time to Sloan personally, not through Kraushaar, meant that she wouldn't be acquiring any of the major city pictures. But by buying at a slow and steady pace from the mid-1930s through 1950 (a year when she was in fact Sloan's only buyer), Martin did amass an impressive collection, one that included some of the artist's best landscapes and portraits. By the time it was exhibited and sold by the Salander-O'Reilly Galleries in New York in 1980, its value was considerable. But more important than her status as a loyal patron, Ruth Martin was a friend who held Dolly in high regard and viewed Sloan as a great American painter.

Appreciation came from a more famous source when Somerset Maugham wrote to Sloan. In April 1937 George Macy, director of the Limited Editions Club of New York, had approached Sloan about doing the illustrations for a new deluxe two-volume set of Maugham's classic, *Of Human Bondage*, to be issued in an edition of fifteen hundred copies. Macy was an admirer of the de Kock etchings from thirty-five years earlier and was eager to have Sloan take on the job; he offered him fifteen hundred dollars for eight etchings for each of the two volumes. Sloan reread the novel with pleasure and set to work on capturing sixteen different moments in Philip Carey's life and career, from his early school days to his time as an art student through his meeting and troubled life with Mildred. Sloan worked well into the summer on the etchings and didn't leave for Santa Fe until August, when he pronounced himself pleased with the results, comprising his last major project as an etcher. "I really have enjoyed my struggles with the etchings," he told a former student, Don Freeman.

Somerset Maugham himself evidently agreed about their quality and wrote to Sloan to say that while he was "lamentably ignorant" of the art of etching, he thought the illustrations "very imaginative and of an ingenious invention." He hung the set of proofs that Sloan sent him on the walls of the house he was staying in that year in South Carolina.

Sloan's break with Helen Farr had been difficult for him, but it had been a torturous experience for her. Since 1935 she had been working as an art teacher at Nightingale-Bamford, a private girls' school in Manhattan, and since the fall of 1936 she had been grappling with the new reality of her situation with Sloan. En route home from a late-summer visit to relatives in California in 1937, Helen stopped off in Santa Fe. Despite Dolly's disapproval, Sloan wanted her to continue with her work on the book, the projected *Remarks on Art*. He hadn't promised that they would altogether end their professional bond, and in any event Dolly seemed to have calmed down since the time of her convalescence the summer before. She knew enough to take her husband at his word about ending the affair with Helen.

Dolly also seems to have had the idea, or hope, that Helen might become otherwise involved, with someone unattached and closer to her own age. At a gathering that Helen was invited to at the Sloans' the week she was in town, another guest did evince an interest in her. Wyatt Davis, in his early thirties, was recently divorced and had moved to New Mexico with an enthusiasm for the beauties of the area that his brother, Stuart, could never muster. A friend of the Shusters as well, he had long been a feature of the Sloans' life there. By the end of the evening—another occasion for plenty of drinking—Dolly had steered Helen off to her bedroom, where Wyatt was waiting.

What followed from that evening spent with Wyatt in the Sloans' bed had the sad, dazed quality of a dream. Still in love but having concluded that Sloan was lost to her forever, Helen found it hard to imagine what happiness the future could offer. The pain of that thought was impossible to deaden and impossible to live with. Shocking her family and friends, she accepted Wyatt's abrupt proposal and married him in October, commencing a sorry union that lasted not quite five months. From Wyatt's point of view, their equally speedy separation was a matter of deciding that he didn't love Helen after all, that he had been used as a substitute for Sloan. From Helen's probably more realistic perspective, it was a case of money, pure and simple: once they were back in New York, Wyatt Davis had realized that the Farrs weren't anywhere near as wealthy as he thought they were. In fact, Helen had been helping her parents pay some of their bills during a recent tight stretch, drawing on her own savings and teaching salary. Whatever the truth, by spring Wyatt had returned to New Mexico and was seeing his first wife—whom he was to remarry, divorce again, and later marry yet a third time. Helen, meanwhile, was pregnant, and left to cope with the problem on her own. Wyatt was done with her. ("He left me on the table" was her characterization of the break.) She never told Sloan or her parents about her abortion or discussed the emotional devastation that followed. Meeting Stuart Davis not long after, Helen encountered a not especially sympathetic former brother-in-law. What had she been thinking of to marry his younger brother, of all people? Stuart wondered.

Whether or not she had any inkling of what a nightmare the Helen Farr–Wyatt Davis marriage had been, or of its tragic consequences, Dolly continued to rely on Helen in times of need, just as she always had. In the spring of 1938 Sloan was in fine health. He made a trip to Andover, Massachusetts, to talk to the students at Phillips Academy on the occasion of a full retrospective of his career—the first ever—at the Addison Gallery there. (Curator Charles Sawyer remembered Sloan's visit as a successful occasion, even if the artist had to be coaxed out of Manhattan. Sloan struck him as a magnificent, "cantankerous old cuss" who was obviously grateful that his later work had been made a legitimate part of the survey, as he wished it to be.) Dolly, looking not at all well ("a sad figure," Sawyer thought), stayed behind in New York. But on Sloan's return from Massachusetts, it was he and not Dolly who was in need of medical attention. His digestive problems of several years' duration had reached a crisis point. A closing of a duct from the gallbladder required immediate surgery.

Feeling her usual panic, Dolly went out with a female friend, a long-time drinking companion, just before Sloan's operation. She was too nervous to stay at home and contemplate everything that could go wrong. When she finally returned to the apartment, she was, of course, in an even worse state of mind and feared a repetition of her experience in Colorado seven years earlier. She asked Helen to come to the Chelsea. "If you need help, you can count on Pete. You know that," Sloan had reminded his wife when he was admitted to the hospital. "She won't do anything to embarrass you." Helen arrived and got rid of the strychnine Dolly was hoarding and threatening to use. She stayed with her until she seemed steadier, even enduring a visit from Sloan's latest private student and model, Barbara Bernhardt, who wanted to make it apparent to both women that she had been more intimate with Sloan of late than had either Dolly or Helen. "He says I'm the best-dressed woman in New York," Barbara told them. It occurred to Helen then that Dolly must have known about this new affair, however brief and purely physical and unthreatening to her marriage it may have been. The paintings in the studio from the last year gave testimony, if nothing else did: *Bawdy Blonde* with her skirt tucked up toward her midriff, Barbara at her easel, Barbara smoking, Barbara playfully raising her legs on the couch to show her slip above her knees, Barbara fashionably clothed and Barbara crosshatched nude. "So why didn't you just throw her out?" Sloan asked Helen later, when she mentioned how annoying she had found Barbara's manner under the circumstances.

Any warmth Dolly may have felt for Helen in 1938 after Sloan's return from the hospital evaporated pretty quickly the next year, when the long-planned book at last came out. A figure like the tall, blond, self-confident Barbara Bernhardt meant one thing to Dolly; a rival for the position of guardian and soul mate to Sloan as artist was something else entirely. Yet *Gist of Art,* as it was called, gave Sloan's reputation a timely boost in the last weeks of 1939 and was a useful project in and of itself (beginning with a four-thousand-copy first printing in hardcover, it has remained available in paperback through the 1990s), something that both Sloan and Helen wanted to see brought to completion, no matter what price they had to pay with Dolly. And a significant price it was, for Helen. Although she had a contractual arrangement to receive one third of the royalties and was mentioned on the title page as having provided "assistance" in the recording of the book's contents, no one was likely to know that *Gist of Art* had really been her project from first to last, and that was just how Dolly wanted it. The dedication was to Amelia White and to Dolly, and Sloan was coerced into saying to anyone who asked, whether friend or interviewer, that the book was essentially Dolly's. Dolly also let it be known that she was writing her husband's biography and editing a volume of the Henri-Sloan correspondence. Neither undertaking, naturally, existed outside of Dolly's fantasies, but the message was clear: no one else need think of assuming the role.

If Helen was deeply hurt by the circumstances of the book's publication and by her relegation to the shadows that fall, she was pleased by the reviews, the sales, and the effect on a depleted John Sloan. He had worked on no more than half a dozen paintings in the preceding twelve months, was done with the League entirely, and had stumbled his way through a mural for the Bronxville Post Office. But the appearance of *Gist of Art* resulted in some gratifying, invigorating attention. Part of this had to do with the nature of the book. After a decade of third-person textbook-style surveys, readers interested in American art were ready for some "kitchen talk," as Helen had called it when presenting her proposal to publisher Sam Golden of the American Artists Group. Thus *Gist of Art* was designed to bridge two worlds, even more so than Henri's inspirational *Art Spirit* of 1923. It contained enough hands-on instruction and advice—of the kind a teacher would dispense to a class at an art school—to benefit the student, and enough general commentary and random "art philosophy" to captivate the art lover who didn't paint or draw. The last third of the book was given over to illustrations of work from every phase of Sloan's career, with brief comments by the artist next to each picture. (This section also contained, as it turned out, a large number of misdated paintings; in his interviews with Helen, Sloan had made educated guesses and fared no better with exact dates than he usually did.)

The technical part of the book covered a bountiful range: Sloan's remarks, as transcribed by Helen and reported by the dozens of former pupils she had written to, dealt with the arrangement of a palette, the properties of gesso and tempera, anatomy and the posing of a model, visual and isometric perspective, the history of underpainting and glazing, approaches to landscape and murals, tone and texture in drawing, and the paramount separation of form and color in his own recent work. The rest was an effort to re-create the engaging spirit of the man behind the artist and the teacher—jocular, indignant, cocky, opinionated, and almost insatiably concerned with freedom. Above all, Sloan spoke out for seeing art as more than merely the mastery of technique or the understanding of trends; there were enough "space eaters" in the world already, he said, enough pictures by academic types and client pleasers (and whether those clients were conservative patrons or the curators at the Modern made no difference). Art, Sloan maintained, had to involve vision, passion, personality, and unsettling *need*. It was at heart a "response to the living of life." It had nothing to do with parasitic critics or dealers or juries. By now, of course, Sloan's failure to make sufficient money from his painting, once a simple, unfortunate fact of his own life, had hardened into a general principle. Success was a trap that prevented one from following one's own bent. Aesthetic satisfaction could be known only by those who abandoned the desire to succeed commercially and worked to please themselves.

Reviewers tended to like the book almost without exception, not only for its technical information but for the personality it projected—a "shrewd, tart, and aphoristic" temperament, the *Times* critic decided, that fell "somewhere between Will Rogers and Whistler." *Time* ran a lengthy piece replete with the usual factual errors and a photo of Sloan at his easel, as did *Life,* and in the wake of so much favorable press, *Hudson Sky,* one of the earliest landscapes, unexpectedly found a home at the Wichita Museum of Art. Such was the vigor of Sloan's new or, rather, renewed celebrity in 1939 that an editor at Doubleday approached him to do another book, this time a "good, tart, shrewd statement of your feelings about art in America." Wisely, Sloan felt that his performance as an art-world curmudgeon was best kept to the podium from here on in. Taken too far, the role of "crusty commentator," hammering away at a corrupt art scene, threatened to be as restrictive as any other.

For Sloan the author, the pleasure of being lionized—despite the strictures against popular approval that Sloan the teacher was so adamant about—lasted well into the next year. He was invited to lecture in Philadelphia, where he met with Marianna for the first time since Bessie's death, in 1930, and even went so far as to do something he would never have considered only a few years earlier: he accepted an invitation from the city officials of Lock Haven to return to his birthplace, the central Pennsylvania logging town he had left at the age of five, to be feted in the local-boy-makes-good tradition. Rebecca Gross, the editor of the town's paper, escorted the Sloans on their tour that autumn afternoon and introduced Sloan at the dinner held in his honor. While she was struck by how fanatically possessive Dolly seemed, never letting her husband out of her sight or allowing him a minute's conversation on his own with anyone else, Miss Gross had the impression that Sloan himself was tickled by the whole experience. She drove him to North Grove Street to see the house where he had been born and to the cemetery where his grandfather was buried with a splendid view of the Susquehanna River. Nothing about the old homestead was familiar, he said. In fact, Sloan joked, the place looked annoyingly middle-class to his eyes, and he wondered if they couldn't find some more disreputable house that he might claim as his starting-point in life.

Houses and domestic stability were much on Sloan's mind in 1940. That spring he had made a decision that required considerable resolve and energy. Dolly was a much-loved figure in Santa Fe. Since the late 1920s, she had been a principal organizer of the Hysterical Parade, a kind of parody extravaganza that was staged each summer in comic tandem with the more traditional Historical Parade, a downtown celebration of the Spanish conquest of the area. She and Witter Bynner often led their parade in one crazy costume or another. But his wife's sociability and her illness overlapped too easily now, Sloan felt, and in her early sixties, she was seeing her last reserves of will collapse. The opportunities for drinking binges away from the house on Garcia Street were simply too great, worse than in New York, and Sloan himself was too old to be wandering the streets at night to find her and guide her home. So, unwilling as they both were to abandon New Mexico altogether, they agreed on a safety measure. Sloan bought several acres six miles north of town from Joe Bakos, a painter and good friend who had homesteaded the land many years before, and then he designed the simple house he wanted built there —two bedrooms, a kitchen and dining area, an ample living room, and a studio—and Bakos saw to its construction. By taking a small loan and renting out their house in town, Sloan hoped they would just be able to manage the new arrangement. Now when they went in to Santa Fe, it would be together, by car, on a joint visit or an errand. There would be no more solo outings downtown for Dolly, no more excursions with friends or acquaintances with the same tendency to lose control. The very primitiveness of the Sloans' new lodgings in the Southwest struck some people as odd, but as Sloan approached the age of seventy, it was hard to underestimate either his ability to economize on daily expenses or his loathing for gentrified living. Sinagua, the name they gave to the house, said it all: with no plumbing into the city lines, they were indeed *sin agua,* or "without water." For that matter, they were without electric lights and a telephone as well.

The drawbacks of Sinagua were apparent from the start. In so remote an area, the house was bound to be broken into every winter (and it was). Sixty pounds of ice might be reduced to twenty by the time the drive from town was completed, and rainwater had to be carefully collected.

The silence could be eerie, though beautiful. Still, the Sloans professed to be happy with their decision, and John Sloan felt rejuvenated to the point of painting eleven landscapes that summer, several of them of better quality than he had produced in some time. What one of their earliest visitors from the East thought of her rustic accommodations isn't known, but her brief stay at Sinagua was surely Juliana Force's first and last experience of "roughing it" in the desert.

Sloan's second operation for an obstruction in his gallbladder, in February 1941, put all the last year's joys and frustrations in a new light. He developed pneumonia while in the hospital, necessitating a much longer stay than anticipated, and emerged much thinner and with a pile of hospital bills that left him staggered. He was too weak to paint at all that year, and the income from his private students barely covered the rent. Dolly nervously tried to interest Amelia White in buying *Three A.M.,* a painting she had always liked, but Miss White had to admit that she couldn't afford it. Mrs. Force was more successful in seeing that a major painting, *The Picnic Grounds,* entered the Whitney collection, which put twelve hundred dollars toward the medical bills after Kraushaar's commission. Friends did their best to raise Sloan's spirits—a testimonial at Petipas celebrated the twenty-fifth anniversary of the Society of Independent Artists and the twenty-fourth of its esteemed president; Amelia White and Oliver La Farge threw a fortieth-wedding-anniversary bash for John and Dolly in Santa Fe that summer; the New Mexico Museum held a big Sloan show; and dear souls such as Raphael Soyer and Philip Evergood let him know how much he meant to them—but it was hard for him to feel elated in the face of an old age that promised only genteel poverty after fifty years of labor. When Sloan was elected to the prestigious Academy of Arts and Letters, in 1942, he wondered how many other members were in the same boat; they looked like a prosperous bunch. He had recently been forced to sell his beloved Daumier lithographs for cash to live on. The Gericault drawing had gone the same route in the thirties, and he and Dolly were beginning the ordeal of opening their library to the book dealers who paid decent prices.

It was while he was in this odd position, and the mood that came with it, that John Sloan—called the "dean of American painters" now, in the press—became involved in the nuttiest project of his entire career. On the face of it, the Art Appreciation Movement and its Hall of Art were just an extension of the same philosophy that animated the Society of Independent Artists, a means of opening doors for talented men and women who had yet to make a place for themselves within the system. In truth, it went considerably beyond the Society—or, put another way, fell considerably short.

The Society itself had become a largely amateur, ragtag operation by the 1940s. Very few artists of note regularly exhibited in the annual show other than Sloan himself, Baylinson, and Pach. (Theresa Bernstein, Louise Bourgeois, Philip Evergood, and William Zorach were the last of the other significant holdouts—a group that defines the phrase "strange bedfellows.") Reviews were perfunctory. Everyone but Sloan and the participants seemed to feel that it was an idea, admirable and even exciting in its first decade, that had long since outlived its purpose. But if eyebrows were raised by Sloan's stubborn loyalty to the Society, that ugly duckling of the Manhattan art world, the Art Appreciation Movement was truly an amateur's bacchanal, a source of mirth and fury among professionals.

The "movement" was the brainchild of Max Pochapin, a middle-aged entrepreneur straight from Central Casting. A former promoter of dolls, alarm clocks, and bazookas, he had done well for himself in the culture line by selling classical-music records in bulk at reduced prices. All had gone well with Music Appreciation, Inc., until Pearl Harbor, when the rationing of shellac, crucial to the production of records, began substantially to curtail the mass-market profits. Pochapin accordingly decided to make the switch to the visual arts, accurately reasoning that the number of impoverished or Sunday painters in America and the number of "common folk" interested in owning an original representational painting were both large enough to constitute a mutually beneficial market. His idea was to open a "Hall of Art" that would eventually have branches in many cities, in storefronts, hotel suites, department stores, or wherever suitable space could be found; he would pack the rooms from top to bottom, bargain-basement style, with paintings, and advertise prices affordable to the man on the street who had never imagined he could own an art work: from a starting price of ten dollars to a top of two hundred. The manager's take on all sales would be a healthy 50 percent. What he needed, though, Pochapin knew, was the imprimatur of a few art-world personages. The inhibiting "gallery aura" was finally going to be dispelled from the business of buying and selling art, but a certain level of class would be required all the same—which led Max Pochapin to John Sloan. In the end, the founder of the Art Appreciation Movement got what he wanted: Sloan, Walter Pach, Reginald Marsh, and two other lesser-known artists all agreed to serve on the "Board of Judges" of the movement, with Sloan as chairman, and to do their part to stimulate the involvement of artists and the interest of the public. Their first act was to send a letter to every artist listed in *Who's Who* and other directories to solicit his or her participation. There was a clear understanding that this was not going to be a discriminating enterprise; the Hall of Art would make the open-door Society of Independent Artists look as restrictive and elitist as the old Academy. Anyone who had ever put brush to canvas in a coherent way was welcome, or actually urged, to send in paintings. Pochapin wanted a massive stockpile of the stuff, and the sooner the better. To Sloan, a kind of Rubicon was being crossed here. The world of "high art" had turned its back on him. He had nothing to lose, or so he felt, by linking his name with that of a no-nonsense businessman. What, he wanted to know, were dealers, anyway, for all their pretensions to the contrary? Hadn't he always stood for making the experience of art more democratic, less sacrosanct? And if Pochapin was willing to offer him a small monthly salary to be the chairman of the Board of Judges, a position that involved no judging of anything, then so be it. He had bills to pay.

Reaction in the art world to the Sloan-Pochapin alliance was predictable. Fellow artists and reputable dealers were dismayed at this latest instance of John Sloan's eccentricity. The most vehement letter he received was from Stuart Davis, by then established as one of the most important abstract painters in America. This promotional deal that Sloan had involved himself in was a "phony of the first order," Davis angrily wrote to his old friend, "which calls for condemnation, not support, by any artist of integrity." It was just a "cheap commercial exploitation of artists and public alike" and a slap in the face to men and women of talent. In fairly scathing terms, Davis went on to remind Sloan that the historical role of the authentic artist was to struggle against wheeler-dealers like Pochapin and the flooding of the market with bad pictures at low prices. That artists "of supposed integrity" could be induced to become part of such a scheme was amazing to him, Davis wrote, adding (rather disingenuously) that he was not making a gratuitous comment on Sloan's personal affairs but simply noting his protest "for the record."

Obviously, the happy summer days of Gloucester outings were long past for Sloan and Ed Davis's son. Artists like Ivan Albright made merciless fun of the project in letters-to-the-editor columns, and even friends such as Will Shuster and Alice Bradley Davis of the *Chicago Sun* worried that Sloan had got himself involved in a questionable deal. (As "Shus" prophetically asked, what protection did the artists have under this system? With such a volume of trade, who was to know what Pochapin really sold anything for and whether the payment made to the artist was fair and accurate?) With the air filled with catcalls, Reginald Marsh bailed out pretty quickly, but Sloan—no surprise to anyone who knew him—decided to dig in. Moreover, the more vocal or snider the opposition, the greater Sloan's commitment to the project seemed to become.

By the beginning of 1943, ads were appearing in the *New York Post* and other papers featuring Sloan's picture above a statement that this notable artist would vouch for the quality of what patrons would find at the Hall of Art in Midtown Manhattan or at any of its branches, and would "guarantee"—whatever that was supposed to mean in this extralegal context—the value of everything on display. Flyers ("Do You Want to Sell Your Paintings? / Is There a Market for Painting? / Can a Market for Painting Be Created?") were sent far and wide, and Sloan made a radio broadcast appealing to artists to send in their works and to buyers to come have a look. The full impact of what this enterprise meant to a man in Sloan's position is captured well enough in one early receipt in his files: a canceled check, after Pochapin's exorbitant commission and following the Hall's price-restriction guidelines, for $112.50—*for the sale of four Sloan paintings.*

In all, it was a strange winter. Sloan heard good reports about his paintings in the new Corcoran Biennial and in group shows at museums in Indianapolis, Milwaukee, and Utica. Yet he wrote plaintively to his sister of his fear that his current work was nothing but an anticlimax. It was distressing, he told Marianna, to have to live with that sense of himself as a man who had already done the best he had in him to do. A third—and finally successful—operation on the gall duct kept Sloan in bed most days until the spring, and as his weight continued to drop, he wondered (not for the first time), what would become of poor Dolly when he was gone.

But that was not how it was to be. Tuesday, May 4, 1943, was the day of the preview of the Society's annual exhibition, the second-to-last it would ever hold, as the fight for space in wartime New York was getting worse by the year. Dolly was sitting by Sloan's bed after breakfast, talking to him while he rested, when she collapsed and slipped to the floor. To Sloan's horror, she was dead by the time he reached her side.

News of Dolly's heart attack and sudden death, at the age of sixty-six, elicited an outpouring of sympathy and sadness. For all of the demons of temper and deceit brought on by her drinking, and for all of the friends and acquaintances she had alienated over the years, Dolly Wall Sloan had lived a life that was unusual and meaningful in other respects, stretching into areas that many people never knew about. Dr. Mary Halton had cause to recollect her work in fund-raising for the home she helped to run for unwed mothers. The prison chaplain at the Dannemora Prison in Clinton, New York, remembered Dolly as the woman who, since the first time the Society had exhibited the convicts' work, ten years earlier, had made sure that the art classes in the prison were kept properly supplied, even as the state attempted to cut the budget for such "inessentials." Anyone interested in Native American art knew her as a staunch advocate of that cause, and Village regulars and Society participants could hardly imagine how much gaiety they would have missed over the years without Dolly Sloan and her energy, her outlandish costumes, her frantic ticket sales for one event or another, her passion for late nights and festive gatherings. The loss to friends such as Witter Bynner and Ruth Martin was personal and deep; Dolly had been a friend who didn't judge others, who could be charming and ferociously loyal. Max Eastman delivered a eulogy at a memorial service that addressed the heartfelt views of all the old Socialist radicals: this was a woman who had cared about people who suffered and did without, who knew nothing about political theory or ideology but believed in rolling up her sleeves to try to effect change, who had an instinctive sense of injustice and of how badly the world treated those who couldn't defend themselves.

Numb with grief and still enfeebled from his surgery, Sloan was unable to attend the memorial service. Brought to the funeral parlor just before the cremation, he stared at Dolly in her coffin and said simply, "She looks noble." He imagined that he would soon follow her.

Renewal and Decline

(1943–1950)

> *"There is only one success—to be able to spend your life in your own way."*
>
> —CHRISTOPHER MORLEY,
> *Where the Blue Begins*
> (1922)

Life with Dolly had always been difficult, at times tormenting, but life without her promised to be unimaginably bleak. Amelia White took her old friend under her wing and insisted that he come out to New Mexico for the summer, not to hibernate at Sinagua but to live as long as he cared to in the guest house on her property. There he was looked after by the dependable Miss White and her housekeeper, fed and pampered and given privacy to rest, grieve, or paint as his mood dictated. Sloan was so well provided for, and (at a ghostly one hundred pounds) so debilitated, that he decided to remain in Santa Fe through the winter. New York in the cold weather and the Chelsea Hotel with its quiet, empty rooms were painful prospects to contemplate. With his finances in a "very, very low state," as he told a former student, he wasn't at all sure what might become of him in the days ahead.

Sloan's more affluent friends tried to set him at ease on that score, at least. Florence Davey McCormick bought *The White Way* that fall from Kraushaar (and two years later gave it to the Philadelphia Museum of Art), and Amelia White purchased *Woman's Work,* one of the best of the 1912 series of paintings of rooftop women tending to their laundry (she eventually donated it to the Milwaukee Museum of Art), and later *Dolly with a Black Bow.*

The person who was most interested in being of help to Sloan, obviously, was Helen Farr, but she felt it was important that she wait a while longer before getting in touch with him. When she finally summoned up the nerve to write at the end of the year, it was in the form of what she self-consciously described as an "earnest letter." Helen acknowledged that Sloan's friends, herself foremost, longed to see him back in New York, but she said they all understood that he had to stay wherever he could best maintain his health and spirits. Many people took it for granted that Sloan probably wouldn't return from New Mexico now that Dolly was gone, and Helen considered that possibility seriously enough to address her former teacher and lover bluntly, on the gloomy assumption that this might be their last communication. What she wanted to say had to do with art, not romance. "I sincerely believe that you are putting too much *teaching* into the painting," she wrote. "You are working too much with your mind." Pressing the point further, in a way that she might not have under other circumstances or in a face-to-face meeting, Helen worried that Sloan had lost his way with these arid, programmatic portraits that denied his finest qualities: "It is as though you shut yourself off from a great tool when you, who are a feeling person, refrain from putting [into the art] your feelings of enthusiasm, interest, character, sorrow." She ended on a positive note, observing that if Sloan's physical strength could be restored, she was sure he would be able to paint as vibrantly as he ever had.

Sloan wasn't shocked by the well-meant criticism. He admitted to Helen that there were times now when he wished he had never embarked on the glazing experiment. "I seem to have lost the ability to paint directly," he wrote plaintively in mid-January. In this, his eighth month in Miss White's guest house, he also confided that he was leading a "lonely, purposeless life" and had yet to feel truly at home in his present setting. For Helen, eager as she was for some information, some hint as to Sloan's state of mind, that remark was enough. She responded by telling him that she wanted to come out to Santa Fe, and soon. Her "cover" was a proposal by the publisher Sam Golden to reissue *Gist of Art*. Sloan expressed some genuine confusion as to why a reprint of their book should necessitate her taking a train across the country in the middle of winter, and he reminded Helen of how long, tiring, and expensive a trip it was. But Helen was not to be put off. "[She] is en route to Santa Fe!" Sloan noted in his diary, with the air of one throwing his hands up in exhausted wonder. "She has a sort of courage, but I wish she hadn't decided to come."

In truth, no one was thrilled to see Helen Farr on the scene again in New Mexico. If it wasn't clear to Sloan that Helen was still passionately in love with him and interested in becoming the second Mrs. Sloan, others were not so naive. Amelia White was quite happy to be taking care of her old friend by herself and saw no need for unsettling changes. Likewise, the Shusters were wary of the possibility—a good one, they knew—that Helen might appropriate "their" John Sloan and take him back to New York for good. That concern was shared by Wyatt Davis. Now remarried to Miriam, Wyatt cannot have been pleased to see his ex-wife in any case. He and Miriam looked on Helen Farr as untrustworthy and seriously threatening to the even deeper bond they had forged with Sloan since Dolly's death. In their view, Helen was "mousy and manipulative" at the same time, and in appearing so suddenly in New Mexico was clearly up to no good.

Wyatt need not have worried that Helen wanted any further contact with him. At a stopover on the trip west, she stood on the back platform of the train and, in a grand gesture, hurled her wedding ring out onto the Kansas plains. A new life, she hoped, was awaiting her, an unexpected fresh start that would eclipse the old mistakes and the old pain. She arrived in Santa Fe on February 2.

John Sloan and Helen Farr were married on February 5, 1944, by a justice of the peace in Santa Fe. He was seventy-two, and she was just two weeks short of her thirty-second birthday. Reactions from friends and family in the East were hardly less extreme than those in New Mexico. Will Shuster's congratulatory observation to Helen was a threat that if she ever hurt Sloan, as he felt she had hurt Wyatt, he would "break her into a thousand pieces." Dr. and Mrs. Farr in Manhattan were horrified by the telegram they received and by the newspaper coverage of the wedding; Helen had never quite adhered to their expectations either socially or professionally, but marriage to a man even older than her father was beyond the pale. Other, more disinterested friends such as Edward and Jo Hopper had a less volatile response. The Hoppers, who knew Helen well, wrote to Sloan that they were of the opinion that this was the best thing that could have happened to him. Of that, Sloan had no doubt.

Helen's arrival in Santa Fe three days before her wedding had shocked Sloan into a recognition of the turning point that was confronting him.

Helen was clear about her interest in him, certain that he was the only man she was going to love no matter what they decided to do, and confident in her desire and need to help him back onto his feet. They retired on their first afternoon together to the bedroom of the guest house, eager to know if the sexual spark of 1936 was still there. There cannot have been much on any level for Sloan to ponder. He called Helen the next day at the boardinghouse where she was staying and told her that he had thought everything through and was sure of what he wanted. He wanted her to go back to New York as his wife. As Helen was expected back at her teaching job in a few days, she left New Mexico just after the ceremony. The plan was for her to reopen the apartment at the Chelsea prior to her husband's return, with Sloan joining her a few weeks later as his health and stamina improved. Sloan found it hard to contain his delight, and during their separation, he bombarded Helen with boyish, joyful letters full of curiosity about the future and an optimism he hadn't felt in years.

His sudden—if not entirely unexpected—marriage to Helen Farr was more than an important emotional and sexual development in John Sloan's life. He desperately needed·to be taken in hand at this point, to be guided toward the stability that he craved and hadn't known for some years. That kind of nurturing guidance of a temperamental artist was something Helen was both eager and able to provide. Any effort in this direction, however, certainly didn't mean rejecting or ignoring the past, and Helen was confronted by the first reminder of Sloan's long life prior to his remarriage the moment she entered the apartment at the Chelsea, now her own home. Dolly, in the form of the 1909 portrait, stared down from the wall. Dolly's clothes and costumes, her letters and photographs and personal effects—there was so much to sort through. But Sloan and Helen wisely decided that there was nothing to be gained, and a great deal to be lost, by failing to talk about Dolly honestly and to keep her memory with them. "After all, Dolly is part of us, our love and our life together," the new Mrs. Sloan wrote to her husband.

The changes Helen did want to make in Sloan's life were simpler and long overdue. Out went the suits and hats from the twenties, attire that a man accustomed to extreme frugality had never been able to part with. He was induced to buy a few items for a newer wardrobe, to eat a more balanced diet and larger meals (which seemed rather quickly to ease his chronic stomach problems), to go for the eye operation that would cure

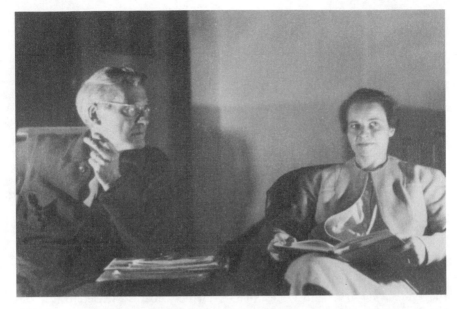

John Sloan and Helen Farr Sloan, circa 1944 (Delaware Art Museum)

his double vision. On the plausible assumption that no one respects anything that is sold too cheaply, the prices for all the oils in Kraushaar's and Erwin Barrie's keeping were doubled. Before the end of the year, *Jefferson Market, Chinese Restaurant* and *Bleecker Street, Saturday Night* had been sold, nicely verifying Helen's thesis. Indeed, over the next two years, with the fortuitous sale of *The Rathskeller* to the Cleveland Museum, *Sun and Wind on Roof* to the Randolph-Macon Women's College, and *Hairdresser's Window* to the Wadsworth Atheneum, Sloan found himself enjoying a healthier income and a renewed museum interest in his pre–Armory Show work.

A related but touchier matter, which Helen knew enough not to press him too hard on, was the Art Appreciation Movement. Sloan's involvement with Max Pochapin was a sore subject for her, as it was for many of his former colleagues and students. Even before Sloan returned from the West that winter, Pochapin had concocted another scheme to expand the Hall of Art setup into six hundred Sears & Roebuck outlets and had approached his titular Head Judge for his approval. To Helen's relief, Sloan decided that Pochapin was moving away from what had been desirable in the original plan and strongly advised him against any expansion. But a certain amount of damage had already been done. Joe Hirshhorn, the tycoon who was in the midst of amassing a vast collection of modern art, paid a visit to the Chelsea in May 1944. He indicated that there were three paintings he wanted and that he was willing to pay eight hundred dollars for all three. Sloan and Helen were insulted by the price and by Hirshhorn's cavalier tone, but some of the blame had to rest squarely on the artist's own shoulders. A painter who sold through the Hall of Art was assumed to be a bargain, someone desperate to make a sale, not a blue-chip investment. To the relief of everyone who knew him, Sloan broke all ties with Pochapin several months later, after he began to suspect that the business's ledgers were not always accurate.

The question of how Sloan was perceived by others, and what measure of respect he was accorded, had always mattered to Helen. Now, as his wife, she could observe at close range what a seesaw experience it was. In 1945 Sloan and Shinn—the last of "The Eight"—were honored by the Philadelphia Museum of Art with an exhibition devoted to the artists of the *Philadelphia Press,* in which twenty-two of Sloan's oils, etchings, and lithographs were on display. (The two men were also asked to provide catalogue essays; to Sloan's mind, Shinn's was embarrassingly "rococo," romanticizing their youth at the newspaper in ways that Sloan found distasteful.) Sloan delivered the Moody Lecture at the Renaissance Society of the University of Chicago on the occasion of a show of his etchings there, and was asked to speak at the Fort Worth Museum in Texas on his way back to New York after the summer in Santa Fe. The book club that had brought out *Of Human Bondage* now wanted him to illustrate its reprint of *The Turn of the Screw* (Sloan ultimately advised them to use the Charles Demuth watercolors), and the University of Georgia expressed interest in having Sloan serve as an artist-in-residence. Once again, he was in demand.

Yet there was also plenty of evidence of a different approach to Sloan. In the winter of 1944–45, the wife of the playwright Clifford Odets studied with him three afternoons a week. Giving no thought to how her remarks might be taken, Mrs. Odets spoke often of the important collection she and her husband were putting together, without ever indicating the least interest in buying so much as a single Sloan etching. When she borrowed an expensive art book from her teacher and was remiss in returning it, Sloan and Helen went to the Odets' apartment on Central Park South to retrieve the volume. They were shown the many Klees the couple had bought—"as a good investment," Mrs. Odets chirped—and then sent on their way.

A similar lack of regard was evinced during an encounter with the grande dame of modern art in Abiquiu, New Mexico, in 1945. Henry Clifford, a curator at the Philadelphia Museum of Art, visited the Sloans that summer on his way out to stay with Georgia O'Keeffe. Sloan and Helen volunteered to drive him the forty miles into the desert, but when they arrived at O'Keeffe's house at midday, Clifford was greeted pleasantly by the owner while Sloan, Helen, and the two friends who had accompanied them were left standing in the broiling sun, barely acknowledged with a nod as O'Keeffe led Clifford to her door. Custom in New Mexico dictated that anyone who made a car trip on any kind of errand in the heat of summer be invited in for a few minutes of shade and a drink of water. Even Clifford understood that O'Keeffe's rudeness was unprecedented and awkwardly insisted that the Sloans be given some water before heading back to Santa Fe. O'Keeffe had no reason to feel any affection for Sloan—she probably knew that he loathed her trademark floral paintings and regularly referred to her as the "Grandma Moses of modern art," a more stylish Bouguereau—but in Helen's view, treating a seventy-four-year-old man of her husband's stature like a chauffeur amounted to unforgivable pettiness. Sloan was not one to forget the slight, either.

The best part of Sloan's gradual rejuvenation in the mid-1940s was that a once-social, once-productive man emerged from the shell that he and Dolly had slipped into over the years and the professional lethargy that had overwhelmed him. More guests were welcomed and more dinner parties held at the Chelsea apartment in the two or three years after Sloan's remarriage than in the entire decade before. Helen was particularly relieved that her family at last came around to seeing that her union with Sloan had been the right choice for her. First her brother and then her cousins, and even her parents, made Sloan's acquaintance and were thoroughly charmed. (Sloan was a little less charmed, perhaps, by Dr. Farr's possessive habit of leaving money for Helen after a visit and, on one early occasion, deep-kissing her in her husband's and mother's presence in a most unfatherly way. The Farr family saga, Sloan perceived, fairly rivaled the neurotic atmosphere of the household he had been raised in.) There were more outings, too, in these years—to see Martha Graham's dance company, the latest O'Neill play (*The Iceman Cometh*), the museum and gallery exhibitions that Sloan had tended to miss in his exhaustion of the late 1930s and early '40s. At a dinner party at Van Wyck Brooks's house, Sloan saw Helen Keller for the first time since her thunderous antiwar lecture at Carnegie Hall in 1916, and at the annual gatherings of the American Academy and the Institute of Arts and Letters, he relished mingling with the extraordinary range of talented people those occasions brought together, from Willa Cather and Theodore Dreiser to Paul Robeson ("a wonderful voice, like an organ," Sloan commented), W. E. B. DuBois, Carson McCullers, Glenway Wescott, Sinclair Lewis, and Thornton Wilder.

Although Sloan was well aware that his powers as a painter were waning—a thought that fueled his periodic depressions—in times of high spirits and quiet confidence he could and did approach his old standard. Charlotte Letteaux, a young woman who had danced with Pavlova, served as his principal model (aside from Helen) for the later crosshatched nudes, some of which have more plausible forms than their predecessors. But it was with one portrait in particular, entitled *Self-Portrait (Pipe and Brown Jacket)*, that Sloan hit the mark one last time. Working in the bathroom, as that room contained the only mirror in the apartment, he abandoned his usual flaxseed tempera for a casein tempera underpainting that he judged "quite satisfying." The shock of white hair flaps over his temples, the facial features are capably modeled, the little stabs of paint that constitute the "linear texture" he still believed in are used to denote the artist's jacket more than his face, the oil-varnish glaze on the panel allows for a rich patina—and the result is an arresting image of the kind Sloan had not produced in years. At seventy-five, his age at the time he painted this last self-portrait, Sloan aimed for the effect of a man at peace with himself, claiming—maybe wishfully—the serenity of a John Butler Yeats or a Robert Henri.

In her diary for February 12, 1947, Helen Farr Sloan entered the sad, terse note, "The postwar Red Hunt is afoot again." Although she was too young to remember the trauma of the Palmer Raids and the anti-Bolshevik hysteria that had followed the Armistice of 1918, her husband had a vivid, angry memory of what a wrenching time it had been.

The "witchhunt" atmosphere of the new postwar America was profoundly disturbing to him—at least as disturbing as the threat of communism itself. For a man who had chafed under the blind patriotism of the McKinley and Wilson years and seen his friends from *The Masses* persecuted by the judicial system, the question in the late 1940s was, Had the United States over the last half century really matured, come to terms with the right to dissent, learned to appreciate independent thought? In many respects, Sloan believed, the answer was no; it was as hard as ever to live in a country with scant use for the misfit, the rebel, the maverick. Between the Stalinists on the one side and the Congress and Catholic Church on the other, he found himself an unhappy citizen of a society prone to fanatical extremes.

Those friends and colleagues who Sloan felt had remained in the shadow of the party, such as Philip Evergood and Rockwell Kent, tended to annoy him now. The policies of the Kremlin were as bankrupt as the dictates of the Vatican, and he assumed that anyone should be able to see that. He was no less disgruntled by the shift to a traditional conservatism on the part of men such as Max Eastman and John Dos Passos. He supported Henry Wallace in 1948, well aware that his chances were nil and that his ability to lead was suspect, and allied himself with those he saw as occupying the sensible middle ground. But what constituted the "middle ground" for Sloan was, by the standard of the day, still rather far to the left. He had served as vice president of the Art Committee of the National Council on American-Soviet Friendship during the last year of the war and in the heyday of the House Un-American Activities Committee was ready to sign any petition against that "disgrace to the nation." He now saw *The New Masses* in a sufficiently favorable light to send its editors some of his etchings for use in their fund-raising auctions. After two decades of keeping a resolutely nonpolitical profile, Sloan was again being talked about in some circles as an unreformed "leftie" or, in the new terminology, a "fellow traveler." The FBI had reactivated its file on the former Socialist and Emma Goldman ally.

Some of Sloan's gestures and statements were a little worrisome to Helen, who was both more vehemently anti-Communist than her husband and more alert to the frightening implications of a new Red Scare. She also had a difficult time coming to grips with his lifelong anti-Catholicism. (She would in fact become a Catholic convert after Sloan's death.) One ridiculous example of the perception of Sloan as a political liability under the new order came up in Santa Fe, when a new organization, the New Mexico Alliance for the Arts, asked him to serve as its president, a largely honorary position. Then enjoying his thirtieth summer in Santa Fe, Sloan was glad to lend his name to any worthwhile cultural cause in the area. He had been intimately involved in the New Mexico Museum's exhibitions, scheduling, and philosophy since the week he arrived back in 1919, and he was much appreciated in the state for his lively interest in the museum. But New Mexico in 1949, conservative and militantly Catholic, was not the same freewheeling place it had been thirty years before. Grumblings were heard about the Alliance's "pinko" president, and sizing up the situation as one that could quickly get out of hand, Sloan deemed it best to bow out of the project. By this time, even with a phone and electric lights added to Sinagua at her insistence, Helen didn't care if she ever set foot in the Southwest again. In her estimation, no one there showed her husband sufficient respect.

Not so in the East. In the spring of 1949, John Sloan enjoyed that unique marker of cultural prominence in America when he was the subject of a *New Yorker* profile. The article, written by Robert Coates and illustrated with a sketch by Reginald Marsh, had been in the works for some time and finally appeared on May 7. It summarized a long, illustrious career and characterized Sloan as he wanted to be seen: "cocky, opinionated, rather biting of humor and intellectually arrogant," but not bitter, and always fully, confidently, devoted to his art. For the umpteenth time, Sloan made much of the fact that he hadn't sold a painting until he was fifty, a partial truth that he now wore as a badge of honor. His credo—"We always regarded contemporary success as artistic failure" —had hardened into an all-purpose line that enabled him to deal with the accumulated rejections of a lifetime and to reinforce a needed self-image as the perennial outsider. By now, the complexity of Sloan's situation, the reality that he was both a formidable insider—indeed, a major player in the art world since 1906—*and* an independent, had been lost along the way. But journalists at this point were inclined to be bland and respectful. At his retrospective exhibition at Kraushaar's the year before, Sloan had been made to feel like a "This Is Your Life" honoree. Edith Glackens, Mary Fanton Roberts, Walter Pach, Holger Cahill, Forbes Watson, Isabel Bishop, Theresa Bernstein, the Hoppers, the Evergoods, the Hamlins, the Soyer brothers, and dozens of other friends had been on hand to applaud the magnitude of Sloan's achievement; Florence Davey McCormick had bought *Spring Planting* for twenty-five hundred dollars; reviewers had made nice comments or refrained from denigrating the late

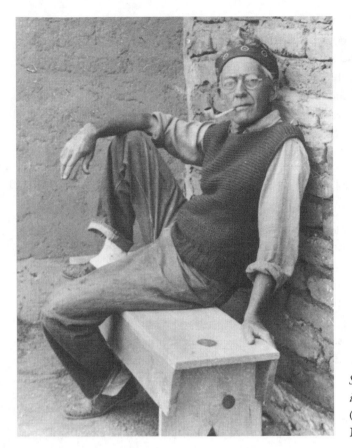

*Sloan at Sinagua
in the late 1940s*
(Delaware Art
Museum)

nudes. The National Academy of Design extended an offer of membership that month. But there was such a thing as being smothered by respect. The biting edge Sloan needed was dulled by time and goodwill and complacent affection.

Sloan sensed this, perhaps sensed his part in the process, too, and at times reacted against it. That reaction took the form of his going out of his way *not* to be ingratiating, to bury Henrietta Sloan's good, quiet little boy once and for all. Sometimes he was merely puckish, as when he told Irene Rice Pereira, a geometric-abstract painter of grids and mazes, that he had lost his mouse in one of her paintings. (Sloan did in fact have a pet white mouse, a quirk Helen learned to live with.) At other times, in public, at dinners or receptions, he could be more belligerent. Sloan disliked Andrew Wyeth's work—he thought it the very epitome of the slickness he had warned his students against—and did his best to keep him out of the Institute of Arts and Letters, even telling Wyeth to his face that he would do better to study Carpaccio and try to produce a less facile art. On the subject of the inhospitable Georgia O'Keeffe, whose name was regularly mentioned for membership in the Institute, Sloan could be critical and argumentative to an extent that embarrassed friends like the Whitney curators Hermon More and Lloyd Goodrich. She was just a product of Stieglitz's hype, Sloan maintained, and the Institute shouldn't be in the business of honoring trendy, second-rate talents—words that surely found their way back to Abiquiu.

In his annual lectures at the Art Students League, Sloan seemed to exhibit most forcefully his need for "fireworks," as Helen called it. Anything was preferable to being designated a "genial old man," the tame historical figure trotted out for the edification of the young. Speaking at the League in the spring of 1949, for instance, Sloan took pains to make a distinction between "modern" and "contemporary." He thought that students needed to study the Modernist movement with care, particularly such early masters as Renoir, van Gogh, and Cézanne, and believed that they would necessarily become capable "contemporary" artists if they knew and appreciated the best of Modernism. But the postwar mania to be "modern," the self-conscious fear of not appearing "modern" enough in one's work, was ruining a generation, he argued. From this perfectly reasonable starting point, then, he launched into the inevitable, the intentional, jibes—a torrent of them, repeated in all of Sloan's last addresses and harking back to his speeches of the 1930s. The Museum of Modern Art had been founded to protect the early investments of its trustees and was now nothing more than the backbone of a narrow propaganda campaign. Art education in most colleges, as far as he could tell, taught the "lingo" but nothing of the soul and reality of art-making. The younger critics formed a "totalitarian authority" as bad as the cadre of reactionary critics of their parents' time. Surrealism was a shallow fad, Dada a one-line joke, and the emerging school of Abstract Expressionism a frightening rejection of the humanity of art. Above all, Sloan upbraided the young for their reluctance to turn their backs on the "party line" of the art magazines, the schools, and the galleries in order to find their own voice. But then everyone was too intent on making a comfortable living out of his or her painting or sculpture, and therein, he felt, lay the real problem.

Sloan's bile, in the view of some, was attributable to jealousy in seeing the children of his friends, such as Stuart Davis and Alexander Calder, take their place in the Modernist canon. But his was a healthy truculence that kept the final defeat of old age at bay and raised some valid objections to an art world that thought in monolithic terms. (Harold Rosenberg's classic phrase a "herd of independent minds" said it all.) Beneath the crankiness was a desire for a less homogenized, more vital approach to art, an assertion that life was not meant to be lived following the right career path and swallowing wholesale the opinions of the day.

Sloan's last opportunity to sound off in a highly visible way on American cultural stupidity came not in New York but in New Mexico. The summer and early autumn of 1950 comprised his last stretch of time in Santa Fe; the following year his health would force him to look for a less strenuous climate and altitude. Just before he and Helen were to close up Sinagua for the winter, an absurd controversy erupted over the art on the exterior of the new state capitol building in Santa Fe, and Sloan leapt at the chance to be heard. The issue concerned a set of terra-cotta plaques commissioned for the outside walls, designed and executed by a local sculptor, William Longley. One depicted a large female nude, an Earth Mother, "about as lacking in erotic quality as possible," according to Oliver La Farge. The brouhaha provoked by its installation was, to Sloan's mind, typical of what went wrong when religious leaders were allowed to throw their weight around unchallenged and when Puritanism and an antipathy toward art came together to block freedom of expression.

A local Baptist minister, acting on behalf of his shocked congregation, had approached Governor Mabry soon after the unveiling to insist that Longley's unclad figure be removed: it was indecent and offensive, he proclaimed. Mabry, happy to oblige any vociferous constituent, was about to comply when a group of artists, including Sloan, Will Shuster, Randall Davey, and Longley himself, demanded a hearing in the governor's office. The conference was as acrimonious as Sloan had hoped it would be. After all, it wasn't every day that one had an adversary as splendidly benighted as the Reverend Robert Brown of the Berean Baptist Church and those of his parishioners who showed up for the meeting at the capitol. Brown admitted that he knew little about art, but he felt he could speak authoritatively on the subject of morals. A naked figure on a public building was immoral. That was the beginning and the end of it. Responding to

Brown's admission that he was ignorant about art, Sloan observed to the group that many people acted as if they were actually proud of that gap in their knowledge. "Would they be proud if they couldn't read?" he wondered. On the question of nudity, Sloan (who seems to have done most of the talking) informed the Baptists that the Sistine Chapel—hardly an immoral setting—was filled with Michelangelo's nudes, though he couldn't swear that the Catholics would tolerate that kind of art now that the Church had "so degenerated" since its glory years. All of the artists agreed that they were best qualified to determine what was pornographic in art and hotly insisted that only a smutty mind would find Longley's statue indecent. A colleague of Brown's then replied that there were other people in the state besides artists whose feelings had to be considered, to which Sloan retorted that those were precisely the fools whom the artists needed to educate. But he was also quick to add that he could educate the good Baptists on their own ground as well: "I could show you things in the Bible that would make this [statue] look like lemonade."

After a sufficient airing of insults and bluster on both sides, Governor Mabry decided that the best thing for him to do was duck the issue entirely and leave the decision with the building's architect. Sloan suggested that a carefully placed fig leaf might do the trick, or perhaps a Republican campaign sticker, but the governor didn't seem to be in the mood for levity. To no one's surprise, "Miss Fertility," as she had been dubbed by the press, was quietly removed a few days later. Diego Rivera and the Rockefellers, William Longley and the Baptists: how little had changed.

In 1950, his seventy-ninth year, Sloan received one of the artistic and intellectual community's most prestigious honors when he was awarded a Gold Medal by the National Academy of Arts and Letters. In a ceremony that also saw the awarding of the Howells Prize for Fiction to William Faulkner, the induction of Robert Sherwood into the Academy, and the induction of Thomas Mann, William Carlos Williams, Robert Penn Warren, and Andrew Wyeth into the Institute of Arts and Letters, Sloan accepted the award for his lifetime of distinguished achievement in the arts. Surely this was a moment to bask in the applause of the most accomplished men and women in the United States, to reflect proudly on how far he had traveled from his stool at Porter & Coates and his desk at

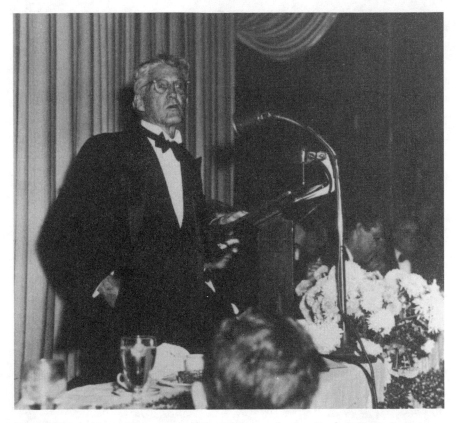

One of Sloan's last public appearances: speaking at the Art Students League's seventy-fifth anniversary celebration at the Waldorf-Astoria, 1950 (Art Students League)

the *Philadelphia Inquirer.* Instead, Sloan found himself fighting off depression and needing all of Helen's solicitous care. It was a little annoying to hear through the grapevine that he had been nominated and chosen "despite rumors of fellow traveling." But the real problem was twofold. On the one hand, Sloan had always disparaged such awards; they implied "establishment approval," something a true artist kept clear of. On the other hand, the-powers-that-be heaped honors on you when you were safely over the hill, Sloan ruefully reflected, and—delightful as it was at the given moment to receive the accolades—that sense of imminent decline was hard to shake. (If it was any consolation, Sloan wasn't the only Academy member to feel uncertain about the implications of the Gold Medal: H. L. Mencken was awarded one as well that year. After his recent stroke, he was too ill to make the trip to New York and had Carl Van

Doren accept for him, after which he became quite angry with himself for not having declined the prize outright. A satirist and critic had no business taking Gold Medals or any other such prizes, he sputtered.)

Sloan was similarly torn when he was approached by the Whitney Museum about mounting a retrospective. The museum's policy throughout the 1930s and '40s had prohibited one-man shows of living artists, a short-sighted rule that meant that some excellent exhibitions, such as the shows devoted to Stuart Davis, Edward Hopper, and Charles Sheeler at the Modern, had been seen elsewhere when they should have been the product of curatorial care at 8 West Eighth Street. In the late 1940s that policy was revoked. Juliana Force was dead, having succumbed to cancer in 1948, and Hermon More had taken over as the museum's director, but plans had been set in motion even before Force's death to survey the careers of John Sloan, Max Weber, and Yasuo Kuniyoshi in the first three retrospectives offered to living painters. The negotiations with More and his curator Lloyd Goodrich to work out the details seemed to take a long time, and Sloan was miffed when Kuniyoshi, not one of his favorite people, was given the first show. He was also rattled by the timetable the Whitney staff was considering: perhaps their new quarters on West Fifty-fourth Street behind the Museum of Modern Art would be ready by late 1951, they speculated, and the Sloan show could open the building. I should live so long to see the move uptown, Sloan grumbled. (A fair comment, given the nature of museum construction goals: the Whitney's Midtown building opened, in fact, in 1954.) If he was going to be studied in depth and "summarized" and patted on the head, he felt, the Whitney might do it with a little more haste. He wasn't going to be around forever. The matter was finally resolved when Sloan put aside his doubts about having to face his career as a completed entity, stopped thinking about the schedule, and accepted the invitation to work with Goodrich. He joked to Hermon More, not without a little of his old facetious anger, that if he didn't live to see the exhibition, he'd settle for having his ashes placed in the cornerstone of the new building.

Dartmouth Summer

(1951)

"I came to admire."

—ROBERT FROST, on visiting
Sloan in the hospital
in New Hampshire

The preparation for the Whitney retrospective necessarily involved Sloan in examining the past, sifting through his files and cabinets —and his own memory—more than was his wont. Urged by Helen and by Lloyd Goodrich to jot down anything that might seem significant about the paintings or the events that Goodrich's catalogue essay would explore, Sloan mused in his journal, "What are the memoirs of a man who admittedly has no memory for the past? I am the same man who loved Balzac's *Human Comedy* sixty years ago. [But] my ideas about art and society have changed."

He well understood that he was one of the few people left with any direct ties to the turn-of-the-century art world, the Village before the war that was supposed to end all wars, or New York in the days of Emma Goldman, John Quinn, Petipas, and the Haymarket. Edith Glackens's incapacitating stroke in the winter of 1951 was a reminder of that fact. Albert Barnes's death, that July, was another, as was the presence of so many interviewers in Sloan's life, scholars or magazine writers or historians who wanted impressions of or information about the "old days." Sometimes it seemed worthwhile to meet with them, if only to set the record straight, as when he assured one young man who was about to write a scholarly article on realism in art and literature that, *no,* he had not read Stephen Crane in his youth and based his early painting on that model of urban naturalism. He didn't want to have anything to do with the "Ash Can" label and thought that his first city paintings probably had little in common with the spirit of Crane, Dreiser, Norris, and others of that school. (As he was enjoying his own American literature phase during these years, devouring Faulkner, Dos Passos, and Richard Wright, Sloan obliged his academic friend by reading most of Crane's fiction—not with much pleasure, he noted.) He was also ready to check the prestige of Everett Shinn whenever he had the chance, having decided that Shinn was at heart a money grubber, a high liver, a society boy more than an artist. "He was an accidental member of 'The Eight'" was his comment as he cast his vote against Shinn's nomination for membership in the Institute of Arts and Letters.

To Helen, as much in love with John Sloan in the seventh year of their marriage as she had been in the first, his interesting past was as much a part of his fascination as the force of his personality, his talent, and his love for her. Ever since coming upon his early diaries in the apartment—the ones begun to "save" Dolly—she had had a keen sense of the importance of preserving as much as she could of Sloan's early history, and took copious notes whenever he was inclined to talk about his life in Philadelphia or New York, the Armory Show, the birth of the Independents, or the artists he had known. A note-taker (still!) and diarist of uncommon diligence, Helen was informed more than once by Sloan that he had no intention of being "Boswelled to death" in his own home. She needed to be discreet and casual with her questions. He had married Helen because it was the right thing to do in the here-and-now; he was happy living with her in a relationship of the kind that had become impossible with Dolly by the end. Sloan wanted a wife, he made clear, not a secretary or an archivist.

Yet he got a secretary and archivist in the bargain, and as he wrote in his own diary on several occasions, he knew that the satisfactions and accomplishments he had enjoyed since 1944 he owed to Helen. Although her own health was often a source of concern to both of them—Helen had a hysterectomy in 1950, at the age of thirty-nine, among other problems —she put his well-being first, screening him from intrusions and seeing to it that he was properly rested and fed and able to paint. Often she and Sloan painted together in the studio, or she served as his model. Helen watched how much Sloan drank and successfully saw him through the trial of quitting smoking in the winter of 1951. Most important for him, she dealt with the problem of what he called his melancholia. Black moods came on him, Sloan had warned Helen that week in Santa Fe when she broached the subject of marriage, and there was nothing to be done about it. In Helen's view, she could be most useful to him by simply keeping any immediate or ostensible cause for depression or exhaustion under control. That meant, above all, a settled homelife, a household of calm, order, intellectual stimulation, and demonstrative affection.

To the extent that Sloan, about to turn eighty, was a person who was drawn to conflict and rancor—the "fireworks"—as much as he craved their opposite, that mission of ensuring calm and order could be a difficult one. In the last speech he ever gave, at an Art Students League benefit in March 1951, Sloan saw himself as being "dusted off and dragged out of my ivory tower" and so determined to give his listeners a good diatribe, consisting in this instance of an unusually vitriolic attack on the influence of Abstract Expressionism on young artists. The thing itself wasn't the problem, he explained; he had seen some fine Pollocks and Gottliebs. The nightmare was the generation of art students who were forsaking draftsmanship and the artist's most important themes—human emotion and interaction—for the sake of paint-smearing and the cult of the new. It was an address, he fervently hoped, to rub some people the wrong way. Asked by Raphael Soyer that month to sign a letter to the board of the Museum of Modern Art, along with several other painters, protesting that institution's dismissal of contemporary American realists from its exhibition program, Sloan proudly added his name. There were few acts in life more important than a heartfelt protest, he believed, even if the protest was apt to fall on deaf ears. A protest for the record had its own kind of nobility. It was the same in politics. The ticker-tape parades for Douglas MacArthur in May were, like all military pageants, "silly, infantile . . . *dreadful*," but the forces of reaction were carrying the day. Sloan's response was quiet, simple, emphatic. He and Helen joined the American Civil Liberties Union.

As summer approached, Helen realized that a decision would have to be made about going to New Mexico. It was clear to her and to Sloan's doctor that the high altitude of Santa Fe would put too great a strain on Sloan's heart. Although he would never admit it, the years were catching up with him. They would have to make other plans for getting out of New York in the heat.

An invitation to spend some time at Dartmouth, in Hanover, New Hampshire, had been extended to Sloan several years before by his Lock Haven cousin John Sloan Dickey, who was the president of the college. Helen thought this would be an excellent alternative. At first Sloan was adamant about not making any changes in a thirty-year pattern. At the least, he said, he wanted to be able to go back to his beloved Sinagua one more time to clean it out ("I want every speck of dust in that place," he complained). Helen insisted that that wouldn't be possible. Angrily, Sloan accused her of trying to separate him from his good friends out West, particularly Will Shuster and Wyatt Davis, but he eventually acceded to her reasoning and to his doctor's strong advice. New Hampshire wasn't a terrible idea, not least because Dartmouth had some positive associations in Sloan's mind: the college's own art gallery had hosted a large Sloan exhibition in 1946, really a sort of retrospective, and had purchased two oils out of the show, *McSorley's Back Room* and one of the early linear-textured nudes from 1929. The fact that the portrait the curators had selected had as its subject one of Sloan's few black models had strongly impressed him at the time; if Antoinette Kraushaar found it hard to sell any of the nudes in the prudish climate of the late 1940s, no one would even look at the black women, it seemed. So New Hampshire it was.

Before leaving New York, Sloan decided to pay one of his infrequent visits to his sister. At their age, the number of times he was likely to see his remaining sibling was probably very limited, he knew, though after the trip to Philadelphia both Sloan and Helen agreed that the usual distance he maintained served a purpose. White-haired and slightly hunchbacked, Marianna ran a used bookshop in the suburb of Germantown and lived a strange, somber life. Since Dolly's death, Sloan had given his unmarried sister several paintings that he hoped she would sell if she ever needed money. But Marianna wasn't interested in talking about her brother—neither his art nor his health nor his summer plans— or much of anything, for that matter, beyond the lonely state of her life and the bitter fantasies she nurtured. She had been destined to be the great painter in the family, she reminded her brother, and had made a sacrifice of her life so that John Sloan could be free to make a name for himself. This version of family history wasn't Sloan's, but by now he knew better than to reason or argue with Marianna.

Once he was used to the idea, Sloan was curious to see what a prolonged stay amid the hills and valleys of northern New England would be like. Arriving in Hanover on June 23, he and Helen intended to remain until mid-September. Their apartment was a sublet in one of the large campus houses on Occum Ridge, a space that didn't entirely suit Sloan as there wasn't an extra free room with the right light to use as a studio. Their initial impressions of the town weren't all to the good, either. Hanover struck Sloan as too affluent, too smug, gentrified beyond what he could stand. He complained of missing the more down-to-earth flavor of Santa Fe, not to mention his friends and his own house there. Helen was relieved to hear him drop the subject once he started browsing in the vast open stacks of Baker Library, from which he brought home books on Constable, Corot, and Millet. She also hoped that he would soon find his way toward trying to paint the new landscape that awaited him, but that proved a problem in itself. Accustomed to the brown, yellow, and reddish hues of the Southwest, Sloan as a painter was disoriented by the lush, unrelenting green he was here expected to grapple with. "The countryside absolutely flabbergasted him," a new friend, Herbert Faulkner West, re-called. To West, a member of Dartmouth's English department who was delighted to make Sloan's acquaintance through President Dickey, Sloan looked that summer a "little bit like an old hawk," shaky on his feet but alert and wise. With his "distinct mop of white hair," lean face, and gleaming, slanting eyes, the "old hawk" knew that his reputation had preceded him, and he lived up to his image as a striking conversationalist. And, too, he made it clear from the beginning that he wasn't thrilled with cozy little Hanover, with the humidity of the Northeast compared to New Mexico, or with all that damn green.

Within a few weeks, though, Sloan's estimation of his new circum-stances had changed. He felt refreshed and challenged and nicely taken care of. West, an aspiring painter, was pleased to drive Sloan wherever he wanted to go and joined him on his first painting expedition. Another former student, the painter Fiske Boyd, lived nearby, and he, too, chauf-feured Sloan about, as did Nan Jones, an out-of-towner who worked for the summer at Baker Library and interviewed Sloan for the local paper. The six landscapes that Sloan completed after these rides through New Hampshire and Vermont—of Mink Brook and the Connecticut River, of a log cabin on the Tweed River and a hilly pasture full of grazing cows, of a Vermont barn and a meadow outside Lebanon—are creditable works. They suggest a painter making the most of a new opportunity, of a kind of light and a combination of colors that he means to understand and master. West also took Sloan to see the Saint-Gaudens Memorial in Cornish, which he thought put him "in a disapproving mood," while Fiske Boyd accompanied him on a visit to the house of Maxfield Parrish, who lived a few miles away. "When you reach our age, Sloan, you have to live as though you had thirty years ahead," Parrish told his guest, whom he hadn't seen since their Philadelphia days in the nineties. Sloan wasn't any more charmed by Parrish's comfortable home than he had been by Augustus Saint-Gaudens's property and bronze reliefs. The men were two of a kind in his eyes, purveyors of formula goods, not artists. If he and Helen decided to buy property in New Hampshire, he said—something he was seriously considering now—his choice would be some good old run-down house in Union Village that they'd fix to their liking. He was keeping his eye out for such places, the more derelict the better.

The longer the Sloans stayed in Hanover, the more people they met and the more socializing their vacation involved. A summer away from Shuster, Davis, Miss White, and the Santa Fe crowd hadn't meant a summer of isolation after all. During the week before his eightieth birthday on August 2, Sloan was the guest of honor at several dinner parties in town. At the party at his own apartment on the second, the guests included his cousin John Sloan Dickey, Herbert West and his wife, the artist Harry Wickey (a friend of the Farr family and an old colleague of Sloan's at the Art Students League who spent his summers nearby), and a few other convivial neighbors. "We had a stiffish punch and a good time," Sloan reported to Will Shuster. To Lloyd Goodrich, he sent one of the postcard/sketches he was renowned for, this one showing the artist sliding in a cloud of dust into a home plate marked "80th Year." Beneath the drawing, he scrawled happily, "Made it, by gosh!"

"Made it," yes—but barely. Only two weeks later, Sloan needed to be examined by a local doctor. He had been bleeding from the rupture of a small nodule by the rectum and assumed he needed only the most perfunctory of examinations. The doctor determined, however, that the bleeding Sloan was aware of when he moved his bowels was not entirely external. A tumor was discovered in the bowel, and a biopsy determined that it was cancerous. Sloan entered Mary Hitchcock Memorial Hospital on August 23 to prepare for surgery. He took a pile of art books borrowed from the Dartmouth library and his copy of Charles Lamb's *Essays of Elia*. "I've had a lot of illness in my life and I don't think I've ever complained," Sloan had said to Helen before leaving their apartment, and he was determined now to be just as stoical. But after a conference with the doctors involved in his case, all of whom had come highly recommended, neither of the Sloans felt that much stoicism or anxiety was called for. By any standard, the procedure was a simple one, and the cancer had been detected in an early, far from dire stage. When Kent Crane came over from Manchester, Vermont, to visit—Kent, now a middle-aged painter himself, was the son of George Luks whom Sloan and Dolly had once doted on—he found Sloan in good spirits, entertaining a stream of visitors.

The only agitation during Sloan's week in the hospital before the operation came when he received a letter from Will Shuster, bearing news that infuriated him. The annual exhibition of contemporary art at the New Mexico Museum, an open-door show in all the years it had been in existence, was to become a juried affair that summer. Sloan, who had looked forward to this show every year with the enthusiasm of a mentor, always happy to see the artists of the state having their turn to be seen, was livid. So on the eve of his surgery, John Sloan was granted one last chance to display the indignation he had felt and expressed on so many occasions since the time of "The Eight" and the *Masses* and the attacks on the Indian dances. "Robert Henri and Edgar Hewett will turn in their graves," Sloan wrote in a telegram that he fired off to Shuster, a telegram that he knew would be circulated in Santa Fe. With the Society of Independent Artists defunct since 1944, the great distinction of the New Mexico Museum's annual show had been its very openness to all styles, themes, and ranges of talent—but now, Sloan fulminated, "watch the miserable, puny, stinking, pallid efforts to show twentieth-class imitations of the current fashions." The jury would be a narrow, self-perpetuating entity, a cabal of insiders and logrollers. Let his protest be recorded. Given the unlikelihood of his ever seeing Santa Fe again, Sloan accepted that this battle, if there was to be one, would be Shuster's. He signed off in gladiator fashion: "I who am about to be operated on Wednesday, salute thee, with love."

The following day, Sloan's last visitor before his surgery came by the room. Robert Frost, a longtime friend of Herbert West's, happened to be staying in the same hospital recovering from extensive facial surgery. When he heard that Sloan was also a patient, he asked West to escort him to Sloan's room so he could pay his respects. Swathed in bandages that left only his eyes, nose, and mouth visible, and speaking through swollen lips, the normally fastidious poet quipped to Sloan, "I am here for Operation Save Face," alluding to a recent military term for the Korean action. Sloan responded with a laugh. "I'm here for Operation Shave Tail," he told Frost. They chatted amicably for a while and agreed to meet under better circumstances when they were both on their feet again. As he walked with West to the door, Frost turned to Sloan and commented, "I came to admire."

By the next evening, Helen was able to send telegrams to the Shusters and various friends around the country announcing the good news that Sloan had pulled through with "amazing vitality." The surgeon had removed the tumor and anticipated a quick recovery.

To the surprise of everyone on the staff at the hospital, however, and to Helen's horror, events took a radically different course. Each day after the operation, Sloan seemed inexplicably weaker. He found the indignity of the temporary colostomy difficult to bear and the many tubes in him annoying. He had no appetite. His mood was dark and cranky, then quiet and resigned. The doctors were at a loss and expressed their concerns to Helen. On the afternoon of Friday, September 7, he started to slip into a coma. "I'm so tired," he told Helen, who had been by his side the whole time. He worried that he would have to paint the next day. Helen assured him that he wouldn't. "It's a fight, isn't it?" he asked, and he fell asleep. That night, shortly before midnight, Sloan died.

Remembering her husband's dislike for elaborate rituals, especially funeral rites, Helen decided to hold a brief memorial service at Dartmouth later that week, after Sloan's cremation. She asked Lloyd Goodrich, who had come to know her husband well that year as he prepared for the exhibition, to deliver the eulogy. Friends from New York and members of Helen's family gathered in a garden near the campus along with President Dickey, Herbert West, and the many new acquaintances the Sloans had made in Hanover. At the ceremony, Goodrich aptly observed that they had come together that day to honor a remarkable individual, "that rare being, a man who saw things with his own eyes, thought his own thoughts, and spoke in his own words." With a simplicity and brevity that Sloan would have appreciated, Goodrich reviewed the events of a productive life in painting, politics, and art education, and the hallmarks of a personality that would be hard for those who had known him to forget—a delicious wit, a fierce sense of conviction, a youthful curiosity, a passionate concern for neglected artists, a great capacity for work and for the enjoyment of life. He concluded his remarks with the words of consolation that any painter or poet, composer or novelist, would want spoken at the end: "The artist is not like most mortals; when he dies he leaves behind that undying distillation of his whole life—his art. Long after those who were fortunate enough to know him have themselves gone, John Sloan's art will continue to move and delight future generations." At the Whitney Museum of American Art the following winter, that distillation would be presented with impeccable care to a large and appreciative audience.

Four months after Sloan's death, and several days after the opening of the retrospective, Helen made the four-hour trip by herself from New York City to Lock Haven, Pennsylvania, to the mountaintop cemetery overlooking the Susquehanna. Sloan had once described to her the day in 1940 when he had visited his birthplace and been taken by his hostess and guide, Rebecca Gross, to his grandfather's grave. He remembered standing with Dolly on the hill and being entranced with the view, looking down the steep slope of graves, past the trees, to the winding river below them. There, on the raw morning of January 20, 1952, by the monument of John French Sloan—dead the very month his grandchild and namesake was born—the ashes of John and Dolly Sloan were opened in their separate urns, mixed, and gently scattered in the winter wind.

Source Notes

ABBREVIATIONS

JSNYS   *John Sloan's New York Scene* (New York; Harper & Row, 1965). Published diaries of John Sloan, 1906–1912

JSD   John Sloan's unpublished diaries, 1944–1951

JSN   John Sloan Notes: 350 pages of verbatim remarks collected and transcribed by Helen Farr Sloan, in the John Sloan Collection of the Delaware Art Museum

HFSD   Helen Farr Sloan's diaries, 1944–1955

HFSN   Unpaginated journals and notebooks kept sporadically by Helen Farr Sloan throughout the 1950s

(Note: at the time of publication, only the "John Sloan Notes" among the unpublished materials listed above are owned by the Delaware Art Museum. Helen Farr Sloan's diaries and journals and John Sloan's late diaries are the property of Mrs. Sloan.)

PROLOGUE: TO WEST EIGHTH STREET

xix–xx   Christopher Gray, "Rebels of Eighth Street Redux," *New York Times,* 12 September 1993, Real Estate sec., p. 7.

xxi   Maugham's praise: quoted in Morse, *John Sloan's Prints,* p. 312.

xxii   "highly successful effort": *The New Yorker,* 19 January 1952, pp. 58–59.

xxii   Not surprisingly: naturally, not all of the reviews were favorable. Milton Brown delivered what was perhaps the most critical assessment in "The Two John Sloans" *(ArtNews,* January 1952), in which he wrote of Sloan as a "tragic case of an artist who outlives his time of creativity."

xxii   "painter laureate of Manhattan": *Cue,* 12 January 1952, p. 13.

xxii   "important historian . . .": Margaret Breuning, *The Art Digest,* 15 January 1952, p. 7.

xxii   "Sloan was one of the first American artists . . .": *Washington Post,* 16 March 1952.

xxii   "[Sloan's] influence . . .": *New York Times,* 13 January 1952.

xxii   "great and courageous personality": *New York Herald Tribune,* 13 January 1952, sec. 4, p. 9.

EARLY DAYS

1   "just about the time the French . . .": Coates Interview Notes, p. 2, on file at the Delaware Art Museum.

2   "a born punster": JSN, pp. 157, 243.

3   Marianna, the most high-strung of the three: JSN, p. 12.

4   On visiting the Philadelphia Centennial Exposition: JSN, p. 155.

5   "weary and aching mass of unemployed": Nevins, *The Emergence of Modern America,* p. 304.

5   "Mother's family got him a job": JSN, p. 105.

6   "it makes such rich-looking garbage": JSN, p. 156.

6–7   John Sloan always maintained that his sister Marianna: interview with Helen Farr Sloan.

9   Alexander "occasionally imbibed a trifle too much": JSN, pp. 109, 164.

12   It was after a fierce snowstorm: quoted in Morse, p. 22, from "Marianna Sloan, Recollections," on file at the Delaware Art Museum.

13   "They knew I was afraid of them": JSN, pp. 108, 185.

14   Philadelphia's version of Cooper Union: Brooks, *John Sloan,* p. 13.

14   "Other boys my age": JSN, p. 4.

16   "very plain piece of work": JSN, p. 203.

A MENTOR

18   "As you will see": letter copied out in JSN, p. 125.

19   "most enterprising sheet in Philadelphia": Mott, *American Journalism*, p. 37.

19   As far back as the Civil War: Starr, *Bohemian Brigade*, p. 242.

20   "all the fun and no examinations": quoted in Brooks, *John Sloan*, p. 21.

21   "unruffled academic slumber": Perlman, *Robert Henri: His Life and Art*, p. 23.

26   As his notes from the time put it: Henri's Charcoal Club Notes (June 1893), quoted in Perlman, *Robert Henri: His Life and Art*, p. 25.

26   John Sloan on the Charcoal Club: JSN, pp. 111, 263.

32   "The work of Mr. John Sloan": Penn, "Newspaper Artists," p. 50.

33   "pull[ing] my religious tooth": JSN, p. 242.

34   "Henri could make anyone": Helen Farr Sloan.

35   "We came to the realistic conclusion": JSN, pp. 316–317.

35   "We should turn our eyes from Paris and Rome": Moore, *Modern Painting* p. 214.

PHILADELPHIA: JOURNALISM AND BEYOND

38   it was estimated that over a thousand artists: *City Life Illustrated*, p. 16.

39   "a journal *intime* wherein the artists": *Moods*, on the first page of the magazine.

41   "Cheret, Hardey, Beardsley": *New York Sun*, 3 February 1895.

42   When a colleague in the office: John Sloan to Helen Farr Sloan, February 1944, Helen Farr Sloan's correspondence files.

43   "It is not hard to recall": John Sloan in *Artists of the Philadelphia Press*, p. 7.

43   "I have one wheel out of the rut": John Sloan to Robert Henri, December 1895, Beinecke Library, Yale University, quoted in Goodrich, *John Sloan*, p. 10.

44   did his "share in painting": John Sloan to Robert Henri, 7 February 1897, Beinecke Library, Yale University.

44–45   "simple and direct": quoted in Perlman, *Robert Henri: His Life and Art*, p. 32.

46   "prophet of the new": *Philadelphia Inquirer,* 24 October 1897, quoted in Perlman, *Robert Henri: His Life and Art,* p. 36.

46   "moral character and high Sunday school class average": Robert Henri to John Sloan, 3 September 1898, Beinecke Library, Yale University.

47   *Sloan* was the past participle of *slow:* quoted in Brooks, *John Sloan,* p. 20.

49–52   Accounts of Sloan's meeting with Dolly Wall and Dolly's background: HFSN and conversations with Helen Farr Sloan.

52   In later years Dolly was wont to say: "MARRY HIM, HER ADVICE," *New York World-Telegram,* 24 October 1939, (interview with Dolly Sloan).

CONFUSION AND COMMITMENT

53–54   On the Spanish-American War, pacifism, and patriotism: JSN, pp. 187–188.

54   When Dolly bought him a puppy: Helen Farr Sloan.

54   "You want to be a great artist": Robert Henri to John Sloan, September 1898, Beinecke Library, Yale University.

54–55   "Don't think that I have been unable . . .": John Sloan to Robert Henri, 30 October 1898, Beinecke Library, Yale University.

55   "a big frog": ibid.

55–56   On Dr. Collier Bower: Helen Farr Sloan.

57   Sloan's reluctance to date the "loose," insinuating women: JSN, p. 108.

59   "extraordinary strength": *Philadelphia Press,* 8 December 1900.

59   "witness the advent": ibid.

60   These are "rhythmic excursions": Scott, *John Sloan,* p. 26.

61   Sloan later acknowledged that his mind-set: HFSN, quoted in Rowland Elzea, *John Sloan's Oil Paintings,* vol. 1, p. 33.

64   His "debut in paint": Robert Henri's diary entry for 9 February 1901, Archives of American Art.

64   "You will be able to appreciate . . .": John Sloan to Robert Henri, November 1900, Beinecke Library, Yale University.

64   Charles FitzGerald review: *New York Sun,* 11 April 1901.

64–65   "dropped [an] attempt at portrait [painting]": John Sloan to Robert Henri, 28 May 1901, Beinecke Library, Yale University.

65   "If you get the figures below": Robert Henri to John Sloan, 15 June 1901, Beinecke Library, Yale University.

65   a brief, complimentary mention of "J. Sloan of Philadelphia": Hartmann, *A History of American Art,* p. 259.

65   What followed was vintage Hartmann: correspondence from Hartmann to Sloan in John Sloan Collection.

66   On Sloan's first married days: Helen Farr Sloan.

71   Charles de Kay's review: *New York Times,* 20 January 1904.

71   Arthur Hoeber's review: *Commercial Advertiser,* 20 January 1904.

NEW YORK, 1904

73   "a great girl": JSNYS, pp. 185–186.

73–75   On early-twentieth-century New York City: see Lloyd Morris, *Incredible New York* (New York: Random House, 1951); Richard O'Connor, *Hell's Kitchen* (Philadelphia: Lippincott, 1958); Gilfoyle, *City of Eros;* Santé, *Low Life;* Scherman, *Girl from Fitchburg.*

77   "The sense of responsibility": John Sloan to Robert Henri, 1904, Beinecke Library, Yale University.

77   On George Bellows's snub: Sloan told Helen Farr Sloan about this episode after their marriage. It certainly makes for a plausibly tense beginning to an awkward twenty-year relationship, though dating the class at which this momentary rudeness took place is somewhat difficult, as Sloan was notoriously bad at remembering exact years and Bellows attended Henri's classes many times circa 1904–1908. However, it is inconceivable that Bellows would have acted toward Sloan in this way once he knew how close he and Henri were (1906–1908), and not likely that he would have done so once Sloan was "established" with his Carnegie Institute Honorable Mention in 1905. In 1904 Sloan was still no one of note as far as George Bellows was concerned. Only once, to my knowledge, did Sloan publicly allude to Bellows's arrogance toward him, in a speech given at the Art Students League on 23 March 1950.

77–78   On Dolly's awkwardness with the other artists' wives: Helen Farr Sloan and *New York World-Telegram,* 24 October 1939.

78–79   On the episode at Edith Glackens's apartment and Sloan's contracting venereal disease: Helen Farr Sloan.

82–83   On Robert Henri/Robert Cozad: Brooks, *John Sloan,* p. 17; Homer, *Robert Henri and His Circle,* pp. 7–20; Perlman, *Robert Henri:*

His Life and Art, pp. 1–7. It was not until after Henri's death, in 1929, however, that Sloan was able to put together all of the pieces and understand his friend's background and family history.

84   "a non-impressionistic impression": Sloan, *Gist of Art,* p. 206.

85   "showing themselves and criticizing others": quoted in Morse, *John Sloan's Prints,* p. 137.

THE "ASH CAN" MYTH

92   "Ash Can realism": the origins of this term are a little murky. It appears in print in 1934 in *Art in America in Modern Times* by Alfred Barr, Jr., and Holger Cahill, a close friend of Sloan's from the 1920s. The artist Art Young complained in 1916 about Sloan and his friends' wanting to "run pictures of ash cans" instead of good Socialist propaganda in their magazine the *Masses.* George Bellows's February 1914 drawing for the *Masses,* showing hungry vagrants picking through some refuse, is entitled *Disappointments of the Ash Can.* It should be noted that the term "ash can" originally referred to curbside receptacles *for ashes,* but as it is used in this context it refers to any garbage or trash can—that is, a symbol of low life in the big city.

92–93   On realism in the arts: An example of the view of Sloan and the painters as necessarily lesser figures than Riis and the photographers is Matthew Baigell's article "Notes on Realistic Painting and Photography, c. 1900–1910" *(Arts Magazine,* November 1979, pp. 141–143), which chides Sloan, among others, for not being the kind of artist he never intended or wanted to be—a gritty social chronicler, a visual Zola, or another version of Riis and Lewis Hine.

92   As Luc Santé points out: Santé, *Low Life,* pp. 36–37.

93   His most recent biographer: Perlman, *Robert Henri: His Life and Art,* p. 57.

95   Dr. Bower suggested: Helen Farr Sloan.

96   "nightly vigils": John Sloan, *Gist of Art,* p. 220; JSN; HFSN.

98   On the radicalism of Sloan's prostitutes: Gilfoyle, *City of Eros,* pp. 279–282.

99–101   "To give art the complexion of our time": Hartmann, "A Plea for the Picturesqueness of New York," in Harry W. Lawton and George Knox, eds., *The Valiant Knights of Daguerre* (Berkeley: University of California Press, 1978), pp. 56–63.

102   "sensitive souls": JSNYS, p. 33.

102   "Gone to seed": quoted in Glackens, *William Glackens and The Eight,* p. 65.

103   On the astronomical salaries of Howard Pyle, Maxfield Parrish, etc.: Milroy, *Painters of a New Century,* p. 54.

103   "his millions of readers": JSNYS, p. 47.

104   "best picture on view": *New York Sun,* 27 December 1906.

106   "often been a sufferer": *New York Sun,* 21 March 1907.

106   "excellent and healthy act": *Collier's,* 6 April 1907, p. 12.

106   "advisability of a split exhibition": JSNYS, p. 112.

106   "The spirit to push the thing through": JSNYS, p. 118.

107   On the damage to *The Wake of the Ferry:* Helen Farr Sloan.

107–108   On Sloan's following the woman on Fourteenth Street: JSNYS, p. 131.

108   "wonderful work": JSNYS, p. 112.

108   "a fattish, demi-monde looking girl": John Sloan to Dolly Sloan, 21 July 1907, Delaware Art Museum.

108   Description of Coney Island: John Sloan to Dolly Sloan, 22 July 1907, Delaware Art Museum.

110   "smoky city": John Sloan to Dolly Sloan, 19 December 1907, Delaware Art Museum.

111   The "false alarm" letter: Dolly Sloan to John Sloan, December 1907, Delaware Art Museum.

AN EVENT AT MACBETH'S

112   "The work of American artists": quoted in Owens, "Art and Commerce," p. 62, from the Macbeth Gallery scrapbooks in the Archives of American Art.

113   "Instead of bewailing lost opportunities": William Macbeth, *Art Notes,* January 1897, p. 36, quoted in Owens, "Art and Commerce," p. 66.

113   Macbeth as a "charming" and "decent" man: JSNYS, p. 152.

114   "men of the rebellion": *New York Herald,* 2 February 1908.

115   "palette of crushed jewels": quoted in Mahonri Young, *The Eight,* p. 79.

116   "Davies is a man . . .": Huneker, *The Pathos of Distance,* p. 112.

117   On Jerome Myers: JSN, p. 298; HFSN.

117   On Hawthorne's exclusion from "The Eight": McCausland, *Charles W. Hawthorne,* p. 20.

117	On Albert Sterner: Albert Sterner to Robert Henri, undated, Beinecke Library, Yale University.
118	"already sick of the damn exhibition": quoted in Glackens, *William Glackens and The Eight,* p. 84.
118	On Sloan's visit to Luks: JSNYS, pp. 182–183.
118	"working like Lucifer": Green, Eleanor, *Maurice Prendergast,* p. 54.
119	"as usual in these affairs": JSNYS, p. 190.
119	One particularly helpful person: Giles Edgerton, "The Younger American Painters: Are They Creating Our Much-Discussed National Art?" *The Craftsman,* February 1908, pp. 512–532.
120	"Packed like an Academy reception": quoted in Perlman, *Robert Henri: His Life and Art,* p. 84.
121	"not of the prosperous aspect": JSNYS, p. 191.
121	Davies's reaction: JSNYS, pp. 192, 197.
122	"A loud chorus of disapproval": William Macbeth, *Art Notes,* March 1908, p. 545.
123	"I feel almost as glad . . .": JSNYS, p. 198.
123	"I defy you to find anyone . . .": quoted in Glackens, *William Glackens and The Eight,* p. 89.
123	"sermon advis[ing] us . . .": JSNYS, pp. 192–193.
123–124	"palm for handing out . . .": *American Art News,* 8 February 1908, p. 6.
124	"It is regrettable that these art writers . . .": JSNYS, p. 193.
124	"clashing dissonances": quoted in Perlman, *The Immortal Eight,* p. 178, from the Macbeth Gallery scrapbook.
124	"gloated in the controversy": JSNYS, p. 197.
125	On the party after the opening: JSNYS, p. 192.
125	On Mrs. Luks's visit and Luks's drinking: JSNYS, p. 199.
126	"freak wall": quoted in Perlman, *The Immortal Eight,* p. 182.
126	"gesture of initiative": Arnold Friedman, unpublished essay on the exhibition in the collection of the Museum of Modern Art.
126	"so different from the 'regular picture game' ": JSNYS, p. 205.

THE PUBLIC AND THE PRIVATE

127	John Trask, "though affable": JSNYS, p. 203.
128	"their painting teems . . .": *Philadelphia Press,* 9 March 1908.
128	"these strong men will no doubt . . .": *Philadelphia Inquirer,* 31 January 1909.

128   "I came near it again": JSNYS, p. 213.

130   "making first-class idiots . . .": quoted in Glackens, *William Glackens and The Eight,* p. 107.

130–131   "No one knew Henri was married . . ." quoted in Glackens, *William Glackens and The Eight,* pp. 110–112.

132   "with joy": JSNYS, p. 220.

134   "I get a joy from these healthy girls . . .": JSNYS, p. 227.

134   "group of eccentric painters": *Chicago Art Institute Bulletin,* October 1908, p. 18.

135   "extremely vigorous . . .": *Chicago Record Herald,* 20 September 1908.

135   "Bewilderment and disappointment": *Chicago Post,* 12 September 1908.

135   "things of quite such radical import . . .": clipping in Chicago Art Institute file; unclear which paper it is from.

135   "BIG SENSATION AT THE ART MUSEUM": *Port Hanson Herald,* undated clipping from Toledo Art Museum scrapbooks for 1908.

135–136   George Stevens's remarks: *Toledo Blade,* 8 October 1908.

136   "resemble bits of ancient tapestry": *Toledo News Bee,* 8 October 1908.

136   "Toledo visitors to the Art Museum . . .": *Toledo Sunday Journal,* 18 October 1908.

136   "impressive originality": *Toledo News Bee,* 15 October 1908, p. 7.

136   The *Blade* critic: *Toledo Blade,* 8 October 1908.

137   Bertha O'Brien's remarks: *Detroit Free Press,* 29 November 1908.

137   The dilemma with the *Press:* JSNYS, pp. 265–266. By this time Sloan probably knew his days as a puzzle-maker were numbered, anyway. Readers had begun to complain that his word puzzles were too hard, either in the clues used or in the answers expected (opera titles, etc.), complaints to which Sloan was not particularly sympathetic.

137   She was a "conventional 'Bohemian' ": JSNYS, p. 267.

138   "one of the most interesting collections": *Indianapolis News,* 9 January 1909, p. 4.

139   "[each] of the artists . . .": *Cincinnati Commercial Tribune,* 7 February 1909, p. 9.

139   "wonderfully fine arrangement": *Cincinnati Enquirer,* 14 February 1909.

139   "gross roué": *Cincinnati Commercial Tribune,* 7 February 1909, p. 9.

139   "seek[ing] diversion among bricklayers": *Pittsburgh Bulletin,* 20 March 1909.

139   "vibrates with humanity": *Pittsburgh Dispatch,* 14 March 1909.
139   The writer for the *Newark Evening News:* 8 May 1909, sec. 2, p. 4.
139–140   "In taking their art directly to the American public": Zilczer,
           "The Eight on Tour, 1908–1909," p. 38. In a field of study in
           which everything seems to be judged by its impact in New York
           and one or two other large cities, it is worth noting that Zilczer's
           essay is one of the few solid research accounts in American art
           history of what the rest of the country was thinking about art and
           artists before the Armory Show.
140   "After I came home . . .": JSNYS, p. 316.
141–142   On Dolly's pregnancy: Sloan spoke of this traumatic episode in
           his life only once, to Helen Farr Sloan, not long before his death.
           It was evident to Mrs. Sloan that the memory of it was still a
           source of anguish and embarrassment for her husband, and she
           never questioned him further about the abortion or referred to it
           in any way. The only thing about this matter that remains un-
           clear is its exact date. It seems most likely to have occurred in
           late 1908 or early 1909, in that Dolly's trips to her doctor for her
           many ambiguous "treatments" sharply increased in 1909, and
           she needed that year to consult a woman physician who special-
           ized in gynecological problems. Dolly's discomfort with the
           pregnancy of Rockwell Kent's wife in 1911 becomes even more
           understandable in this light, as does her interest in sheltering the
           children of the Lawrence strike in 1912 and in entertaining the
           children of Gloucester circa 1914–1918.

CALL TO ACTION

144–145   "Happiness rather than misery . . .": JSNYS, p. 13.
146   "most Christ-like man . . .": Helen Farr Sloan note in JSNYS,
           p. 382.
146   "four more years . . .": JSNYS, p. 259.
146   "as great a depiction . . .": Barrell, "The Real Drama of the
           Slums," p. 563.
146   "Now we are 'Reds' ": JSNYS, p. 381.
147   on one occasion Sloan went to the rectory: Helen Farr Sloan.
148   "To leave New York . . .": John Butler Yeats to William Butler
           Yeats, 9 May 1908, quoted in Hone, *J. B. Yeats,* p. 104.
148   "Why do birds migrate?": John Butler Yeats to Ruth Hart, 22
           November 1913, quoted in Hone, *J. B. Yeats,* p. 165.

149   "All that happens in Dublin . . .": John Butler Yeats to Lily Yeats, 19 February 1921, quoted in Murphy, *Prodigal Father,* p. 333.

149   "kindly and well informed": JSNYS, p. 324.

149   On the Thanksgiving dinner: JSNYS, p. 355.

150   "very dear and interesting": JSNYS, p. 360.

150   "a scheme of color": *JSNYS,* p. 318.

152   forcing his students to devote time: Perlman, *Robert Henri: His Life and Art,* p. 104.

152   "The light on the brick": HFSN.

152   "God Bless the Maratta Colors": JSNYS, p. 514.

153   "It has beauty . . .": Sloan, *Gist of Art,* p. 220.

153–154   On the voyeurism episode: JSNYS, p. 549, and Helen Farr Sloan.

154   "The voyeuristic concerns dominating Sloan's iconography . . .": Baker, "Voyeurism in the Art of John Sloan," p. 383.

154   "Surely," Sloan noted: JSNYS, p. 443.

154–155   "PANIC AVERTED IN ART SHOW CROWD": *New York Mail and Express,* 2 April 1910.

155   The long, elaborate story of the efforts to secure a space for the Independents Show is recounted in Homer, *Robert Henri and His Circle,* pp. 152–153; Perlman, *Robert Henri: His Life and Art,* pp. 92–95; and Mary Ellen Conner's master's thesis on the subject (Delaware Art Museum).

156   "[the] fact that there are a great many good pictures . . .": *New York Sun,* 3 March 1910.

156   "like slipping a pair of men's drawers . . .": JSNYS, p. 396.

156   "cut me from the exhibition game": ibid.

156–157   Walter Pach suggested: JSNYS, p. 399.

157   On Paul Dougherty: JSNYS, pp. 186, 190.

157   "mark[ed] an epoch . . .": *New York Mail and Express,* 4 April 1910.

157   "much finer than the paintings": *New York Times,* 4 April 1910.

157   a "peculiarly classic" merit: ibid.

157   the *Call*'s Socialist response: *The Call,* 29 May 1910.

157   Huneker's response: *New York Sun,* 7 April 1910.

158   Wallace Stevens's reaction to the National Academy of Design: Holly Stevens, ed., *Letters of Wallace Stevens* (New York: Knopf, 1966), p. 116.

159   The pitiful resolution to the whole contretemps: JSNYS, p. 505. It would seem that the Robert Henri–Dolly Sloan relationship was not without its twists and turns, either, though Sloan was

reluctant to record anything specific in his diaries about their more difficult moments. (He would note, for instance, that cross words were exchanged but would not always elaborate as to their cause.) Henri certainly appreciated Dolly's care during his depressed periods after Linda's death, but he very likely ran out of patience with her, as did most of Sloan's friends from Philadelphia, as the years went by. (Also see JSNYS, p. 195.)

159   Kent was a "hard liver": JSNYS, p. 469.

160   On Kent's philanderings and relations with the Sloans: Traxel, *An American Saga,* pp. 59, 65, and JSNYS, p. 496, 498.

161   "smiling like Elijah . . .": quoted in Reid, *The Man from New York,* p. 86.

161–162   On the individuals in *Yeats at Petipas:* for a long time it was assumed that the third figure from the right in the picture was Anne Squires, but as she was not a regular at Petipas until much later, that identification was never too likely. Eulabee Dix, a model and miniature painter, was a part of the Yeats-Sloan group circa 1910 (see letter from Joan Gaines, Dix's daughter, to Rowland Elzea, Delaware Art Museum).

162   Yeats later said: Rowland Elzea, *John Sloan's Oil Paintings,* vol. 1, p. 107.

163   "brainless cowards": JSNYS, p. 583.

163–164   On Dolly's distressing meeting with William Butler Yeats: Brooks, *Scenes and Portraits,* p. 175, and Murphy, *Prodigal Father,* p. 415.

165   Miss Finch's "staggering" goodwill: JSNYS, p. 578.

166   "after a wild struggle . . .": JSNYS, p. 125.

166   "another all day attempt . . .": JSNYS, p. 282.

166   [Katherine] does her part . . .": JSNYS, p. 342.

166   "There is nothing so improving . . .": John Butler Yeats to John Sloan, 11 January 1912, Princeton University Library.

166–168   Sloan's descriptions of his time in Omaha: letters to Dolly, December 1911–January 1912, Delaware Art Museum.

AN INDEPENDENT PATH

169   Dolly's Christmas with Sloan's family: Dolly to John Sloan, January 1912, Delaware Art Museum.

169   "soak in something to paint": JSNYS, p. 597.

171   "ritual cleansing and renewal . . .": Hills, "John Sloan's Images of Working-Class Women," pp. 175, 177.

172   the "strike was dramatized . . .": Symes and Clement, *Rebel America,* p. 272.

173   "Where's the man with the permit to parade?": Vorse, *A Footnote to Folly,* p. 1.

173   wanted to "use" the children: JSNYS, p. 602.

173   "I interrupted [him] . . .": JSNYS, pp. 607–608.

174   "It is a big thing . . .": JSNYS, p. 615.

174   On the Union Square episode: *New York Times,* 3 May 1912.

176   On the Ettor-Giovannitti Carnegie Hall rally: Poole, *The Bridge,* pp. 197–198, and a May 1943 letter from Poole to John Sloan on the occasion of Dolly's death, Delaware Art Museum. Poole was one of many in the movement who would remember with affection and admiration Dolly's spirit on behalf of the "cause."

177   "written *for* the masses . . .": *The Masses,* March 1911, p. 3.

177–178   As Young later recalled in his memoirs . . . : Art Young, *On My Way,* pp. 275–276.

178   the "John Barrymore of American radicalism": Symes and Clement, *Rebel America,* p. 282.

179   with the exception, years later, of the sexually touchy Ernest Hemingway: all biographies of Hemingway and Eastman narrate their infamous encounter in the office of Max Perkins at Scribners, where Hemingway, feeling that Eastman had impugned his masculinity in a review, demanded to see how much hair Eastman had on his chest and proceeded to beat him up. While it was not one of the more distinguished moments in Hemingway's life, Eastman was later typically gracious about the whole unsavory matter.

179   On salaries: JSNYS, p. 627. Eastman was eventually paid $25 a week for his labors, according to Sloan.

179   "brilliant untrammeled thinker": JSNYS, p. 633.

180   "a revolutionary and not a reform magazine . . .": *The Masses,* January 1913, p. 2.

180   "I hope to do my share . . .": John Sloan to John Quinn, 24 November 1912, Quinn Papers, New York Public Library.

180   "I think it is too bitter in tone . . .": John Quinn to John Sloan, 1 January 1913, Quinn Papers, New York Public Library.

181   Vorse's view of the magazine: quoted in Zurier, *Art for "The Masses,"* p. 50.

182   "Bourgeois pigs!": Art Young, *On My Way,* p. 281.

182 "found no trouble in mixing Socialism . . .": quoted in Shannon, *The Socialist Party in America,* p. 57.

184–185 When Norman Hapgood: Hawkes, p. 24.

185 "The strange thing was . . .": JSN, p. 290.

185 Full of praise: John Butler Yeats, "The Work of John Sloan," *Harper's Weekly,* 22 November 1913, pp. 20–21.

185 "He engages in a war of opinion . . .": ibid.

A NEW VISION

186 He told Quinn: John Sloan to John Quinn, 13 April 1913, Quinn Papers, New York Public Library.

187 On Sloan's lack of interest in the Association of American Painters and Sculptors: JSNYS, pp. 628–629.

187 "of fastidiously aristocratic bearing . . .": Brown, *The Story of the Armory Show,* p. 57.

188 On Davies and Pach's treatment of Henri: Perlman, *Robert Henri: His Life and Art,* p. 108.

188 He brusquely shrugged off Sloan's qualms: Reid, *The Man from New York,* p. 404.

189 "silent, poetic type . . .": Helen Farr Sloan.

189 On Sloan's feelings about Stieglitz: Brooks, *John Sloan,* pp. 129–130.

190 William Glackens hit the nail on the head: Glackens, *William Glackens and the Eight,* p. 181.

190 As Maurice Prendergast put it: quoted in Brooks, *John Sloan,* p. 135.

190–191 he paradoxically began to reflect: Helen Farr Sloan; this is an observation repeated more than once in JSN and HFSN.

192 On visiting Albert Barnes: Schack, *Art and Argyrol,* p. 78.

193–196 On the Paterson Strike Pageant: see Martin Green, *New York 1913.*

196 As Malcolm Cowley noted: Cowley, *Exile's Return,* p. 66.

198 "When people marry . . .": John Butler Yeats to John Quinn, 27 October 1912, Quinn Papers, New York Public Library.

199 "But for her, he'd talk nothing else . . .": quoted in Murphy, *Prodigal Father,* p. 429.

199 Emma Bellows thought her a scandal: Morgan, *George Bellows,* p. 207.

199 a "little frump, a dreadful woman": quoted in Bowers and Hale, *Leon Kroll,* p. 48.

199 "The horrible Mrs. Sloan" and the subsequent quotations from Quinn about Dolly: quoted in Murphy, *Prodigal Father,* pp. 497–498, 533.

200 "If only he will let his feelings show . . .": Marianna Sloan to Dolly, 1914, Delaware Art Museum.

200 Quinn advanced the money: John Quinn to Dolly Sloan, 2 July 1914, Quinn Collection, New York Public Library.

201 the docks of Provincetown: John Sloan to Randall Davey, 1914, Delaware Art Museum.

202 "Italian wife beaters": JSN, p. 169.

202 Elizabeth Oakes Colford: Crews, *The Red Cottage,* unpaginated.

202 Once in a while: HFSN.

202 the "habit of working": HFSN.

207 "one of the odd corners of America": HFSN.

207 "The vials of wrath were full": quoted in Robert K. Massie, *Dreadnought* (New York: Viking, 1992), p. 855.

209 On Davey's reactions: Morgan, *George Bellows,* p. 203.

211 On Mrs. Whitney, Mrs. Force, and the Immigrant in America exhibition: Berman, *Rebels on Eighth Street,* pp. 118–120, and Friedman, *Gertrude Vanderbilt Whitney,* p. 373.

211–212 On Jennie Doyle: Doyle's letters are in the Sloan Collection at the Delaware Art Museum.

1916: OPENED DOORS

213 On the letter mishap: Berman, *Rebels on Eighth Street,* p. 122, and Friedman, *Gertrude Vanderbilt Whitney,* p. 375.

214 "The dealers in the city": John Sloan to Gertrude Vanderbilt Whitney, 7 January 1916, Whitney Museum of American Art.

214 On John Weichsel: see Gail Stavitsky, "John Weichsel and the People's Art Guild," *Archives of American Art Journal* 31, no. 4, pp. 12–19.

215 McBride's review: *New York Sun,* 30 January 1916.

215–216 Bowdoin's review: *New York Evening World,* 27 March 1916.

216 On the portrait of Juliana Force: Berman, *Rebels on Eighth Street,* p. 124.

216–217 On the Egner fiasco: Rowland Elzea, *John Sloan's Oil Paintings,* vol. 1, p. 128.

217–220   On the artists' conflicts with the editors of the *Masses:* the mem-
             oirs of Dell, Eastman, and Art Young; Fishbein, pp. 21–22;
             Zurier, *Art for "The Masses,"* pp. 51–57; *New York Sun,* 8 April
             1916, and other clippings in the Sloan Collection, and JSN, pp.
             193–194.

217   the "pictures are always first rate": quoted in Zurier, *Art for "The
             Masses,"* p. 42.

217   "those rude, raw drawings . . .": ibid.

218   "roars as gently as a sucking dove": quoted in "RADICAL EDITORS
             FIGHT OVER MAGAZINE POLICY," *New York Morning Telegram,* 8
             April 1916.

218   "Somebody spilled the apple cart": ibid.

218   "[Men such as John Sloan and Stuart Davis] . . .": quoted in
             New York Sun, 8 April 1916.

219   "Max, when thy right hand offendeth thee . . .": quoted in
             Eastman, *Enjoyment of Living,* p. 555.

220   On Floyd Dell's view of the artists' demands: by the time he
             wrote his memoirs, *Homecoming,* in 1933, Dell had come around
             to a more benign perspective on Sloan's break with the *Masses.*
             Insisting that Sloan was at heart as much a propagandist as any-
             one on the magazine, he questioned how much he really wanted
             to sever his ties with the cause and implied that he had acted
             more as a spokesman for men less articulate than he—that is,
             defending the artists who weren't very good at speaking up for
             themselves rather than making demands he himself cared about.
             There may be something to this (Sloan loved defending the un-
             derdog), but Sloan's desire to be completely unfettered in his
             painting and drawing was also stronger than Dell ever realized.

220   "Dear Sloan . . .": Eastman, *Enjoyment of Living,* p. 556.

220   To a reporter: *New York Morning Telegraph,* 8 April 1916.

220–221   On the Hotel Brevoort fete for Goldman: Drinnon, *Rebel in Para-
             dise,* p. 168.

221   In inscribing: a copy of Goldman's memoirs, personally inscribed
             to the Sloans, is in the Sloan Collection in the library of the
             Delaware Art Museum.

221   On Juliana Force: Berman, *Rebels on Eighth Street,* pp. 124–128.

223   The artist Adolph Dehn: quoted in Zurier, *Art for "The Masses,"*
             p. 189, from the Dehn Papers in the Archives of American Art.

226   On Elsie Driggs's reactions to Sloan: many conversations
             with the author, a friend of the Driggs/Gatch family, in the
             1980s.

226   "For the study of composition . . .": quoted in John Loughery, "Blending the Classical and the Modern: The Art of Elsie Driggs," *Woman's Art Journal,* Fall 1986–Winter 1987, p. 22.

227   On the Christmas-week flare-up: Murphy, *Prodigal Father,* p. 457.

BOHEMIA'S BORDERS

228   The Washington Square Arch outing: recounted in many histories of Greenwich Village, including Parry, *Garrets and Pretenders,* pp. 275–277, and Allen Churchill, *The Improper Bohemians* (New York: Dutton, 1959), p. 107. Sloan also spoke of it to Helen Farr Sloan after their marriage.

229   a "spiritual haven . . . a sort of liberal/radical small town": Judith Schwarz, *Radical Feminists of Heterodoxy,* p. 29.

230   a hectic "gathering place . . .": Untermeyer, *Bygones,* p. 37.

230   the "curse of conformity": quoted in Humphrey, *Children of Fantasy,* p. 6.

230   "I doubt if ever in America . . .": Scherman, *Girl from Fitchburg,* p. 60.

232   "more than justify the big faith . . .": *New York Evening Mail,* 26 March 1917.

233   the "prosaic and even ugly nature of his subjects": Royal Cortissoz, *New York Tribune,* 1 April 1917.

233–234   On the early history of the Independents: see Marlor, "A Quest for Independence" and *The Society of Independent Artists,* and Naumann, "The Big Show."

234   "Do you mean," Kent exclaimed . . . : quoted in Naumann, "The Big Show," part 1, p. 37, from Beatrice Wood's memoir *I Shock Myself.*

234   "suppressed adolescence": ibid.

235   On the urinal: the fate of the urinal itself is a tad obscure. The story of Glackens's "accident" with Mutt's art work comes from the book about "The Eight" written by Glackens's son, Ira, who heard this tale from John Kraushaar (or so he told Helen Farr Sloan). Some letters in the Katherine Dreier Collection at Yale seem to verify this account, at least indirectly. Avis Berman reports in *Rebels on Eighth Street* (p. 135) that the urinal was rescued and given sanctuary in Stieglitz's studio, which makes sense con-

sidering that Stieglitz photographed it for the magazine *The Blind Man.* Of course, the photograph could have been made prior to Glackens's indelicate handling of *Fountain,* or, since all urinals look alike, Stieglitz may even have photographed a counterfeit *Fountain* (though an Independents entry ticket is visible in the photo, attached to the urinal). Duchamp claimed, none too plausibly, that the collector Walter Arensberg bought the urinal and later lost it. All one can safely conclude is: how Duchamp would have loved this speculation!

236 On Helen Keller's outspoken antiwar lecture tour and appearance in New York: Morgan, *George Bellows,* p. 207, and Lash, *Helen and Teacher,* pp. 423–429.

237 Ed Davis was actually "keen for the war": John Sloan to Robert Henri, 7 June 1917, Beinecke Library, Yale University.

237 "I love him because . . .": John Butler Yeats to Dolly Sloan, 30 March 1917, Princeton University.

237 "Unhappy . . . restless . . . quarrelsome": John Butler Yeats to Dolly Sloan, 9 August 1917, Delaware Art Museum.

238 On Dolly's fund-raising for Tom Mooney: clipping of 9 May 1917 (which newspaper is unclear), Delaware Art Museum.

238 a "woman of stone": Helen Farr Sloan.

238 On the neurologist's recommendation: Helen Farr Sloan.

242–243 On the early structure and ambitions of the Society: See Marlor, *The Society of Independent Artists:* pp. 1–24.

243 As Theresa Bernstein later observed: interview with the author.

244–245 On the *Masses* trials: Dell, *Homecoming,* pp. 313–319; Eastman, *Love and Revolution,* pp. 58–63; Hillquit, *Loose Leaves from a Busy Life,* pp. 224–230; Art Young, *On My Way,* pp. 292–300; and Zurier, *Art for "The Masses,"* pp. 59–64. Dell also wrote an account of the trial for the *Liberator* (June 1918, pp. 7–18).

244 "a scene," Dell noted: "The Story of the Trial," *The Liberator* (June 1918), p. 11.

245 "[Dolly's] pungent testimony . . .": ibid.

245 The near-miss for the prosecution in the April 1918 trial did not, unfortunately, signal an end to the government's desire to punish the staff of the *Masses* for its radical views. A second conspiracy trial took place in October 1918, only weeks before the Armistice was signed. This time Eastman took a more forceful position on the issues, particularly in defense of Socialism and the right to free speech. The jury voted 4 for conviction and 8 for acquittal, and there the matter finally ended.

245–246   On the wartime atmosphere in Gloucester: see Kenny, *Cape Ann: Cape America;* Garland, *Eastern Point;* and the *Gloucester Daily Times,* particularly 11 July 1918, p. 6, and 29 July 1918, p. 1.

246   On Dolly's brush with the authorities: Helen Farr Sloan.

THE OTHER AMERICA

249   "our trip to see America": Dolly's journal, Delaware Art Museum.

249–250   On the trip to New Mexico: Holcomb, "John Sloan in Santa Fe"; Kraft, *John Sloan in Santa Fe;* Brooks, *John Sloan,* pp. 153–154; Sloan's letters to Robert Henri, at Yale; JSN; HFSN.

251   On Marsden Hartley: Ludington, *Marsden Hartley,* pp. 56–57.

251   On Mrs. Eva Feynes: Udall, "Marsden Hartley's Self-Portrait," p. 32.

251   "contrary to my usual custom . . .": John Sloan to Robert Henri, 26 August 1919, Beinecke Library, Yale University.

253   "desert forms, so serene and clear": quoted in Kraft, *John Sloan in Sante Fe,* p. 37.

254   "simple, unimitative, but profound": Sloan, *Gist of Art,* p. 263.

255   "We have before this had occasion . . .": Royal Cortissoz, *New York Tribune,* 15 February 1920.

256   "heaviness of touch . . .": *Brooklyn Daily Eagle,* 22 February 1920.

256   "priceless inheritance . . .": Sloan, quoting Edgar Hewett, in Society of Independent Artists catalogue, 1920.

256–257   On the Hamilton Easter Field imbroglio: Marlor, *The Society of Independent Artists,* p. 16–19.

257   "Your complexion is so bad . . .": John Butler Yeats to John Sloan, 27 May 1920, Princeton University.

258   the "clouds hanging round the peaks . . .": John Sloan to Robert Henri, 3 July 1920, Beinecke Library, Yale University.

258   On Dolly's visit to the fortune teller: JSN, p. 331, and HFSN.

259   "one of the most vigorous . . .": *Vanity Fair,* May 1921.

259–260   A few months later, Sadakichi Hartmann: the Hartmann letters, at the Delaware Art Museum, and JSN, p. 343.

260   "courage to be himself . . .": Yeats, "A Painter of Pictures," p. 401.

260   "My own father's death . . .": John Sloan to Lily Yeats, 7 February 1922, quoted in Hone, *J. B. Yeats,* p. 289.

260   "great warm glow has gone": ibid.

261   Rollin Kirby's remarks about Yeats: JSNYS, p. 418.

YEARNINGS

263–265   On the Hamlin sale and Sloan's audit: Helen Farr Sloan; JSN, p. 33; and Sloan's financial records, at the Delaware Art Museum.

266–267   On the censorship trial of J. Francis Kaufman's painting: Marlor, *The Society of Independent Artists,* pp. 19–21, and 1923–1924 news clippings, Delaware Art Museum.

267–270   On the censorship of Indian dances: see Hecht, *Oliver La Farge and the American Indian;* Kelly, *The Assault on Assimilation;* McNickle, *Indian Man;* and Sloan, "The Indian Dance from an Artist's Point of View." John Collier's *Indians of the Americas* (Mentor, 1947) also gives a good account of the discrimination the tribes faced.

269   "I think I am in a position": Sloan, *Gist of Art,* p. 270.

270   "rank tenderfoot": Henry McBride, *New York Herald,* 22 April 1923.

271   On Stuart Davis's reaction to New Mexico: Sims, *Stuart Davis,* p. 166.

272–273   On Lee Gatch in Sloan's class: conversations with Elsie Driggs Gatch.

273   "Once in class I was in a terrible dilemma . . .": Jennie Slaughter to Helen Farr, n.d. (1932), Helen Farr Sloan correspondence files.

273   To one student whose drawings: Brooks, *John Sloan,* p. 143, and Easoni Martin letters to Helen Farr Sloan, circa 1952, Delaware Art Museum; also JSN, p. 25. (Sloan seems to have made this tart suggestion to more than one facile student.)

273–274   On Theodore Dreiser's visit: Brooks, *John Sloan,* p. 188; Lingeman, *Theodore Dreiser,* p. 37; JSN, p. 182.

274   "[He] had the most valuable influence . . .": quoted in Sackler, "Interview with Adolph Gottlieb," p. 23.

274   "The academic point of view . . .": *Forum,* 23 April 1925.

274   On Easoni Martin: Martin corresponded at great length with Helen Farr Sloan after John Sloan's death; the letters containing his recollections of Sloan's classes are at the Delaware Art Museum.

275 "I think that the people he did the most for . . .": Cummings, "Interview with Katherine Schmidt," p. 20.

275 "contagion of naïveté": Henry McBride, *The Dial*, June 1924, p. 565.

276 "If the Society . . .": Sloan, *Gist of Art*, p. 14.

276 "John Sloan has always been a sort of Cyrano de Bergerac . . .": *Pittsburgh Post*, 4 April 1924.

277 On Gertrude Vanderbilt Whitney's assistance: Berman, *Rebels on Eighth Street*, p. 136.

277–278 On the Abraham Walkowitz and Max Weber flare-ups: JSN, p. 221, and Helen Farr Sloan.

278 "evening gown and the sweater . . .": undated clipping, Delaware Art Museum.

278–279 On the Inje-Inje: In *Revolution and Tradition in American Art* (pp. 28–29), John I. H. Baur treats this episode—"half, or perhaps three-quarters, serious"—as a "movement." Certainly to Cahill it may have taken on that aspect, but to Sloan the Inje-Inje business was strictly a practical joke. Baur is in error when he accepts Cahill's assertion that this South American tribe with a two-syllable/one-word vocabulary did in fact exist.

279 "third-rate painter": quoted in Murphy, *Prodigal Father*, p. 498.

280 "Most of our museums are on the wrong trail . . .": quoted in *ArtNews*, 21 February 1925.

281 "From the list, I gather . . .": quoted in Townsend Ludington, *John Dos Passos: An American Odyssey* (New York: Dutton, 1980), p. 237.

281 "obedient priests . . .": Eastman, *Love and Revolution*, p. 494. Eastman in this volume provides a good account of the efforts of the *New Masses* crowd to denigrate the work of the earlier magazine and to brand Eastman himself as a bourgeois dilettante.

281 "I have no intention of being used . . .": Helen Farr Sloan.

282 On Dolly's lack of interest in sex in the 1920s: Helen Farr Sloan and HFSD (1948). Sloan's erotic drawings are in the collection of the Delaware Art Museum; a selection of similar work was given by Mrs. Sloan to the Lock Haven State University art collection in Lock Haven, Pennsylvania.

283 "a very jolly affair": quoted in Morse, *John Sloan's Prints*, p. 252.

283 "beautifully theatrical" effect: ibid.

OLD BATTLES, NEW RESOLVE

284   "to have to scuttle out like rats . . .": John Sloan to Will Shuster, 18 January 1927, Archives of American Art.

285   "on a sudden impulse": Sloan, *Gist of Art,* p. 285.

285–286   "not so persuasive": *New York Tribune,* 20 February 1927.

286   "one is apt to think of Mr. Sloan . . .": *New York Times,* 20 February 1927.

287   "terrible shuffling ordeal": John Sloan to Will Shuster, 4 March 1927, Archives of American Art.

287   "a heavenly abode . . .": ibid.

287   Hopper's article: Edward Hopper, "John Sloan and the Philadelphians," *The Arts,* April 1927, pp. 169–178.

288   On the origins of *The Lafayette Hotel* sale idea: HFSN and Helen Farr Sloan.

288–289   Information on the donations: Avis Berman, from her Juliana Force files.

289   "credit [for the gift] should go to . . .": Duncan Phillips to John Sloan, Delaware Art Museum.

289   Henri's reservations about the idea: Helen Farr Sloan.

290   "strange combination of religious fanatic and unscrupulous financier . . .": Simpson, *Artful Partners,* pp. 193–202. The scarcely plausible Carl Hamilton is also discussed, a little more discreetly, in Meryle Secrest's book *Being Bernard Berenson* (New York: Holt Rinehart Winston, 1979) and in the second volume of Ernest Samuels's biography of Berenson (Cambridge: Harvard University Press, 1979). In 1926 Mary Berenson wrote that Hamilton was reporting that he was prosperous again, having paid off two million dollars in debts, "but we have ceased to believe him" (*Mary Berenson: A Self-Portrait from Her Diaries and Letters,* p. 261).

291   On the Owen Cattell loan: HFSN and Helen Farr Sloan.

292   "with a kind of lumpy grandeur": HFSN.

293   "I have very few things to teach you . . .": HFSN.

293   "oh, so amusing": Tarbell, *Peggy Bacon,* p. 9. Bacon, an exceptionally talented and witty graphic artist, was one of Sloan's earliest students at the League; she was of a temperament to appreciate Sloan's humor as well as anyone, but she also knew the bite of his tongue. When criticizing one of her drypoints, Sloan remarked on the fact that only one person in the picture had been portrayed in an attractive light (i.e., the artist) and that only an egotist

would subject everyone else to caricature while sparing herself. It took Bacon twenty-five years and a few cocktails to let Sloan know that the pretty girl in the drawing had been her classmate, the artist Katherine Schmidt.

293 Even for someone such as Alexander Calder: Helen Farr Sloan and Marter, *Alexander Calder,* pp. 25–26, 33–34, 69–70, 79.

294 "man of universal vision . . .": Art Young, *On My Way,* pp. 279–280. Dolly, he wrote, was "one of the estimable women who aided in many a crisis when the law was holding us up or scouts were needed to raise money." Young inscribed his copy of his memoirs to the Sloans "In memory of the romantic days."

295 "this splendid gesture of appreciation": Sloan, "My Recent Encounter," p. xliv.

296 On John Kraushaar's Coney Island suggestion: Fred Shane to Helen Farr, 24 July 1932, Helen Farr Sloan's correspondence files, and JSN, p. 32.

296–297 On the shift in Sloan's style and interests: the best and most detailed account is in Rowland Elzea, *John Sloan's Oil Paintings,* vol. 1, pp. 27–30.

297 "clinching reality . . . the plastic power": JSN, p. 351.

297 "The nudes I painted before . . .": ibid.

298 "abstract motives": JSN, p. 144.

299 "You're here to show your figure, not your ignorance": Mrs. A. K. Weld (Yosene Balfour Ker) to Rowland Elzea, Delaware Art Museum. My thanks to Iris Snyder for calling this note to my attention.

299 On Henri's disapproval: Helen Farr Sloan.

299 "You will be alone now . . .": John Sloan to Marianna Sloan, April 1930, Delaware Art Museum.

301 "born of theory, not enthusiasm": *ArtNews,* 12 April 1930.

301–305 On the summer of 1930: Helen Farr Sloan; HFSN.

305 "Sloan is the most vituperative person in New York": Frances Beisel quoting Dolly in a letter to Helen Farr, 1932, in Helen Farr Sloan's correspondence files.

305–306 Sloan's illness and Dolly's suicide attempt: Helen Farr Sloan; HFSN.

306 "I guess you do know . . .": Dolly Sloan to Helen Farr, 28 September 1931, in Helen Farr Sloan's correspondence files.

307 Designed to "win aesthetic appraisal of Indian art . . .": Tribal Arts Exposition press release, 1931.

306–309 On the Tribal Arts Exposition show: files concerning all aspects of the project (finances, list of art works, publicity, etc.) at the Delaware Art Museum.

309   "affair of uncommon interest": Royal Cortissoz, *New York Herald Tribune,* December 1931 clipping, Delaware Art Museum.

309   "awakened appreciation . . .": *The Nation,* 6 May 1931, pp. 501–503.

309   "[receiving] more publicity . . .": John Sloan to Will Shuster, December 1931, Archives of American Art.

FEAR ITSELF

311   "Who can describe the hopelessness . . .": quoted in Berman, *Rebels on Eighth Street,* p. 309.

312   Government and business had little interest: "SLOAN DEPLORES U.S. APATHY IN FOSTERING ART," *New York Herald Tribune,* 31 March 1932.

312   On Jackson Pollock: Naifeh and Smith, *Jackson Pollock,* pp. 237–238.

312–313   On Sloan's displeasure with the Art Students League: HFSN; Helen Farr Sloan; interview with David W. Scott.

313–315   On the George Grosz episode: clipping file (20–24 April, 1932), Delaware Art Museum; the election at the League was prominently covered in New York City's newspapers and the art magazines that spring. Also see Brooks, *John Sloan,* pp. 201–205.

316–317   On the summer of 1932 in Santa Fe: Helen Farr Sloan.

319–320   On the Diego Rivera cause célèbre: Wolfe, *The Fabulous Life of Diego Rivera,* pp. 317–340 and Brooks, *John Sloan,* pp. 170–171.

320   As Sloan mused: *Time,* 11 December 1933.

321   she and Dolly weren't getting along: Hecht, *Oliver La Farge and the American Indian,* p. 65.

321–322   On the Evergoods: Kendall Taylor, *Philip Evergood,* pp. 80–82.

322   "warm brown torso": Sloan, *Gist of Art,* p. 312.

323   "rated it with anything in the nude line . . .": ibid., p. 319.

323   Dolly arrived home from work early: Helen Farr Sloan.

324   "alarming procedure . . .": *ArtNews,* 6 January 1934, p. 6.

324–325   The PWAP scandal: clipping file (spring 1934), Delaware Art Museum.

326   In New York one afternoon in 1935: HFSN.

326   On NYU's eviction: Helen Farr Sloan; JSN, p. 266. The NYU

administration responded to Sloan's request to keep his apartment under the guise of being a student or lecturer at the school by pontificating on the "deception" his request involved. Sloan fumed, "You wouldn't think [a big operation like] N.Y.U. could be run without some deception!"

327   Mary Regensberg remembered: interview with the author.

329   "I believe that . . .": Quoted in James Miller, *The Passion of Michel Foucault* (New York: Simon and Schuster, 1993), p. 19.

ART: *GIST* AND STRUGGLE

330–331   "Eakins' strong realism . . .": Lewis Mumford, *The Brown Decades* (Reprint. New York: Dover, 1971), pp. 107–108.

331   "had no rivals worthy of notice": Thomas Craven, *Men of Art* (New York: Simon & Shuster, 1931), p. 512.

331   "one of the most deeply thoughtful . . .": La Follette, *Art in America,* p. 324.

331   "I hate that painting": quoted in *The Chelsean,* December 1939.

332   "facet of Fascism": "SLOAN CRITICAL OF INTENSE INTEREST IN 'AMERICAN' ART," *New Rochelle Standard Star,* 9 November 1937.

332   "mausoleum of Modernism": JSN, p. 176.

332   "from the abstract . . .": Helen Farr Sloan.

332   "gentle rain of malice": "JOHN SLOAN SAYS WHAT ART NEEDS IS A BAN ON IT," *New York Herald Tribune,* 16 November 1939.

332   "art punchers": JSN, p. 208.

333   On Mrs. Force's purchase of two Sloan paintings: Helen Farr Sloan.

334   "Dust Gathers at the Whitney Museum": *Brooklyn Daily Eagle,* 14 February 1937.

334   Irving Howe, Afterword to *Germinal* (New York: New American Library, 1970), p. 429.

334   On Sloan's final teaching days: interviews with Mary Regensberg and David W. Scott.

335   On Ruth Martin: Helen Farr Sloan and the Salander-O'Reilly Galleries' catalogue for the sale of the Ruth Martin collection, with an essay by Grant Holcomb, March 4–April 5, 1980.

335–336   On the etchings illustrating *Of Human Bondage:* Morse, *John Sloan's Prints,* p. 312.

336–337   On her marriage to Wyatt: Helen Farr Sloan.

337   "cantankerous old cuss": Charles Sawyer interview, 21 June
           1991, in the Archives of American Art, and letter to the author.
337–338   Helen's relationship with Dolly circa 1938–1939: Helen Farr
           Sloan.
340   "shrewd, tart, and aphoristic": Charles Poore, *New York Times,*
           undated clipping, Delaware Art Museum.
340   as did *Life:* not surprisingly, the *Life* magazine article of 11 De-
           cember 1939 was the purest hokum, complete with corny photos
           of the "colorful" artist (*Life*'s favorite slant on the subject of art
           in America), inaccurate dates, and the astounding information
           that Sloan and "The Eight" had been the organizers of the Ar-
           mory Show.
340   "good, tart, shrewd statement . . .": to John Sloan, 1930, Dela-
           ware Art Museum.
340–341   Sloan's visit to Lock Haven: interview with Rebecca Gross.
342–345   On the Art Appreciation Movement: clipping file, Delaware Art
           Museum (see especially Lowell Brentano, "Pictures for Every-
           body," *Saturday Evening Post,* 14 August 1943, p. 27); JSD;
           HFSN; Helen Farr Sloan. Stuart Davis's rebuke to Sloan (10 June
           1942) is in the correspondence file at the Delaware Art Museum.
346   On Dolly's death: John Sloan to Vivian Organ, 27 May 1943,
           Beinecke Library, Yale University.
346   Max Eastman: undated newspaper clipping (1943), Delaware Art
           Museum.
346   "She looks noble": HFSN.

DECLINE AND RENEWAL

347   "very, very low state": John Sloan to Don Freeman, 16 August
           1943, Delaware Art Museum.
348   "earnest letter": Helen Farr to John Sloan, 26 November 1943.
348   "I seem to have lost the ability . . .": John Sloan to Helen Farr,
           14 January 1944.
348   "[She] is en route to Santa Fe!": JSD (28 January 1944).
349   "mousy and manipulative": conversation with Earl Davis, Stuart
           Davis's son and Wyatt Davis's nephew, 15 February 1993.
349   "break her into a thousand pieces": Helen Farr Sloan and HFSD
           (20 August 1948).
349   On the Hoppers' happiness for Sloan: Jo Hopper to John Sloan,
           26 February 1945, Delaware Art Museum.

350 "After all, Dolly is part of us . . .": Helen Farr Sloan to John Sloan, 11 February 1944.
351–352 On Joe Hirshhorn's visits: JSD (27 May 1944); HFSD (27 May 1944); JSN, p. 202.
352 Shinn's was embarrassingly "rococo": HFSN.
352–353 On Mrs. Odets: JSD (11 May 1946) and HFSD (11 May 1946).
353 On the visit to Abiquiu: Helen Farr Sloan and JSD (12 August 1945), in which Sloan wryly notes, "[O'Keeffe] is not an easy hostess."
353 Sloan's view of O'Keeffe as an artist: JSN, p. 8.
354 "a wonderful voice, like an organ": JSD (19 May 1944).
354 "quite satisfying": JSD (30 May 1946).
354–355 On Sloan's politics in the late 1940s: HFSD (e.g., 4 May 1945, 1 and 10 April 1948); JSN, pp. 17–19.
355–356 On the New Mexico Alliance for the Arts: Helen Farr Sloan.
356 unique marker of cultural prominence: Coates, "Profiles."
357 On Irene Rice Pereira: JSN, p. 46.
357–358 On Andrew Wyeth: Brooks, *John Sloan*, p. 234; Helen Farr Sloan.
358 On Georgia O'Keeffe: JSD (13 December 1948). References to O'Keeffe throughout Sloan's diaries are none too complimentary.
358 annual lectures: The typescripts of several of Sloan's League speeches are in the collection of the Delaware Art Museum.
359–360 On the "Miss Fertility" controversy: La Farge, pp. 394–398.
362 On Mencken's response to the award: Fred Hobson, *H. L. Mencken: A Life* (New York: Random House, 1994), p. 516.
362 On preparing for the Whitney's retrospective and the joke to More: JSD (21 March 1950).

DARTMOUTH SUMMER

363 "What are the memoirs of a man . . .": JSN, p. 184.
364 not with much pleasure, he noted: HFSD (20 December 1948).
364 "He was an accidental member of 'The Eight' ": Helen Farr Sloan.
364 "Boswelled to death": Helen Farr Sloan.
365 The last speech he ever gave: the text is in the Delaware Art Museum library.
365 "silly, infantile . . . *dreadful*": JSD (19 May 1951).
365 "I want every speck of dust in that place": HFSN.

366   On Marianna's delusions: Helen Farr Sloan; JSD (4 May 1951).

366–370   The essence of Sloan's time in New Hampshire can be found in
               Herbert Faulkner West's thirty-two-page chapbook, *John Sloan's
               Last Summer,* privately printed in 1952.

368   "When you reach our age . . .": Helen Farr Sloan.

368   "We had a stiffish punch": John Sloan to Will Shuster, 5 August
               1951, Archives of American Art.

368   Goodrich postcard: Delaware Art Museum.

368–369   "I've had a lot of illness in my life": quoted in Helen Farr Sloan
               to Emily Genauer, 16 January 1952, copy of the letter at Dela-
               ware Art Museum.

369   The only agitation: *Santa Fe New Mexican,* 2 September 1951,
               sec. B, p. 6, and the Sloan-Shuster letters for August 1951.

369   "Robert Henri and Edgar Hewett . . .": John Sloan to Will
               Shuster, 27 August 1951, Archives of American Art.

369–370   The Sloan-Frost moment is from West, *John Sloan's Last Summer,*
               p. 30–32.

370   "I'm so tired . . .": Helen Farr Sloan; HFSN.

370–371   Goodrich's eulogy: typescript in the Delaware Art Museum.

371   On the mixing and scattering of Sloan's and Dolly's ashes: HFSN
               (20 January 1952).

Bibliography

Adams, Philip Rhys. *Walt Kuhn, Painter: His Life and Art.* Columbus: Ohio State University Press, 1974.

Artists of the Philadelphia Press. Exhibition catalogue. Philadelphia: Philadelphia Museum of Art, October 14–November 18, 1945.

Baigell, Matthew. "Notes on Realistic Painting and Photography, c. 1900–1910." *Arts Magazine,* November 1979, 141–143.

Baker, John Howard. "Voyeurism in the Art of John Sloan: The Psychodynamics of a 'Naturalistic' Motif." *Art Quarterly,* Autumn 1978, 379–395.

Baldwin, Neil. *Man Ray: American Artist.* New York: Clarkson Potter, 1988.

Barrell, Charles Wisner. "The Real Drama of the Slums, as Told in John Sloan's Etchings." *The Craftsman,* February 1909, 559–564.

Baur, John I. H. *Revolution and Tradition in American Art.* Cambridge: Harvard University Press, 1951.

Baury, Louis. "The Message of Bohemia." *The Bookman,* November 1911, 256–266.

Beard, Rick, and Leslie Cohen Berlowitz, eds. *Greenwich Village: Culture and Counterculture.* New Brunswick: Rutgers University Press, 1993.

Berman, Avis. "Artist as Rebel: John Sloan vs. the Status Quo." *Smithsonian,* April 1988, 74–84.

———. *Rebels on Eighth Street: Juliana Force and the Whitney Museum of American Art.* New York: Atheneum, 1988.

Berry-Hill, Henry, and Sidney Berry-Hill. *Ernest Lawson: American Impressionist, 1873–1939.* Leigh-on-Sea, England: F. Lewis, 1968.

Biddle, George. *An American Artist's Story.* Boston: Little, Brown, 1939.

Bohrod, Aaron. "On John Sloan." *College Art Journal,* Fall 1950, 3–9.

Bolger, Doreen. "Hamilton Easter Field and the Rise of Modern Art in America." Master's thesis, University of Delaware, 1973.

Bowers, Fresdon, and Nancy Hale, eds. *Leon Kroll: A Spoken Memoir.* Charlottesville: University of Virginia Press, 1983.

Breitenbach, Edgar. *The American Poster.* Exhibition catalogue. American Federation of the Arts, October House, Inc., 1967–1969.

Brentano, Lowell. "Pictures for Everybody." *Saturday Evening Post,* 14 August 1943.

Broder, Patricia Janis. *The American West: The Modern Vision.* Boston: New York Graphic Society, 1984.

Brooks, Van Wyck. *Days of the Phoenix: The Nineteen-Twenties I Remember.* London: Dent, 1957.

———. *John Sloan: A Painter's Life.* New York: Dutton, 1955.

———. *Scenes and Portraits.* New York: Dutton, 1954.

Brown, Milton. *American Painting from the Armory Show to the Depression.* Princeton: Princeton University Press, 1955.

———. "The Ash Can School." *American Quarterly,* Summer 1949, 127–134.

———. *The Story of the Armory Show.* New York: Abbeville, 1988.

———. "The Two John Sloans." *Art News,* January 1952, 24–27.

Bullard, John Edgar III. "John Sloan and the Philadelphia Realists and Illustrators, 1890–1920." Master's thesis, University of California at Los Angeles, 1965.

Caffin, Charles. *The Story of American Painting.* New York: Frederick Stokes, 1907.

Calder, Nanette. *Thoughts of A. Stirling Calder on Art and Life.* New York: Privately printed, 1947.

Cantor, Milton. *Max Eastman.* New York: Twayne, 1970.

City Life Illustrated, 1890–1940: Sloan, Glackens, Shinn—Their Friends and Followers. Exhibition catalogue. Wilmington: Delaware Art Museum, September 7–November 23, 1980.

Clark, Eliot. *A History of the National Academy of Design.* New York: Columbia University Press, 1954.

Clayton, Douglas. *Floyd Dell: The Life and Times of an American Rebel.* Chicago: Ivan Dee, 1994.

Coates, Robert. "Profiles: After Enough Years Have Passed." *The New Yorker,* 7 May 1949, 36–51.

Coke, Van Deren. *Taos and Santa Fe: The Artist's Environment.* Albuquerque: University of New Mexico Press, 1963.

Colman, David Elliot. "The Social Commentary of John Sloan in the Context of

American Progressivism." Master's thesis, University of California at Berkeley, 1972.

Conner, Mary Ellen. "The 1910 Exhibition of Independent Artists." Master's thesis, University of Delaware, 1990.

Conrad, Peter. *The Art of the City: Views and Versions of New York.* New York: Oxford University Press, 1984.

Corn, Wanda. "The New New York." *Art in America,* July/August 1973, 58–65.

Cowley, Malcolm. *Exile's Return.* New York: Penguin, 1969.

Crews, Britt. *The Red Cottage.* Exhibition catalogue. Gloucester, Massachusetts: Cape Anne Historical Association, May 29–September 26, 1992.

Crunden, Michael C. *American Salons.* New York: Oxford University Press, 1993.

Cummings, Paul. "Interview with Katherine Schmidt." *Archives of American Art Journal* 13 (1973): 20.

Dell, Floyd. *Homecoming: An Autobiography.* New York: Farrar and Rinehart, 1933.

———. "Memories of the Old Masses." *American Mercury* 68 (April 1949): 481–487.

———. "Rents Were Low in Greenwich Village." *American Mercury* 65 (December 1947): 662–668.

———. "The Story of the Trial." *The Liberator,* June 1918, 7–18.

DeShazo, Edith. *Everett Shinn, 1876–1953, A Figure in His Time.* New York: Clarkson Potter, 1974.

Dijkstra, Bram. *Cubism, Stieglitz, and the Early Poetry of William Carlos Williams.* Princeton: Princeton University Press, 1969.

Dispenza, Joseph, and Louise Turner. *Will Shuster: A Santa Fe Legend.* Santa Fe: Museum of New Mexico Press, 1989.

Doezema, Marianne. *George Bellows and Urban America.* New Haven: Yale University Press, 1992.

———. "John Sloan at Santa Fe: Representing the American Indian." Paper presented at the annual convention of the American Studies Association, Costa Mesa, California, November 1992.

Drinnon, Richard. *Rebel in Paradise: A Biography of Emma Goldman.* Reprint. New York: Harper & Row, 1976.

Dunn, Dorothy. *American Indian Painting.* Albuquerque: University of New Mexico Press, 1968.

Eastman, Max. *Enjoyment of Living.* New York: Harper and Brothers, 1948.

———. "For Dolly Sloan." *New Leader,* 15 May 1943, 4.

———. *Love and Revolution: My Journey through an Epoch.* New York: Random House, 1964.

Egbert, Donald Drew. *Socialism and American Art.* Princeton: Princeton University Press, 1967.

Eldredge, Charles C., Julie Schimmel, and William H. Truettner. *Art in New Mexico, 1900–1945: Paths to Taos and Santa Fe.* Washington and New York: National Museum of American Art and Abbeville Press, 1986.

Elzea, Betty. *The Wards and the Sloans.* Occasional Paper No. 3. Wilmington: Delaware Art Museum, 1990.

Elzea, Rowland, and Elizabeth Hawkes. *John Sloan: Spectator of Life.* Exhibition catalogue. Wilmington: Delaware Art Museum, 1988.

———. *John Sloan's Oil Paintings: A Catalogue Raisonné.* 2 vols. The American Art Series. Newark, Del.: University of Delaware Press, 1992.

Falk, Peter Hastings. *The Annual Exhibition Record of the National Academy of Design, 1901–1950.* Madison, Conn.: Sound View, 1990.

The Fiftieth Anniversary of the Exhibition of Independent Artists in 1910. Exhibition catalogue. Wilmington Delaware Art Center, 1960.

Fishbein, Leslie. *Rebels in Bohemia: The Radicals of "The Masses," 1911–1917.* Chapel Hill: University of North Carolina Press, 1982.

Fitzgerald, Richard. *Art and Politics: Cartoonists of "The Masses" and "Liberator."* Westport, Conn.: Greenwood, 1973.

Folk, Thomas. "The Western Paintings of John Sloan." *Arts & Antiques,* March/April 1982, 100–107.

Forwood, William L. "John Sloan, Japonisme, and the Art Nouveau." Master's thesis, University of Delaware, 1970.

Friedman, B. H. *Gertrude Vanderbilt Whitney.* Garden City, N.Y.: Doubleday, 1978.

Gallatin, A. E. *John Sloan.* New York: Dutton, 1925.

Garland, Joseph E. *Eastern Point.* Petersborough, N.H.: Noone House, 1971.

Gibson, Arrell Morgan. *The Santa Fe and Taos Colonies: Age of the Muses, 1900–1942.* Norman: University of Oklahoma Press, 1983.

Gilfoyle, Timothy J. *City of Eros: Prostitution, New York City, and the Commercialization of Sex, 1790–1920.* New York: Norton, 1992.

Glackens, Ira. *William Glackens and The Eight: The Artists Who Freed American Art.* New York: Horizon, 1983.

Goldin, Amy. "The Eight's Laissez-Faire Revolution." *Art in America,* July/August 1973, 42–49.

———. "How Are the Prendergasts Modern?" *Art in America,* September/October 1976, 61–67.

Goldman, Emma. *Living My Life.* 2 vols. New York: Knopf, 1931.

Goodman, Helen E. "Robert Henri: The Teacher." Ph.D. diss., New York University, 1975.

Goodrich, Lloyd. *John Sloan.* New York: Whitney Museum of American Art, 1952.

Gordon, Robert. *John Butler Yeats and John Sloan: The Records of a Friendship.* Dublin: Dolman, 1978.

Gray, Christopher. "Rebels of Eighth Street Redux." *New York Times,* 12 September 1993, Real Estate sec., 7.

Green, Eleanor. *Maurice Prendergast: An Art of Impulse and Color.* Exhibition catalogue. College Park, Maryland: University of Maryland, 1976.

Green, Martin. *New York 1913.* New York: Scribners, 1988.

Grosz, George. *A Little Yes and a Big No: The Autobiography of George Grosz.* New York: Dial, 1946.

Hamerton, Philip Gilbert. *The Etcher's Handbook.* Boston: Roberts Brothers, 1881.

Handy, Elizabeth. "H. G. Maratta's Color Theory and Its Influence on the Painters Robert Henri, John Sloan, and George Bellows." Master's thesis, University of Delaware, 1969.

Hart, John. *Floyd Dell.* New York: Twayne, 1971.

Hartmann, Sadakichi. *A History of American Art.* New York: L. C. Page & Co., 1901; rev. ed., 1934.

Hawkes, Elizabeth. *John Sloan's Illustrations in Magazines and Books.* Wilmington: Delaware Art Museum, 1993.

Haywood, Bill. *Bill Haywood's Book.* 1929. Reprint. Westport, Conn.: Greenwood, 1983.

Hecht, Robert A. *Oliver La Farge and the American Indian.* Metuchen, N.J.: Scarecrow, 1991.

Heller, Adele, and Lois Rudnick, eds. *1915: The Cultural Moment.* New Brunswick: Rutgers University Press, 1991.

Hillquit, Morris. *Loose Leaves from a Busy Life.* New York: Macmillan, 1934.

Hills, Patricia. "John Sloan's Images of Working-Class Women: A Case Study of Roles and Interrelationships of Politics, Personality, and Patrons in the Development of Sloan's Art, 1905–1916." *Prospects,* 1980, 157–196.

———. *Turn-of-the-Century America.* Exhibition catalogue. New York: Whitney Museum of American Art, June 30–October 2, 1977.

Hirschfeld, Charles. " 'Ash Can' vs. 'Modern' Art in America." *Western Humanities Review* 10 (Autumn 1956): 363–365.

Historic Lock Haven. Clinton County Historical Society, 1979.

Historical Review of Philadelphia: 1896. Philadelphia: *Philadelphia Inquirer* International Edition, 1896.

Holcomb, Grant. *Focus I: John Sloan, "The Wake of the Ferry, II."* Essay and exhibition checklist. San Diego: Timken Art Gallery, October 2–December 2, 1984.

————. *John Sloan: The Gloucester Years.* Exhibition catalogue. Springfield, Mass.: Springfield Library and Museums Association, 1980.

————. "John Sloan and 'McSorley's Wonderful Saloon.' " *The American Art Journal,* Spring 1983, 5–20.

————. "A Painter's First Commission: The Portraits of Mr. and Mrs. Gottlieb Storz of Omaha." *Nebraska History,* Fall 1976, 423–429.

Homer, William Innes. "The Exhibition of 'The Eight': Its History and Significance." *American Art Journal,* Spring 1969, 53–64.

————. *Robert Henri and His Circle.* Ithaca: Cornell University Press, 1969.

————. *Thomas Eakins: His Life and Art.* New York: Abbeville, 1992.

Hone, Joseph, ed. *J. B. Yeats: Letters to His Son William Butler Yeats and Others, 1869–1922.* New York: Dutton, 1946.

Hoopes, Donelson F. "Randall Davey: The New York/Santa Fe Connection." *American Arts & Antiques,* January–February 1979, 42–49.

Humphrey, Robert E. *Children of Fantasy.* New York: Wiley, 1978.

Huneker, James. *The Pathos of Distance.* New York: Scribners, 1913.

Jeffers, Wendy. "Holger Cahill and American Art." *Archives of American Art Journal* 31 (4 November 1991): 2–11.

Karpiscak, Adeline Lee. *Ernest Lawson, 1873–1939.* Exhibition catalogue. Phoenix: University of Arizona, 1979.

Kelly, Lawrence C. *The Assault on Assimilation.* Albuquerque: University of New Mexico Press, 1983.

Kenny, Herbert. *Cape Ann: Cape America.* Philadelphia: Lippincott, 1971.

Kent, Rockwell. *It's Me, O Lord: The Autobiography of Rockwell Kent.* New York: Dodd, Mead, 1955.

Kiehl, David. *American Art Posters of the 1890s.* With essays by Phillip Dennis Cate, Nancy Finlay, David Kiehl. New York: Metropolitan Museum of Art, 1987.

Kinser, Suzanne. "Prostitutes in the Art of John Sloan." *Prospects* 9 (1984): 231–254.

Kraft, James. *John Sloan: A Printmaker.* Exhibition catalogue. Washington: International Exhibitions Foundation, 1984.

Kraft, James, and Helen Farr Sloan. *John Sloan in Santa Fe.* Exhibition catalogue. Washington: Smithsonian, 1981.

Kwait, Joseph J. "John Sloan: An American Artist as a Social Critic, 1900–1917." *Arizona Quarterly,* Spring 1954, 52–64.

LaFollette, Susan. *Art in America.* New York: Norton, 1929.

Landgren, Michael E. *Years of Art: The Story of the Art Students League of New York.* New York: Robert McBride, 1940.

Larkin, Oliver. *Art and Life in America.* New York: Rhineboat, 1949.

Lash, Joseph P. *Helen and Teacher.* New York: Delacorte, 1980.

Lingeman, Richard. *Theodore Dreiser: An American Journey, 1908–1945.* New York: Putnam, 1990.

Loughery, John. "The Mysterious George Luks." *Arts Magazine,* December 1987, 34–35.

———. "The *New York Sun* and Modern Art in America: Charles FitzGerald, Frederick James Gregg, James Gibbons Huneker, Henry McBride." *Arts Magazine,* December 1984, 77–82.

Love, Richard H. *John Barber: The Artist, the Man.* Chicago: Haase-Mumm, 1981.

Ludington, Townsend. *Marsden Hartley: The Biography of an American Artist.* Boston: Little, Brown, 1992.

Margolin, Victor. *American Poster Renaissance.* New York: Watson-Guptill, 1975.

Marlor, Clark. "A Quest for Independence: The Society of Independent Artists." *Art and Antiques,* March/April 1981, 75–80.

———. *The Society of Independent Artists: The Exhibition Record, 1917–1944.* Park Ridge, N.J.: Noyes Press, 1984.

Marter, Joan M. *Alexander Calder.* Cambridge: Cambridge University Press, 1991.

Mathews, Nancy Mowll. *Maurice Prendergast.* Exhibition catalogue. Williamstown, Mass.: Williams College Museum of Art, 1991.

May, Henry F. *The End of American Innocence.* New York: Knopf, 1959.

McCausland, Elisabeth. *Charles W. Hawthorne: An American Figurative Painter.* New York: American Artists Group, 1947.

McCoy, Garnett. "Arthur B. Davies and Robert Henri: An Unstable Alliance." In *Dream Vision: The Work of Arthur B. Davies.* Exhibition catalogue. Boston: Institute of Contemporary Art, March 17–May 10, 1981.

McNickle, D'Arcy. *Indian Man: A Life of Oliver La Farge.* Bloomington: Indiana University Press, 1971.

Meech, Julia, and Gabriel P. Weisberg. *Japonisme Comes to America: The Japanese Influence on the Graphic Arts, 1876–1925.* New York: Abrams and Rutgers University Press, 1990.

Mellquist, Jerome. *The Emergence of an American Art.* New York: Scribners, 1942.

Meyer, Susan. "Eric Sloane's America." *American Artist,* June 1977, 40–45.

Milroy, Elizabeth. *Painters of a New Century: The Eight and American Art.* Exhibition catalogue with essays by Milroy and Gwendolyn Owens. Milwaukee: Milwaukee Art Museum, September 6, 1991–September 21, 1992.

Moore, George. *Modern Painting.* New York: Scribners, 1893.

Morgan, Charles H. *George Bellows: Painter of America.* New York: Reynal, 1965.

Morse, Peter. "John Sloan's Etching Technique: An Example." *Smithsonian Journal of History* 2 (Fall 1967): 17–34.

————. *John Sloan's Prints: A Catalogue Raisonné of the Etchings, Lithographs, and Posters.* New Haven: Yale University Press, 1969.

Mott, Luther. *American Journalism: A History, 1690–1960.* New York: Macmillan, 1962.

Murphy, William M. *Prodigal Father: The Life of John Butler Yeats.* Ithaca: Cornell University Press, 1978.

Myers, Jerome. *Artist in Manhattan.* New York: American Artists Group, 1940.

Naifeh, Steven, and Gregory White Smith. *Jackson Pollock: An American Saga.* New York: Clarkson Potter, 1990.

Naumann, Francis. "The Big Show: The First Exhibition of the Society of Independent Artists." Parts 1, 2. *Artforum,* February, April 1979, 34–39, 49–53.

Nevins, Allan. *The Emergence of Modern America, 1865–1878.* New York: Macmillan, 1927.

Norman, Dorothy. *Alfred Stieglitz: An American Seer.* New York: Aperture, 1973.

O'Neill, William L., ed. *Echoes of Revolt: "The Masses," 1911–1917.* Chicago: Quadrangle Books, 1966.

————. *The Last Romantic: A Life of Max Eastman.* New York: Oxford University Press, 1978.

O'Toole, Judith H. *George Luks: An American Artist.* Exhibition catalogue with essays by O'Toole, Stanley Cuba, and Nina Kasanof. Wilkes-Barre, Penn.: Sordoni Art Gallery, Wilkes College, May 3, 1987–March 5, 1988.

Owens, Gwendolyn. "Art and Commerce: William Macbeth, The Eight, and the Popularization of American Art." In Milroy, *Painters of a New Century,* 61–85.

Pach, Walter. "The Etchings of John Sloan." *Studio,* 14 August 1926, 102–105.

————. "John Sloan Today." *Virginia Quarterly Review,* July 1925, 196–204.

————. *Queer Thing, Painting: Forty Years in the World of Art.* New York: Harper & Brothers, 1938.

Parry, Albert. *Garrets and Pretenders.* New York: Covici Friede, 1933.

Pène du Bois, Guy. *John Sloan.* New York: Whitney Museum of American Art, 1931.

Penn, F. "Newspaper Artists: John Sloan." *Inland Printer,* October 1894, 50–52.

Perlman, Bennard B. *The Golden Age of Illustration: F. R. Gruger and His Circle.* Westport, Conn.: North Light, 1978.

————. *The Immortal Eight.* Westport, Conn.: North Light, 1979.

————. *The Immortal Eight and Its Influence: The Art Students League of New York.* Exhibition catalogue. New York: Art Students League, 1983.

————. *Robert Henri: His Life and Art.* New York: Dover, 1991.

————. *Robert Henri: Painter.* Exhibition catalogue. Wilmington: Delaware Art Museum, 1984.

Phillips, Sandra S. "The Art Criticism of Walter Pach." *Art Bulletin,* March 1983, 106–122.

Poole, Ernest. *The Bridge: My Own Story.* New York: Macmillan, 1940.

Reich, Sheldon. *Andrew Dasburg: His Life and Art.* Cranbury, N.J.: Associated University Presses, 1989.

———. *Graphic Styles of the American Eight.* Exhibition catalogue. Salt Lake City: Utah Museum of Fine Arts, February 29–April 11, 1976.

———. "Randall Vernon Davey (1887–1964): A Forgotten American Artist." Unpublished essay, New Mexico Historical Library, Santa Fe.

Reid, B. L. *The Man from New York: John Quinn and His Friends.* New York: Oxford University Press, 1968.

Rich, Daniel Catton, ed. *The Flow of Art: Essays and Criticisms of Henry McBride.* New York: Atheneum, 1975.

Richardson, E. P. *Painting in America.* London: Constable, 1956.

Robertson, Bruce. *Reckoning With Winslow Homer: His Late Paintings and Their Influence.* Cleveland: Cleveland Museum of Art, 1990.

Robertson, Edna, and Sarah Nestor. *Artists of the Canyons and Caminos: Santa Fe, the Early Years.* Layton, Utah: Peregrine Smith, 1976.

Robinson, Roxana. *Georgia O'Keeffe: A Life.* New York: Harper & Row, 1989.

Rose, Barbara. *American Art Since 1900.* New York: Holt, Rinehart, and Winston, 1975.

Rosenstone, Robert A. *Romantic Revolutionary: A Biography of John Reed.* New York: Knopf, 1975.

Rueppel, M. L. "The Graphic Art of Arthur B. Davies and John Sloan." Ph.D. diss., University of Wisconsin, 1955.

The Ruth Martin Collection of Paintings by John Sloan. Exhibition catalogue with essay by Grant Holcomb III. New York: Salander-O'Reilly Galleries, March 4–April 5, 1980.

Sackler, Dorothy. "Interview with Adolph Gottlieb." *Archives of American Art Journal* 13 (1973): 23.

Santé, Luc. *Low Life: Lures and Snares of Old New York.* New York: Farrar, Straus & Giroux, 1991.

Schack, William. *Art and Argyrol: The Life and Career of Dr. Albert C. Barnes.* New York: Thomas Yoseloff, 1960.

Scherman, Bernadine Kielty. *Girl from Fitchburg.* New York: Random House, 1964.

Schrader, Robert Fay. *The Indian Arts and Crafts Board.* Albuquerque: University of New Mexico Press, 1983.

Schwab, Arnold. *James Gibbons Huneker: Critic of the Seven Arts.* Stanford: Stanford University Press, 1963.

Schwartz, Constance H. *The Shock of Modernism in America: The Eight and Artists of the Armory Show*. Exhibition catalogue. Rosyln Harbor, N.Y.: Nassau County Museum of Fine Art, April 29–July 29, 1984.

Schwartz, Sanford. "When New York Went to New Mexico." pp. 85–94 in *The Art Presence*. New York: Horizon, 1976.

Schwarz, Judith. *Radical Feminists of Heterodoxy: Greenwich Village, 1912–1940*. Lebanon, N.H.: New Victoria Press, 1982.

Scott, David W. *"The City from Greenwich Village." Studies in the History of Art, 1971–1972* (National Gallery of Art), 106–119.

———. *John Sloan*. New York: Watson-Guptill, 1975.

Scott, Gail. *Marsden Hartley*. New York: Abbeville, 1988.

Shannon, David. *The Socialist Party in America*. Chicago: Quadrangle Books, 1967.

Sims, Lowery Stokes, et al. *Stuart Davis, American Painter*. New York: Metropolitan Museum of Art, 1991.

Simpson, Colin. *Artful Partners: Bernard Berenson and Joseph Duveen*. New York: Macmillan, 1986.

Sloan, Helen Farr, ed. *John Sloan: New York Etchings*. New York: Dutton, 1978.

Sloan, John. "Artist, Dealer, and Buyer." *Creative Art,* February 1928, xxxvii–xxxviii.

———. *Gist of Art*. New York: American Artists Group, 1939.

———. "An Independent, an Open Door." *The Arts,* April 1927, 187–188.

———. "Indian Art." *Rotarian,* March 1941, 18–21.

———. "The Indian as Artist." *Survey,* 1 December 1931, 243–246.

———. "The Indian Dance from an Artist's Point of View." *Arts & Decoration,* January 1924, 17, 56.

———. Introduction to Ira Moskowitz and John Collier, *Patterns and Ceremonials of the Indians of the Southwest*. New York: Dutton, 1949.

———. "My Recent Encounter." *Creative Art,* May 1928, xliv–xlv.

———. "The Process of Etching." *Touchstone,* December 1920, 238–240.

———. "Randall Davey." *New Mexican Quarterly Review,* Spring 1951, 22–23.

Sloan, John, and Oliver La Farge. *Introduction to American Indian Art*. New York: Exposition of Indian Tribal Arts, 1931. Reprint. Glorieta, N.M.: Rio Grande Press, 1971.

St. John, Bruce. *John Sloan*. New York: Praeger, 1971.

———. "John Sloan in Philadelphia, 1888–1904." *Archives of American Art Journal,* Fall 1971, 80–87.

———. *John Sloan's New York Scene: From the Diaries, Notes, and Correspondence, 1906–1913*. New York: Harper & Row, 1965.

Starr, Louis M. *Bohemian Brigade*. New York: Knopf, 1954.

Stavitsky, Gail. "John Weichsel and the People's Art Guild." *Archives of American Art Journal* 31 (4 November 1991): 12–19.

Symes, Lillian, and Travers Clement. *Rebel America: The Story of Social Revolt in the United States.* Reprint. Boston: Beacon Press, 1972.

Tarbell, Roberta K. *Peggy Bacon: Personalities and Places.* Washington: National Collection of Fine Arts, 1975.

Taylor, Joshua C. *The Fine Arts in America.* Chicago: University of Chicago Press, 1975.

Taylor, Kendall. *Philip Evergood: Never Separate from the Heart.* Cranbury, N.J.: Associated University Presses, 1983.

Traxel, David. *An American Saga: The Life and Times of Rockwell Kent.* New York: Harper & Row, 1980.

Udall, Sharyn Rohlfsen. "Marsden Hartley's Self-Portrait." *El Palacio,* Spring 1993, 32–35.

———. *Modernist Painting in New Mexico, 1913–1935.* Albuquerque: University of New Mexico Press, 1984.

Untermeyer, Louis. *Bygones.* New York: Harcourt, Brace, and World, 1965.

———. *From Another World.* New York: Harcourt Brace, 1939.

Vanderlip, Dianne Perry. *John Sloan/Robert Henri: Their Philadelphia Years, 1886–1904.* Exhibition catalogue. Philadelphia: Moore College of Art, October 1–November 12, 1976.

Vorse, Mary Heaton. *A Footnote to Folly: Reminiscences of Mary Heaton Vorse.* New York: Farrar and Rinehart, 1935.

Watson, Forbes. "John Sloan." *Magazine of Art,* February 1952, 62–70.

———. "Realism Undefeated." *Parnassus* 9 (March 1937): 11–14.

Watson, Stephen. *Strange Bedfellows.* New York: Abbeville, 1991.

Weber, Bruce. "The Prowed Tower: Early Images of the Flatiron Building." Exhibition essay. New York: Berry-Hill, Inc., 1991.

Weeks, Barbara Anne. "The Artist John Sloan's Encounter with Socialism." Master's thesis, University of West Florida, 1973.

Weigle, Marta, and Kyle Fiore. *Santa Fe and Taos: The Writer's Era, 1916–1941.* Santa Fe: Ancient City Press, 1982.

West, Herbert Faulkner. *John Sloan's Last Summer.* Iowa City: Prairie Press, 1952.

Winterich, John T. "The Imprints of A. Edw. Newton & Co., 1887–1893." *The Colophon* 1, no. 4 (Spring 1936): 510–522.

Wolfe, Bartram D. *The Fabulous Life of Diego Rivera.* New York: Stein & Day, 1963. Scarborough House edition.

Wright, Brooks. *The Artist and the Unicorn: The Lives of Arthur B. Davies.* New City, N.Y.: The Historical Society of Rockland County, 1978.

Yeats, John Butler. "A Painter of Pictures." *The Freeman,* 4 January 1922, 401–402.

———. "The Work of John Sloan." *Harper's Weekly.* 22 November 1913, 20.

Young, Art. *Art Young: His Life and Times.* New York: Sheridan House, 1939.

————. *On My Way.* New York: Horace Liveright, 1928.

Young, Mahonri. *The Eight.* New York: Watson-Guptill, 1973.

Zilczer, Judith K. "Anti-realism in the Ashcan School." *Artforum,* March 1979, 44–49.

————. "The Eight on Tour, 1908–1909." *American Art Journal* 16, no. 3 (Summer 1984): 20–49.

Zorach, William. *Art Is My Life.* Cleveland: World Publishing, 1967.

Zurier, Rebecca. *Art for "The Masses": A Radical Magazine and Its Graphics, 1911–1917.* Philadelphia: Temple University Press, 1988.

Acknowledgments

Some years ago John Rewald, the art historian and Cézanne biographer, remarked in conversation about the difficulties of what he termed the "artist's widow syndrome," that unfortunate practice that some wives of deceased painters engage in when they seek to control their husband's posthumous reputations, usually to the detriment of that reputation. In such situations, documents are mysteriously edited, material is withheld, questionable information is released, and freedom of thought is impinged upon by various ploys. This is a problem I have encountered on one or two occasions, though not—I am happy to note—in the writing of John Sloan's life story.

In fact, for anyone engaged in such an endeavor, it would be hard to imagine a more helpful and generous woman than Helen Farr Sloan. She had the sense to save all of her husband's papers and to see that they came to rest in one accessible archive, the vision to encourage diverse scholarship and frank inquiry, and the faith in those of us who have written about her husband to leave us to follow our bent. Very early on in my research, Mrs. Sloan made it clear that she would be honest in her discussions with me, would never be found peering over my shoulder, would open every door she could. I nodded pleasantly at the time and hoped for the best. That she did just what she said comes as no surprise to me today, and I am sure that as a biographer I will never have it so good again. I am grateful not only for the many hours of sensitive interviews Mrs. Sloan granted over a period of two years but for her trust in making available to me private papers, letters, journals, and later diaries of hers and her husband's that were not yet a part of the archive that houses the Sloan Collection.

In Wilmington, Delaware, where I spent the spring of 1992 and a part of

1993 studying the extensive John Sloan Collection at the Delaware Art Museum, I accrued numerous debts in addition to those owed Mrs. Sloan. Rowland Elzea, at that time the principal curator of the museum and the director of the Sloan archive (and the author of a masterful catalogue raisonné of Sloan's oil paintings, published in 1992), helped me in many ways, as did Steve Bruni, the museum's director; Jeanette Toohey, the current curator of the Sloan Collection; the former librarian, Iris Snyder, and the current librarian, Harriet Memeger; the assistant librarian, Beth Davis; the archivist, Lee Ann Dean; the registrar, Mary Holahan; the photographer, Jon McDowell; and Elizabeth McLaughlin, formerly of the rights and reproductions department. Indeed, everyone on the staff of the Delaware Art Museum was both friendly and helpful. My thanks, also, to Charles and Judy Powell, proprietors of the Boulevard in Wilmington, for accommodations that would exceed any traveling scholar's expectations.

In Gloucester, Massachusetts, I was assisted in my work by Britt Crews, former curator of the Cape Ann Historical Society, whose timely exhibition The Red Cottage in the summer of 1992 gave me the chance to see not only more paintings by John Sloan and Stuart Davis but also works by some of the friends —Paul Cornoyer, Alice Beach Winter, Charles Allan Winter, Randall Davey, and Stuart Davis's mother—who shared the Sloans' cottage. I am also grateful to Virginia Smith for showing me the actual red cottage, now her home, that Sloan rented during his five productive summers in Gloucester between 1914 and 1918, and to the librarians at the Sawyer Free Library in that town.

In Santa Fe, New Mexico, Sandra D'Emilio, curator of the New Mexico Museum of Fine Arts, showed me the works by Sloan that that museum owns; librarian Phyllis Cohen at the museum and librarian Orlando Romero at the Santa Fe Historical Society pointed me in the right direction when I was perusing the files and stacks of their institutions; and Steve Modzelewski, the painter who now lives in Sloan's old studio on Garcia Street, graciously let this rather pushy stranger into his home to see where the subject of his book worked for so many summers in the 1920s and '30s and to examine the evidence of Sloan's craftsmanship as carpenter and decorator. As an Easterner who had never set foot in New Mexico, I found my time in that state—working in Santa Fe and scouting about for the sites of Sloan's paintings of reservations and mesas—an especially pleasurable aspect of writing this book.

In Lock Haven, Pennsylvania, I was able to see Sloan's birthplace, the cemetery in which his relatives are buried and his own ashes scattered, the paintings and personal effects of his that are now in the town's library, and the etchings owned by the Lock Haven State University—all thanks to Rebecca Gross, a consummate tour guide even in her late eighties. Her recollections of the Sloans, whom she met in 1940, were vivid and informative.

In New York City, Carole Pesner, Katherine Kaplan, and Al Fraser of the Kraushaar Gallery showed me the many fine paintings that are still a part of the John Sloan Trust, as well as the Sloan-Kraushaar correspondence in their files. Their interest in this project was helpful in many ways from the very start. I also made use of the resources of the New York Public Library, the Archives of American Art, the Art Students League, the Mercantile Library, the libraries of the Whitney Museum of American Art and the Metropolitan Museum of Art, and the New-York Historical Society, and I owe a debt of gratitude to the directors and librarians in each of those institutions.

For information and research suggestions provided in correspondence, personal interviews, or phone conversations, or for help in enabling me to see works by John Sloan that are not readily on view, I am indebted to Sidney Berger, Martha Blocker, Cecilia Chin, Earl Davis, Miriam Davis, Harvey Dinnerstein, Marianne Doezema, the late Elsie Driggs, Mary Regensberg Feist, Joan Gaines, the late Ira Glackens, the late Lloyd Goodrich (many years before I imagined I would ever be writing about Sloan, we had several good talks about him and other artists of his generation), Herbert Greenwald, Jerry Hackman, Elizabeth Hawkes (author of the excellent *John Sloan's Illustrations in Books and Magazines),* Cathy Henderson, Fred Hill, Robert Hunter, James Kraft, Ms. Pele de Lappe, Janet LeClair, Gail Levin, Mr. and Mrs. Hirschl Levine, Andrea Luks, Joan Marter, Theresa Bernstein Meyerowitz, Elizabeth Milroy, Judith O'Toole, Michael Owen, Raymond Pach, David Palmquist, Bennard Perlman, F. Warren Peters, Sister Emily Phelan, Sheldon Reich, W. Jackson Rushing, Charles Sawyer, Judith Ann Schiff, Jeanne Schinto, Elizabeth Schmidt, Lowery Stokes Sims, Will South, Gail Stavitsky, Harry Sternberg, Wendy Thomas, Sharyn Rohlfsen Udall, Katharine J. Watson, Mrs. Betts Wolk, Judith Zilczer, and Rebecca Zurier. The interest Avis Berman showed in this project from its inception was especially important to me, and our wanderings through the labyrinthine corridors of the old Whitney Museum on West Eighth Street to see the rooms where Sloan's paintings were first hung and where he conferred with the inimitable Juliana Force are a vivid memory. As always, Avis was a remarkable source for suggestions on archives and individuals to consult.

My archival sources for this biography, beyond the several thousand documents and personal effects—letters, diaries, clippings, catalogues, and photographs—in the John Sloan Collection in Wilmington, have included the John Sloan–Robert Henri letters at the Beinecke Rare Book and Manuscript Library at Yale University, Sloan letters in the collection of the Ransom Humanities Center at the University of Texas in Austin, the John Quinn Collection at the New York Public Library, the John Butler Yeats Collection at the Princeton University Library, the Juliana Force files at the Whitney Museum of American

Art, and the correspondence and transcribed interviews at the Archives of American Art of Adolph Gottlieb, Katherine Schmidt, Everett Shinn, Will Shuster, Raphael Soyer, Harry Wickey, and numerous other artists who knew Sloan. Correspondence and clippings files at the Carnegie Institute, the Chicago Art Institute, the Indianapolis Museum of Art, and the Toledo Museum of Art were also very useful.

The enthusiasm for this project shown by my literary agent, Faith Hamlin of Sanford J. Greenburger Associates, was an important impetus when I was in the early stages of my work. The process of seeing the book to completion was immeasurably aided by the suggestions and insights of Jack Macrae at Henry Holt, an exemplary editor and provocative thinker.

My thanks to those friends and relatives whose interest and support was vital: in Connecticut and New York, Mary Allen, Stewart Galanor, Thomas Gatch, Curtis and Degi Jennings, Marion Kern, Ron Koury, Kevin Lally, Helen Loughery, Virginia Loughery, Ruth Pegolo, Maria Soares, Patricia Timm, Melissa Timm—and Angie and Ty Florie (in whose exhilarating high school English class I first heard extolled the talents of John Sloan and his contemporaries Hopper, Marin, and Dove).

Finally, this biography is dedicated to the person I met in my American literature class in our long-gone school days and who has helped me in my research and shared and enriched the last nineteen years of my life: Thomas Orefice.

John Loughery
1994

Index

Page numbers in **boldface** refer to illustrations.